Evolutionary Case Formulation

Álvaro Quiñones Bergeret

Evolutionary Case Formulation

Developing a Unified Language for the Practice of Psychotherapy

Springer

Álvaro Quiñones Bergeret
Department of Social Sciences
University of Tarapacá
Iquique, Chile

ISBN 978-3-031-67414-3 ISBN 978-3-031-67412-9 (eBook)
https://doi.org/10.1007/978-3-031-67412-9

The original submitted manuscript has been translated into English. The translation was done using artificial intelligence. A subsequent revision was performed by the author(s) to further refine the work and to ensure that the translation is appropriate concerning content and scientific correctness. It may, however, read stylistically different from a conventional translation.

This Springer imprint is published by the registered company Springer Nature Switzerland AG
The registered company address is: Gewerbestrasse 11, 6330 Cham, Switzerland

Preface

We psychotherapists suffer from a lack of common language in psychotherapy and its various implications are a major problem that we can no longer ignore. To illustrate, I remember an anecdote from a psychological care center more than two decades ago. It involved an adult person who consulted a therapist for a psychological problem and after the evaluation, the therapist informed them of a psychological diagnosis and treatment to follow; and after a few days, the same person decided to seek a second opinion from another therapist, who informed them of a different psychological diagnosis and treatment. It should be clarified that both therapists were from different psychological schools.

This person, who saw two therapists, was left confused and told a third therapist at the psychological care center about their situation of uncertainty. In the end, I heard the anecdote, and I must say that it did not surprise me in the slightest. In summary, such a person was left somewhere on a continuum of "less to more confusion."

As we know, psychotherapists not only differ in the hypothetical origin of the psychological problem (e.g., crisis, lack of purposes in life, our biological/body/brain chemistry, traumas, our dysfunctional family, social relationships, etc.) but they understand the psychotherapeutic process in different ways and propose different psychological formulations and therefore a diversity of interventions and evaluations and more.

All of the above, at least, is a consequence of the numerousness of psychotherapies and to illustrate this problem, Eisner (2000) estimated at the end of the twentieth century that there were more than 500. Ultimately, the landscape has not changed at the beginning of 2024, since the field of psychotherapy, paraphrasing Marks, "remains fragmented into fiefdoms and a federal union seems to be far in the future" (2000, p. 329), but there is hope despite the prevailing pessimism in my opinion.

The *therapists ideally* (I underline "ideally") guide their practice by theoretical systems that should be a well-organized, structured, and coherent set of nomothetic and idiographic information with an empirical basis and possible to refute. But it is well known that this has not happened for various reasons and interests of different nature.

Clearly, there is a lack of consensus on what constructs, criteria, and indicators, among others, we should take into consideration to evaluate and achieve more effective and efficient help for the patients who request our help. In other words, an excess of generalities and absence of specificity due to the abuse of ideology that several psychological systems continue to defend despite many refutations of all kinds. Apparently, we psychotherapists have lost sight of what Kurt Lewin stated quite some time ago, that "there is nothing more practical than a good theory."

Now, in the field of psychotherapy, a conceptual framework is needed that is not artificial, that is, a unified theory (common language) and of progressive complexity (that incorporates the advances of knowledge in different fields of knowledge), that is sensitive and gives response to psychological problems from the observation and systematic evaluation of complete psychotherapeutic processes. Therefore, the dialectic between quantitative and qualitative psychotherapy research, systematized clinical practice, measurable results, and the commensurable follow-up of the patient's self-perception are fundamental to advance in achieving a theory with consistent practice that facilitates effective and efficient treatments.

What is this book about? It proposes a case formulation model with an evolutionary stamp[1] that arises from the research of complete psychotherapeutic processes, relates the nomothetic and idiographic, combines the paradigmatic (scientific logical) and narrative, cybernetics, incorporates common factors, specific factors, transdiagnostic factors, and the evolutionist/intersubjective processes of meaning creation that are organized in narratives.

The book *Evolutionary Case Formulation: Developing a Unified Language for the Practice of Psychotherapy,* that the reader has in their hands, is, in the first place, the result of the development of a research program in adult patients of the neurotic spectrum (Quiñones et al., 2015, 2017; Quiñones, 2014a, b). It present a case formulation model which was first presented in the Spanish edition of this book, published in 2021 (Quiñones, 2021). This English edition is a fully revised and updated version of the original Spanish edition. More specifically, the case formulation protocol presents a series of innovations that are not present in the Spanish edition. In other words, it is a protocol that includes numerous clarifications in the intersubjective knowledge domains, making this book different. The conceptual development emerged from the analysis of textual data in complete psychotherapy processes. And certainly, the importance given to the analysis of textual data was not a coincidence, and essentially obeyed to the fact that I supposed a significant gap between what the therapists said they did and what they effectively did in session (Quiñones, 2011a, b, 2013; Quiñones et al., 2012). And, in the second place, the evolutionist seal of the formulation model that is presented are the dimensions of intersubjective meaning elaboration that are a product of our evolution as a species (Self System, Cognition, Emotion, Interpersonal, Imagination, Corporeality, Sexuality, and

[1] The evolutionary stamp is inspired by the fact that Homo sapiens are cultural, social, and cooperative creatures wired to function in such a way. They are active processors of information/meaning, social knowledge, transmitters of elements of culture, and accumulation of cultural knowledge (see Quiñones, 2024)

Religiosity/Spirituality) and that are a common language to understand psychological suffering and its possible changes toward healthy intersubjective regulation trajectories. In coherence with the above, a terminology of first- and second-order intersubjective domains is proposed to indicate a hierarchical relationship of information processing and meaning creation in an intersubjective matrix.

Continuing with the proposal in the present text, a model of first- (Self System) and second-order (cognition, emotion, interpersonal, imagination, corporeality, sexuality, and religiosity/spirituality) intersubjective knowledge domains is proposed that facilitates in the first place to delimit parsimoniously what happens to the patient at the Idiographic/Nomothetic level. It is important to emphasize that the intention is not to provide an exhaustive review of each of the intersubjective knowledge domains, as this would be impossible given the rapid advancements in research across different fields of knowledge (psychology, psychopathology, neuroscience, etc.) but rather, these developments are presented to situate a case formulation proposal with an evolutionary perspective.

In the second place, at the idiographic level, it designs intervention strategies "tailored to the patient" in the synergistic dynamics of the dysfunctional intersubjective knowledge domains that are articulated in the *Self System*. In the third place, it guides the therapist to generate an intersubjective space of sensitive listening and understanding that allows *thematizing* the psychological suffering of the patient in a "Dysfunctional Intersubjective Theme" that is manageable to start the process of personal change. And fourth, the therapist guides the emergence of gradual change through a general strategy of *Narrative Scaling* and other *Techniques* specific based on understanding for the intersubjective knowledge domains that present discomfort and/or psychological deregulation involved with the generic objective of achieving a disarticulation of the dysfunctional intersubjective theme, and thus, facilitate the emergence of a new *Functional Narrative*.

To conclude, the book is structured in two parts. The first part describes the conceptual bases of the Evolutionary Case Formulation (ECF) model in 11 chapters. The second part, which consists of three chapters, presents the step-by-step application of the Evolutionary Case Formulation protocol in a successful psychotherapy process of 29 sessions, as well as a concluding chapter. The complete Evolutionary Case Formulation protocol is included as an Appendix at the end of the book.

Iquique, Chile
March 2024 — Álvaro Quiñones Bergeret

References

Eisner, D. A. (2000). *The death of psychotherapy: From Freud to alien abductions*. Greenwood Publishing Group.

Marks, I. (2000). Forty years of psychosocial treatments. *Behavioral and Cognitive Psychotherapy*, *28*, 323–334.

Quiñones, A. (2011a). Modificación del significado personal: Perspectivas de un programa de investigación de procesos en psicoterapia. *Rivista di psichiatria*, *46*(5–6), 319–325.

Quiñones, A. (2011b). Pauta de Reconstrucción de Malestar Psicológico: Aplicaciones a un caso clínico. *Revista de Psicoterapia*, *88*, 97–130.

Quiñones, A. (2013). *Indicadores de procesos en psicoterapia asociados a éxito*. [Tesis de Doctorado, Universidad Autónoma de Barcelona]. Repositorio Institucional – Universidad Autónoma de Barcelona.

Quiñones, A. (2014a). Un nuovo modelo di formulazione dei casi clinici: Parte I. En Quiñones, A., Cimbolli, P., & Pascale, A. (Eds.), *La psicoterapia dei processi di significato personale dei disturbi psicopatologici*. Manuale Teórico e Practico (pp. 67–109). Casa Alpes.

Quiñones, A. (2014b). Applicazione del modello di formulazione dei casi clinici RMPS: Parte II. En Quiñones, A., Cimbolli, P., & Pascale, A. (Eds.) (Eds.), *La psicoterapia dei processi di significato personale dei disturbi psicopatologici*. Manuale Teórico e Practico (pp. 131–156). Casa Alpes.

Quiñones, A. (2021). *Formulación de caso evolucionista: Un lenguaje común en psicoterapia*. Ril editores.

Quiñones, A. (2024). Perspectiva evolucionista para la formulación de caso: Un sistema abierto. En A. Quiñones, & C. Caro (Eds.), *Formulación de Caso: Hacia una Psicoterapia de precisión* (pp. 84–122). UNED editorial.

Quiñones, A., Ceric, F y Ugarte, C. (2015). Flujos de información en zonas de tiempo subjetivo: Estudio de un proceso psicoterapéutico exitoso. *Revista Argentina de Clínica Psicológica*, *24*(3), 255–266.

Quiñones, A., Ceric, F., Ugarte, C., & Pascale, A. (2017). Psychotherapy and psychological time: a case study. *Rivista di Psichiatria*, *52*(3), 109–116.

Quiñones, A., Melipillán, R., & Ugarte, C. (2012). Indicadores de procesos de éxito en psicoterapia cognitiva. *Revista Argentina de Clínica Psicológica*, *21*(3), 247–254.

Acknowledgments

I would like to express my deepest gratitude to psychologist Carla Antonia Ugarte Pérez for her invaluable help. Her insightful suggestions, reflections, and cooperation in improving the figures have been fundamental. Especially, I value the enriching conversations we had about the text.

During the writing of this book, I received very valuable feedback from colleagues in Spain, Italy, the United States, Argentina, and Chile regarding the evolutionary case formulation model presented in various academic contexts. Their contributions have greatly enriched this work.

I take this opportunity to express my special gratitude to Bruno Fiuza and the Springer editorial team, who made the publication of my first book in English possible. Additionally, I thank psychologist Silvana Milozzi for her excellent work in reviewing the English translation, carried out by Springer.

Finally, I wish to express my deepest gratitude to the patients I have had the opportunity to help in my professional life both in Chile and in Spain. I deeply appreciate the special human connection that occurs in the intersubjective space of the psychotherapy process.

Contents

Part I
Conceptual Bases of the Evolutionary Case Formulation Model

Chapter 1
Introduction

The book "*Case Formulation from an Evolutionary Perspective: a common language in psychotherapy*" is the product of the development of a research program in individual psychotherapy processes. In this context, and including a temporal perspective, the initial question was What do we therapists (*participant observers*) do to facilitate change in a therapeutic process? Subsequently, other questions arose: *What do we understand by therapeutic process? What should we observe session by session? How can we describe and assess a therapeutic process over time?* In the end, we arrived at the question What do we understand by "changes" in a psychotherapeutic process? In sum, many questions with partial answers depending on the school one adheres to in psychotherapy.

The main objective of the research program was to construct, from what occurs in the intersubjective space[1] called psychotherapy, a model of Case Formulation from an evolutionary perspective [ECF] that would help therapists from a common language to thematically understand psychological suffering (Idiographic/Nomothetic—see Fig. 1.1: Theming and nomothetic and idiographic integration), organize clinical information (Nomothetic), propose an intervention design (Nomothetic/Idiographic), and monitor the entire process including the patient's active feedback[2] (Idiographic).

In every psychotherapy process, the focus is to understand the psychological imbalance that the patient experiences. In the model of Evolutionary Case Formulation, such *psychological imbalance* is understood as a dynamic and complex process of flows of information and self-referential knowledge that is called "*Dysfunctional intersubjective theme.*"

On the other hand, making a bit of general history, it is worth noting that case formulation models seek the following:

[1] Jürgen Habermas (1970) says "the intersubjectivity of understanding means both an individual capacity and a social domain."

[2] The term patient is used in the book (from Latin *patiens*: the one who suffers or endures).

Á. Quiñones Bergeret, *Evolutionary Case Formulation*,
https://doi.org/10.1007/978-3-031-67412-9_1

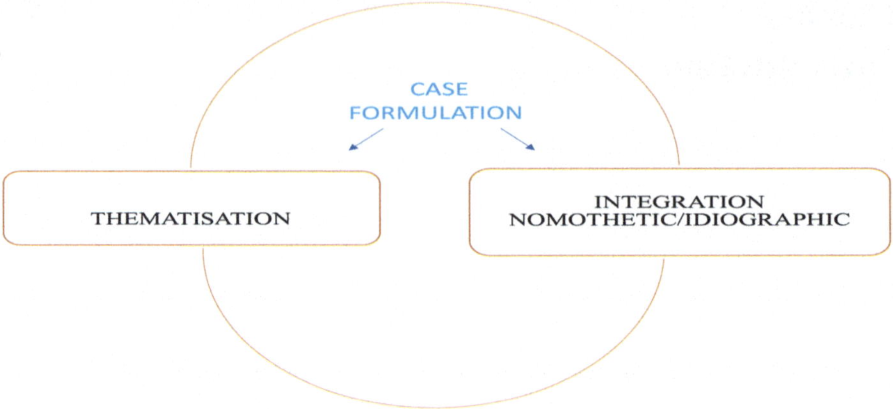

Fig. 1.1 Theming and nomothetic and idiographic integration

1. Formulation is a co-construction based on genuine human collaboration.
2. It establishes a bridge between theory and the practice of psychotherapy and helps to make sense of the patient's psychological problem (Dysfunctional Intersubjective Theme).
3. Psychological conceptualization, in itself, is therapeutic since it is a way to understand, probabilistically predict, and normalize the patient's problems.
4. It provides a structure for psychotherapy and guides the choice of possible interventions.
5. It allows monitoring of the process.
6. It increases the effectiveness of treatment.
7. It serves to manage problems that arise in the therapeutic relationship.
8. It improves the therapist's empathy and this contributes to the outcome of the psychotherapeutic process.
9. It allows understanding and redirecting a psychotherapeutic process that is failing in a timely manner.

There are several definitions of *Case Formulation* that allow for a global overview (see Table 1.1).

It should be noted that the most widely disseminated publications on *Case Formulation* have been written by psychiatrists and aimed primarily at English-speaking readers (see Bruch & Bond, 1998; Eells, 1997; Weerasekera, 1996).

However, the ***Evolutionary Case Formulation*** proposed in this book is defined as follows:

In general, it is a psychological methodology that allows organizing clinical information and is based on the collaboration between a person seeking help and a psychotherapist. In addition, it is a time-limited relationship that occurs in an intersubjective/cultural context and aims to describe and explain the psychological alteration in a way that is understandable to the patient. Specifically, in terms of the psychotherapeutic process:

Table 1.1 Definitions of case formulation

Author	Definition
Lazare	*Case formulation is a conceptual scheme that organizes, explains, or makes sense of large amounts of data and influences the treatment decisions* (1976, p. 77)
Eells	*Case formulation in psychotherapy is essentially a hypothesis about the causes, precipitants, and maintaining influences of a person's psychological, interpersonal, and behavioral problems* (1997, p. 1)
Aveline	*The formulation explains how and why the patient's equilibrium has become disturbed and how the problems or symptoms have arisen and are maintained. From it, a logical course of therapy can be deduced, taking into account the probable consequences of change (losses and gains) and the likelihood of achieving change. The formulation, therefore, serves both as a map for therapy and a guide to which map to choose* (1999, p. 202)
Division of clinical psychology	*Formulation is the summation and integration of the knowledge that is acquired by the assessment process (which may involve a number of different procedures). This will draw on psychological theory and data to provide a framework for describing a problem, how it developed and is being maintained* (2001, p. 3)

First, it facilitates the psychotherapist, as a participant observer, to have a conceptual map.
Second, it describes nomothetic processes and transitions to the idiographic as it identifies a Dysfunctional Intersubjective Theme.
Third, it proposes a co-constructed hypothesis and communicated through gradual psychological formulations.
Fourth, it develops a flexible and adjustable intervention plan that facilitates achieving successful therapeutic results according to agreed therapeutic objectives.
Fifth, objectify the trajectory of the psychotherapeutic process with co-constructed indicators.

The *Evolutionary Case Formulation Model* is configured by intersubjective knowledge domains (first and second order). The first order domain is the Self System and the second order domains are Cognition, Emotion, Interpersonal, Imagination, Corporeality, Sexuality, and Religiosity/Spirituality (see Fig. 1.2). Domains can behave in a functional or dysfunctional way. Each intersubjective knowledge domain is understood as active and prepared information that has possibilities for increasing personal knowledge.

In the case of dysfunctional behavior of several or all domains, they are integrated and expressed in a Dysfunctional Intersubjective Theme (example: Grandiosity, Self-sabotage, etc.). Each of the dysfunctional intersubjective knowledge domains is evaluated according to two dimensions (Psychological Distress-Psychological Well-being[3] [D-W] and Psychological Regulation-Psychological

[3]Anyone with good mental health not only enjoys not having psychological problems and/or mental illnesses, but also presents a dynamic and stable psychological well-being. In this sense, it is appropriate to remember what the World Health Organization says "Mental health is a state of

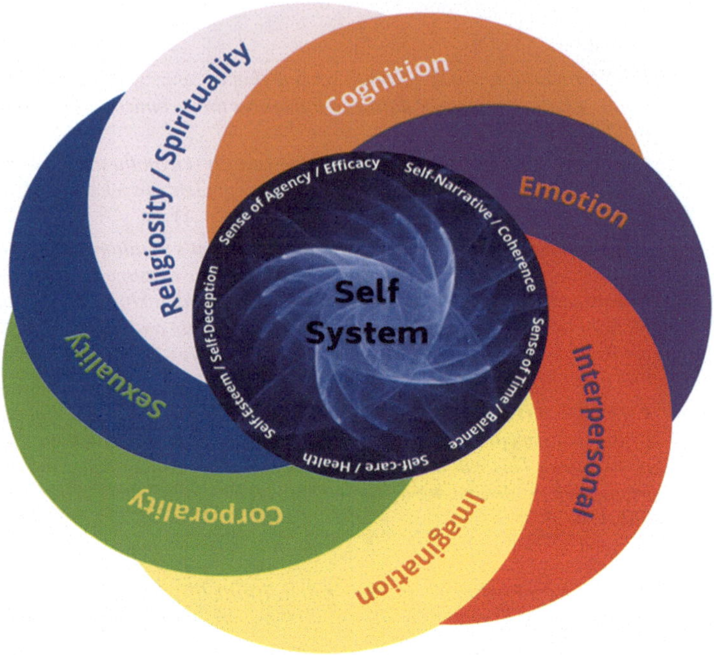

Fig. 1.2 Intersubjective knowledge domains of the evolutionary case formulation model

Table 1.2 Psychological distress and psychological well-being

Psychological dysregulation				Psychological regulation		
High	Moderate	Mild	Neutral	Mild	Moderate	High
−3	−2	−1	0	1	2	3

Dysregulation [R-D]) (see Tables 1.2 and 1.3). To be considered dysfunctional, they must be evaluated in the area of Psychological Distress (examples: −1, −2, −3) and/or in the area of Psychological Dysregulation (examples: −1, −2, −3).

I must point out that using two axes of evaluation ([D-W] and [R-D]) is due to being parsimonious.[4] Specifically, I follow the principle of Occam's razor (the law

well-being in which the individual realizes his own abilities, can cope with the normal stresses of life, can work productively and fruitfully, and can make a contribution to his community" (World Health Organization, 2001). On the other hand, it is essential to consider the research tradition on well-being in both its hedonic and eudaimonic form (See Ryan & Deci, 2001; Fredrickson, 2001, 2016).

[4] Inference in psychotherapy is part of the work of all therapists. However, assessing on a Likert scale aims to facilitate understanding and metacognition in psychotherapeutic work in order to achieve well-being and psychological regulation in the case formulation model presented in this book.

Table 1.3 Psychological dysregulation and psychological regulation

Psychological distress				Psychological well-being		
High	Moderate	Mild	Neutral	Mild	Moderate	High
−3	−2	−1	0	1	2	3

of parsimony) to avoid the proliferation of the number of evaluation axes. Therefore, I have proposed a minimum number of two axes to take into account a maximum number of psychopathological phenomena. The main practical consequences of this are, on the one hand, to facilitate the work of the therapist and, on the other hand, to be understandable to the patient.

The first axis is called *psychological distress/well-being.* It is in a certain sense easier to evaluate since people have quite an intuition and training in their daily life about it. The therapist asks and evaluates without much difficulty (examples: Do you feel good most of the time?, Are you satisfied with the decisions you have made this year?, Do you think you have developed as a person?, Do you feel in harmony with yourself?, Do you feel at peace with yourself?, How did you feel at the moment you realized you were not as usual?, How uncomfortable do you feel when you do not meet your proposed objectives?, How does the feeling that you lost harmony affect you?, etc.). Only when a severe condition is present, the evaluation can be difficult and take quite a lot of time.

The second axis is called *psychological dysregulation/psychological regulation.* It is an assessment of a greater difficulty as it requires the patient not to present deficits in cognitive processing (examples: metacognition and executive functions). The therapist must explore and assess with attunement and expertise. In general, my clinical experience and that of other colleagues informs us of the importance of being very attentive to assess feedback (examples: Did the intense anger you felt at that moment have the consequence you expected?, Did the anger help you solve the problem?, How did you feel seen by your sister at that moment of alteration?, etc.). Clearly this axis is of greater severity when we hypothesize that the patient values himself at "−3." High intensity is usually present in more complex problems, for example, patients with personality disorders and different types of comorbidity.

In addition, the inter-domain psychological evaluation allows to represent the domains of second-order intersubjective knowledge. As shown below, the therapist can represent based on the scores the following plane that shows four possible quadrants: I Dimensional psychological regulation; II Dimensional intrapersonal psychological dysregulation; III High dimensional psychological dysregulation; IV Interpersonal dimensional psychological dysregulation (see Fig. 1.3), and also, the dysfunctionality in the three following quadrants (II, III, and IV) is visualized as a dynamic, complex, and synergistic constellation called "Dysfunctional Intersubjective Theme."

It should be noted that the name of the quadrants is based on the severity. Now, quadrant I is the healthy one and is called "Dimensional Psychological Regulation," and quadrant III is the one that presents the most dysfunctionality and is called

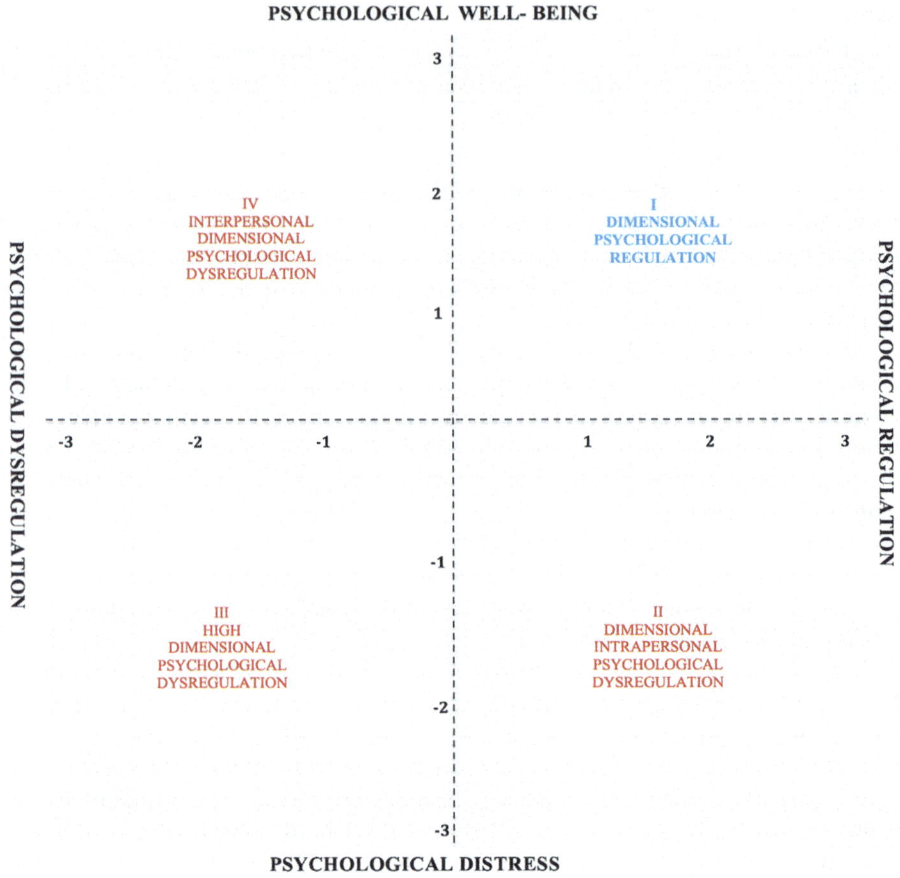

Fig. 1.3 Quadrants of psychological evaluation

"High Dysfunctional Psychological Dysregulation." Finally, the remaining two quadrants (II and IV) present different alterations based on the two axes.

From a therapeutic process perspective, the *Evolutionary Case Formulation* [ECF] has three sections to conceptualize, represent, monitor, and evaluate the psychotherapeutic process: Case Formulation-Evaluation [ECF-E], Case Formulation-Intervention [ECF-I] and Psychotherapy Process Assessment Interview [PPAI]. Such sections can be reviewed in detail in the Appendix and their applications in the second part of this book, titled "Psychotherapy Process."

On another note, there are nine conceptual aspects about the *evolutionary case formulation model* that will be presented in detail in this book:

1. The human being is understood as a self-organized and complex system in a cultural intersubjective matrix. An individual system with identity (dimensions of continuity) that develops enabled by a dynamic organization that is a bodily, energetic, psychological, temporal, social, and cultural process.

2. The Self System functions in an embodied way and essentially allows intentionality, self-regulation, proactivity, and intersubjectively and culturally situated self-reflection. It is ubiquitous in information processing and individual meaning creation throughout the life cycle. It consists of Self-narrative/Coherence, Sense of Agency/Efficacy, Sense of Time/Balance, Self-esteem/Self-deception, and Self-care/Health. It is the primary and inclusive (first-order) domain that acts as an articulator ("narrative center of gravity") of the seven second-order intersubjective knowledge domains. In addition, each dimension of the Self System combines in multiple ways with the second-order domains, for example, the improvement of the sense of agency/efficacy that implies self-management and the patient's emotional regulation will have a positive impact on their interpersonal relationships.
3. The seven second-order intersubjective knowledge domains (Cognition, Emotion, Interpersonal, Imagination, Corporeality, Sexuality, Religiosity/Spirituality) belong to different phenomenological domains and interact with each other articulated by the Self System. Namely, they are "intersubjective sensors" that are prepared to provide meaning and regulation in social life. They are our evolutionary potential ("our intentional biological machinery") for living in cultural intersubjectivity.
4. Psychological problems are conceptualized as regulation difficulties that manifest through themes that have nomothetic and idiographic characteristics.[5]
5. The *dysfunctional intersubjective theme* [DIT] is understood as a pattern ("Gestalt") of individual information and knowledge in a cultural intersubjective network. It emerges from the synergy of the intersubjective knowledge domains that function dysfunctionally and which is identified as a dysfunctional narrative that implies intersubjective tension.
6. Each dysfunctional intersubjective knowledge domain can be evaluated individually (own dynamics with possible "intra" configurations) and in relation to other domains (synergy and complexity).
7. Propose psychological clinical hypotheses with a common language. Presenting a comprehensible hypothesis that allows for a joint work plan is fundamental to generating knowledge, commitment, and hope on the part of the patient to achieve desired changes. In the protocol of Case Formulation from an evolutionary perspective [ECF-E) it is specified in "a.4" (see Appendix).
8. All intersubjective knowledge domains can contribute to the narrative escalation that the Self System regulates, articulates, and enables to emerge a functional and healthy narrative. The *Narrative Escalation* refers to the therapist-guided process that begins with an emerging narrative (in the profile of all or some of the patient's dysfunctional intersubjective knowledge domains) and gradually ends in a dynamic functional narrative (see Fig. 2.1, in Chap. 2).

[5] Research informs us that human beings are similar (Nomothetic) and different (Idiographic) at the same time, and at this intersection they present certain universal conflicts ("conflicting psychological plots").

9. The *dimensional psychological regulation and adaptive intersubjective sense of reality* is what is intended to be achieved in a successful therapeutic process. Such an outcome is identified with quadrant I ("Dimensional Psychological Regulation," see Fig. 1.3). By *Dimensional Psychological Regulation,* it refers to various possibilities of well-being and individual psychological regulation (such results are identified with various possibilities depending on the profile of second-order intersubjective knowledge domains in quadrant I, see Fig. 1.3). In other words, it is what is understood as psychological health in the case formulation model from an evolutionary perspective (ECF), and by *Adaptive Intersubjective Sense of Reality,* it refers to the synergistically articulated and fluid functioning of the intersubjective knowledge domains (first and second order) that allow the self-organized system "human being" to have a conscious existential sense and regulation in social life. Such a sense of reality is researched in intentionality, self-regulation, proactivity, and intersubjectively and culturally situated self-reflection on the part of the individual human system.

References

Aveline, M. (1999). The advantages of formulation over categorical diagnosis in explorative psychotherapy and psychodynamic management. *European Journal of Psychotherapy, Counselling and Health, 2*(2), 199–216.

Bruch, M., & Bond, F. W. (1998). *Beyond diagnosis: Case formulation approaches in cognitive-behavioural therapy*. Wiley.

Division of Clinical Psychology. (2001). *The core purpose and philosophy of the profession*. British Psychological Society.

Eells, T. D. (Ed.). (1997). *Handbook of psychotherapy case formulation*. Guilford Press.

Fredrickson, B. L. (2001). The role of positive emotions in positive psychology. The broaden-and-build theory of positive emotions. *The American Psychologist, 56*(3), 218–226.

Fredrickson, B. L. (2016). The eudaimonics of positive emotions. In J. Vittersø (Ed.), *Handbook of eudaimonic well-being* (pp. 183–190). Springer International.

Habermas, J. (1970). A theory of communicative competence. In H. P. Dreitzel (Ed.), *Recent sociology* (Vol. No. 2). Macmillan.

Lazare, A. (1976). The psychiatric examination in the walk-in clinic: Hypothesis generation and hypothesis testing. *Archives of General Psychiatry, 33*, 96–102.

Ryan, R. M., & Deci, E. L. (2001). On happiness and human potentials: A review of research on hedonic and eudaimonic well-being. *Annual Review of Psychology, 52*(1), 141–166. https://doi.org/10.1146/annurev.psych.52.1.141

Weerasekera, P. (1996). *Multiperspective case formulation: A step towards treatment integration*. Krieger.

World Health Organization. (2001). *Strengthening mental health promotion*. World Health Organization.

Chapter 2
Narratives and Initial Precisions for Case Conceptualization

The purpose of this section is to begin to define what will be understood by narratives in Case Formulation from an evolutionary perspective [ECF].

Homo Sapiens *are active processors of information*[1] *and social knowledge*, and therefore, they are capable of detecting, generating information, receiving information, storing information, and transforming it into personal knowledge in a context of cultural intersubjective fabric. It is important to note that information and knowledge are not synonymous. The information is the basis of knowledge and not all information is automatically converted into knowledge. In other words, the information "digested" by the mental "metabolism" (unconscious and conscious processing) of Homo Sapiens transforms it into "personal contextualized and cultural" knowledge and consequently human knowledge is intentional, it is a "know-how," it is solving problems of existence and more.

Language is a powerful evolutionary "instrument" of social coordination, collaboration, self-interpretation, and interpretation of others, which allows at an individual level to distinguish and organize information and knowledge of different "potentially meaning-generating self-referential modalities" (cognition, emotion, interpersonal, imagination, corporeality, sexuality, and religiosity/spirituality) and which are integrated into a *Self-System*. In addition, language provides diverse possibilities of meaning,[2] as it allows to be in the world intersubjectively in different possible idiographic patterns of conscious self-understanding through narratives about oneself and others with degrees of agency. Therefore, the interpretive possibilities of language enable the transformation of the self-generated information by

[1] A core aspect of the human mind is an embodied and relational process that regulates the flow of energy and information within the brain and between brains (Siegel, 2012, p. 3).

[2] The symbolic ability to understand, predict, and alter the course of events confers considerable functional advantages. The evolutionary emergence of language and abstract and deliberative cognitive abilities provided the neuronal structure to supplant aimless environmental selection by cognitive agency (see Bandura, 2006).

Á. Quiñones Bergeret, *Evolutionary Case Formulation*,
https://doi.org/10.1007/978-3-031-67412-9_2

the person and received from others into personal knowledge with degrees of continuity and coherence in a narrative identity in process (*that is, narrative of who one was, who one is and who one can become*).

It is important to fully acknowledge that psychotherapy is carried out in an explicit culture, an aspect very little considered by the different psychotherapeutic models that debate between the paradigmatic and narrative; and we still cannot agree, and we are "in debt."

Culture refers to the common ways in which individuals interpret the meaning of themselves and their possible worlds (Bruner, 1986, 1990; La Roche & Christopher, 2009). Members of the same culture share knowledge, music, dance, values, beliefs, religious and spiritual beliefs, customs, sports, rituals, myths, stories, etc. The entire dynamic of cultural elements creates a shared sense of identity and common and public meanings that we must consider. It is necessary to clarify this point further for the understanding of the complexity that implies always doing psychotherapy in a cultural context. I quote Marsella and Yamada (2010) to better glimpse the link between culture and human behavior that every therapist must consider. They define culture:

> Culture is shared learned behavior and meanings that are socially transmitted for purposes of adjustment and adaptation. Culture is represented externally in artifacts (e.g., food, clothing, music), roles (e.g., the social formation), and institutions (e.g., family, government). It is represented internally (i.e., cognitively, emotionally) by values, attitudes, beliefs, epistemologies, cosmologies, consciousness patterns, and notions of personhood. Culture is coded in verbally, imagistically, proprioceptively, viscerally, and emotionally resulting in different experiential structures and processes. (2010, p. 105)

Similarly, it is noteworthy that the content of human cognition is always intersubjective and, in this sense, the cultural sensitivity of Homo Sapiens is of the utmost relevance in the meaning expressed mainly through narratives and being with others in the construction of contextual and cultural meaning (Quiñones, 2013). At this point, let's look a little more finely at this matter of working with another person to guide them towards the desired change and we can pose the following reflective question "How do we understand ourselves and others?" Mainly through narration, with all its limitations, which arises in an active body and temporarily situated in an intersubjective-cultural framework. Now, narration is part of our evolutionary history as a species. It is a common way of communication that allows experiencing introspection and reflection of one's own life and that of others in a fabric of cultural collaboration. In fact, there are varieties of cultural forms of narrative (story, novel, opera, dance, folklore, poem, drama, cinema, mythology, history, etc.) and all have consequences in the own narratives of each member of the culture. In summary, "we are social narrating beings" that are interconnected in an intersubjective and cultural network as long as our biological existence lasts.

We know that the narratives that people construct about events contribute to the ability to extract meanings from them, which is considerably facilitated when the narratives are more coherent (Brockelman, 1985; Linde, 1993; Siegel, 1999) and enable self-awareness and self-regulation, among other aspects. In this sense, people tell stories for many reasons, for example, to understand some moment of their lives, to have fun, to play, to inform, to teach, to learn, to deceive, to ask for an interpretation, to persuade, to seduce, to defend themselves, understand a dream, etc. All of the above is known, but a very relevant aspect is the *intelligibility* of what is told by the person for the person themselves and for others, so that a *credible themed narrative* is constructed that facilitates inter-subjective regulation. Therefore, helping people to appropriate themselves through a narrative that allows them self-regulation, health, coherence, self-esteem and agency for example, is a "cornerstone" in psychotherapeutic efforts to gradually achieve a change that implies at the same time well-being and psychological regulation.

As a general framework of integration on language, self-narrative and self, Theodore Sarbin argued:

> The self-narrative need not appear as a remote hypothetical construct. It can be seen as an emergent from our grammatical rule for using first person singular pronouns. The pronouns, I and me (and their equivalents in other European languages), were accented by James, Mead, Freud, and others in the effort to give meaning to that vague but indispensable construct, the self. Their strategy was to uncover the references for I and me. They substantiated the pronouns by adding the definite article, thus rendering it possible to speak of *the I* and *the me*. In substantiating the pronouns in the context of the grammatical rules that govern the use of I as subject and me as object, these writers (perhaps unwittingly) introduced a narrative metaphor. The uttered pronoun, *I*, stands for the author, *me* stands for the actor, the character in the drama, the narrative figure. The self as author, *the I*, imaginatively constructs a story in which the narrative figure, *the me*, is the protagonist. Such narrative construction is possible because the self as author can imagine the future and reconstruct the past (see Mancuso & Sarbin, 1983, and Crites, this volume). In the same way that a person may become overinvolved in a narrative figure portrayed in a novel, play, biography, folktale, or film, so may that person become overinvolved in the narrative figure (*the me*) created by the self as author (*the I*). (1986, p. 18)

In addition to the above, I highlight the systematic contributions of developmental psychology research on narratives and self-organization of meaning. Specifically, there is growing evidence that a narrative function appears in the third year of life in children, allowing them to create stories about the events they experience in their daily lives (Nelson, 1989; Haden et al., 1997; Siegel, 1999). In this sense, Daniel J. Siegel (2012) argues that a narrative function appears in children that allows them to create stories about the events they experience in everyday life:

> These narratives are sequential descriptions of people and events that condense numerous experiences into generalizing and contrasting stories. New experiences are compared to old ones. Similarities are noted in creating generalized rules, and differences are highlighted as memorable exceptions to these rules. The stories are about making sense of events and the mental experiences of the characters. Filled with the elements of the characters' internal experience in the context of interactions with others in the world, these stories appear to be functioning to create a sense of coherent comprehension of the individual in the world across time. (p. 364)

Two researchers with many points of convergence on the narrative conception of identity are Jerome Bruner and Dan P. McAdams. It is noteworthy that Bruner (2004) defends a distributed and narrative conception of the self (See later in Chap. 4). He characterizes narratives as a tool to justify, argue, understand, communicate, or reflect on various ranges of human themes, emphasizing the possibility of creating narratives in the form of autobiographies. In other words, the narrative allows connecting the past, the present, and the future through an active synthesis, according to the autobiographical identity. McAdams and Olson, characterize the self as a story and identity as a life story:

> Narrative identity is the storied understanding that a person develops regarding how he or she came to be and where he or she is going in life. It is a narrative reconstruction of the autobiographical past and imagined rendering of the anticipated future, complete with demarcated chapters, key scenes (high points, low points, turning points), main characters, and intersecting plot lines. (McAdams & Olson, 2010, p. 527)

He also specifies that self-authorship is not just telling a story:

> Self-authorship, however, requires more than merely telling stories about what happened yesterday or last year. To construct a narrative identity, the person must envision his or her entire life—the past reconstructed and the future imagined—as a story that portrays a meaningful sequence of life events to explain how the person has developed into who he or she is now and may develop into who he or she may be in the future. (McAdams & Olson, 2010, p. 527–528)

Now, to more precisely define the term "narrative" in psychotherapy, I emphasize the perspective and orientations of Donald Polkinghorne (1988):

> ...narrative is a meaning structure that organizes events and human actions into a whole, thereby attributing significance to individual actions and events according to their effect on the whole. Thus, narratives are to be differentiated from chronicles, which simply list events according to their place on a time line. Narrative provides a symbolized account of actions that includes a temporal dimension. (p. 18)

Particularly the *narrative mode of knowing* consists of organizing experience with the help of a scheme assuming the intentionality of human action (Polkinghorne, 2001). In this proposal, the narrative organizational scheme is of particular importance for understanding human activity. It is the scheme that shows the purpose and direction in human affairs and makes individual human life understandable as a whole (Polkinghorne, 1988).[3] Consequently, narratives are presented as a specific tool for internalizing human processes and reflecting on one's own life stories that take the form of present psychological plots that can be problematic and maladaptive (which I call Dysfunctional Intersubjective Theme—DIT) or adaptive and enrich the understanding of one's own life and provide perspective.

Now, the plot allows a set of specific events to be brought into a comprehensive whole. Polkinghorne, with his usual sharpness, says:

> The organizing theme that identifies the significance and the role of the individual events is normally called the "plot" of the narrative. The plot functions to transform a chronicle or listing of events into a schematic whole by highlighting and recognizing the contribution that certain events make to the development and outcome of the story. Without the recognition of significance given by the plot, each event would appear as discontinuous and separate, and its meaning would be limited to its categorical identification or its spatiotemporal location. (1988, p. 18–19)

---

[3]The narrative scheme serves as a lens through which seemingly independent and disconnected elements of existence are seen as related parts of a whole (see Polkinghorne, 1988).

In a similar direction, Carrithers also upheld the importance of mental and social understanding from the understanding of the plot, and he put it this way:

> So when we understand a plot, we understand changes of mind and of relationship, changes brought about by acts. Moreover, we are able to link acts, thoughts, and their consequences together so that we grasp the metamorphosis of each other's thoughts and each other's situations in a flow of action. In this perspective character and plot are indivisible, for we understand character only as it is revealed to us in the flow of action, and we only understand plot as the consequence of characters acting with characteristic beliefs and intentions. With such narrative understanding people orient themselves and act in accountable manner, sensibly, effectively, and appropriately, creating and re-creating complex skeins of social life. (1992, p. 84)

It is relevant and clarifying to remember Polkinghorne's point of view on the dynamics of the plot and change, he held:

> When they come to the therapeutic situation, clients already have life narratives, of which they are both the protagonist and author. The life narrative is open- ended: future actions and occurrences will have to be incorporated into the present plot. (1988, p. 182)

Problematic psychological plots, we often observe in patients who present typical plots, for example, people with chronic depression. They usually create plots that order and configure their life events with the hallmark of being centered on loss and/or hopelessness. In other words, they order the events of their life as part of a tragic plot in which the protagonist (oneself) is abandoned or without hope to achieve their own objectives.

In the field of psychotherapy, there is a bulky agreement among psychotherapists of some orientations, in maintaining that the psychological understanding of the patient requires the identification of the different "experiential events" and the reflective analysis of them, with the aim of a new integration of these events emerging in a new plot without inflections that makes them understandable in the context in which they occurred (García Haro et al., 2024; Quiñones et al., 2015, 2017; Dimaggio & Semerari, 2004; McAdams & Janis, 2004; Polkinghorne, 1988, 2001, 2004; Guidano, 1999, Lakoff, 1987; Haskell, 1987). This process allows for new trajectories of adaptive personal meaning, which implies a new causal and temporal articulation of the involved events, an emergence of a clear judgment about what happened accompanied by different purposes and a sense of agency, among others.

In summary, from an evolutionary perspective, narratives are fundamental for understanding human existence and are part of our evolutionary history as a species. They particularly allow us to understand how people come to mentally represent culturally anchored events about themselves over time (past, present, and future perspective), about others, about the real and virtual world in which they live in the twenty-first century.

On the other hand, the perspective on narratives in the case formulation model from an evolutionary perspective [ECF] has several characteristics that I list in a general and introductory way. First, the narrative is assumed as a source of analysis, clarification, existential positioning, reflection, and synthesis that facilitates achieving continuity in the *narrative identity.* Second, it is fundamental to overcome a psychologically difficult and painful theme called *Dysfunctional Narrative.* This means, it is essential to make accessible and re-articulate past and present experiences (and their ingredients in the "profile of dysfunctional intersubjective knowledge domains") that are active in the narrative that traps the person.

Third, the process of psychological change guided by the ECF involves generating conditions for sequential elaboration (descriptive narrative) and reflection (reflective narrative) through the process of *Narrative Scaling*[4] in order to achieve a Functional Narrative (Fig. 2.1). That is, the different "evolutionary ingredients" (profile of dysfunctional intersubjective knowledge domains) now behave in synergy as a new "Gestalt of Transformative Understanding."

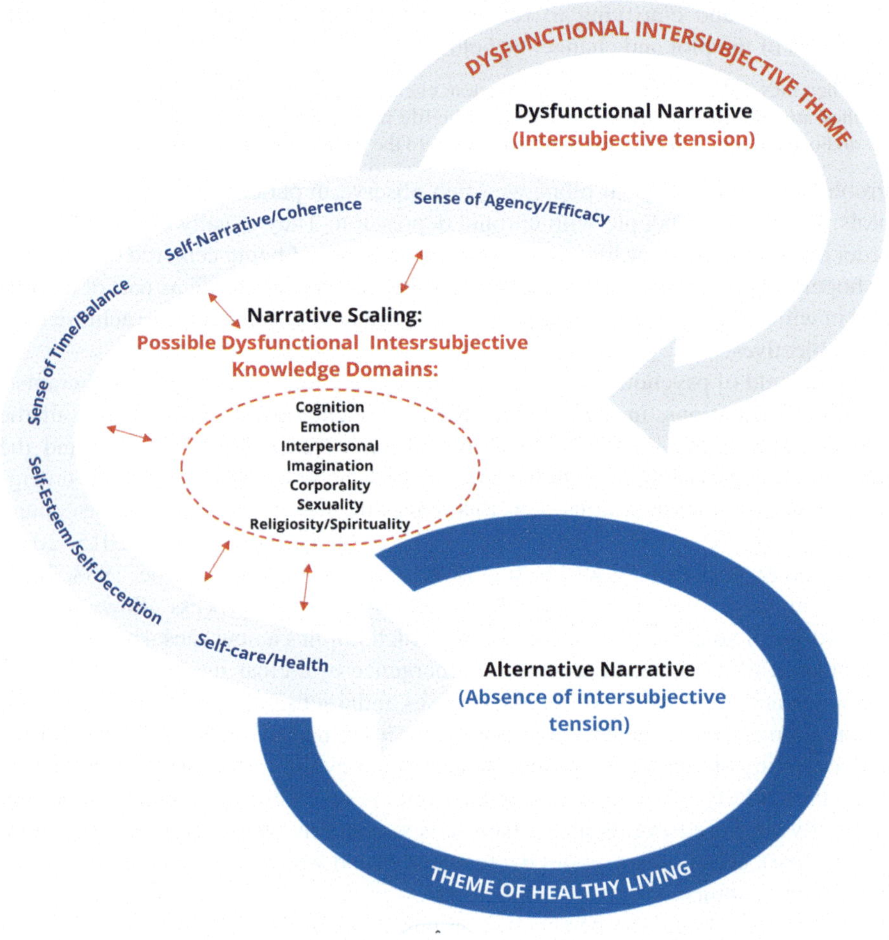

Fig. 2.1 Narrative scaling

[4] *Narrative Scaling* refers to the therapist-guided process that begins with an emerging narrative (in the profile of all or some of the patient's dysfunctional intersubjective knowledge domains) and gradually ends in a dynamic functional narrative.

To summarize, the narrative in the *Case Formulation from an evolutionary perspective*, is conceived as a "powerful evolutionary tool" that organizes events and vital actions into an intentional symbolic structure that is ubiquitous, and that particularly allows to describe, understand, reflect, and explain the flow of temporal existence in an "intersubjective and cultural fabric." Therefore, without constantly working on the narrative, adaptive psychological change is not possible.

References

Bandura, A. (2006). Toward a psychology of human agency. *Perspectives on Psychological Science, 1*(2), 164–180. https://doi.org/10.1111/j.1745-6916.2006.00011.x

Brockelman, P. (1985). *Time and self. Phenomenological explorations*. The Crossroad Publishing Company.

Bruner, J. (1986). *Actual minds, possible worlds*. Harvard University Press.

Bruner, J. S. (1990). *Acts of meaning*. Harvard University Press.

Bruner, J. (2004). The narrative creation of self. In E. L. Angus & J. McLeod (Eds.), *The handbook of narrative and psychotherapy: Practice, theory, and research* (pp. 3–14). Sage.

Carrithers, M. (1992). *Why humans have cultures: Explaining anthropology and social diversity*. Oxford University Press.

Dimaggio, G., & Semerari, A. (2004). Disorganized narratives: The psychological condition and its treatment. In E. L. Angus & J. McLeod (Eds.), *The handbook of narrative and psychotherapy: Practice, theory, and research* (pp. 263–282). Sage.

García Haro, J., Quiñones, A., & Ugarte, C. (2024). Formulación de caso en conducta suicida: una perspectiva evolucionista para la regulación y bienestar psicológico. In A. Quiñones & C. Caro (Eds.), *Formulación de Caso: Hacia una Psicoterapia de precisión* (pp. 381–431). UNED editorial.

Guidano, V. F. (1999). Psicoterapia: Aspectos metodológicos, cuestiones clínicas y problemas abiertos desde una perspectiva postracionalista. *Revista de Psicoterapia, 37*, 95–105.

Haden, C. A., Haine, R. A., & Fivush, R. (1997). Developing narrative structure in parent-child reminiscing across the preschool years. *Developmental Psychology, 33*, 295–307.

Haskell, R. E. (1987). Structural metaphor and cognition. In R. E. Haskell (Ed.), *Cognition and symbolic structures: The psychology of metaphoric transformation* (pp. 241–256). Ablex.

La Roche, M. J., & Christopher, M. S. (2009). Changing paradigms from empirically supported treatment to evidence-based practice: A cultural perspective. *Professional Psychology: Research and Practice, 40*(4), 396–402.

Lakoff, G. (1987). *Women, fire and dangerous thing: What categories reveal about mind*. University of Chicago Press.

Linde, C. (1993). *Life stories: The creation of coherence*. Oxford University Press.

Marsella, A. J., & Yamada, A. M. (2010). Culture and psychopathology: Foundations, issues, directions. *Journal of Pacific Rim Psychology, 4*(2), 103–115. https://doi.org/10.1375/prp.4.2.103

McAdams D. P., & Janis, L. (2004). Narrative identity and narrative therapy. EL Angus, J. Mcleod The handbook of narrative and psychotherapy: Practice, theory, and research (pp. 159–173). : Sage.

McAdams, D. P., & Olson, B. D. (2010). Personality development: Continuity and change over the life course. *Annual Review of Psychology, 61*, 517–542. https://doi.org/10.1146/annurev.psych.093008.100507

Nelson, K. (Ed.). (1989). *Narratives from the crib*. Harvard University Press.

Polkinghorne, D. E. (1988). *Narrative knowing and the human sciences*. State University of New York Press.

Polkinghorne, D. (2001). The self and humanistic psychology. In K. J. Schneider, J. Bugental, & J. Pierson (Eds.), *The handbook of humanistic psychology: Leading hedges in theory, research and practice* (pp. 81–100). Sage.

Polkinghorne, D. E. (2004). Narrative therapy and postmodernism. E L. Angus, J. Mcleod The handbook of narrative and psychotherapy: Practice, theory, and research (pp. 53–67). : Sage.

Quiñones, A. (2013). *Indicadores de procesos en psicoterapia asociados a éxito.* [Tesis de Doctorado, Universidad Autónoma de Barcelona]. Repositorio Institucional – Universidad Autónoma de Barcelona.

Quiñones, A., Ceric, F., & Ugarte, C. (2015). Flujos de información en zonas de tiempo subjetivo: estudio de un proceso psicoterapéutico exitoso. *Revista Argentina de Clínica Psicológica, 24*(3), 255–266.

Quiñones, A., Ceric, F., Ugarte, C., & Pascale, A. (2017). Psychotherapy and psychological time: A case study. *Rivista di Psichiatria, 52*(3), 109–116.

Sarbin, T. R. (1986). The narrative as the root metaphor for contextualism. In T. R. Sarbin (Ed.), *Narrative psychology: The storied nature of human conduct* (pp. 3–22). Praeger.

Siegel, D. J. (1999). *The developing mind: How relationships and the brain interact to shape who we are* (1st ed.). Guilford Press.

Siegel, D. J. (2012). *The developing mind: How relationships and the brain interact to shape who we are* (2nd ed.). Guilford Press.

Chapter 3
Thematization: Beginning of Case Conceptualization

The proposed model focuses on a thematic conceptualization. Therefore, the Case Formulation from an evolutionary perspective [ECF] begins by identifying a "*Dysfunctional Intersubjective Theme*"and the profile of the dysfunctional intersubjective knowledge domains involved (see Box 3.1). In this context and by way of order, I point out two particularities:

Firstly, a *Dysfunctional Intersubjective Theme* (DIT) is understood as an active dynamic of information and knowledge that occurs in the patient's intersubjective representation and is operationalized as a profile of *Dysfunctional Intersubjective Domains* that interfere with psychological regulation and psychological well-being. More precisely, the DIT refers to experiences that accumulate and integrate into memory and are experienced with intersubjective tension in the *existential present* through a dysfunctional narrative.[1] In other words, it is a sort of "area of information and knowledge in narrative format" that presents degrees of *psychological deregulation and psychological distress.*

Secondly, a *Dysfunctional Intersubjective Theme* ***is idiographic*** and arises in a historical (personal), contextual, and cultural framework. Therefore, the themes are also ***nomothetic***, for example, grandiosity, hypercontrol, procrastination, self-sabotage, inauthenticity, etc. (see Box 3.2). It is revealed in a *Dysfunctional Narrative* and takes shape through a problematic psychological plot based on personal history and culture.

On the other hand, in doing psychotherapy, a question that every therapist asks themselves about a patient is "What is psychologically happening to the patient who communicates psychological suffering?". The first thing that should be attempted is to capture the intimate meaning by understanding the self-narrative. However, this question must be specified in terms of psychological processing to be partially

[1] Examples of TID: "trapped by not feeling emotionally in tune with her partner"; "pleasing the partner in an automatic and indiscriminate way and feeling distressed at different times."

Á. Quiñones Bergeret, *Evolutionary Case Formulation*,
https://doi.org/10.1007/978-3-031-67412-9_3

Box 3.1: Thematization

EVOLUTIONARY CASE FORMULATION - EVALUATION

Name: .... Date: ....

Carried out in session No.: ____ (integration of information)

Reason for consultation (in patient's own words):

....

....

I. THEMATIC CONCEPTUALIZATION

Dysfunctional Intersubjective Theme (co-construction): ....

....

(mark presence: x)

Specify thematic axis(es):
Psychological intimacy ☐ Death/Finitude of existence ☐ Surrender ☐ Greatness ☐ Inferiority ☐ Avenger ☐ Power ☐ Failure ☐ Loss ☐ Complacent ☐ Inauthenticity ☐ Freedom ☐ Uncontrollability ☐ Certainty ☐ Mistrust ☐ Perfectionism ☐ Betrayal ☐ Opposition ☐ Loneliness ☐ Limitation ☐ Sabotage ☐ Transcend ☐ Contempt ☐ Hypercontrol ☐ Hypercriticism ☐ Discrimination ☐ Jealousy ☐ Compete ☐ Postponement ☐ Uprooting ☐ Self-sacrifice ☐ Sexualization ☐ Unworthy ☐ Abandonment ☐ Incompetence ☐ Moral superiority ☐ Fear of aging ☐ Paternal deprivation ☐ Maternal deprivation ☐ Technological addiction ☐
Others:________________

Dysfunctional Narrative:

....

....

Beginning of the Theme(s)? Course?

....

....

Are there relevant life events and/or precipitating stressors?

....

....

Is there frustration of basic psychological needs: competence, autonomy, relationship?

....

....

What strengths do you identify in the person?

....

....

SISTEMA SELF: valoración clínica
(marcar presencia: X)

SENSE OF AGENCY/EFFICACY: Alteration ☐
Describe:...

....

SELF-NARRATIVE/COHERENCE: Alteration ☐
Describe:...

....

SENSE OF TIME/BALANCE: Alteration ☐
Describe:...

....

SELF-ESTEEM/SELF-DECEPTION: Alteration ☐
Describe:...

....

SELF- CARE/ HEALTH: Alteration ☐
Describe:...

....

Box 3.2: Specify Thematic Axis [Nomothetic]

(marcar presencia: X)

Specify thematic axis(es):
Psychological intimacy ☐ Death/Finitude of existence ☐ Surrender ☐ Greatness ☐ Inferiority ☐ Avenger ☐ Power ☐ Failure ☐ Loss ☐ Complacent ☐ Inauthenticity ☐ Freedom ☐ Uncontrollability ☐ Certainty ☐ Mistrust ☐ Perfectionism ☐ Betrayal ☐ Opposition ☐ Loneliness ☐ Limitation ☐ Sabotage ☐ Transcend ☐ Contempt ☐ Hypercontrol ☐ Hypercriticism ☐ Discrimination ☐ Jealousy ☐ Compete ☐ Postponement ☐ Uprooting ☐ Self-sacrifice ☐ Sexualization ☐ Unworthy ☐ Abandonment ☐ Incompetence ☐ Moral superiority ☐ Fear of aging ☐ Paternal deprivation ☐ Maternal deprivation ☐ Technological addiction ☐
Others: ______________________

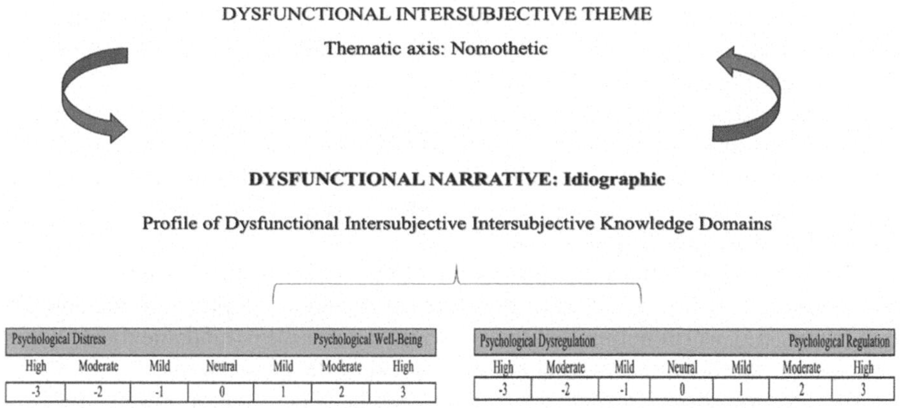

Fig. 3.1 Process diagram in psychotherapy

answered at the beginning of the psychotherapeutic process by patient and therapist, in order to propose a comprehensible hypothesis that allows for a joint work plan.

A directed path to begin answering the aforementioned question is to probe, explore, sound out, and investigate the "psychological ingredients" that appear in the story and reason for consultation and their subsequent thematic co-construction in the process of evaluation (Dysfunctional Intersubjective Theme). In "this hermeneutic back and forth," the Dysfunctional Intersubjective Knowledge Domains are analyzed and evaluated through the two axes: Psychological Distress-Psychological Well-being and Psychological Deregulation-Psychological Regulation (see Fig. 3.1).

On the other hand, there are aspects to highlight in the ECF that facilitate the observation and joint reflection of the Therapist/Patient dyad to generate the ***theming*** that facilitates self-understanding in the patient. Thus, the therapist is assisted

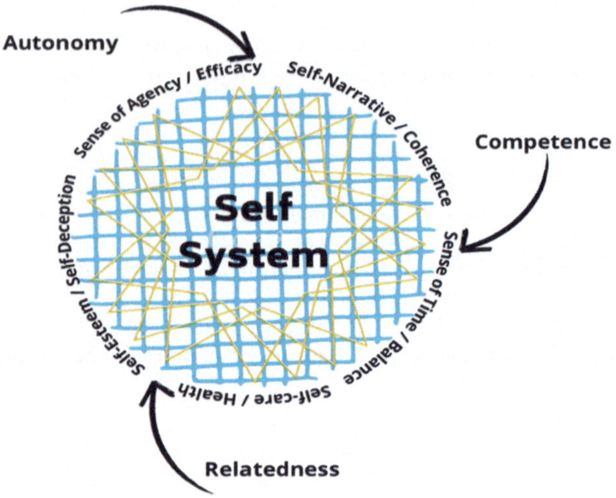

Fig. 3.2 Self system and interaction with psychological needs. (Adapted from Quiñones, 2024)

with possible thematic axes that are nomothetic (see Fig. 3.2). Obviously, both clinical experience and therapeutic training are the main factors when defining a Dysfunctional Intersubjective Theme (Idiographic).

As observed in *"specify thematic axis,"* there are several possibilities of dysfunctional Themes that are common in the West. We can name "loss" with a dysfunctional narrative "I always end up alone"; "injustice" with a dysfunctional narrative "I can't stand inequality"; "opposition" with a dysfunctional narrative "I always look for inconsistency to attack", etc.

The following questions are then asked: "Start of the theme?" "Course?". Both questions refer to the evaluation of the chronology and development of the conflictive theme. It is worth noting that the descriptive narrative is fundamental to begin to place the psychological problem in the context of the person's life.

The question about relevant events that affect the person and/or present stressors continues: "Are there relevant life events and/or precipitating stressors?"

Elucidating this aspect is fundamental, since stressors affect existence and personal well-being depending on the severity, for example, a chronic illness, divorce, death of a loved one, etc.

Penultimately, the question is asked about possible psychological needs that are not being met. "Is there frustration of basic psychological needs: competence, autonomy, relationship?". This penultimate question of the first part of the ECF-E refers to the theory of basic psychological needs (Ryan & Deci, 2017) which establishes the existence of three psychological needs (competence, relationship, and autonomy) that need to be satisfied by people for their psychological development and optimal personal well-being (Deci & Ryan, 2000). In addition, basic needs when frustrated are the source of a variety of maladaptive forms as has been well documented (Ryan & Deci, 2017).

It should be noted that people can differ in terms of how subjectively prominent these needs are or how centrally the needs are represented in their personal goals and lifestyles, and these individual differences can affect the satisfaction of needs. However, the essential assumption is that greater satisfaction of the basic need will result in better well-being, and greater frustration of the need will decrease well-being, regardless of these conditional factors (Ryan & Deci, 2017). Consequently, it is important to start answering this question from the beginning because the *Dysfunctional Intersubjective Theme* [TID] also develops in a context of frustration of the psychological needs of competence, autonomy, and relationship.

In relation to the Self System and its interaction with psychological needs (see Fig. 3.2) always present, it is necessary to delve a little deeper. In particular, the dimensions of the Self System and its wiring with second-order intersubjective domains have a strong relationship with the satisfaction of psychological needs (autonomy, competence, and relationship)[2] and stress coping (see Fig. 3.2). The emergence of unhealthy trajectories, such as the presence of a dysfunctional intersubjective theme, depends on this self-organizing interaction. We must not lose sight of the fact that motives arise from psychological needs to energize, direct, and sustain the behavior necessary to advance towards greater personal growth and optimal well-being in life (Ryan & Deci, 2017).

Finally, exploration is made of the strengths observed in the person **"What strengths do you identify in the person?"**. This is a question that the therapist must keep in mind and elucidate in the psychotherapy process.

In addition, this aspect is very useful because the strengths that every human being has are of great help to promote changes and also to bring to the present the necessary agency to start working on dissolving the *Dysfunctional Intersubjective Theme.*

In summary, thematization is a dynamic process that involves the emergence of a dysfunctional narrative articulated by the Self System (and includes a profile of second-order domains), in a context of possible stressors and alterations of basic psychological needs. In other words, a TID is an emerging dysfunctional/maladaptive possibility in a complex system, which can be transient or chronic.[3]

3.1 Guiding the Development of Healthy Narratives in Psychotherapy

Thematizing the psychological problem (see "Specify thematic axis", ECF-Evaluation) is the first step for the patient to delimit his problematic theme. With the ECF-Intervention, the guided process begins for the patient to progressively explore and understand his conflictive theme (TID).

---

[2] Psychological needs (autonomy, competence, relationship) refer to an inherent (innate) psychological process that underlies the proactive desire to seek interactions with the environment that can promote personal growth, social development, and psychological well-being (Reeve, 2017).

[3] For example, see depression from an evolutionary theory perspective (Gilbert, 1992).

In particular, the conflictive psychological plots that need to be reconstructed in a psychotherapeutic process involve reordering the narrative through the distinction of descriptive narrative and reflective narrative (Quiñones, 2013).

By *Descriptive Narrative,* we understand a narrative that refers to external and interpersonally situated aspects of what happened to the person who experienced degrees of psychological discomfort and psychological deregulation. It implies a sequential and linear description of a fact and answers the following possible questions: What happened?, Who were there?, Where did it happen?, How did it start?, How did it develop?, How did it end? and How long did it last?" In the maladaptive dimension, it indicates an elaboration that shows different types of deficits and/or absence in the proper sequential and linear description. As a consequence, it does not serve the patient to obtain a representation that contributes to having a panorama that facilitates a healthy significance; therefore, he remains trapped in the conflictive plot. On the contrary, in the adaptive case, there is an adequate sequential and linear description of what happened.

By *Reflective Narrative,* we understand a narrative that refers to aspects of internal elaboration situated intersubjectively that facilitates the reflective analysis of what happened and processed the person. In the adaptive case, it implies an elaboration of meaning and articulation of what happened and answers the following possible questions: What were your intentions? What were the intentions of those present? What bodily sensations did you experience? What emotions did you identify in yourself? Do you have an explanation for why the event occurred? Were you focused on the present during the event, or were you thinking about your past or future? Did you feel comfortable afterward? What does the event hypothetically mean to you? What does it hypothetically mean to the others present? What new insights do you recognize now when you look back at the event? If we reflect together now, has something similar happened to you before? What possible consequences do you infer now after reflecting with me?

In the practical dimension of psychotherapy, when a patient begins to successfully (adaptively) elaborate his psychological conflict through a dialectic of *descriptive and reflective narratives "strengthened in quantity and quality progressively,"* new causal connections, stable sense of agency, positive self-deception, adequate emotional decoding, interpersonal awareness, temporal awareness, body awareness, narrative coherence, social reference, etc., emerge and consolidate. In summary, a functional narrative emerges. On the contrary, in the maladaptive case, the elaboration is deficient; therefore, it indicates absence of transformation of the *Dysfunctional Narrative* that continues "trapping the person."

Lastly, for narratives that need to be reconstructed because they are part of the *Dysfunctional Intersubjective Theme* (TID), it is suggested to use the Format for Narrative Reconstruction (see Appendix).

Appendix: Format for Narrative Reconstruction

RECONSTRUCTED SITUATION [Dysfunctional Narrative] **Session:___**

We will call the situation: "________________________________"

Descriptive Narrative:

What happened? ……………………………………………………………………
……………………………………………………………………………………
Who were present? ………………………………………………………………
……………………………………………………………………………………
Where did it happen? ……………………………………………………………
……………………………………………………………………………………
How did it start?…………………………………………………………………
……………………………………………………………………………………
How did it unfold?………………………………………………………………
……………………………………………………………………………………
How did it end?…………………………………………………………………
……………………………………………………………………………………
How long did it last?……………………………………………………………
……………………………………………………………………………………

Reflective Narrative:

What were your intentions?……………………………………………………
……………………………………………………………………………………
What were the intentions of those present? ……………………………………
……………………………………………………………………………………
What bodily sensations did you experience?……………………………………
……………………………………………………………………………………
What emotions do you identify in yourself? ……………………………………
……………………………………………………………………………………

What emotions do you identify in those present?………………………………
……………………………………………………………………………………

Do you have an explanation for why what happened occurred? ………………
……………………………………………………………………………………

In what happened, are you focused on the present or are you thinking about your past or future? ……………………………………………………………………………
……………………………………………………………………………………

Did you feel comfortable afterwards?……………………………………………
……………………………………………………………………………………

What does what happened mean to you? ………………………………………
……………………………………………………………………………………

What does it mean to the others present? ....
....

Continuation

What do you realize if you observe the panorama of what happened?.................
....

And if you look at the moment when you move to "_________"?..................................
....

Has something similar happened to you before?..
....

What consequences do you observe now upon reflecting with me?...............................
....

Effects of the reconstruction according to therapist and patient (deferred):

What changes are observed in the Dysfunctional Narrative?...............................
....
....

Does a Functional Narrative emerge? Yes: ☐ No: ☐
....
....

What characteristics does the emerging Functional Narrative have?
....
....

Are there behavioral changes associated with Functional Narrative emerging in everyday life? Yes: ☐ No: ☐
....
....

Observations
....
....

References

Deci, E. L., & Ryan, R. M. (2000). The "what" and "why" of goal pursuits: Human needs and the self-determination of behavior. *Psychological Inquiry, 11*(4), 227–268. https://doi.org/10.1207/S15327965PLI1104_01

Gilbert, P. (1992). *Depression. The evolution of powerlessness*. Guilford Press.

Quiñones, A. (2013). *Indicadores de procesos en psicoterapia asociados a éxito*. [Tesis de Doctorado, Universidad Autónoma de Barcelona]. Repositorio Institucional – Universidad Autónoma de Barcelona.

Quiñones, A. (2024). Perspectiva evolucionista para la formulación de caso: Un sistema abierto. In A. Quiñones & C. Caro (Eds.), *Formulación de Caso: Hacia una Psicoterapia de precisión* (pp. 107–135). UNED Editorial.

Reeve, J. (2017). *Understanding motivation and emotion*. Wiley.

Ryan, R. M., & Deci, E. L. (2017). *Self-determination theory: Basic psychological needs in motivation, development, and wellness*. Guilford Press.

Chapter 4
Self System: First Order Knowledge Domain

The Self System[1] is ubiquitous in the processing of information and creation of individual meaning in a cultural intersubjective matrix, and it is characterized by being a permanent embodied process, dynamic, synergistic, multimodal, historical, and contextual.

In the model of case formulation from an evolutionary perspective [ECF], it is the primary and inclusive domain, which acts as an articulator ("narrative center of gravity"[2]) of the seven domains of second order intersubjective knowledge (Cognition, Emotion, Interpersonal, Imagination, Corporeality, Sexuality, Religiosity/Spirituality).

As a frame of reference, Bruner's work is very relevant for what follows, and it is the approach of the Self as a system (Bruner, 1997a; Bruner & Kalmar, 1998) would have two functions that facilitate a delimitation and understanding of the complexity of what is called "Self": (1) function of intersubjective communicability and (2) function of individuation. The first highlights the evolutionary perspective and understands Homo Sapiens as a species that shares symbolic representations and consensual ways of orienting itself in the social world and at the same time is capable of having private experiences, and the second, promotes the development of individuation and would basically consist in creating and maintaining subjectivity as protected privacy.

An essential premise is that the Self System is a process. Clearly this aspect is highlighted by Paul Brockelman, he says:

> Far from being a thing, the self is in fact a complex set of relations. It is a dynamic process, a set of intentional activities reflectively aware of itself as such. I am a relation which is temporal, but I am also conscious of that. (1985, p. 79)

[1] In the text, I use "self," "I," "oneself," "self-awareness," "identity," interchangeably. On the other hand, the first systematic treatment of the study of the self concept in psychology was carried out by William James in his book Principles of Psychology.

[2] See Daniel Dennett (1991).

Á. Quiñones Bergeret, *Evolutionary Case Formulation*,
https://doi.org/10.1007/978-3-031-67412-9_4

Similarly, the centrality of the Self for social functioning[3] is crucial to make viable the life in groups and in cultural complexity. Complementary to the previous, and paraphrasing Gallagher and Zahavi, the self is present to itself when it is in the world. They maintain:

> The self is present to itself precisely and indeed only when it is engaged in the world. It would consequently be a decisive mistake to interpret the phenomenological notion of a core, or minimal, self as a Cartesian-style mental residuum, that is, as some kind of self-enclosed and self-sufficient interiority. The phenomenological notion of self is fully compatible with a strong emphasis on the fundamental intentionality, or being-in-the-world, of consciousness. (2008, p. 204)

As a historical context, the understanding of the self (self-awareness) in the field of psychology has a long tradition of debate and research (Gallagher & Zahavi, 2012; Gallagher, 2000a, b; Bruner, 1990, 1997a, 2004; Bruner & Kalmar, 1998; Neisser, 1988, 1993; Guidano, 1992; Guidano & Liotti, 1983; Lewis, 1994, 2010, 2011; Markus, 1977; Lewis & Brooks-Gunn, 1979a, b; James, 1890). However, it is also noteworthy that in the twenty-first century, there is still no formal definition of Self.

On the other hand, from the perspective of neuroscience, it is argued that the brain has likely developed different mechanisms to know ourselves, understand how others respond to us, detect threats within the social group, and regulate actions to avoid being excluded from these groups (Krendl & Heatherton, 2009). It is relevant to highlight that the Self, from an evolutionary perspective, makes us what we are as a unique species.

One of the prominent researchers in the field of evolutionary psychology is Michael Lewis (1994, 2010, 2011). He emphasizes the importance of understanding the Self as a complex system.[4]

On his question "What is a Self?", Lewis points out:

> The claim has been made that it is possible to know of all things related to the self; for example, the yogi's belief in the control of much of our autonomic nervous system function. Although it might be true that I could know more of some parts of myself if I chose to, it is nonetheless the case that what is known by myself is greater than what I can state I know.
>
> If such facts are true, then, it is fair to suggest a metaphor of myself. I imagine myself to be a biological machine that is an evolutionarily fit complex of processes: doing, feeling, thinking, planning, and learning. One aspect of this machine is the idea of me. If I were an Eastern mystic, I would perhaps draw this idea as an eye, like some all-seeing thing. Not being such a metaphysician, I prefer the metaphor of a protoplasmic mass, perhaps resembling the frontal lobes. It is this mass that knows itself and knows it does not know all of

---

[3] For context, there are two sociologists who deserve special mention in relation to the topic of the self and who have been very important for psychology. First, Charles Horton Cooley (1864–1929) introduced the term *looking-glass self* to suggest that other people serve as a mirror in which we see ourselves. Expanding on this idea, George Herbert Mead (1863–1931) added that we often know ourselves by imagining what others think of us and then incorporate these perceptions into our personal concepts.

[4] It poses four questions that are fundamental to understanding the Self: "What is a self?, How do we measure a self?, Are there cultural and historical differences in a self?, What does a self do?".

> itself! The me that recognizes me in the mirror is located in that particular mass. The self, then, is greater than the me, the me being only a small portion of myself. If the metaphor drawn is unsatisfactory, the difference between self and me can be understood from an epistemological point of view. The idea that I know is not the same as the idea that I know I know. The me aspect of the self that I refer to is that which knows it knows. (1994, p. 21)

From his perspective, the Self consists of at least two main aspects: the machinery of the self which is implicit consciousness and includes regulatory functions and even high-order learning, and the mental state of me[5] which is explicit consciousness. Lewis states:

> The ontogenetic and phylogenetic coherences found to date support the idea that in order to understand the concept of self, we need to disentangle the common term self into at least two aspects. These I have called the machinery of the self and the idea of me. They have been referred to by other terms, for example, I have referred to the idea of me as objective self- awareness and the machinery of self as subjective self-awareness (Lewis, 1990, 1991, 1992). They both are biological events. The same objective-subjective distinction has been considered by others (see, for example, Duval & Wicklund, 1972). In any consideration of the concept of self, especially in regard to adult humans, it is important to keep in mind that both aspects exist. There is, unbeknownst to us most of the time, an elaborate complex of machinery that controls much of our behavior, learns from experience, has states, and affects our bodies, most likely including what and how we think. The processes are, for the most part, unavailable to us. What is available is the idea of me. (1994, p. 24)

The two aspects of the Self, implicit and explicit consciousness,[6] allow for a more precise understanding of the idea of the narrative Self. Lewis (2010) on life narratives and continuity, indicates:

> These life narratives also fit with our notion of causality, in that events that happen earlier affect events that happen later. Our personal life narratives must explain how we got from one point to another, so they are likely designed to eliminate discontinuities. Our narratives are, by their nature, attempts at continuity because it is our nature, at least in this age, to think of ourselves as a unity even though we may contain conflicting parts. No matter how difficult these parts may be to reconcile, in the picture we paint of ourselves, all the disparate parts somehow get together and form a single me, a personality we can understand. We need to maintain our identity, and our narratives serve that need by showing how we are the same or, if we are different, how that difference came about. (p. 664)

Jerome Bruner is another fundamental researcher on the Self and is relevant in the present framework to unambiguously assume that the human being is not an "island" but lives in intersubjectivity. Bruner on intersubjectivity, maintains:

> Let me conclude this part of our discussion by noting only that the presence of human intersubjectivity and the gifts that it brings—like symbolic standing for—allows us to use others as guides in adapting, to the world and, indeed, to operate jointly with others in

[5] In the latter half of the second year of life, the child acquires the idea of me. The emergence of the idea of me allows for the representation of self and other (Lewis, 1994).

[6] A "theory of mind," such as social cognition, implies an explicit awareness of one's own and others' mental states. In such a context, the development of explicit awareness for Lewis (2010, 2011), there would be at least four aspects of its development: Knowing or I know"; "is I know I know"; "is I know you know", "as I know, you know, I know".

> constructing, a world to which we are able to adapt. I also want to argue that such intersubjectivity is a condition for language and its use, that it is the heart of the "standing for" relation without which there could be no symbolic language. Without these things, the cultural adaptation would be impossible. (1997b, p. 88)

Clearly, Bruner is a strong advocate that culture prescribes its own genres for self-construction, that is, ways in which we can legitimately conceive of ourselves and others. In other words, identity is deeply relational, therefore it implies the other. He says:

> Rather, we continually construct and reconstruct a Self, as required by the situations we encounter, guided by our memories of the past and our experiences and fears for the future. Talking about ourselves to ourselves is like inventing a story about who and what we are, what happened, and why we are doing what we are doing. (Bruner, 2003, p. 93. Free translation by the author)

A huge contribution from Bruner to the understanding of the Self was his proposal of nine indicators of the Self that show social presence ("thus placing the Self within the locus of social behavior") and the quality of self-narratives (Bruner, 1997a; Bruner & Kalmar, 1998). Such indicators of the self are what people take as signals that the Self is present and at the same time allow us to contrast ourselves with others and realize many of our own characteristics. In addition, they are helpful in focusing on dysfunctional narratives and promoting change in psychotherapy. Bruner and Kalmar maintain "They trigger a sense of our own Self or of Selfhood in others. Taken together, they suggest the domain of functioning within which Self seems to operate" (Bruner & Kalmar, 1998, p. 310).

The nine indicators are briefly defined below, paraphrasing Bruner (Bruner, 1997a; Bruner & Kalmar, 1998), and I add brief reflections for therapists:

1. *Agency Indicators*: Refers to voluntary acts of free choice, initiatives freely undertaken in pursuit of a goal. Fundamentally: "The sense of optativity, of the need to weigh alternatives, signals Selfhood in our own private consciousness" (Bruner & Kalmar, 1998, p. 311).

   Reflection for therapists: In psychotherapy, therapists witness in our patients low agency or unstable agency. Therefore, every psychotherapeutic process should seek to dissolve the "constrained agency" and contribute to the emergence of agency.
2. *Commitment Indicators*: Essentially, they inform us about the tenacity of human beings. They indicate hierarchy, tenacity, delay of gratification, sacrifice of what we like, and perseverance at various times. In other words, "following one's own projects and purposes that each one imposes on oneself." Bruner points out "Commitment indicators are about an agent's adherence to an intended or actual line of action, an adherence that transcends momentariness and impulsiveness" (1997a, p. 149).

   Reflection for therapists: In psychotherapy, commitment to oneself, in its various forms, is fundamental to achieving well-being and effecting change in psychotherapy when necessary.

3. *Resource Indicators*: Refers to the contribution made by the individual to achieve their commitments.

   In the words of Bruner:

   > Resource indicators speak to the powers, privileges, and goods that an agent seems willing to bring or actually brings to bear on his commitments. They include not only such "external" resources as power, social legitimacy, and sources of information, but "inner" ones as well, like patience, perspective, forgiveness, persuasiveness and the like. (1997a, p. 149)

   Reflection for therapists: In psychotherapy, personal contribution to conduct life is fundamental for psychological well-being. Just like dealing with what needs to be changed in a successful psychotherapy process.
4. *Social Reference Indicators*: Points to the relevance of the social reference that people use to value and legitimize their own actions. Bruner and Kalmar (1998) point out "They signal that others are in mind, whether these are real people, cognitively constructed reference groups, or some sort of normative "law and order"" (p. 311).

   Reflection for therapists: In psychotherapy to understand a person's life at the present time, it is necessary to consider and understand such indicators accurately (example: hierarchy of social references).
5. *Evaluation Indicators*: They point out the process of valuing ourselves and others in intersubjectivity. In the words of Bruner:

   > Evaluation indicators provide signs of how we or others value the prospects, outcomes, or progress of intended, actual, or completed lines of endeavor. They may be specific (as with signs of being satisfied or dissatisfied with a particular act) or highly general (as with a sense that some large enterprise as a whole is satisfactory or not). These indicators tell about situated affect as it relates to the conduct of life in the small or large. (1997a, p. 149)

   Reflection for therapists: In psychotherapy, personal and others' evaluation plays an important role in certain sensitivity to judgment scenarios, for example, in the spectrum of anxiety disorders.
6. *Qualia Indicators*: They signal the "feel" of existence in a broad sense. To illustrate: daily humor and its variations, the daily rhythm in the work week and the weekend, the dejection that happens to all of us in certain circumstances, the enthusiasm that invades us at certain opportunities, etc. Bruner highlights "Qualia indicators are signs of the "feel" of a life-mood, pace, zest, weariness, or whatever. They are signs of the subjectivity of selfhood" (1997a, p. 149).

   Reflection for therapists: From a nomothetic point of view, in patients who present mood disorders and impulsivity, this indicator is often altered.
7. *Reflexivity Indicators*: They inform us about the reflective activity directed at self-examination in various areas of personal life, the constant self-construction in the intersubjective world, the self-evaluation of successes and failures, and the perspective that provides us metacognition. Bruner points out that fundamentally "Reflexive indicators speak to the more metacognitive side of Self, to the reflective activity invested in self-examination, self-construction, and self-evaluation" (Bruner, 1997a, p. 150).

Reflection for therapists: This indicator in the space of psychotherapy needs to be promoted throughout the process of dissolving a Dysfunctional Intersubjective Theme [TID] that implies discomfort and psychological dysregulation.

8. *Coherence indicators*: They refer to the integrity of a person's actions, their multiple commitments, the management of resources to carry out personal projects, self-evaluations over time, etc. Bruner asserts "These indicators are taken to reveal the internal structure of a larger self-concept and are presumed to indicate how the particulars of various endeavors cohere in a "life as a whole""(1997a, p. 151).

   Reflection for therapists: In psychotherapy, the therapist values the sense of personal identity that depends on the content and cohesion of the life story, which the patient constructs in the life cycle.

9. *Positioning indicators*: They reveal how an individual locates himself in the real world, which translates into social coordinates, his vital time, and the social order in which he lives. Bruner points out: "Most usually, positional indicators become salient when we sense a discrepancy between our own sense of position and some publicly prescribed one-as when we act out of role, or somebody is seen as 'uppity'"(1997a, p. 150).

   Reflection for therapists: This indicator in the special intersubjective space that occurs in psychotherapy is relevant to make the necessary and timely adjustments in situations of possible discrepancies.

In the context of psychotherapy, each *Self Indicator* moves on a continuum. I will give an example of high commitment and low commitment in academic work. A person with high commitment in their academic work would reveal a very efficient and professional person who postpones gratification in function of academic achievements such as writing articles for indexed journals, books, and preparing their postgraduate classes. Even excessive commitment over time could affect their mental health.

In the case of low commitment in academic work, it would show us a person who does not feel challenged by academia, feels levels of annoyance in relation to the different university tasks (researching, teaching, attending students, etc.) for some time. Such a situation, if it persists over time, can contribute to a depressive picture.

To conclude, the nine Self indicators proposed by Bruner help the therapist with an additional map for narrative understanding (identity as a life story in evolution) and thus achieve the emergence of possible new adaptive meanings (psychological well-being and psychological regulation according to the case formulation model from an evolutionary perspective).

The work of Daniel Dennett and his remarkable and permanent contribution to the understanding of the Self is essential as a frame of reference for case formulation. His proposal of a Self "as a center of narrative gravity," a position coinciding with the twenty-first century neurosciences of how the brain works, is another complementary way of understanding the *Self System* (Sense of Agency/Efficacy, Autonarrative/Coherence, Sense of Time/Balance, Self-esteem/Self-deception, Self-care/Health). He says:

> A self is an abstract object, a theorist's fiction. The theory is not particle physics but what we might call a branch of people-physics; it is more soberly known as phenomenology or hermeneutics, or soul-science (Geisteswissesnschaft). The physicist does an interpretation, if you like, of the lectern and its behavior, and comes up with the theoretical abstraction of a center of gravity, which is then very useful in characterizing the behavior of the lectern in the future, under a wide variety of conditions. The hermeneuticist, or phenomenologist—or anthropologist—sees some rather more complicated things moving about in the world—human beings and animals—and is faced with a similar problem of interpretation. It turns out to be theoretically perspicuous to organize the interpretation around a central abstraction: Each person has a self (in addition to a center of gravity). In fact we have to posit selves for ourselves as well. The theoretical problem of self-interpretation is at least as difficult and important as the problem of other-interpretation. (Dennett, 1992, p. 105)

The *narrative center of gravity* would be the concept that explains the experience of a unifying center that is agent and object of words. It is clarifying to understand what is meant by "Self," as Dennett argued in 1991:

> A self, according to my theory, is not any old mathematical point, but an abstraction defined by the myriads of attributions and interpretations (including self-attributions and self-interpretations) that have composed the biography of the living body whose Center of Narrative Gravity it is. As such, it plays a singularly important role in the ongoing cognitive economy of that living body, because, of all the things in the environment an active body must make mental models of, none is more crucial than the model the agent has of itself. (1991, pp. 426–427)

It is also worth noting that the Self is conceived as an evolutionary product that arises with language through narratives and as a result of the need for self-representation for oneself and for others. He also makes it clear that the narrative self is not substantially real, but rather an empty abstraction. Ultimately, for Dennett (1991) the self is a "center of narrative gravity" and consists of the abstract and mobile point at which the various stories that the subject tells about himself meet.

A practical aspect before finishing is to make explicit that the dimensions of the Self System are surely several more than those proposed, but it is important to consider parsimony in any case formulation that is made in a psychotherapy process. The time and dedication to each patient on the part of a therapist must be adequate ("and not excessive") so as not to lose and/or diminish the understanding of the complexity of the psychological problem. In this sense, in my opinion, therapists should evaluate at least the five proposed dimensions: Self-narrative/Coherence, Sense of Time/Balance, Sense of Agency/Efficacy, Self-esteem/Self-deception, and Self-care/Health (Fig. 4.1).

To conclude the framework of the Self System as a first order knowledge domain, before going into detail on the dimensions of the Self, it is appropriate to remember what Eugène Minkowski said at the beginning of the twentieth century about the Self: "The madness . . . does not originate in the disorders of judgment, perception or will, but in a disturbance of the innermost structure of the self" (1997, p. 114. Originally published in 1928. *Free translation by the author*[7]).

---

[7] "la folie [...] ne consiste pas ni dans un trouble du jugement, ni de la perception, ni de la volonté, mais dans une perturbation de la structure intime du moi"

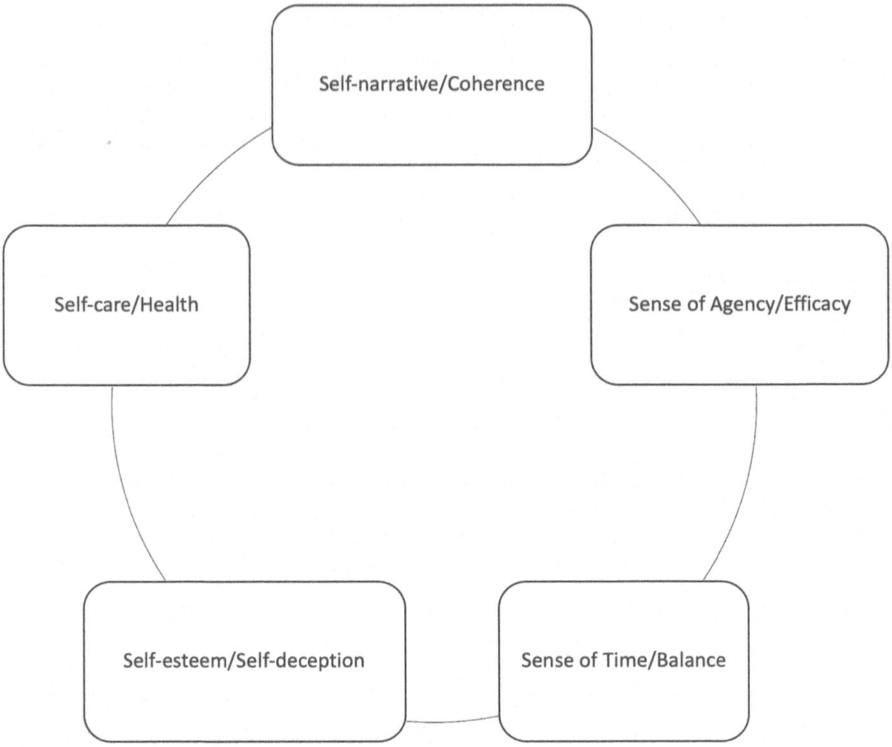

Fig. 4.1 Five dimensions of the self system

I highlight the absence of the Self in the case formulation models in the twenty-first century. It is a matter that should at least call us to reflection. It is difficult to imagine an existential problem or a panic attack, without a subject who experiences it.

4.1 Sense of Agency/Efficacy

We therapists pay high attention when patients report that they "lose the meaning of their life," "feel helpless," "their thoughts or actions do not come from themselves," "their thoughts are not under their control," among other possibilities. This is what the sense of agency in the field of psychotherapy is about.

An evolutionary perspective provides a more precise understanding of the role that agency plays in our interconnected life in an intersubjective matrix:

> Human forebears evolved into a sentient agentic species. Their advanced symbolizing capacity enabled humans to transcend the dictates of their immediate environment and made them unique in their power to shape their life circumstances and the course of their lives. (Bandura, 2006 p. 164)

The concept of human agency (Self as a doer) is a transtheoretical construct. It has received increasing attention from researchers in psychology, both as a fundamental aspect of Social Cognitive Theory (Bandura, 1986, 2001), Self-Determination Theory (Ryan & Deci, 2017; Deci & Ryan, 2000, Deci & Ryan, 1991), in psychopathology (Frith, 2005; Lind et al., 2018; Kristmannsdottir et al., 2019) and as a mechanism of change in psychotherapy (Levitt et al., 2016; Mackrill, 2009; Quiñones, 2013; García Haro et al., 2024; Tallman & Bohart, 1999), among others.

We know that agency (sense of agency) can be observed differentially in normality and abnormality since it is considered a crucial part of mental health. For this reason, the interruption and/or alteration in the sense of agency can characterize psychological problems of various nature (Schizophrenia,[8] Depression, Borderline Personality Disorder, Obsessive Compulsive Disorder, Eating Disorder, Suicide, Addictions, etc.) and in severe cases, for example, the delusion of control can occur (Frith, 2005; Blakemore et al., 2002). And last but not least, the alteration of agency by stress situations (examples: unexpected divorce, unexpected wealth, a chronic illness, job loss, loss of home, exile, political persecution, etc.) should be considered.

Now, optimizing the patient's agency is an essential goal in various psychotherapeutic traditions; however little empirical guidance based on research has been generated on how to facilitate and strengthen the sense of agency during the psychotherapeutic process (García Haro et al., 2024; Wahlström & Seilonen, 2016; Quiñones, 2013; William & Lewitt, 2007).

Let's start in general terms with some delimitations of what is understood by agency:

- Paul Brockelman (1985), in relation to agency, maintains that the essential thing is "Being able" and that it also constitutes a defining characteristic of personal identity.
- Albert Bandura (2001) defines agency as an intentional act that he considers as the initial key to the power to originate actions in given purposes.
- Edward Deci and Richard Ryan (1995) argue that human agency refers to those motivated behaviors that emanate from the integrated self.
- Shaun Gallagher maintains that the sense of agency is the experience that it is I who is causing or generating the action (Gallagher, 2000a, b).

Albert Bandura's Social Cognitive Theory is a powerful framework for conceptualizing what it means to be an agent. For Bandura (2001, 2006, 2008), agent behavior consists of four interrelated properties. The first is *intentionality*, that is, people form intentions that include action plans and strategies to carry them out and secondly, *foresight* which implies the temporal extension of agency. In other words, it refers to the visualization of goals and the anticipation of the likely outcomes of possible actions. The third property is *self-reactiveness* and it refers to the fact that agents are not only planners and forecasters but also self-regulators. In other words,

[8] Different research groups agree in reporting that patients with positive symptoms of schizophrenia (hearing voices, experiencing hallucinations and delusions) have difficulties in reflecting on their own agency (Jeannerod, 2009; Synofzik et al., 2010; Voss et al., 2010).

people compare their performance with personally valued goals and standards, with the aim of reducing the discrepancy between them. The fourth property is *self-reflection*, which implies the active evaluation of motivations, values, and one's own performance. Bandura asserts:

> People are not only agents of action. They are also self-examiners of their own functioning. Through functional self-awareness, they reflect on their personal efficacy, the soundness of their thoughts and actions, and the meaning of their pursuits, and they make corrective adjustments if necessary. The metacognitive capability to reflect upon oneself and the adequacy of one's thoughts and actions is the most distinctly human core property of agency. (2006, p. 165)

Within the framework of social cognitive theory, it is pointed out that efficacy beliefs are the foundation of human agency and refer to the person having clear goals and being able to define their life goals. A high sense of agency implies that the person fulfills his/her purposes. Bandura defines the perception of self-efficacy as "Perceived self-efficacy refers to beliefs in one's capabilities to organize and execute the courses of action required to produce given attainments" (1997, p. 3).

Therefore, people who believe that through their actions they cannot produce the desired results will have little incentive to act and persevere when facing different problems and/or tensions in social life.

Specifically in psychotherapy, the *efficacy expectations*[9] and *outcome expectations*[10] (Bandura, 1997) are essential for parsimoniously monitoring the sense of agency. Paraphrasing Bandura (1991), the *efficacy expectations* and *outcome expectations* are independent causal determinants for the initiation and regulation of behavior. Likewise, both types of expectations must be reasonably high before behavior acquires energy and is directed towards the goal.

Another frame of reference is Deci and Ryan's Self-Determination Theory (Deci & Ryan, 2000; Ryan & Deci, 2017) which aims to explain motivation and behavior based on individual differences in motivational orientations, contextual influences, and interpersonal perceptions. The theory allows understanding how the agent power in human beings is promoted or discouraged. The essential arguments are that (1) humans are more agents and perform better when motivation is experienced as autonomous or intrinsic; (2) autonomous motivation is more likely when the basic psychological needs of competence (i.e., self-efficacy), relatedness, and autonomy are met; and (3) environmental conditions can support or frustrate the satisfaction of such needs (Ryan & Deci, 2017). Therefore, the fundamental point is that the most complete expression of agency occurs when behavior is intrinsically motivated or when external regulations have been fully internalized (i.e., integrated regulation) and, consequently, the reasons for behavior are experienced as autonomous. Ultimately, when evaluating a patient, it is important to assess the type and quality of motivation.

---

[9] By *expectation of efficacy* it is understood to be a judgment about one's own ability to perform a particular act or course of action. The question is: "Can I do it?".

[10] By *expectation of result* we understand a judgment about a certain action, once carried out, will produce a particular result. The question is: "Will what I do work?".

The patient who is in a process of psychotherapy, to some degree, has a diminished, constrained, or inhibited sense of agency. This can be communicated explicitly or between the lines by the patient and the therapist must evaluate it and make it explicit in collaborative attunement. For example, it can be seen in the case of an adult patient with a depressive disorder: *"I don't know what to do with my life... I feel lost, but I keep going..."*

For therapists, defining a patient's sense of being an agent involves exploring and identifying the self-perception of how much they feel and perceive that they voluntarily lead their life in a cognitively self-regulated way. Similarly, it is crucial that the psychological interpretations and reformulations provided by the therapist to have a possible positive effect need to "touch" a degree of agency in the patient; otherwise they are doomed to failure.

Possible indicators of healthy agency include proper planning, necessary motivation, adjusted prediction, adequate assessment of future possibilities, adequate self-assessment of the present, voluntary acts of free choice, developing talents, cultivating interests, exercising and developing skills, taking initiatives freely undertaken in the pursuit of a goal, monitoring behavior to face environmental challenges and to pursue short- and long-term goals, etc.

Within this framework, the therapist in the psychotherapy process has to seek that the person in the psychotherapy process, gradually becomes in their life "a self-regulated protagonist." In the logic of the proposed case formulation model, a successful process would imply achieving dimensional psychological regulation (various possibilities of well-being and psychological regulation. See Table 1.3 in Chap. 1).

In summary, the "sense of healthy agency/effectiveness" is understood as the optimal level of perception of one's own sense of effective conduct of one's own life (the person feels and values themselves as the protagonist of their desired initiatives and actions). On the contrary, an "altered sense of agency/effectiveness," either minimal or non-existent, is observed at times when the patient communicates the desire to be "liberated," "improved," "rescued," etc. Therefore, this dimension of the altered Self System indicates the presence of a potential Dysfunctional Narrative that informs us of a possible *Dysfunctional Intersubjective Theme* (See Appendix 4.1).

4.2 Self-Narrative/Coherence[11]

It is transcendental to keep in mind that both language and narratives are part of our evolutionary history as a species, and in particular, they have had an impact on the progressive achievement of an increasingly sophisticated intersubjective and existential self-understanding in the twenty-first century. In this sense, it is important to

[11] In Chap. 2 "NARRATIVES AND INITIAL PRECISIONS FOR CASE CONCEPTUALIZATION," there are several conceptual developments that are complementary to what is exposed in this Sect. 4.2.

underline that the essential evolution of the brain gave us the ability to tell stories in the first person about oneself and to do so in a narrative form (Fischer, 1987). Therefore, knowledge (epistemology) and existence (ontology) are inseparable and are essentially organized in narrative terms, and this is because language transforms the modulation of immediate experience into patterns of conscious self-understanding through narratives about oneself (Guidano, 1999; Mahoney, 1991). Hence, people have idiosyncratic ways of organizing their knowledge and this is expressed in different types of narratives, that is, in a kind of narrative framework that facilitates the organization of experience (see the nine indicators of the Self proposed by Jerome Bruner for example), and special attention deserves the term "experience" in a context of history, and for this I quote Stephen Crites. He says:

> Many such things register in my consciousness, are perceived but not experienced, heard but not listened to. Here I must acknowledge a terminological quibble. I think it is useful to reserve the word "experience" for what is incorporated into one's story, and thus owned, owned up to, appropriated. It will follow from this usage that many things are experienced retroactively. The close air, my labored breath, my co-worker's agitation had to be sensed at the time or they could not have dawned on me later, and of course it is common to use the word "experience" for all such sensations. But then we would need another word to signify the conscious appropriation, since the distinction is too crucial to be left muddled. I prefer to say that most of the things that are sensed are never experienced, and that only those that are attended to are experienced, some things only slowly clarifying themselves as I become aware of their significance for my story. From this point of view "experience" is a single, vast story-like construct, containing many subplots, richly illustrated by visual images and accompanied by sounds and rhythms that may already be forming themselves into a kind of music. This narrative construct, furthermore, is constantly changing, shifting its accents; some episodes that had seemed important becoming trivial and others emerging from obscurity into central importance. (Crites, 1986, p. 160–161)

Various researchers emphasize that the characteristics of coherence[12] constitute a substantial aspect of a high-quality narrative, and it encompasses the general structure, flow, and meaning of the narrative (Baerger & McAdams, 1999; Reese et al., 2011; Sarbin, 1981). Therefore, narrative coherence[13] contributes to locating a specific narrative in time and place and incorporates intentions, imagination, motivations, thoughts, and feelings within the narrative (Linde, 1993; Reese et al., 2011).

The concept of narrative self implies a diachronic and complex structure that depends on the possibilities provided by the ability to reflect (metacognition) and

[12] It is relevant to bear in mind the remarkable development of Leon Festinger (1957) on the reduction of cognitive dissonance as the main driver in cognitive functioning to maintain coherence. Such a contribution is very relevant and current in the twenty-first century since it points to unity in multiplicity and if it is not achieved, intersubjective tension arises.

[13] The sense of self coherence is inspired by the dynamics that William James (1890) sustained about the "I" that acts and experiences (the experiencing «I») and the "Me" that observes and evaluates (the appraising «Me»).

the modalities of information processing in a cultural and situated context. According to the narrative perspective, people constitute their own identity by formulating autobiographical narratives in "life stories" (Schechtman, 1996) that involve life themes, but dysfunctional themes can also arise, which in the Case formulation model from an evolutionary perspective is called *Dysfunctional Intersubjective Theme* [DIT].

Now, it is noteworthy that the interpretation process that emerges from the I/Me dynamic is linked among other aspects to memory, time, and metacognition. It is relevant in such a context, what is held by Gallagher (2003) about the interpretation process that normally shapes episodic-autobiographical memories into a narrative structure depends on the capacity for reflective metacognition. In this regard, he states:

> A life event is not always meaningful in itself, but depends on a narrative structure that lends it context and sees in it significance that goes beyond the event itself. To form a self-narrative, one needs to do more than simply remember life events. One needs to consider them reflectively, deliberate on their meaning and decide how they fit together semantically. Metacognition allows for that reflective process of interpretation. (Gallagher, 2003, p. 349)

In particular, according to Gallagher (2003), there are at least four cognitive abilities that condition the formation of narrative self, and if any of these abilities were to fail, it would be noticeable in the person's narrative:

1. An ability to integrate temporal information.
2. A minimal self-reference ability.
3. An ability to encode and retrieve episodic-autobiographical memories.
4. An ability to engage in reflective metacognition.

Therefore, any of the four abilities observed to be altered informs us of possible difficulties in the sense of narrative coherence in the patient and can be very helpful in guiding during moments of reconstruction of the *Dysfunctional Intersubjective Theme* [DIT].

In conclusion, the sense of coherence of a narrative refers to the own perceived self-coherence of a sequence of events chosen as relevant by the person. Events with a strong autobiographical component chosen as significant and that inform how the person interprets their life, roles, priorities, and responsibilities (examples: work, family, social, sports, vital, charitable, etc.), among others. Therefore, the congruence and correspondence remembered, integrated, and narrated for oneself and others is of utmost importance for self-identity. In other words, the feeling of coherent narrative involves "being true to oneself" or if preferred "honest with oneself," in order to give meaning to one's "own life."

Therefore, this altered dimension of the Self System indicates the presence of a potential Dysfunctional Narrative that informs us of a possible *Dysfunctional Intersubjective Theme* (See Appendix 4.2).

4.3 Sense of Time/Balance

Psychologists have progressively become interested in the study of time perception because all human beings organize, prioritize, and plan their different activities in the present and in their probable future horizon (James, 1890; Lewin, 1942; Fraisse, 1967; Tulving, 2002; Grondin, 2010; Loose et al., 2017, 2019; Quiñones et al., 2018).

In the psychological field, the temporal nature of human behavior appears with explanatory relevance in different areas of knowledge: stress (Papastamatelou et al., 2015), attention deficit and hyperactivity (Toplak et al., 2003), anxiety (Bar-Haim et al., 2010), depression (Åström et al., 2019), eating disorders (Garcia et al., 2017), patients in psychiatric contexts (van Beek et al., 2011), problematic alcohol consumption (McKay et al., 2018), religiosity (Lowicki et al., 2018), psychological well-being (Garcia et al., 2016); job satisfaction (Bajec, 2018), research in psychotherapy processes (Quiñones et al., 2012, 2015, 2017), case formulation in psychotherapy (García Haro et al., 2024), risk behaviors (Boyd & Zimbardo, 2005), and type II diabetes mellitus (Quiñones et al., 2018), among others.

I will begin this thorny topic by quoting Frederick T. Melges, well known for his contributions to the study of temporal perspective. He asserts:

> Temporal perspective refers to how a person construes and experiences the past, present, and future. It refers to the span of awareness into the past and future as well as the relative attention given to the past, present, or future. For a person to make adequate distinctions between these divisions of "time's arrow," he or she has to have intact sequential thinking in which the present is differentiated from the past and future. (Melges, 1990, p. 256)

Concerning the case formulation presented in this book, I will start with a general framework to introduce myself to psychological temporality and the imbalance observed in certain profiles of information processing and meaning creation in different types of patients. For this, I will open the topic by quoting philosopher Paul Brockelman, who maintains the following about the sense of time and human activity:

> The unique sense of time we are pointing to here is the fact that human activity is a reaching out of the past and present toward anticipated goals. Actions is not "in" time nearly as much as it embodies the movement of time itself! Putting it another way, we can no more understand an action outside the horizon of the flow and dimensions of time than we can understand breathing without oxygen and lungs. Time—the flow or movement itself—is a necessary condition of our behaviour and lives. (1985, p. 22)

And I also add what Brockelman asserts about self-awareness and time. He says:

> Self-consciousness means reflective awareness of oneself as a temporal relation. But it also means becoming reflectively conscious that we are just such a double relation of temporality and reflection. As we have seen, reflection is itself a kind of temporal doing within the stream of our temporal activities and thus itself is retained and reflectively recallable. (1985, p. 77)

What Brockelman points out are powerful reflections for therapists and the possibilities it opens in the field of psychotherapy. It is not minor, to conceive that human beings self-organize in time and its dimensions.[14]

The Self and temporality are inseparable since "we have an embodied sense of time." Thus, human life occurs in parallel temporal dimensions, for example: chronological time shared with others (clocks, calendars, etc.) and internal time (various temporal profiles). We know little about how temporal perspectives are organized in people and only recently have we begun to make progress in answering this question.

At present, we know without a doubt that maintaining a sense of continuity (identity over time) is crucial for psychological adaptation throughout the course of life (Sneed & Whitbourne, 2003; Staudinger, 2001). However, the sense of continuity essentially takes shape through the "evolutionary instrument" that makes us unique as a species, which is language, and it is what would allow us to make our experience coherent over time. Having said that, the narrative self is fundamental to understanding personal identity as continuity over time. It is clear that the essence of self-awareness and the quality of continuity lies in the ability to observe oneself over time (Tulving, 1985, 2002; Tulving & Szpunar, 2012; Melges, 1990).

We know that time is inherent to human self-awareness. In this sense, the concept of autonoetic consciousness[15] ("mental time travel") proposed and developed by Endel Tulving (Tulving, 1985, 2002; Tulving & Szpunar, 2012) is relevant. It consists of the type of consciousness that is necessary to think about oneself in the context of subjective time, that is, its prolonged existence over time (its own remembered past and imagined future). In Tulving's words:

> A normal healthy person who possesses autonoetic consciousness is capable of becoming aware of her own past as well as her own future; she is capable of mental time travel, roaming at will over what has happened as readily as over what might happen, independently of physical laws that govern the universe. (1985, p. 5)

It is important to note that impaired autonoetic consciousness leads to problems with planning, prospective memory, episodic future thinking, and general thinking about one's own future (See Bar, 2011). Therefore, therapists' attention to this dimension of human processing can be very important depending on the case and when understanding a psychological problem.

All of the above allows us to assert that human life has a situated temporal structure, or in other words: "the sense of time is synonymous with embodied life." According to Gallagher (2003), the normal generation of a narrative self depends on

---

[14] In borderline personality disorders, it is common to observe problems with the hierarchy of daily time to perform different roles.

[15] Unlike autonoetic consciousness, the *noetic consciousness* refers to the person's ability to be aware of information about the world in the absence of any kind of memory. It implies awareness of symbolic representations of reality without consciousness of reliving the past.

the correct functioning of a variety of cognitive abilities, including capacities for short-term temporal processing (working memory), self-awareness, episodic memory, and reflective metacognition. Specifically, we humans require the ability to integrate temporal information for proper formation of the narrative self, and this implies that the sense of time we have is a dynamic of intersubjective meaning that connects us with who we have been, who we are, and who we aspire to be.

Regarding research in psychotherapy, the sense of self and temporality are inseparable processes in the patient's psychological system and have been observed in complete psychotherapy processes (See Quiñones et al., 2015, 2017). Briefly, the research by Quiñones et al. (2017) was the first to evaluate and compare the perception of subjective time in complete video-recorded psychotherapy processes using a mixed methodology. It consisted of a comparative case study within the framework of psychotherapy process research and described the perception of subjective time in two psychotherapy processes, one successful and one unsuccessful. Two cognitive-oriented psychotherapy processes were studied, video-recorded and transcribed in all their sessions. First, a qualitative coding (Top-down) was applied to identify the types of subjective time categories, depending on psychological well-being. These were past, present, and future, each in a positive and negative form. Secondly, two types of quantitative statistical analyses were applied: one of content analysis, which allowed observing the frequencies for the six categories and in another, a cumulative frequency analysis that allowed identifying a differential pattern in the two cases analyzed. From these data, different temporal profiles were evidenced for both cases, differentiated by categories, a finding that would allow tracking the process of subjectivity in terms of specific components in relation to the success of psychotherapy (see Fig. 4.2. Adapted from Quiñones et al., 2017).

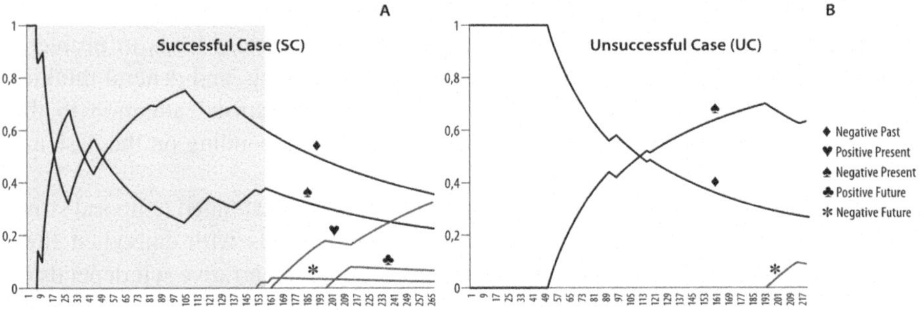

Fig. 4.2 Cumulative frequencies of time categories versus speaking turnThis figure shows the cumulative frequency of possible time categories: past, present, and future, and each of their positive and negative variants. The X-axis shows the registered turns for both therapeutic processes. These turns have been sequentially selected from therapy sessions. The Y-axis shows the relative frequencies of the time categories. The 1A figure corresponds to the Successful Case (SC) and the 1B corresponds to the Unsuccessful Case (UC). In the SC there was no presence for the category Positive Past and for the UC, there was no presence for categories: Positive Future, Positive Present, and Positive Past. The gray area in the Fig. 1A (SC) corresponds to the period where the Negative Reflexive Narrative predominates and in the following period, roughly from the turn 161, the Positive Reflexive Narrative predominates

In short, the aforementioned research aimed to explore indicators of subjective time perception (patient's speaking turns) associated with therapeutic success (subjective perception, agreement between client and therapist on the fulfillment of objectives, therapist's assessment and psychological tests at different times), using textual data obtained in naturalistic clinical practice. It is noteworthy that the importance of temporal profiles was evidenced in the research. Different temporal profiles were observed for both cases, successful versus unsuccessful, in relation to psychological well-being. In addition, the phenomenological analysis of the experience of the patients analyzed in the case research shows that the perception of psychological time (temporal profile) has an impact on psychological distress versus psychological well-being.

In the theoretical field of psychotherapy, the self and psychological time is the ontology that must be taken into consideration and not "lose sight of" in the participant observation that every therapist performs in the co-construction of the therapeutic focus with an "other who suffers psychologically" and seeks to facilitate change. To be more specific, when there is an alteration of the temporal perspective, degrees of disorganization of psychological processing and possible evolutions towards Dysfunctional Intersubjective Themes (examples: hypercontrol, self-sabotage, discomfort with relationships, etc.) are originated. If the alteration is stable over time, clinical pictures of various complexity are produced (examples: "excess orientation to the past" is observed in depression, "excess orientation to the hedonistic present" in addiction, "excess orientation to the present" in stress, "excess orientation to the future" in anxiety; "unbalanced time profile" in psychological distress, etc.). From a look at the process of change in psychotherapy, the perspective of psychological time is conceptualized as an indicator of the organization of the experience of the continuity of the sense of self in the cultural intersubjective matrix. Therefore, if the dynamics of subjective time is altered in the understanding that it produces psychological deregulation, we will observe alterations of various nature that interfere with the adaptation of the psychological system (for example, problems of hierarchy that translate into not distinguishing the urgent from the important in everyday life).

The evidence indicates that the temporal perspective observed in a person at a given moment can become a relatively stable personality trait and, therefore, transform into a particular temporal bias that predominates in the perspective and behavior of that subject. In this sense, when people often exhibit a dominant temporal orientation, they can become dysfunctional and present a series of psychological problems (Boniwell, 2005; Boniwell & Zimbardo, 2004).

Zimbardo and Boyd (1999) promoted the ideal of "Balanced Temporal Profile"[16] as optimal for individual psychological health and social functioning. This profile is defined as the mental ability to flexibly switch between different dimensions of temporality depending on the conditions of the situation. Particularly, the balanced

---

[16] Balanced temporal profile refers to low scores in the negative past and fatalistic present, as well as moderate to high scores in the positive past, hedonistic present and perspectives of future time (Boniwell & Zimbardo, 2004; Zimbardo & Boyd, 2008).

time perspective hypothesizes that an unbalanced time perspective (one that is too focused on one of the dimensions of time: past, present, or future) can compromise the ability to promote well-being. In this sense, the balanced time perspective is defined as the mental ability to easily switch between the dimensions of the time perspective, depending on the demands of the task, situational considerations, and personal resources (Boniwell & Zimbardo, 2004). It is argued that a person with a balanced profile possesses temporal harmony and functions optimally within a flexible set of all temporal frameworks depending on the demands of a situation, their values, and needs (Stolarski et al., 2015; Zimbardo & Boyd, 2008).

In the process of psychotherapy, the assessment of the time perspective is subtle and complex, as we live and are time. The presence or absence of alteration of psychological temporality is assessed with questions and observations: Are you stuck in your past?, How committed are you to your present?, How does the person emotionally experience his/her past, present, and future horizon?, Are they able to observe themselves (self-awareness/mental journey) through time?, Is there an appropriate chronology of events in the story that causes psychological distress? Is the sense of reality of time maintained?, What is the relationship between internal time and chronological time? Is there an alteration in the future time perspective?, Is there a presence of a balanced profile?, Do they organize their time in a way that they can accomplish what is planned in everyday life?, etc.

Similarly, the therapist must assess whether the patient reflects on their existential time in a flexible and adaptive way, for example, they live the present as possibilities and decisions; they live the past as information and not a destiny; they have hope in the future; they present a balanced temporal profile, etc. Let's look at a brief example of a transcribed session from an adult patient:

Therapist What is the problem that at this moment you find most notable?

Patient My lack of time to do my things.

Therapist Can you tell me more about that?

Patient Sure. My family consists of my wife and three children. My three children are boys and they have an excess of energy... they absorb a lot of my time. They leave me very little time to do everything that I need to do. So, it confuses me.

Therapist In what sense does it "confuse" you?

Patient In that I have to do things outside of normal hours. You could say that during the day I have to do what is related to my job and in the afternoon when I return home I must help my wife, play with my three children (6, 8, and 10 years old) for 1 h and a half so they can expend their energy. After dinner, I help my wife with the children's homework and I feel tired. In general, I have to stay up until 1:00 am to finish my work tasks. I sleep very little on weekdays. The consequence is that I feel irritable... and many times I can't concentrate on what I have to do and I "freeze."

Therapist I understand, what do you mean by "I freeze"?

Patient It's as if I observe myself... and I don't do anything during that time. It's for several minutes... it's strange. Then, I go to the bedroom and watch television. And on many occasions, I stay thinking about what I didn't do. It's unpleasant.

We are time in process and therefore a flexible temporal balance in every human being is necessary for adequate adaptation and psychological well-being in a dynamic intersubjective reality. Therefore, it is altered dimension of the Self System indicates the presence of a potential Dysfunctional Narrative that informs us of a possible *Dysfunctional Intersubjective Theme* (See Appendix 4.3).

4.4 Self-Esteem/Self-Deception

As a context, the nature and function of self-esteem is one of the oldest and probably most studied topics in psychology (Muris & Otgaar, 2023; Orth & Robins, 2022); however, it still has controversial aspects.

The word esteem comes from the Latin "aestimare," which means "to estimate or value." From a psychological perspective, William James (1890) held the following about self-esteem while describing the qualities of the Self:

> So our self-feeling in this world depends entirely on what we back ourselves to be and do. It is determined by the ratio of our actualities to our supposed potentialities; a fraction of which our pretensions are the denominator and the numerator our success: thus, Self-esteem = Success/Pretensions. Such a fraction may be increased as well by diminishing the denominator as by increasing the numerator. (p. 248)

It is necessary to emphasize that William James' definition is dynamic since the ratio can change. Also, it shows us that it is possible to modify self-esteem by increasing the frequency of success, decreasing the degree of aspiration or shifting attention to other significant areas of life in which one is more competent and, therefore, is more likely to be successful.

Crocker and Park (2003), based on James' definition, constructed a model of self-esteem based on *contingencies* of value that regulate and motivate behavior. For these researchers, firstly, individual competence is key to self-esteem, because succeeding over time requires the ability to acquire and use skills relevant to the domains of life that are linked to the sense of identity. That is, we care deeply about success and failure in areas that are personally important to us. Secondly, this perspective is very useful when we try to understand why people can seem so motivated to succeed and so fearful of failing. Similarly, understanding the "being defensive" in circumstances where their personal identity is threatened in some dimension that matters to them.

Paraphrasing Crocker and Wolfe (2001), self-esteem is a multifaceted construct—it can not only be high or low, but also people differ in their self-esteem contingencies, or what they believe they must be and do to have value and worth as a person. As several researchers point out in response to the question "What self-esteem contingencies are optimal?". The given answer alludes to the fact that external self-esteem contingencies, such as basing self-esteem on appearance, approval and consideration from others, or academic success or other achievements (example: business success), are associated with more negative outcomes than relatively internal sources of self-esteem (See Crocker, 2002; Pyszczynski et al., 2002).

Christopher Mruk defines self-esteem as "...self-esteem is the lived status of one's competence at dealing with the challenges of living in a worthy way over time" (2013a, p. 27).

Mruk highlights the importance of understanding self-esteem as a balanced relationship between competence and worthiness, and he points out that both aspects should always be considered in relation as they are present, regardless of whether one stands out more than the other. Also, an advantage in defining self-esteem in terms of competence and worthiness is that the cognitive and affective dimensions can be observed since *competence* alludes more to the cognitive and *worthiness* more to the affective (see Murk, 2013b).

Today, it is important to pay attention to cultural differences and their impact on self-esteem (Mruk, 2013a; Cai et al., 2007). Self-esteem is a strong predictor of subjective well-being in individualistic cultures, but not so much in collectivist cultures (Diener & Diener, 1995). Similarly, there is a substantial difference in how emotions are valued across cultures and to what extent emotional excitement is desired.[17]

The evidence shows that self-esteem is essential for maintaining a stable and coherent sense of self and connections with others and is also necessary to allow the Self to grow (See Mruk, 2013a). People in different parts of the world need and strive at the same time to feel comfortable and good about themselves.

In a current meta-analytic review of the literature on self-esteem, Orth and Robbins concluded "The findings of this review indicate that having high (vs. low) self-esteem has wide-ranging positive consequences, including better social relationships, more success at school and work, better mental and physical health, and less antisocial behavior" (2022, p. 5).

Regarding the defensive dimension of self-esteem, the concept of *self-deception* is pertinent. Self-deception has a history in psychology and philosophy. There is a popular saying that facilitates its quick understanding and says "Out of sight, out of mind"; it is a good way to capture this dynamic aspect of defensive meaning in everyday life.

As a framework of evolutionary reference on the dynamics of deception and self-deception, I quote Trivers:

> In our own species, deceit and self-deception are two sides of the same coin. If by deception we mean only consciously propagated deception—outright lies—then we miss the much larger category of unconscious deception, including active self- deception. On the other hand, if we look at self-deception and fail to see its roots in deceiving others, we miss its major function. (2011, p. 3)

Deception is an activity deeply rooted in the social life we know. It is a characteristic that has been selected throughout evolution and has taken complex forms in its expression (Trivers, 2011; Humphrey, 1986; Lewin, 1988; Sarbin, 1981, 1986). Likewise, Triandis (2009) argues that self-deception is due to humans using their

[17] Eid and Diener (2001) report that guilt is of greater importance in collectivist cultures, while pride is more valued in individualistic cultures.

hopes, needs, and desires to "construct" their way of seeing the world. For example, a boy thinks that the girl he likes is playing "hard to get" and invites her out for the fourth time, even though it is evident to everyone that she is completely ignoring him.

It is also important to note that there are several types of self-deception. For example, biased information search strategies, partial interpretive processes, biased memory processes (example: selective amnesia), mental health problems (example: anorexic ignores her potential fear of public rejection), maladaptive attitudes, overconfidence in oneself (Trivers, 2011; von Hippel & Trivers, 2011; Triandis, 2011; Westland & Shinebourne, 2009; Guidano, 1992), means to disengage moral self-sanctions from harmful behavior (Bandura, 2016).

Theodore Sarbin in the mid-1980s indicated to us, with his usual acuity, the essential to capture self-deception:

> To understand the process of self-deception, then, requires that the observer inquire into the person's self-narrative and identify the features of the self as narrative figure or protagonist (as distinguished from the self as narrator or story maker). The observer must be ready to recognize the inconsistency or absurdity of the story if the narrator were to spell out engagements that appeared to violate the integrity of the self as narrative figure. (1986, p. 17)

Self-deception applied to psychotherapy is relevant and useful, as it has allowed progress in understanding the daily incoherence observed in human relationships and psychological problems. However, in my view, it has not been given enough attention, and some researchers and psychotherapists who share an evolutionary and narrative view are an exception.

Self-deception can also be understood as a dynamic relationship between knowledge and consciousness (Guidano, 1992). From a dynamic of Self, it is argued that self-awareness does not correspond to an objective knowledge or image of oneself, but would be a way of "putting the pieces in their place," a way of manipulating the data distinguished in immediate experience with the "purpose" of achieving an acceptable self-esteem as a result of self-assessment. Therefore, self-deception processes are related to self-esteem (self-assessment) and refer to biases and/or omissions to achieve the coherence of information in order to maintain an image of oneself acceptable to oneself and an image projected and believed by others.

Similarly, self-deception has been studied as a dimension in mental health: low, medium, and high, an aspect that has been described by several researchers and psychotherapists from different perspectives that are useful (Bandura, 2016; Bonanno & Siddique, 1999; Sarbin, 1986; Taylor, 1989; Guidano, 1992). Briefly:

- Sarbin (1986) interpreted self-deception as a narrative reconstruction in which the person is the agent of the reconstruction.
- Taylor argues that moderate self-deceptions are associated with good mental health (Taylor, 1989).
- Guidano (1992) from a view of the dynamics of the self (I/ME) argued that excessive self-deception raises the impossibility of classifying immediate experience to critical levels of the uncontrollable, while reduced self-deception increases self-reference processes excessively, easily reaching in the dynamics of sameness to levels of complexity that are difficult to handle.

- Bonanno and Siddique (1999) describe maladaptive attitudes and behaviors as pretexts, evasions, and denials of the "truth" of their situation. They also indicate the presence of contradictory attitudes with respect to their own process of change in psychotherapy (example: avoids taking responsibility for oneself, has problems with self-understanding, participates little in their psychotherapy, etc.).
- Bandura (2016) argues that acting in a way that keeps one uninformed about unwanted information is a self-deception, and in relation to the functionality of self-deception, it serves as a means to disengage moral self-sanctions from harmful behavior. He argues that there are eight mechanisms of moral disengagement: (1) moral justification, (2) euphemistic labeling, (3) advantageous comparison, (4) displacement of responsibility, (5) diffusion of responsibility, (6) ignoring or distorting the consequences, (7) dehumanization, and (8) attribution of blame.

Negative self-deception, which implies *dimensional psychological deregulation,*[18] refers to the narrative inconsistencies that are accompanied by loss, omission, falsehood, distortion, and/or reduction of information that is not integrated into a consistent narrative and therefore negatively affects personal identity. In such a context, for example, if we pay attention to psychopathology, symptoms and signs are indicators that the quality of reflective consciousness is diminished and deficient. Indicators of *self-deception* are Incoherence between "saying" and "doing," Self-contradictions, Excessive self-confidence, Illusion of control, Disdain for others, False self-narratives, Projection, Denial, Moral superiority, Blinding power, Ignoring relevant information, Avoids disappointment, Avoids taking responsibility for oneself, Defends the image of another significant, Omission of personal information to avoid incoherence, etc.

On the other hand, in positive self-deception that presents dimensional psychological regulation, biases, omissions, distortions, and forgetfulness of information do not generate problems in the continuity of identity. Personal. In other words, the different losses of information do not cause problems in the articulation of intersubjective knowledge in biographical self-narrative, since the integration of information into a meaning that flows in a temporally balanced way allows for different healthy dynamics. Therefore, the sense of *Self-esteem/Self-deception* that all human beings need to live in society is understood in a dynamic and narrative way. In such a context, the two-factor model in self-esteem (competence and dignity) complemented with the diversity of self-deception (narrative) is of great clinical utility because it allows understanding the interpersonal dimension from an evolutionary perspective.

[18] *Dimensional Psychological Regulation* refers to various possibilities of well-being and individual psychological regulation (such results are identified with various possibilities depending on the profile of second-order intersubjective knowledge domains in quadrant I, see in Chap. 1, Fig. 1.3). In other words, it is what is understood as psychological health in the case formulation model from an evolutionary perspective (ECF).

To conclude, this altered dimension of the Self System indicates the presence of a potential Dysfunctional Narrative that informs us of a possible *Dysfunctional Intersubjective Theme* (see Appendix 4.4).

4.5 Self-Care/Health

Self-care/Health is a dimension of the self system and refers to consciously and informedly taking care of oneself. People have to be aware of the relevance of developing self-responsibility for their health and well-being at different times in their life cycle as it is essential for their optimal psychological functioning and the energy/vitality in everyday life.

Schroeder (2007) estimated that 40% of deaths in Western societies are caused by the long-term consequences of acting based on desires, such as consuming tobacco, sex, alcohol, recreational drugs, and unhealthy foods.

Research on self-care and quality of life is robust and growing. In fact, self-care is considered by the WHO as "the ability of individuals, families, and communities to promote health, prevent disease, maintain health, and cope with illness and disability with or without the support of a healthcare provider" (World Health Organization, 2019, X).

Taking care of oneself is living better, and it is evident in the twenty-first century the awareness of information to promote self-care (examples: more nutritional information on food in different countries, public policies of time change to take advantage of light, anti-tobacco public policies, etc.) and this goes hand in hand with technological developments increasingly available to more and more people (examples: devices to monitor health indicators such as smartwatches, smartphone, etc.). In other words, it is necessary to consider the *health literacy* that each person has at the time of consulting (Simonds, 1974; World Health Organization, 2013), and this implies, delimiting the ability to obtain, process, and understand the information and know the basic health services that should be consulted to make optimal health decisions, and no less important, to take care of and monitor their vitality on a day-to-day basis.

Clearly self-care has a fundamental relevance for health (Wilkinson & Whitehead, 2009), prevention, and for the care of chronic diseases (adherence to treatments) that emerge in the life cycle (Quiñones et al., 2018). Therefore, valuing and weighing the patient's self-care ("positive practices") in different areas of personal and social life is of the utmost relevance. This implies dietary habits, work/rest balance, frequent exercise, physical activity, diet, avoiding sedentary lifestyle, daily hours dedicated to sleep, quality of sleep, ability to relax, enjoy leisure, recreation with family and friends, avoid self-medication, low or no alcohol consumption and none of tobacco, adequate space of the dwelling, acoustic isolation of the dwelling, thermal isolation of the dwelling, suitable place to work, physical safety, etc.

Self-care and mental health are closely related and are observed in different dimensions of human functioning. For example, studies show that quality of life and severity of depressive symptoms are inversely associated in depressive disorder (Saarijarvi et al., 2002; de Leval, 1999) and the same relationship is observed in bipolar disorder (Simjanoski et al., 2023).

"Physical activity" is defined as any movement of the skeletal muscle that results in energy expenditure (Epel et al., 2016). Research differentiates between physical activity and sedentary behaviors (examples: watching television, sitting all day at work, spending a long time in front of a computer), as there is growing evidence that they independently predict health and disease (Chomistek et al., 2013; Katzmarzyk, 2010).

From the review of scientific literature, it is clear that depression and physical activity are intimately connected.[19] Depressed and anxious people are less likely to be physically active (Goodwin, 2003; Ströhle, 2009) and more likely to remain more sedentary (Teychenne et al., 2010).

The time adults spend sedentary or simply "sitting for a long time" has recently been proposed as a problem that has harmful effects on health outcomes. It has been shown that sedentariness has specific metabolic consequences, even among those who comply with moderate to vigorous physical activity guidelines. There is evidence of higher rates of morbidity and mortality among those who spend more time being sedentary, regardless of whether or not they engage in regular physical activity (Wu et al., 2022; Thorp et al., 2011; Wilmot et al. 2012).

The evidence is overwhelming about the negative aspects of a sedentary lifestyle as it increases the risk of developing numerous health problems, such as cardiovascular diseases, hypertension, type 2 diabetes, colon and breast cancer, osteoporosis, and depression (Morrow et al., 1999; Oja & Borms, 2004; US Department of Health and Human Services, 1996, 2000). There is also a direct positive association between health, quality of life, and physical activity (Bize et al., 2007). In the same direction, it has been found that regular physical exercise can be an effective treatment for anxiety and depression (Peden, 2013) and other benefits.

In humans and all mammals, sleep is a fundamental biological requirement. Experimental data indicate that, on average, 7–8 h of nighttime sleep are needed to optimize human neurobehavioral performance (Penev, 2013). In turn, the National Sleep Foundation recommends sleeping 7–9 h per day for adults (18–64 years) and 7–8 h for older adults (≥65 years) (Hirshkowitz et al., 2015). It is noteworthy that a recent systematic review concludes that a sleep duration of 7–8 h per day is most favorably associated with health among adults and older adults (Chaput et al., 2020).

Sleep occupies approximately one third of adult life (Lakhan & Finesmith, 2013). Both NREM and REM sleep are associated with dynamic changes in the cardiac, cerebral, respiratory, vascular, endocrine, thermoregulatory, enteric nervous, procreative, and immune systems (Rama et al., 2005).

[19] See the interesting research by Verhoeven et al. (2023) on antidepressant medication and career therapy for patients with depressive and anxiety disorders.

The fundamental organization of normal sleep occurs through a complex process of two stages: NREM sleep (non-rapid eye movement) occupies 75–80% of total sleep time, is linked to the homeostatic process, and involved in physical rest (Rama et al., 2005). The REM stage (rapid eye movement) corresponds to 20–25% of total sleep, appears to be related to mental function, and is therefore necessary for psychological, emotional rest and memory (Lockley & Foster, 2012; Rama et al., 2005). Many physiological functions undergo significant changes during sleep and depend on the NREM (non-rapid eye movement) and REM (rapid eye movement) phase, for example, blood pressure, heart rate, cardiac function, autonomic nervous system, among others.

We know that the quality of sleep is essential for the quality of life and health, and also for cognitive processes, such as learning, memory, problem-solving, and decision-making. The effects of sleep deprivation include excessive daytime sleepiness, lower attention levels, memory problems, impaired decision-making, reduced motivation, fatigue, irritability, poor declarative and procedural learning, and generally reduced neurocognitive functioning among others (Curcio et al., 2006). Insufficient sleep has a strong negative impact on quality of life and may be related to serious emotional, social, academic, professional, and health difficulties (Gaultney, 2010; Taylor et al., 2013) and also to the use of various stimulants (Lohsoonthorn et al., 2013).

Sleep disturbance is especially associated with major depressive disorder (Baglioni et al., 2010, 2011), anxiety disorders (Cox & Olatunji, 2016; Roth et al., 2006), bipolarity, schizophrenia, generalized anxiety, post-traumatic stress, and panic disorder (Nofzinger, 2005). In particular, insomnia has been identified as a risk factor, a comorbid condition, and a transdiagnostic symptom for mood/anxiety disorders and schizophrenia (Palagini et al., 2022).

In general, irritability, anxiety, lack of motivation, and symptoms of depression are often seen in people with insufficient sleep. Cognitive problems include poor concentration, slower reaction times, distraction, forgetfulness, and lack of coordination (Lakhan & Finesmith, 2013). Several studies have shown that there is also a higher risk of hypertension, coronary disease, and obesity (Jike et al., 2018).

Prospective studies have shown that substance use disorder and anxiety disorders predict sleep disorders and vice versa (Batterham et al., 2012; Pieters et al., 2015). Similarly, although sleep disturbance is a known consequence of intoxication, chronic substance use, and substance withdrawal symptoms (García & Salloum, 2015), people with substance use disorder may also use substances to mitigate sleep disturbance. For example, chronic substance users abuse stimulants to reverse sleepiness (Roehrs & Roth, 2015). Particularly, alcohol consumption affects sleep (Song & Walker, 2023; Foster, 2013).

Similarly, there is research indicating that lack of sleep is a factor in the increasing prevalence of obesity. The relationship between sleep restriction, increased appetite, and weight gain could stem from alterations in the metabolism of hormones that regulate appetite and cause a decrease in energy expenditure (Covassin et al., 2022; Magee et al., 2010). It should be considered that the demands and opportunities of modern life mean that many people habitually sleep less than 6 h per night and epidemiological and experimental studies show an association between such short sleep and a higher risk of obesity (Covassin et al., 2022; Garaulet et al., 2011; Nishiura et al., 2010). In sum, so relevant is it in the clinic, that sleep disturbance is proposed as a possible transdiagnostic factor in psychopathological problems (Harvey et al., 2011).

In general, the broad knowledge of our functioning is generating a wide spectrum of self-care interventions that are promising for preventing health problems, improving health and well-being of people.

Self-care/Health should guide the therapist to pay attention to a series of indicators: Enjoyment of life, Work capacity, Physical health, Quality of sleep, Sexual life, Rest, Healthy eating, Body care, Physical activity/Exercise, Leisure/Free time, Social support, Sufficient energy for daily life, General vitality, Social relationships, Personal relationships, Safety in daily life, Body weight, Low alcohol consumption, Low caffeine consumption, Comfortable living space, Sufficient money to cover your needs, etcetera.

In conclusion, this altered dimension of the Self System indicates the presence of a potential Dysfunctional Narrative that informs us of a possible *Dysfunctional Intersubjective Theme* (See Appendix 4.5).

As a summary of the five proposed dimensions of the Self System, normative orientations are pointed out below that do not intend to be exhaustive. The relevant thing to consider is that the embodied Self System and its intersubjective articulation through its five dimensions can generate healthy, unhealthy, or unhealthy trajectories at times in the life cycle (see Table 4.1).

Table 4.1 Self system and some normative orientations

Self system	Guiding normative objectives
Self-narrative/coherence "self-story"	Decrease inconsistencies and/or dilemmas in dominant narratives that interfere with adaptive trajectories that contribute to existential purposes and the care of quality close relationships.
Sense of agency/efficacy	Increase the sense of capacity-authorship, will and motivation in everyday life.
Sense of time/balance	Articulate and re-organize autobiographical memories and stressful events that hinder the sense of the present and future.
Self-esteem/self-deception	Recognize and understand what has been little or not recognized in the history of personal relationships.
Self-care/health	Decrease behaviors that affect health, energy, vitality and dissatisfaction of psychological needs (competence, autonomy and relationship) and control and cope with stress.

Adapted from Quiñones (2024)

Boxes 4.1 and 4.2 show the first order intersubjective knowledge domain "**SELF SYSTEM**" in the case formulation protocol (the Case Formulation-Evaluation and the Case Formulation-Intervention are shown).

Box 4.1: Case-Evaluation Formulation—SELF SYSTEM: Clinical Assessment

(mark presence: x)

SENSE OF AGENCY/EFFICACY: Alteration ☐
Describe:..
....
....

SELF-NARRATIVE/COHERENCE: Alteration ☐
Describe:..
....
....

SENSE OF TIME/BALANCE: Alteration ☐
Describe:..
....
....

SELF-ESTEEM/SELF-DECEPTION: Alteration ☐
Describe:..
....
....

SELF-CARE/HEALTH: Alteration ☐
Describe:..
....
....

Observations:..
....
....

Box 4.2: Case Formulation—SELF SYSTEM: Clinical Assessment

(mark presence: x)

SENSE OF AGENCY/EFFICACY: Alteration ☐ Progress ☐ Regulation ☐
Describe:..
....
....

SELF-NARRATIVE/COHERENCE: Alteration ☐ Progress ☐ Regulation ☐
Describe:..
....
....

SENSE OF TIME/BALANCE: Alteration ☐ Progress ☐ Regulation ☐
Describe: ....
....
....

SELF-ESTEEM/SELF-DECEPTION: Alteration ☐ Progress ☐ Regulation ☐
Describe:..
....
....

SELF-CARE/HEALTH: Alteration ☐ Progress ☐ Regulation ☐
Describe:
....
....
....

Observations:..
....
....

4.6 Appendices

Appendix 4.1: Therapist's Guide: Sense of Agency/Efficacy

- Sense of Agency/Efficacy refers to people's ability to attribute thoughts, feelings and behaviors to themselves, as well as their ability to take initiative, persistence and responsibility for their own actions in everyday life. In other words, it is how people "self-manage their daily lives".
- Alteration of the Sense of Agency/Efficacy, possible implications:

  1. They lose their sense of life "I am without a compass".
  2. They feel helpless.
  3. They feel demotivated.
  4. Difficulty and possible disorganization in making decisions.

5. They feel incapable.
6. Their thoughts or actions do not come from themselves (psychotic).

- In order to assess the Sense of Agency/Efficacy, the narrative is analyzed thematically.

Exploratory questions based on dysfunctional subject matter:

1. Do you presently have purposes that you perceive, feel, and believe you can achieve?
2. Do you perceive, feel and believe that you make your own decisions?
3. Do you organize action plans and regulates these plans and actions to achieve the desired results?
4. Does your own motivation influence your personal goals?
5. Do you self-direct when you perceive difficulties and/or setbacks in your daily life?
6. Do you have the conviction that you are realizing your personal potential? How do you perceive yourself in the face of challenges?

Appendix 4.2: Therapist's Guide: Sense of Self-Narrative/Coherence

- The sense of Self-narrative/Coherence is an essential aspect of a narrative that enables psychological health (regulation and well-being).

We know that people structure their experience through stories to give meaning to their existence.

Alteration of sense of Self-Narrative/Coherence, possible implications:

1. Degrees of misunderstanding of themselves and others in different roles.
2. Fluctuating psychological distress.
3. Fluctuating psychological dysregulation.

- To assess parsimoniously the sense of self-narrative/coherence, the narrative is analyzed thematically.

Exploratory questions based on dysfunctional subject matter:

1. Do you perceive coherence in what you feel, think and do in the present?
2. Does the meaning of experiences from your past help you make sense of experiences in the present?
3. Does the meaning of present experiences help you think about your future without discomfort?
4. Do you have personal goals that you feel and think are consistent with your personal well-being?
5. Have you ever felt that you are a burden to yourself and/or your loved ones?
6. Do you incorporate possible lessons learned from your adverse experiences?

Appendix 4.3: Therapist's Guide: Sense of Time/Balance

Sense of Time/Balance refers to how a person interprets and experiences the past, present and future with degrees of existential balance in the present.

- Alteration of the Sense of Time/Balance, possible implications:

  1. Degrees of behavioral disorganization in the present (e.g., impulsivity).
  2. Difficulty and/or disorganization in achieving goals and purposes.
  3. Difficulty and/or disorganization in fulfilling commitments at agreed times in various roles.

- To assess the Sense of Time/Balance parsimoniously, the narrative is analyzed thematically.

Exploratory questions based on dysfunctional subject matter:

1. If you had to describe yourself how you live your subjective time, what adjective would you use?
2. When you experience a disagreement (e.g., a heated argument) with another person, how do you temporarily organize yourself?
3. How do hypothetically anticipated consequences influence your behavior?
4. When you have several difficulties in a single day, do you organize yourself according to "urgent" / "important" / "can wait"?
5. Do you sacrifice your personal well-being to achieve future results?
6. What is the rhythm of your thinking like?

Appendix 4.4: Therapist's Guide: Sense of Self-Esteem/Self-Deception

- The Sense of Self-esteem/Self-deception alludes to the dynamics of processes of self-knowledge and self-awareness. Such processes are related to self-esteem (self-worth) and coherence (personal knowledge) in order to maintain a self-image acceptable to oneself and believed by one's interpersonal environment.

- Altered Sense of Self-esteem/Self-deception, possible implications:

  1. Discrepancies of their social self-image (stress).
  2. Difficulties in weighing their actions with others in tense interpersonal situations.
  3. Existential self-doubts.
  4. Doubts about his competences.

- In order to assess parsimoniously the Sense of Self-esteem/Self-deception, the narrative is analyzed thematically.

Exploratory questions based on dysfunctional subject matter:

1. Do you feel satisfied with yourself?
2. What do you consider to be your weaknesses?
3. Do you feel that you are authentic in your different roles?
4. Does the self-image you have of yourself coincide with the self-image of significant others?
5. Do you perceive that you tend to exaggerate about yourself?
6. Do you feel tension when you talk about what you have done and could have done?
7. Do you feel that your social image corresponds to what people say about you?

Appendix 4.5: Therapist's Guide: Sense of Self-Care/Health

- Sense of Self-Care/Health refers to taking informed care of oneself (based on information acquired and actively sought) throughout the life cycle.

Self-responsibility for one's own health and well-being at different points in the life cycle is essential for optimal psychological functioning.

- Alteration of the Sense of Self-Care/Health, possible implications:

1. Anti-health discourse and/or irony related to self-care ("you have to die of something").
2. Difficulties with energy to carry out chores.
3. Easily exhausted "run out of gas on a daily basis".
4. Perception of oscillating vitality.

- To assess parsimoniously the Sense of Self-Care/Health, the narrative is analyzed thematically.

Possible exploration questions based on dysfunctional subject matter:

1. What self-care activities do you do frequently?
2. How is the quality of your sleep?
3. What is your energy level like throughout the day?
4. How many meals do you eat during the day?
5. How important is it to you to be informed about your health status?
6. Do you consider that you take care of your health in a timely manner? What do you usually do to do this?
7. Do you consider your health and care according to your age?

References

Åström, E., Rönnlund, M., Adolfsson, R., & Grazia Carelli, M. (2019). Depressive symptoms and time perspective in older adults: Associations beyond personality and negative life events. *Aging & Mental Health, 23*(12), 1674–1683. https://doi.org/10.1080/13607863.2018.1506743

Baerger, D. R., & McAdams, D. P. (1999). Life story coherence and its relation to psychological well-being. *Narrative Inquiry, 9*(1), 69–96. https://doi.org/10.1075/ni.9.1.05bae

Baglioni, C., Spiegelhalder, K., Lombardo, C., & Riemann, D. (2010). Sleep and emotions: A focus on insomnia. *Sleep Medicine Reviews, 14*(4), 227–238.

Baglioni, C., Battagliese, G., Feige, B., Spiegelhalder, K., Nissen, C., Voderholzer, U., et al. (2011). Insomnia as a predictor of depression: A meta-analytic evaluation of longitudinal epidemiological studies. *Journal of Affective Disorders, 135*(1–3), 10–19.

Bajec, B. (2018). Relationship between time perspective and job satisfaction. *International Journal of Human Resources Development and Management, 18*(1/2), 145–165.

Bandura, A. (1986). *Social foundations of thought and action: A social cognitive theory.* Prentice-Hall.

Bandura, A. (1991). Self-regulation of motivation through anticipatory and self-reactive mechanisms. In R. A. Dienstbier (Ed.), *Nebraska symposium on motivation, 1990: Perspectives on motivation* (pp. 69–164). University of Nebraska Press.

Bandura, A. (1997). *Self-efficacy. The exercise of control.* W.H. Freeman.

Bandura, A. (2001). Social cognitive theory: An agentic perspective. *Annual Review of Psychology, 52,* 1–26. https://doi.org/10.1146/annurev.psych.52.1.1

Bandura, A. (2006). Toward a psychology of human agency. *Perspectives on Psychological Science, 1*(2), 164–180. https://doi.org/10.1111/j.1745-6916.2006.00011.x

Bandura, A. (2008). The reconstrual of "free will" from the agentic perspective of social cognitive theory. In J. Baer, J. C. Kaufman, & R. F. Baumeister (Eds.), *Are we free? Psychology and free will* (pp. 86–127). Oxford University Press.

Bandura, A. (2016). *Moral disengagement: How people do harm and live with themselves.* Macmill.

Bar, M. (Ed.). (2011). *Predictions in the brain: Using our past to generate a future.* Oxford University Press.

Bar-Haim, Y., Aya Kerem, A., Lamy, D., & Zakay, D. (2010). When time slows down: The influence of threat on time perception in anxiety. *Cognition and Emotion, 24*(2), 255–263.

Batterham, P. J., Glozier, N., & Christensen, H. (2012). Sleep disturbance, personality and the onset of depression and anxiety: Prospective cohort study. *Australian and New Zealand Journal of Psychiatry, 46*(11), 1089–1098.

Bize, R., Johnson, J. A., & Plotnikoff, R. C. (2007). Physical activity level and health-related quality of life in the general adult population: A systematic review. *Preventive Medicine, 45,* 401–415.

Blakemore, S., Wolpert, D., & Frith, C. (2002). Abnormalities in the awareness of action. *Trends in Cognitive Sciences, 6*(6), 237–242.

Bonanno, G. A., & Siddique, H. I. (1999). Emotional dissociation, self-deception, and psychotherapy. In J. A. Singer & P. Salovey (Eds.), *At play in the fields of consciousness: Essays in honor of Jerome L. Singer* (pp. 249–270). Lawrence Erlbaum Associates Publishers.

Boniwell, I. (2005). Beyond time management: How the latest research on time perspective and perceived time use can assist clients with time-related concerns. *International Journal of Evidence Based Coaching and Mentoring, 3*(2), 61–74.

Boniwell, I., & Zimbardo, P. G. (2004). Balancing time perspective in pursuit of optimal functioning. In P. A. Linley & S. Joseph (Eds.), *Positive psychology in practice* (pp. 165–178). Wiley.

Boyd, J., & Zimbardo, P. (2005). Time perspective, health and risk taking. In A. Strathman & J. Joireman (Eds.), *Understanding behavior in the context of time* (pp. 85–107). LEA.

Brockelman, P. (1985). *Time and self. Phenomenological explorations.* The Crossroad Publishing Company.

Bruner, J. S. (1990). *Acts of meaning*. Harvard University Press.

Bruner, J. (1997a). A narrative model of self-construction. *Annals of the New York Academy of Sciences, 818*, 144–161.

Bruner, J. S. (1997b). *Fundamentals of human caregiving: The early beginnings. Discurs d'Investidura d'Hoctor Honoris Causa de la UdG*. Girona: Universitat de Girona. https://www.udg.edu/Portals/9/Publicacions/Llibre_hc1197_BRUNER.pdf

Bruner, J. (2003). *La fábrica de historias*. Derecho, literatura, vida. Fondo cultura económica.

Bruner, J. (2004). The narrative creation of self. In E. L. Angus & J. Mcleod (Eds.), *The handbook of narrative and psychotherapy: Practice, theory, and research* (pp. 3–14). Sage.

Bruner, J., & Kalmar, D. (1998). Narrative and metanarrative in the construction of self. In M. Ferrari & R. Sternberg (Eds.), *Self-awareness* (pp. 308–331). Guilford Press.

Cai, H., Brown, J. D., Deng, C., & Oakes, M. A. (2007). Self-esteem and culture: Differences in cognitive self-evaluations or affective self-regard? *Asian Journal of Social Psychology, 10*, 162–170.

Chaput, J. P., Dutil, C., Featherstone, R., Ross, R., Giangregorio, L., Saunders, T. J., Janssen, I., Poitras, V. J., Kho, M. E., Ross-White, A., & Carrier, J. (2020). Sleep duration and health in adults: An overview of systematic reviews. *Applied Physiology, Nutrition, and Metabolism, 45*(10 (Suppl. 2)), S218–S231. https://doi.org/10.1139/apnm-2020-0034

Chomistek, A. K., Manson, J. E., Stefanick, M. L., Lu, B., Sands-Lincoln, M., Going, S. B., et al. (2013). Relationship of sedentary behavior and physical activity to incident cardiovascular disease: Results from the Women's health initiative. *Journal of the American College of Cardiology, 61*(23), 2346–2354.

Covassin, N., Singh, P., McCrady-Spitzer, S. K., St Louis, E. K., Calvin, A. D., Levine, J. A., & Somers, V. K. (2022). Effects of experimental sleep restriction on energy intake, energy expenditure, and visceral obesity. *Journal of the American College of Cardiology, 79*(13), 1254–1265. https://doi.org/10.1016/j.jacc.2022.01.038

Cox, R. C., & Olatunji, B. O. (2016). A systematic review of sleep disturbance in anxiety and related disorders. *Journal of Anxiety Disorders, 37*, 104–129. https://doi.org/10.1016/j.janxdis.2015.12.001

Crites, S. (1986). Storytime: Recollecting the past and projecting the future. In T. R. Sarbin (Ed.), *Narrative psychology: The storied nature of human conduct* (pp. 152–173). Praeger Publishers/Greenwood Publishing Group.

Crocker, J. (2002). The costs of seeking self-esteem. *Journal of Social Issues, 58*(3), 597–615. https://doi.org/10.1111/1540-4560.00279

Crocker, J., & Park, L. E. (2003). Seeking self-esteem: Construction, maintenance, and protection of self-worth. In M. R. Leary & J. P. Tangney (Eds.), *Handbook of self and identity* (pp. 309–326). The Guilford Press.

Crocker, J., & Wolfe, C. T. (2001). Contingencies of self-worth. *Psychological Review, 108*(3), 593–623. https://doi.org/10.1037/0033-295x.108.3.593

Curcio, G., Ferrara, M., & De Gennaro, L. (2006). Sleep loss, learning capacity and academic performance. *Sleep Medicine Reviews, 10*, 323–337.

de Leval, N. (1999). Quality of life and depression: Symmetry concepts. *Quality Life Research, 8*(4), 283–291. https://doi.org/10.1023/a:1008970317554

Deci, E. L., & Ryan, R. M. (1991). A motivational approach to self: Integration in personality. In R. Dienstbier (Ed.), *Nebraska symposium on motivation: Perspectives on motivation* (Vol. 38, pp. 237–288). University of Nebraska Press.

Deci, E. L., & Ryan, R. M. (1995). Human autonomy: The basis for true self-esteem. In M. H. Kernis (Ed.), *Efficacy, agency, and self-esteem* (pp. 31–49). Plenum Press.

Deci, E. L., & Ryan, R. M. (2000). The "what" and "why" of goal pursuits: Human needs and the self-determination of behavior. *Psychological Inquiry, 11*(4), 227–268. https://doi.org/10.1207/S15327965PLI1104_01

Dennett, D. C. (1991). *Consciousness explained*. Little, Brown and Co.

Dennett, D. C. (1992). The self as a center of narrative gravity. In F. Kessel, P. Cole, & D. Johnson (Eds.), *Self and consciousness: Multiple perspectives* (pp. 103–115). Erlbaum.
Diener, E., & Diener, M. (1995). Cross-cultural correlates of life satisfaction and self-esteem. *Journal of Personality and Social Psychology, 68*, 653–663.
Eid, M., & Diener, E. (2001). Norms for experiencing emotions in different cultures: Inter- and intranational differences. *Journal of Personality and Social Psychology, 81*, 869–885.
Epel, E., Prather, A. A., Puterman, E., & Tomiyama, A. J. (2016). Eat, drink, and be sedentary: A review of health behaviors' effects on emotions and affective states, and implications for interventions. In L. F. Barrett, M. Lewis, & J. M. Haviland-Jones (Eds.), *Handbook of emotions* (4th ed., pp. 685–706). Guilford Press.
Festinger, L. (1957). *A theory of cognitive dissonance*. Row Peterson.
Fischer, R. (1987). On fact and fiction – The structure of stories that the brain tells itself about itself. *Journal of Social and Biological Structures, 10*, 343–351.
Foster, J. (2013). Alcohol and sleep. In V. R. Preedy, V. B. Patel, & L.-A. Le (Eds.), *Handbook of nutrition, diet and sleep* (pp. 341–351). Wageningen Academic Publishers.
Fraisse, P. (1967). *Psychologie du temps*. PUF (deuxième édition).
Frith, C. (2005). The self in action: Lessons from delusions of control. *Consciousness and Cognition, 14*(4), 752–770. https://doi.org/10.1016/j.concog.2005.04.002
Gallagher, S. (2000a). Philosophical conceptions of the self: Implications for cognitive science. *Trends in Cognitive Science, 4*(1), 14–21. https://doi.org/10.1016/s1364-6613(99)01417-5
Gallagher, S. (2000b). Self-reference and schizophrenia: A cognitive model of immunity to error through misidentification. In D. Zahavi (Ed.), *Exploring the self: Philosophical and psychopathological perspectives on self-experience* (pp. 203–239). John Benjamins.
Gallagher, S. (2003). Self-narrative in schizophrenia. In T. Kircher & A. David (Eds.), *The self in neuroscience and psychiatry* (pp. 336–357). Cambridge University Press.
Gallagher, S., & Zahavi, D. (2008). *The phenomenological mind: An introduction to philosophy of mind and cognitive science*. Routledge.
Gallagher, S., & Zahavi, D. (2012). *The phenomenological mind: An introduction to philosophy of mind and cognitive science* (2nd ed.). Routledge.
Garaulet, M., Ortega, F. B., Ruiz, J. R., Rey-Lopez, J. P., Beghin, L., Manios, Y., Cuenca-Garcia, M., Plada, M., Diethelm, K., Kafatos, A., Molnar, D., Al-Tahan, J., & Moreno, L. A. (2011). Short sleep duration is associated with increased obesity markers in European adolescents: Effect of physical activity and dietary habits. The HELENA study. *International Journal of Obesity (London), 35*, 1308–1317.
García Haro, J., Quiñones, A., & Ugarte, C. (2024). Formulación de caso en conducta suicida: una perspectiva evolucionista para la regulación y bienestar psicológico. In A. Quiñones & C. Caro (Eds.), *Formulación de Caso: Hacia una Psicoterapia de precisión* (pp. 381–431). UNED editorial.
García, A. N., & Salloum, I. M. (2015). Polysomnographic sleep disturbances in nicotine, caffeine, alcohol, cocaine, opioid, and cannabis use: A focused review. *The American Journal on Addictions, 24*(7), 590–598.
Garcia, D., Sailer, U., Nima, A. A., & Archer, T. (2016). Questions of time and affect: A person's affectivity profile, time perspective, and well-being. *PeerJ, 4*, e1826. https://doi.org/10.7717/peerj.1826
Garcia, D., Granjard, A., Lundblad, S., & Archer, T. (2017). A dark past, a restrained present, and an apocalyptic future: Time perspective, personality, and life satisfaction among anorexia nervosa patients. *PeerJ, 5*, e3801. https://doi.org/10.7717/peerj.3801
Gaultney, J. F. (2010). The prevalence of sleep disorders in college students: Impact on academic performance. *Journal of American College Health, 59*(2), 91–97.
Goodwin, R. D. (2003). Association between physical activity and mental disorders among adults in the United States. *Preventive Medicine, 36*(6), 698–703.
Grondin, S. (2010). Timing and time perception: A review of recent behavioral and neuroscience findings and theoretical directions. *Attention, Perception & Psychophysics, 72*, 561–582.

Guidano, V. F. (1992). *Il sé nel suo divenire*. Bollati Boringhieri.
Guidano, V. F. (1999). Psicoterapia: Aspectos metodológicos, cuestiones clínicas y problemas abiertos desde una perspectiva postracionalista. *Revista de Psicoterapia, 37*, 95–105.
Guidano, V. F., & Liotti, G. (1983). *Cognitive processes and emotional disorders*. Guilford Press.
Harvey, A. G., Murray, G., Chandler, R. A., & Soehner, A. (2011). Sleep disturbance as transdiagnostic: Consideration of neurobiological mechanisms. *Clinical Psychology Review, 31*(2), 225–235.
Hirshkowitz, M., Whiton, K., Albert, S. M., Alessi, C., Bruni, O., DonCarlos, L., et al. (2015). National Sleep Foundation's updated sleep duration recommendations: Final report. *Sleep Health, 1*, 233–243. https://doi.org/10.1016/j.sleh.2015.10.004
Humphrey, N. (1986). *The inner eye*. Faber and Faber.
James, W. (1890). *The principles of psychology*. Henry Holt.
Jeannerod, M. (2009). The sense of agency and its disturbances in schizophrenia: A reappraisal. *Experimental Brain Research, 192*(3), 527–532.
Jike, M., Itani, O., Watanabe, N., Buysse, D. J., & Kaneita, Y. (2018). Long sleep duration and health outcomes: A systematic review, meta-analysis and meta-regression. *Sleep Medicine Reviews, 39*, 25–36. https://doi.org/10.1016/j.smrv.2017.06.011
Katzmarzyk, P. T. (2010). Physical activity, sedentary behavior, and health: Paradigm paralysis or paradigm shift? *Diabetes, 59*(11), 2717–2725.
Krendl, A. K., & Heatherton, T. F. (2009). Self versus others/self-regulation. In G. G. Berntson & J. T. Cacioppo (Eds.), *Handbook of neuroscience for the behavioral sciences* (pp. 859–878). Wiley.
Kristmannsdottir, G., Keski-Rahkonen, A., & Kuusinen, K. L. (2019). Changes in the sense of agency: Implications for the psychotherapy of bulimia nervosa- a case study. *Journal of Clinical Psychology*, 1–14.
Lakhan, S. E., & Finesmith, R. B. (2013). Nutritional supplements and sleep: An overview. In V. R. Preedy, V. B. Patel, & L.-A. Le (Eds.), *Handbook of nutrition, diet and sleep* (pp. 401–414). Wageningen Academic Publishers.
Levitt, H., Pomerville, A., & Surace, F. (2016). A qualitative meta-analysis examining clients' experiences of psychotherapy: A new agenda. *Psychological Bulletin, 142*, 801–830.
Lewin, K. (1942). Time perspective and morale. In G. Watson (Ed.), *Civilian morale*. Houghton Mifflin.
Lewin, R. (1988). *In the age of manking*. Simithsonian Books.
Lewis, M. (1994). My self and me. In S. T. Parker, R. W. Mitchell, & M. L. Broccia (Eds.), *Self-awareness in animals and humans* (pp. 20–34). Cambridge University Press.
Lewis, M. (2010). The emergence of consciousness and its role in human development. In R. Lerner & W. Overton (Eds.), *Cognition, biology, and methods. The handbook of lifespan development* (Vol. 1, pp. 628–670). Wiley.
Lewis, M. (2011). The origins and uses of self-awarenesss or the mental representation of me. *Consciousness and Cognition, 20*, 120–129.
Lewis, M., & Brooks-Gunn, J. (1979a). Toward a theory of social cognition: The development of self. In I. Uzgiris (Ed.), *New directions in child development: Social interaction and communication during infancy* (Vol. 1979, pp. 1–20). Jossey-Bass.
Lewis, M., & Brooks-Gunn, J. (1979b). *Social cognition and the acquisition of self*. Plenum.
Lind, M., Jørgensen, C. R., Heinskou, T., Simonsen, S., Bøye, R., & Thomsen, D. K. (2018). Patients with borderline personality disorder show increased agency in life stories after 12 months of psychotherapy. *Psychotherapy, 56*, 274. https://doi.org/10.1037/pst0000184
Linde, C. (1993). *Life stories: The creation of coherence*. Oxford University Press.
Lockley, S., & Foster, R. (2012). *Sleep: A very short introduction* (1st ed.). Oxford University Press.
Lohsoonthorn, V., Khidir, H., Casillas, G., Lertmaharit, S., Tadesse, M. G., Pensuksan, W. C., Rattananupong, T., Gelaye, B., & Williams, M. A. (2013). Sleep quality and sleep patterns in relation to consumption of energy drinks, caffeinated beverages, and other stimulants among Thai college students. *Sleep & Breathing, 17*(3), 1017–1028. https://doi.org/10.1007/s11325-012-0792-1

Loose, T., Acier, D., Andretta, J., Cole, J., McKay, M., Wagner, V., & Worrell, F. (2017). Time perspective and alcohol-use indicators in France and the United Kingdom: Results across adolescents, university students, and treatment outpatients. *Addiction Research & Theory, 26*, 143. https://doi.org/10.1080/16066359.2017.1334202

Loose, T., Du Pont, L., Acier, D., & El-Baalbaki, G. (2019). Time perspectives mediate the relationship between personality traits and alcohol consumption. *Time & Society, 28*(3), 1148–1166.

Lowicki, P., Witowska, J., Zajenkowski, M., & Stolarski, M. (2018). Time to believe: Disentangling the complex associations between time perspective and religiosity. *Personality and Individual Differences, 134*, 97–106.

Mackrill, T. (2009). Constructing client agency in psychotherapy research. *Journal of Humanistic Psychology, 49*(2), 193–206.

Magee, C., Xu-Feng, H., Iverson, D., & Caputil, P. (2010). Examining the pathways linking chronic sleep restriction to obesity. *Journal of Obesity, 2010*, 821–710.

Mahoney, M. J. (1991). *Human change processes*. Basic Books.

Markus, H. R. (1977). Self-Shemata and processing information about the self. *Journal of Personality and Social Psychology, 35*, 63–78.

McKay, M. T., Perry, J. L., Cole, J. C., & Worrell, F. C. (2018). What time is it? Temporal psychology measures relate differently to alcohol-related health outcomes. *Addiction Research & Theory, 26*(1), 20–27.

Melges, F. T. (1990). Identity and temporal perspective. In R. A. Block (Ed.), *Cognitive models of psychological time* (pp. 255–266). Lawrence Erlbaum Associates.

Minkowski, E. (1997). Du symptome au trouble générateur. (originally published in *Archives suisses de neurologie et de psychiatrie,* 1928; 22). In *Au-delà du rationalisme morbide.* Éditions L'Harmattan.

Morrow, J. R., Jackson, A. W., Bazzarre, T. L., Milne, D., & Blair, S. N. (1999). A one-year follow-up to physical activity and health. A report of the surgeon general. *American Journal of Preventive Medicine, 17*(1), 24–30.

Mruk, C. J. (2013a). *Self-esteem and positive psychology: Research, theory, and practice* (4th ed.). Springer Publishing Company.

Mruk, C. J. (2013b). Defining self-esteem as a relationship between competence and worthiness: How a two-factor approach integrates the cognitive and affective dimensions of self-esteem. *Polish Psychological Bulletin, 44*(2), 157–164.

Muris, P., & Otgaar, H. (2023). Self-esteem and self-compassion: A narrative review and meta-analysis on their links to psychological problems and well-being. *Psychology Research and Behavior Management, 16*, 2961–2975. https://doi.org/10.2147/PRBM.S402455

Neisser, U. (1988). Five kinds of self knowledge. *Philosophical Psychology, 1*(1), 35–59.

Neisser, U. (1993). *The perceived self: Ecological and interpersonal sources of self-knowledge.* Cambridge University Press.

Nishiura, C., Noguchi, J., & Hashimoto, H. (2010). Dietary patterns only partially explain the effect of short sleep duration on the incidence of obesity. *Sleep, 33*, 753–757.

Nofzinger, E. A. (2005). Psychiatric insomnias. In A. N. Rama, C. Cho, & C. A. Kushida (Eds.), *Handbook of clinical neurophysiology* (Vol. 6, pp. 317–326). Elsevier.

Oja, P., & Borms, J. (2004). Health enhancing physical activity. In P. Oja & J. Borms (Eds.), *Perspectives – The multidisciplinary series of physical education and sport science* (Vol. 6). Meyer & Meyer Sport (UK) Ltd..

Orth, U., & Robins, R. W. (2022). Is high self-esteem beneficial? Revisiting a classic question. *American Psychologist, 77*(1), 5–17. https://doi.org/10.1037/amp0000922

Palagini, L., Hertenstein, E., Riemann, D., & Nissen, C. (2022). Sleep, insomnia and mental health. *Journal of Sleep Research, 31*(4), e13628. https://doi.org/10.1111/jsr.13628

Papastamatelou, J., Unger, A., Giotakos, O., & Athanasiadou, F. (2015). Is time perspective a predictor of anxiety and perceived stress? Some preliminary results from Greece. *Psychological Studies, 60*, 468–477.

Peden, A. (2013). Tackling depressed mood through exercise. *Healthcare Counselling & Psychotherapy Journal, 13*(3), 34–35.

Penev, P. D. (2013). Sleep deprivation and human energy metabolism. In V. R. Preedy, V. B. Patel, & L.-A. Le (Eds.), *Handbook of nutrition, diet and sleep* (pp. 193–208). Wageningen Academic Publishers.

Pieters, S., Burk, W. J., Van der Vorst, H., Dahl, R. E., Wiers, R. W., & Engels, R. C. (2015). Prospective relationships between sleep problems and substance use, internalizing and externalizing problems. *Journal of Youth and Adolescence, 44*(2), 379–388. https://doi.org/10.1007/s10964-014-0213-9

Pyszczynski, T., Greenberg, J., & Goldenberg, J. (2002). Freedom in the balance: On the defense, growth, and expansion of the self. In M. R. Leary & J. Tangney (Eds.), *Handbook of self and identity* (pp. 314–343). Guilford.

Quiñones, A. (2013). *Indicadores de procesos en psicoterapia asociados a éxito.* [Tesis de Doctorado, Universidad Autónoma de Barcelona]. Repositorio Institucional – Universidad Autónoma de Barcelona.

Quiñones, A. (2024). Perspectiva evolucionista para la formulación de caso: Un sistema abierto. In A. Quiñones & C. Caro (Eds.), *Formulación de Caso: Hacia una Psicoterapia de precisión* (pp. 107–135). UNED editorial.

Quiñones, A., Melipillán, R., & Ugarte, C. (2012). Indicadores de procesos de éxito en psicoterapia cognitiva. *Revista Argentina de Clínica Psicológica, 21*(3), 247–254.

Quiñones, A., Ceric, F., & Ugarte, C. (2015). Flujos de información en zonas de tiempo subjetivo: estudio de un proceso psicoterapéutico exitoso. *Revista Argentina de Clínica Psicológica, 24*(3), 255–266.

Quiñones, A., Ceric, F., Ugarte, C., & Pascale, A. (2017). Psychotherapy and psychological time: A case study. *Rivista di Psichiatria, 52*(3), 109–116.

Quiñones, A., Ugarte, C., Chávez, C., & Mañalich, J. (2018). Variables psicológicas asociadas a adherencia, cronicidad y complicaciones en pacientes con diabetes mellitus II. *Revista Médica de Chile, 146*, 1151–1158.

Rama, A. N., Cho, C., & Kushida, C. A. (2005). NREM-REM sleep. In C. Guilleminault (Ed.), *Clinical neurophysiology of sleep disorders. Handbook of clinical neurophysiology* (Vol. 6, pp. 21–29). Elsevier.

Reese, E., Haden, C. A., Baker-Ward, L., Bauer, P., Fivush, R., & Ornstein, P. A. (2011). Coherence of personal narratives across the lifespan: A multidimensional model and coding method. *Journal of Cognition and Development, 12*(4), 424–462. https://doi.org/10.1080/15248372.2011.587854

Roehrs, T. A., & Roth, T. (2015). Sleep disturbance in substance use disorders. *Psychiatry Clinics of North America, 38*(4), 793–803.

Roth, T., Jaeger, S., Jin, R., Kalsekar, A., Stang, P. E., & Kessler, R. C. (2006). Sleep problems, comorbid mental disorders, and role functioning in the national comorbidity survey replication. *Biological Psychiatry, 60*(12), 1364–1371.

Ryan, R. M., & Deci, E. L. (2017). *Self-determination theory: Basic psychological needs in motivation, development, and wellness.* Guilford Press.

Saarijarvi, S., Salminen, J. K., Toikka, T., & Raitasalo, R. (2002). Health-related major quality of life among patients with major depression. *Nordic Journal of Psychiatry, 56*, 261–264.

Sarbin, T. R. (1981). On self deception. *Annals of New York Academy of Sciences, 364*, 220–235.

Sarbin, T. R. (1986). The narrative as the root metaphor for contextualism. In T. R. Sarbin (Ed.), *Narrative psychology: The storied nature of human conduct* (pp. 3–22). Praeger.

Schectman, M. (1996). *The constitution of selves.* Cornell University Press.

Schroeder, S. A. (2007). We can do better: Improving the health of the American people. *New England Journal of Medicine, 357*, 1221–1228.

Simjanoski, M., Patel, S., Boni, R., Balanzá-Martínez, V., Frey, B. N., Minuzzi, L., Kapczinski, F., & Cardoso, T. A. (2023). Lifestyle interventions for bipolar disorders: A systematic review and meta-analysis. *Neuroscience and Biobehavioral Reviews, 152*, 105257. https://doi.org/10.1016/j.neubiorev.2023.105257

Simonds, S. K. (1974). Health education as social policy. *Health Education Monographs, 2*(Suppl. 1), 1–25.
Sneed, J. R., & Whitbourne, S. K. (2003). Identity processing and self-consciousness in middle and later adulthood. *The Journals of Gerontology Series B: Psychological Sciences and Social Sciences, 58*(6), P313–P319. https://doi.org/10.1093/geronb/58.6.P313
Song, F., & Walker, M. P. (2023). Sleep, alcohol, and caffeine in financial traders. *PLoS One, 18*(11), e0291675. https://doi.org/10.1371/journal.pone.0291675
Staudinger, U. M. (2001). Life reflection: A social–cognitive analysis of life review. *Review of General Psychology, 5*(2), 148–160. https://doi.org/10.1037/1089-2680.5.2.148
Stolarski, M., Wiberg, B., & Osin, E. (2015). Assessing temporal harmony: The issue of a balanced time perspective. In M. Stolarski, N. Fieulaine, & W. van Beek (Eds.), *Time perspective theory: Review, research and application* (pp. 57–71). Springer International Publishing.
Ströhle, A. (2009). Physical activity, exercise, depression and anxiety disorders. *Journal of neural Transmission (Vienna, Austria: 1996), 116*(6), 777–784. https://doi.org/10.1007/s00702-008-0092-x
Synofzik, M., Thier, P., Leube, D. T., Schlotterbeck, P., & Lindner, A. (2010). Misattributions of agency in schizophrenia are based on imprecise predictions about the sensory consequences of one's actions. *Brain: A Journal of Neurology, 133*(Pt 1), 262–271. https://doi.org/10.1093/brain/awp291
Tallman, K., & Bohart, A. C. (1999). The client as a common factor: Clients as self- healers. In M. A. Hubble, B. L. Duncan, & S. D. Miller (Eds.), *The heart and soul of change: What works in therapy* (pp. 91–131). American Psychological Association.
Taylor, S. E. (1989). *Positive illusions: Creative self-deception healthy mind*. Basic Books.
Taylor, D. J., Bramoweth, A. D., Grieser, E. A., Tatum, J. I., & Roane, B. M. (2013). Epidemiology of insomnia in college students: Relationship with mental health, quality of life, and substance use difficulties. *Behavior Therapy, 44*(3), 339–348. https://doi.org/10.1016/j.beth.2012.12.001
Teychenne, M., Ball, K., & Salmon, J. (2010). Sedentary behavior and depression among adults: A review. *International Journal of Behavioral Medicine, 17*(4), 246–254. https://doi.org/10.1007/s12529-010-9075-z
Thorp, A. A., Owen, N., Neuhaus, M., & Dunstan, D. W. (2011). Sedentary behaviors and subsequent health outcomes in adults: A systematic review of longitudinal studies, 19962011. *American Journal of Preventive Medicine, 41*(2), 207–215.
Toplak, M. E., Rucklidge, J. J., Hetherington, R., John, S. C., & Tannock, R. (2003). Time perception deficits in attention-deficit/ hyperactivity disorder and comorbid reading difficulties in child and adolescent samples. *Journal of Child Psychology and Psychiatry, and Allied Disciplines, 44*(6), 888–903. https://doi.org/10.1111/1469-7610.00173
Triandis, H. C. (2009). *Fooling ourselves: Self-deception in politics, religion, and terrorism*. Praeger.
Triandis, H. C. (2011). Culture and self-deception: A theoretical perspective. *Social Behavior and Personality, 39*(1), 3–14.
Trivers, R. (2011). *The folly of fools: The logic of deceit and self-deception in human life*. Basic Books.
Tulving, E. (1985). Memory and consciousness. *Canadian Psychology, 26*, 1–12.
Tulving, E. (2002). Chronesthesia: Conscious awareness of subjective time. In D. T. Stuss & R. T. Knight (Eds.), *Principles of frontal lobe function* (pp. 311–325). Oxford University Press.
Tulving, E., & Szpunar, K. (2012). Does the future exist? In B. Levine & F. Craik (Eds.), *Mind and the frontal lobes: Cognition, behavior, and brain imaging* (pp. 248–263). Oxford University Press.
U.S. Department of Health and Human Services. (1996). *Physical activity and health: A report of the surgeon general*. Atlanta, GA: U.S. Department of Health and Human Services, Centers for Disease Control and Prevention, National Center for Chronic Disease Prevention and Health Promotion. Report no. 1.

U.S. Department of Health and Human Services. (2000). *Healthy people 2010* (conference edition in 2 Vols.). US Department of Health and Human Services. Retrieved July 2013 from: http://www.health.gov/healthypeople

van Beek, W., Berghuis, H., Kerkhof, A., & Beekman, A. (2011). Time perspective, personality and psychopathology: Zimbardo's time perspective inventory in psychiatry. *Time & Society, 20*(3), 364–374. https://doi.org/10.1177/0961463X10373960

Verhoeven, J. E., Han, L. K. M., Lever-van Milligen, B. A., Hu, M. X., Révész, D., Hoogendoorn, A. W., Batelaan, N. M., van Schaik, D. J. F., van Balkom, A. J. L. M., van Oppen, P., & Penninx, B. W. J. H. (2023). Antidepressants or running therapy: Comparing effects on mental and physical health in patients with depression and anxiety disorders. *Journal of Affective Disorders, 329*, 19–29. https://doi.org/10.1016/j.jad.2023.02.064

von Hippel, W., & Trivers, R. (2011). The evolution and psychology of self-deception. *The Behavioral and Brain Sciences, 34*(1), 1–56. https://doi.org/10.1017/S0140525X10001354

Voss, M., Moore, J., Hauser, M., Gallinat, J., Heinz, A., & Haggard, P. (2010). Altered awareness of action in schizophrenia: A specific deficit in predicting action consequences. *Brain: A Journal of Neurology, 133*(10), 3104–3112. https://doi.org/10.1093/brain/awq152

Wahlström, J., & Seilonen, M. L. (2016). Displaying agency problems at the outset of psychotherapy. *European Journal of Psychotherapy & Counselling, 18*(4), 333–348.

Westland, S., & Shinebourne, P. (2009). Self-deception and the therapist: An interpretative phenomenological analysis of the experiences and understandings of therapists working with clients they describe as self-deceptive. *Psychology and Psychotherapy: Theory, Research and Practice, 82*(4), 385–401. https://doi.org/10.1348/147608309X450508

Wilkinson, A., & Whitehead, L. (2009). Evolution of the concept of self-care and implications for nurses: A literature review. *International Journal of Nursing Studies, 46*(8), 1143–1147.

Williams, D. C., & Levitt, H. M. (2007). Principles for facilitating agency in psychotherapy. *Psychotherapy Research, 17*(1), 66–82. https://doi.org/10.1080/10503300500469098

Wilmot, E. G., Edwardson, C. L., Achana, F. A., Davies, M. J., Gorely, T., Gray, L. J., Khunti, K., Yates, T., & Biddle, S. J. (2012). Sedentary time in adults and the association with diabetes, cardiovascular disease and death: Systematic review and meta-analysis. *Diabetologia, 55*(11), 2895–2905. https://doi.org/10.1007/s00125-012-2677-z

World Health Organization. (2013). *Health literacy the solid facts*. Denmark.

World Health Organization. (2019). *WHO consolidated guideline on self-care interventions for health: Sexual and reproductive health and rights*. World Health Organization.

Wu, J., Zhang, H., Yang, L., Shao, J., Chen, D., Cui, N., Tang, L., Fu, Y., Xue, E., Lai, C., & Ye, Z. (2022). Sedentary time and the risk of metabolic syndrome: A systematic review and dose-response meta-analysis. *Obesity Reviews, 23*(12), e13510. https://doi.org/10.1111/obr.13510

Zimbardo, P. G., & Boyd, J. N. (1999). Putting time in perspective: A valid, reliable individual-differences metric. *Journal of Personality and Social Psychology, 77*(6), 1271–1288. https://doi.org/10.1037/0022-3514.77.6.1271

Zimbardo, P. G., & Boyd, J. N. (2008). *The time paradox: The new psychology of time that will change your life*. The Free Press.

Chapter 5
Cognition

Cognition is a primordial system that evolution has provided us with. Generally, cognition refers to the global and holistic activity of giving meaning in Homo Sapiens. In such a context, rationality (examples: increasingly context-sensitive inferential strategies, inductive and deductive inferences to extract patterns of contextually valid informational relationships, etc.) allowed us as a group to solve problems of various complexity and create progressively complex technologies.

In the case formulation model presented, the intersubjective knowledge domain "Cognition" is evaluated through three axes of analysis: cognitive alterations, metacognitive alterations, and alterations in executive functions (see Fig. 5.1). Both metacognition and executive functions are two domains of cognitive development that play a central role in the development of self-regulated behavior and mental operations. These higher-order cognitive processes allow for flexible operation and efficient adaptation to new and challenging tasks.

5.1 Cognitive Alterations

The first axis is the ***Cognitive Alterations***. Firstly, both *rumination and worry* are considered modes of repetitive negative thoughts (Arditte et al., 2016) and share the fact of being forms of persevering thoughts with difficulties to stop focusing on the negative, and they have as consequences deficits in personal performance, concentration, and attention difficulties (Watkins et al., 2005). In particular, the *repetitive negative thoughts* are considered as cognitive vulnerability factors for various mental health problems (anxiety disorders, mood states, and eating disorders) (Sternheim et al., 2012). This type of thoughts "involve attentive, persevering, frequent, and relatively uncontrollable cognitive activity that focuses on the negative aspects of the self and the world" (Ehring & Watkins, 2008, p.193). In addition, they are

Á. Quiñones Bergeret, *Evolutionary Case Formulation*,
https://doi.org/10.1007/978-3-031-67412-9_5

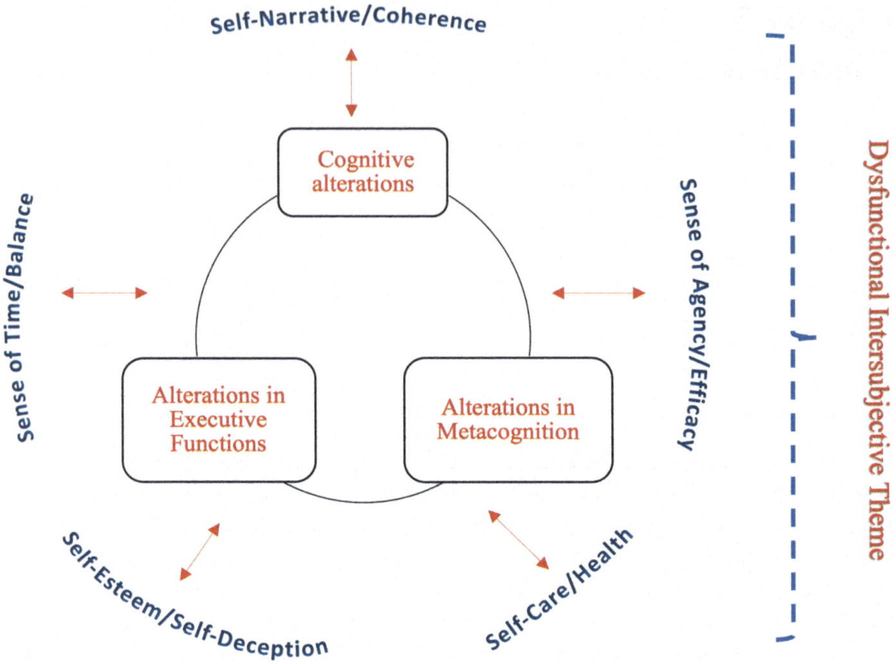

Fig. 5.1 Cognition

considered a common risk factor that would explain the high rates of comorbidity among different emotional disorders (Kalmbach et al., 2016).

The *rumination* is defined as a pattern of thoughts and repetitive behaviors that focus attention on oneself, on depressive symptoms and their causes, meanings, and consequences of these symptoms, instead of actively focusing on a solution to resolve the circumstances surrounding these symptoms (Nolen-Hoeksema & Morrow, 1993, p. 569). Research indicates that rumination is considered a risk factor for depression (Lyubomirsky et al., 2015), anxiety disorder (McEvoy & Brans, 2013), eating disorder (Holm-Denoma & Hankin, 2011), and substance abuse (Watkins, 2015).

Rumination and the characteristics of memory recovery deserve special attention from psychotherapists. In this sense, the *field perspective* versus *observer perspective* (Nigro & Neisser, 1983)[1] are relevant to keep in mind in understanding rumination. There is evidence supporting a link between rumination and memories from the observer's perspective. For example, there are interesting research on this, firstly Williams & Moulds (2007) indicate that dysphoric participants who remembered intrusive memories from an observer's perspective reported more rumination than

[1] "Field perspective" refers to memories remembered in the first person and are phenomenologically rich. On the other hand, third-person memories are called "observer perspective" and contain more descriptive but less affective details (Nigro & Neisser, 1983).

those who reported memories from the field perspective. Secondly, there is evidence that repeated rehearsal of memory transforms field memories into observer memories (D'Argembeau & Van der Linden, 2004; Robinson & Swanson, 1993).

The *worry* is defined as a chain of thoughts or verbal linguistic activity and images (although more the former) loaded with negative affect and relatively uncontrollable. The worry process represents an attempt at mental problem solving on a topic whose outcome is uncertain, although it carries the possibility of one or more negative consequences and is considered very related to the process of fear (Borkovec et al., 1983).

In the field of research, it is an increasingly studied phenomenon in the general and clinical population. Davey et al. (1996) found in the general population that 38% of people worried at least once a day. On the other hand, worry is a central feature of generalized anxiety disorder and is common in other anxiety and mood disorders (McEvoy et al., 2013).

Now, there are several aspects to consider in excessive worry: *Intolerance to uncertainty and overestimation of worry. Intolerance to uncertainty* is an increasingly studied phenomenon and is considered the nuclear aspect to explain the etiology and maintenance of excessive worry (Dugas et al., 2005). Currently, intolerance to uncertainty is a dispositional tendency to experience fear of the unknown and is an important factor in the development and maintenance of anxiety disorders (Bomyea, et al., 2015; Carleton, 2012). In addition, it includes beliefs that uncertainty is threatening and stressful and causes anxiety, as well as the desire to avoid situations where there may be uncertainty and ambiguity (Buhr & Dugas, 2002; Dugas et al., 2001). It is noteworthy, that the most complete conceptual model of the relationships between intolerance to uncertainty and anxiety psychopathology was designed mainly to explain the symptoms of generalized anxiety disorder (Dugas et al., 1998).

Dugas and collaborators suggest that intolerance to uncertainty may represent a causal risk factor for worry. The data Clinical trials show that over the course of treatment for Generalized Anxiety Disorder, changes in intolerance to uncertainty tend to precede changes in worry (Dugas & Ladouceur, 2000; Dugas et al., 1998). Additionally, there is a laboratory study that showed that manipulating intolerance to uncertainty causes changes in worry, with greater intolerance to uncertainty generating more worry and less intolerance leading to fewer worries (Ladouceur et al., 2000).

For those who have a high level of intolerance to uncertainty, the possibility of negative outcomes is proposed as it triggers maladaptive cognitive reactivity and behavior (e.g., greater need for information during decision-making) that serve to increase worry and anxiety (Dugas et al., 2005; Dugas & Robichaud, 2007; Ladouceur et al., 2000). Similarly, intolerance to uncertainty contributes to other problematic cognitive processes, which include poor problem orientation and cognitive avoidance, which paradoxically contribute to maintaining worry and anxiety (Dugas & Robichaud, 2007).

Another indicator is *selective attention (attentional bias).* The concept of selective attention is already observed with William James, who stated "My experience is what I agree to attend to. Only those items which I notice shape my mind—without selective interest, experience is an utter chaos" (James, 1890, p. 402).

Selective attention refers to a process by which specific stimuli, within the external and internal environment, are selected for further processing (See Harvey et al., 2004). Likewise, attention plays a central role in episodic memory because it is necessary for the formation of lasting memory traces (Rock & Gutman, 1981).

In the psychotherapeutic field, *attention* is a fundamental process. From a human development point of view, it is worth remembering that joint attention is considered the greatest cognitive achievement of infancy (Tomasello, 1999). Without joint attention, it is difficult to imagine how a baby's vocabulary can be taught, or indeed, how the baby can be taught to participate in any non-verbal activity (Premack, 1986). As Tomasello (1999) and Hobson (2002) have pointed out, there could be no exchange of cognitive events without joint attention.

In the field of research, there is compelling evidence about the importance of *selective attention* in mental health problems (unipolar depression, bipolar disorder, post-traumatic stress disorder, panic attacks, specific phobia, generalized anxiety, eating disorders, autism, schizophrenia, etc.) and personality variables such as neuroticism and extraversion that are associated with individual differences in the attentional processing of emotional stimuli (Haas et al., 2007; Amin et al., 2004). There is agreement that people with psychological disorders show attentional biases that are closely related to their current concerns and that are of different types (examples: detection of relevant danger signals, reward, safety, confirmation of beliefs, interference with processing of new information, etc.).

According to the review by Harvey et al. (2004), there are three attention processes that can be considered well-established transdiagnostic processes: (1). Selective attention to external stimuli relevant to worry; (2). Selective attention to internal stimuli relevant to worry (focused attention); (3). Attentional avoidance or attention towards sources of safety.

In summary, for practical work, certain interventions aim at attention processes that include reducing attention to negative stimuli, promoting attention to information that can disconfirm problematic beliefs, and improving control over attention.

Another relevant cognitive processing indicator is *expectations*[2] (probabilistic beliefs about the dimension of existential future time) that shape and influence our perception, motivation, emotion, cognition, and behavior in various intersubjective contexts. On the other hand, prediction is a fundamental task of the human brain (Bar, 2007, 2009, 2011; Friston & Kiebel, 2009). In fact, for example, predictions about the future include short-term predictions about what object may appear next in a scene (Bar, 2007) and prediction errors about expected rewards that are crucial for learning (Schultz et al., 1997).

Now, the *expectations* that people have about what will happen and how well they can cope with what happens to them have relevant motivational implications. We know from research in psychology, that the strength with which people try to

[2] Expectation does not have a single definition.

exert personal control depends on the solidity of their expectations that they will be able to achieve it.

One aspect that deserves attention is the relevance of optimism in daily life, which indicates the importance of expectations in psychological well-being. There are several studies that have shown that being optimistic, which is defined as an individual difference characterized by positive future expectations, is related to health benefits (Scheier et al., 1989). It has also been observed that optimism predicts better mental health and less emotional distress (Kwon, 2002; Lench, 2011).

On the other hand, expectations are considered an essential element of any effective psychotherapy (Constantino et al., 2011, 2020, 2021; Connor & Callahan, 2015; ; Frank, 1963; Kirsch, 1985) and even some researchers point out that most psychotherapies are intimately related to the manipulation and revision of patients' expectations (Greenberg et al., 2006). Similarly, it is interesting to note that humans learn from their mistakes and their successes; however, to argue that we learn more from our mistakes than from our good choices is a matter of debate (Klein et al., 2007; Eppinger & Kray, 2011). In such a context, it is relevant to pay attention to the expectation and feedback mechanisms observed in certain types of problems and their consequences in mental health problems. As an illustration, I will mention marital conflict (Ali et al., 2022), specifically women abused by their partners. Although most women in abusive relationships try to leave the relationship at least once, many of them return to their partners (Bell et al., 2007; Goodman et al., 2003). Similarly, approximately half of the women who seek shelter through domestic violence programs return to abusive relationships after leaving the shelter (Tutty, 1996).

Another indicator is the *problematic attributional profile*. Inferring the cause of an event is called *attribution* (Heider, 1944). From a historical perspective, the development of the theory of causal attribution in social psychology led to a concern for attributional style as a personality variable (see Weiner & Graham, 1999).

We know that attributions are a very relevant source of knowledge when understanding how individual intersubjective and contextualized meaning is constructed. We know that one appreciable aspect when experiencing events is judging their causes since inferring a cause informs us if an event was intentional or accidental.

Research indicates that explanatory style has been related with types of depression, performance, health, and other significant life outcomes (See Wise & Rosqvist, 2006; Joiner, 2001). More specifically, the relationship between attributional style and depression is robustly documented (Hu et al., 2015; Gladstone & Kaslow, 1995; Joiner & Wagner, 1995; Sweeney et al., 1986). Hu et al. (2015) conducted a meta-analysis that examined the relationship between attribution style (which included internal, stable, global and composite causes for negative outcomes) and depression. They found overwhelming support for this relationship.

In clinical and student samples, it has been shown that people who characteristically explain negative events in terms of internal, stable, and global causes (pessimistic explanatory style) are more likely to develop depression (particularly, "hopeless depression") than those who tend to make external, unstable, and specific attributions for negative outcomes (Abramson et al., 1989; Alloy et al., 2000). Moreover, attributing positive events to unstable and specific sources is associated with depression, although less strongly than attributions for negative events (Ahrens & Haaga, 1993). In fact, negative attribution styles contribute to a variety of common emotional difficulties, including depression, anxiety, frequent anger, and guilt (Hilt, 2004).

We humans make spontaneous attributions daily ("we explain our behavior and that of others permanently", "we explain events") and they deal with how people explain the origin of their behavior and that of other people. However, if there is a *problematic attribution profile,* it is crucial to identify it in the *Dysfunctional Intersubjective Theme* as it contributes to a quality of mental representation with intersubjective tension.

5.2 Alterations in Metacognition

The second axis of analysis is the ***Alterations in Metacognition***. The concept of metacognition ("reflective function") has a long history in psychology and has different origins, among which cognitive psychology (Theory of Mind) with the pioneering works of Premack and Woodruf, the work of Wilfred Bion, the Theory of Object Relations and Attachment Theory stand out. Specifically, the study of metacognition emerged in the area of developmental psychology and later in the psychology of memory, aging, neuropsychology (Brown, 1978; Flavell, 1976, 1979; Metcalfe & Shimamura, 1994), and cognitive neuroscience of metacognition (Fleming & Frith, 2014).

John Hurley Flavell (1976, 1979) is one of the pioneers in the use of the term metacognition. According to Flavell (1979), metacognition is a system that organizes information, experiences, objectives, and strategies. Flavell (1979) distinguished four components of metacognition that interact in a complex way: (a) metacognitive knowledge, (b) metacognitive experiences, (c) metacognitive goals (or tasks), and (d) metacognitive actions (or strategies).

Recently, metacognition has been examined as a fundamental basis for most or all psychological disorders (Nordahl & Wells, 2018; Semerari et al., 2014, Semerari, 1999; Wells, 1995, 2000, 2013; Wells & Matthews, 1994). While it is true, metacognition has been studied essentially in personality disorders, metacognitive dysfunctions are not present exclusively in individuals with personality disorders (Dimaggio et al., 2007; Bateman & Fonagy, 2004), but have also been found in other psychopathological problems. In fact, Gumley (2011) and others have considered metacognitive dysfunctions as a pathogenic transdiagnostic factor.

In psychotherapy[3] the term Metacognition is often used to indicate the reflective function. It is relevant to keep in mind that the term Metacognition is somewhat

[3] For context, the ability to understand mental states in psychotherapy has been given different names, particularly in the field of personality disorders it is often called "metacognition" (Semerari et al., 2007; Dimaggio & Lysaker, 2010; Carcione et al., 2011) or "mentalization" (Bateman & Fonagy, 2004; Bouchard et al., 2008; Choi-Kain & Gunderson, 2008). These two terms have been

imprecise and in psychotherapy it is no exception both in the definition and in the structure of interventions (see Wells' Metacognitive Therapy, Moritz and Woodward's Metacognitive Training, and Lysaker's MERIT- Metacognitive Reflection and Insight Therapy).

Metacognition has also been used as a general term to describe the processes that allow people not only to experience the world, but also to experience and reflect on themselves as they experience the world (Moritz & Lysaker, 2018). More specifically, metacognition describes a range of interrelated factors comprising any knowledge or cognitive process that is involved in the interpretation, monitoring, or control of cognition. In metacognitive processes, it is important to distinguish between metacognitive knowledge and metacognitive regulation (Harvey et al., 2004). The *metacognitive knowledge* refers to the beliefs and information that people have about their own thought processes and how they work. Such knowledge can take the form of conscious propositional beliefs of different nature or could reflect procedural rules that have been developed over time and learning to guide processing (Wells, 2000).

Metacognitive beliefs include "positive metacognitive beliefs," which emphasize the advantages of certain types of thinking (examples: "thinking that my worry is useful for problem-solving," "I must remember everything and I will know if I am guilty," etc.), and "negative metacognitive beliefs," which emphasize the risks and negative consequences of thoughts (example: "worrying will drive me crazy"). It is important to note that Wells (2000) used the term metacognition to refer to a set of beliefs about mental content, rather than a function that allows us to be aware of mental states as argued by Antonio Semerari's group (Semerari et al., 2007).

It has been found that metacognitive beliefs are positively associated with depression (Wells, 2013; Papageorgiou & Wells, 2001); symptoms of psychosis such as hallucinations (Morrison et al., 2002), obsessions, and compulsions (Solem et al., 2010); health anxiety (Bailey & Wells, 2016); generalized anxiety (Cartwright-Hatton et al., 2004; Wells, 1999); alcohol abuse (Spada & Wells, 2010); and social anxiety (Nordahl & Wells, 2018; Nordahl et al., 2016; Vassilopoulos et al., 2015; Fisak & Hammond, 2013; Wong & Moulds, 2010).

On the other hand, the *metacognitive regulation* involves all the processes that control and monitor cognition, such as the allocation of attention, monitoring, planning, and discrepancy checking. Metacognitive regulation includes the responses or strategies that people use to try to control the activities or the content of their cognitive system (Wells 2000, 2009; Harvey et al., 2004). Both recurrent thinking and thought suppression are examples of such metacognitive control strategies.

In another order of things, personality disorders present difficulties in reasoning about mental states, that is, the metacognitive abilities of individuals are impaired (Dimaggio & Lysaker, 2010; Dimaggio et al., 2015). From the cognitive tradition,

used in numerous studies as similar concepts, and there is broad consensus indicating that they refer to almost the same psychological function (Bo et al., 2014; Semerari et al., 2014; Fonagy & Bateman, 2016).

alterations such as the ability to represent goals, the ability to decenter, the ability to differentiate, the ability to integrate, sharing deficits, and belonging deficits are highlighted.

The *ability to represent goals*. Humans set goals and establish plans to achieve them, this dynamic is part of our nature. However, the element that characterizes the deficit in the representation of goals is what Carcione et al. (1999) point out "The element that characterises this condition is the difficulty of representing in one's own mental scenario a goal with a corresponding plan of action, in the absence of an interpersonal context of reference" (p. 151. Author's free translation).

They also clarify that this alteration is not a black or white response. They argue:

> A lack of representation does not imply that the person lacks goals but that, at least in certain circumstances, he or she does not manage to represent any of them in consciousness in a definite way. Similarly, by over-representation we do not mean the presence in the system of too many goals but the fact that the subject does not manage to make a selection appropriate to the context and circumstance. (Carcione et al., 1999, p. 148. Free translation by the author)

The *ability to decenter* refers to that cognitive function that "in everyday life, allows us to interact with reality and with other human beings, considering the point of view of the other as external and different from our own" (Nicolò, 1999, p. 281. Free translation by the author). When the deficit of decentering is present, the person is unable to assume this perspective (Falcone et al., 2003).

The *ability to differentiate* allows us to recognize our mental states as representations of reality. When this ability is in deficit, the recognition of subjectivity and the fallibility of one's own representations and constructions of the world with respect to reality is altered (Falcone, 1999; Falcone et al., 2003).

The *ability to integrate* refers to the ability to extrapolate links, regularities, or differences between different states and mental processes of oneself and others (Semerari, 2000).

In conclusion, and in order to facilitate possible paths of tuning with patients' representation problems, the importance of having a conceptual map of possible deficits/alterations in the reflective function [metacognitive/mentalizing capacity] is of great help.

The *deficits of belonging* and *deficits of sharing* are frequent according to the Semerari group and alert us to the possibilities of encountering deficient mental states characterized by issues of distancing from others, exclusion and rejection. Firstly, a sense of *belonging* is understood as "the perception of community of mental contents, values, beliefs, experiences, affections, skills, interests, that define a particular group" (Dimaggio et al., 1999, p. 235. Free translation by the author). One aspect of the experience of non-belonging that stands out is the feeling of being particularly visible and observed. Secondly, they define *sharing* as analogous to belonging but with respect to a dual relationship (Dimaggio et al., 1999). An example, generally in borderline personality disorder, the feeling of non-belonging is experienced as an unjust exclusion by others that is associated with the emotion of anger and hostility.

On the other hand, Bateman and Fonagy consider that mentalization[4] is closely related to concepts such as "metacognition" and "theory of mind" (Bateman & Fonagy, 2012). From the perspective of Fonagy and Bateman (2007), the alteration of interpersonal relationships observed in borderline personality disorder is frequent. Namely, Fonagy (Fonagy & Target, 2000) argue that this dimension is related to a deficiency in the ability to accurately perceive the respective mental states of oneself and others, and to differentiate between oneself and others. Similarly, Fonagy and Bateman (2007) argue that the deficiency of interpersonal awareness in the case of borderline personality disorders would imply the underlying absence of an effective and stable differentiation between oneself and others at the level of distinguishing respective mental states.

In summary, today, we know that the reflective function involves different activities related to self-awareness (self-reflexivity), awareness of other mental activities. (awareness of others), the awareness that others have different and valid perspectives (decentering), and the use of metacognitive knowledge to respond to psychosocial challenges. In addition, we know that the presence of a metacognitive deficit or several compromises the fluidity of the interpersonal relationship and awakens in the interlocutor different and particular sensations according to the type of deficit presented.

5.3 Alterations in Executive Functions

The third axis of analysis are the ***Alterations in Executive Functions*** (also labeled as executive control or cognitive control). To begin with, it should be clarified that there is no single definition of *Executive Functions* and also no universally accepted model (see Table 5.1). However, the model of Akira Miyake (Miyake et al., 2000) is of great influence today.

Executive functions refer to a set of higher-order cognitive processes that are responsible for controlling and regulating our thoughts, emotions, and actions. It includes working memory/updating, attention/inhibitory control, and cognitive flexibility (for example, Diamond, 2013; Miyake & Friedman, 2012). In addition to the above, they are understood as sets of cognitive skills that allow the individual to adapt to their circumstances. Changing. More specifically, they are a series of skills capable of regulating action and behavior, through the allocation of cognitive resources aimed at exploring, associating, deciding, controlling, and evaluating situations (Grieve & Gnanasekaran, 2009).

Neuropsychological foundations indicate that their neurological basis in the brain extends into the frontal lobe, especially in the prefrontal cortex (Shannon et al., 2013). Firstly, neuroimaging studies have consistently shown that in children

[4] The ability to attribute to others and to recognize in oneself mental states in terms of thoughts, desires, intentions, emotions, etc., and to realize that behavior is not always equivalent to the mental state (Fonagy et al., 1995).

Table 5.1 Definitions of executive functions

Lezak	Executive functions refer to a collection of interrelated cognitive and behavioral skills that are responsible for purposeful, goal-directed activity, and include the highest level of human functioning, such as intellect, thought, self-control, and social interaction (1995, p. 42)
Anderson	The processes associated with executive functions are numerous, but the principle elements include anticipation, goal selection, planning, initiation of activity, self-regulation, mental flexibility, deployment of attention, and use of feedback (2002, p. 71)
Vriezen and Pigott	Executive function has been defined in a variety of ways but is generally viewed as a multidimensional construct encapsulating higher-order cognitive processes that control and regulate a variety of cognitive, emotional and behavioral functions (2002, p. 296)
Corbett et al.	Executive function (EF) is an overarching term that refers to mental control processes that enable physical, cognitive, and emotional self-control (2009, p. 210)
Dawson and Guare	Executive skills allow us to organize our behavior over time and override immediate demands in favor of longer-term goal (2010, p. 1)
Delis	Neither a single ability nor a comprehensive definition fully captures the conceptual scope of executive functions; rather, executive functioning is the sum product of a collection of higher level skills that converge to enable an individual to adapt and thrive in complex psychosocial environments (2012, p. 14)
Friedman & Miyake	Executive functions "are higher-level cognitive processes that, through their influence on lower-level processes, enable individuals to regulate their thoughts and actions during goal-directed behaviour" (2017, p. 186)

and adults, the prefrontal cortex is strongly activated when performing tasks of executive functions (Wendelken et al., 2012).

Secondly, patients with brain lesions in the prefrontal cortex have shown relatively circumscribed deficits in executive domains, such as attention, working memory, planning, inhibition, interference control, and decision-making (Fuster, 2008). Thirdly, the prefrontal cortex and the behavioral correlates of executive functions show a prolonged development into adolescence and even adulthood (Diamond, 2000; Wendelken et al., 2011).

The development of executive functions begins from birth and extends into adulthood (Wendelken et al., 2011, 2012; Sastre-Riba, 2006) and begins to decline in old age (Roselli et al., 2008). Research has shown that executive functions develop progressively and differentially, for example in terms of the ability to switch from one strategy to another reach adult levels around 10 years old, while planning skills and verbal generation continue their development into adolescence and even during early adulthood (See Roselli et al., 2008).

The essential elements that comprise executive functions are (1) anticipation and development of attention, (2) impulse control and self-regulation, (3) mental flexibility and use of feedback, (4) planning and organization, (5) effective selection of strategies to solve problems, and (6) monitoring (Anderson, 2008). In addition, Zelazo (2015; Zelano et al., 2003, 2004) pointed out that the processes that integrate executive functions vary on a continuum from purely cognitive challenges ("cold executive functions") to motivationally significant situations ("hot executive functions"). These two processes are especially important in novel situations that require a quick and flexible adjustment to the demands of the context (Zelazo et al., 2003).

There are different taxonomies of executive functions but the most used, proposed by Miyake et al. (2000), holds that there are three basic functions: *updating*, *inhibition* and *shifting* (change). The *updating* refers to the ability of working memory to search for information quickly, maintain information in an active state, and protect this information from distractions. The *inhibition* reflects the ability to intentionally inhibit dominant automatic responses when necessary. *Shifting* refers to task switching, which means the ability to switch between tasks or mental sets.

Anderson (2002, 2008) proposes four different domains of executive functions: (1st) The *attentional control* refers to the ability to selectively attend to a specific stimulus; (2nd) The *cognitive flexibility* includes the ability to switch to new activities, cope with changes in routines, learn from mistakes and develop alternative strategies, multitasking and temporary storage processes (working memory), for example, "Can I see this from your point of view?"; (3rd) *Goal setting* It refers to the initiative, conceptual reasoning, and planning ability (anticipating future events, formulating a goal, developing steps to achieve a goal) and organization (ability to organize complex information or sequence the mastery of a strategy in phases in a logical and systematic way); (4th) The *information processing* focuses on speed, fluency, and efficiency in completing new tasks or solving a problem.

A significant number of studies agree in reporting that depressive patients show different alterations in executive functions (Rock et al., 2013; Snyder, 2013; Wagner et al., 2012) and it has also been confirmed that their dysfunction in depression is a predictor of suicidal behavior (Keilp et al., 2013; Onat et al., 2019). To illustrate the importance in depression, Richard-Devantoy et al. (2012) conducted a meta-analysis in depressive disorders and showed a positive association between alterations in cognitive inhibition and suicidal behaviors. In addition to this, Bredemeier and Miller (2015) conducted a systematic review of 43 articles published up to 2014 with different mental disorders and concludes that deficits in executive functions are associated with suicidal behavior. This association is moderated by factors such as the lethality of the suicide attempt and, especially, by the clinical diagnosis since they indicate that 75% of the research that includes patients with depression shows significant results, unlike the data in bipolar disorders (29%) and psychotic disorders (33%). Similarly, deficits in executive functions have been found in borderline personality disorder (Fertuck et al., 2005), obsessive-compulsive disorder (Pedroli et al., 2019; Olley et al., 2007), anxiety disorders (Snyder et al., 2014), obesity (Ugarte, 2019), schizophrenia (Bansal et al., 2019), Externalization Disorders (Petrovic & Castellanos, 2016), Stress (Reising et al., 2018; Quinn & Joormann, 2015), personality traits (Eysenck et al., 2005), among others.

It is relevant to note, that in the review of Garcia-Villamisar et al. (2017), the evidence of deficiencies in executive functions in five personality disorders was analyzed: borderline, obsessive-compulsive, antisocial, narcissistic, and schizotypic. They reported that significant deficits were observed in decision making, working memory, inhibition, and flexibility. For example, patients with Obsessive Compulsive Disorder show dysfunctions in executive functions, especially in cognitive inhibition, which can cause problems when responding to internal and external requirements, by inhibiting the ability to manage and direct the necessary cognitive resources (Pedroli et al., 2019).

Finally, I mention some studies that have examined personality traits and executive functions (Williams et al., 2010). For example, evidence indicates that neuroticism and anxiety are associated with lower inhibition. People with neurotic traits typically exhibit low inhibition capacity, measured through the Stroop task (Luu et al., 2000). Likewise, it has been discovered that anxiety particularly affects inhibition and change (Eysenck et al., 2007; Eysenck & Derakshan, 2011).

Next, the second-order intersubjective knowledge domain "**COGNITION**" is shown in the case formulation protocol (the Case Formulation-Evaluation and the Case Formulation-Intervention are shown in Boxes 5.1 and 5.2).

Box 5.1: Case Formulation—Evaluation

[**COGNITION**] Indicate and weigh which processes contribute to discomfort and/or psychological deregulation: ....

....

(mark presence: x)

Cognitive alterations:

Rumination ☐ Worry ☐ Intolerance to uncertainty ☐ Selective attention ☐

Problematic attributional profile ☐ Absence of realistic expectations ☐

Deficit in problem solving ☐ Others: ____________

Describe: ....

....

Metacognition alterations:

Representation ☐ Differentiation ☐ Decentering ☐ Sharing ☐ Belonging ☐
Integration ☐ Positive metacognitive beliefs ☐

Negative metacognitive beliefs ☐ Others: ____________

Describe: ....

....

Alterations in executive functions:

Cognitive flexibility ☐ Attentional control ☐ Inhibition ☐ Self-monitoring ☐

Planning ☐ Others: _____________

Describe: ....

....

Psychological Distress						Psychological Well-Being
High	Moderate	Mild	Neutral	Mild	Moderate	High
-3	-2	-1	0	1	2	3
Psychological Dysregulation						Psychological Regulation
High	Moderate	Mild	Neutral	Mild	Moderate	High
-3	-2	-1	0	1	2	3

Box 5.2: Case Formulation—Intervention

COGNITION: Indicators of change

(mark presence: x)

Cognitive alterations: Progress ☐ Regulation ☐

Describe: ....

....

Metacognition alterations: Progress ☐ Regulation ☐

Describe: ....

....

Alterations in executive functions: Progress ☐ Regulation ☐

Describe: ....

....

- Functional Narrative Indicator: Integrates knowledge about cognition ☐

- Behavioral Change Indicator: Incorporates changes ☐

Psychological Distress						Psychological Well-Being
High	Moderate	Mild	Neutral	Mild	Moderate	High
-3	-2	-1	0	1	2	3
Psychological Dysregulation						Psychological Regulation
High	Moderate	Mild	Neutral	Mild	Moderate	High
-3	-2	-1	0	1	2	3

Observations: ....

....

References

Abramson, L. Y., Metalsky, F. I., & Alloy, L. B. (1989). Hopelessness depression: A theory based subtype of depression. *Psychological Review, 96*, 358–372.

Ahrens, A. H., & Haaga, D. A. F. (1993). The specificity of attributional style and expectations to positive and negative affectivity, depression, and anxiety. *Cognitive Therapy and Research, 17*, 83–98.

Ali, P. A., McGarry, J., & Maqsood, A. (2022). Spousal role expectations and marital conflict: Perspectives of men and women. *Journal of Interpersonal Violence, 37*(9–10), NP7082–NP7108. https://doi.org/10.1177/0886260520966667

Alloy, L. B., Abramson, L. Y., Hogan, M. E., Whitehouse, W. G., Rose, D. T., Robinson, M. S., et al. (2000). The Temple–Wisconsin cognitive vulnerability to depression (CVD) project: Lifetime history of Axis I psychopathology in individuals at high and low cognitive risk for depression. *Journal of Abnormal Psychology, 109*, 403–418.

Amin, Z., Constable, R. T., & Canli, T. (2004). Attentional bias for valenced stimuli as a function of personality in the dot-probe task. *Journal of Research in Personality, 38*(1), 15–23. https://doi.org/10.1016/j.jrp.2003.09.011

Anderson, P. J. (2002). Assessment and development of executive function (EF) during childhood. *Child Neuropsychology, 8*(2), 71–82.

Anderson, P. J. (2008). Towards a developmental model of executive function. In V. Anderson, R. Jacobs, & P. J. Anderson (Eds.), *Executive functions and the frontal/lobes: A lifespan perspective* (pp. 3–22). Psychology Press.

Arditte, K. A., Sahw, A. S., & Timpano, K. (2016). Repetitive negative thinking: A transdiagnostic correlate of affective disorders. *Journal of Social and Clinical Psychology, 35*(2), 181–201.

Bailey, R., & Wells, A. (2016). Metacognitive beliefs moderate the relationship between catastrophic misinterpretation and health anxiety. *Journal of Anxiety Disorders, 34*, 8–14.

Bansal, S., Robinson, B. M., Leonard, C. J., Hahn, B., Luck, S. J., & Gold, J. M. (2019). Failures in top-down control in schizophrenia revealed by patterns of saccadic eye movements. *Journal of Abnormal Psychology, 128*(5), 415–422. https://doi.org/10.1037/abn0000442

Bar, M. (2007). The proactive brain: Using analogies and associations to generate predictions. *Trends in Cognitive Sciences, 11*, 280–289.

Bar, M. (2009). The proactive brain: Memory for predictions. *Philosophical Transactions of the Royal Society B: Biological Sciences, 364*, 1235–1243.

Bar, M. (Ed.). (2011). *Predictions in the brain: Using our past to generate a future*. Oxford University Press.

Bateman, A., & Fonagy, P. (2004). *Psychotherapy for borderline personality disorder: Mentalization based treatment*. Oxford University Press.

Bateman, A. W., & Fonagy, P. (Eds.). (2012). *Handbook of mentalizing in mental health practice*. American Psychiatric Publishing, Inc.

Bell, M. E., Goodman, L. A., & Dutton, M. A. (2007). The dynamics of staying and leaving: Implications for battered women's emotional well-being and experiences of violence at the end of a year. *Journal of Family Violence, 22*, 413–428.

Bo, S., Abu-Akel, A., Kongerslev, M., Haahr, U. H., & Bateman, A. (2014). Mentalizing mediates the relationship between psychopathy and type of aggression in schizophrenia. *The Journal of Nervous and Mental Disease, 202*, 55–63.

Bomyea, J., Ramsawh, H., Ball, T. M., Taylor, C. T., Paulus, M. P., Lang, A. J., & Stein, M. B. (2015). Intolerance of uncertainty as a mediator of reductions in worry in a cognitive behavioral treatment program for generalized anxiety disorder. *Journal of Anxiety Disorders, 33*, 90–94. https://doi.org/10.1016/j.janxdis.2015.05.004

Borkovec, R., Robinson, E., Pruzinsky, T., & Depree, J. (1983). Preliminary exploration of worry: Some characteristics and processes. *Behaviour Research and Therapy, 21*(1), 9–16.

Bouchard, M.-A., Target, M., Lecours, S., Fonagy, P., Tremblay, L.-M., Schachter, A., & Stein, H. (2008). Mentalization in adult attachment narratives: Reflective functioning, mental states, and affect elaboration compared. *Psychoanalytic Psychology, 25*(1), 47–66. https://doi.org/10.1037/0736-9735.25.1.47

Bredemeier, K., & Miller, I. W. (2015). Executive function and suicidality: A systematic qualitative review. *Clinical Psychology Review, 40*, 170–183. https://doi.org/10.1016/j.cpr.2015.06.005

Brown, A. L. (1978). Knowing when, where, and how to remember: A problem of metacognition. *Advances in Instructional Psychology, 1*, 77–165.

Buhr, K., & Dugas, M. J. (2002). The intolerance of uncertainty scale: Psychometric properties of the English version. *Behaviour Research and Therapy, 40*, 931–946.

Carcione, A., Nicolò, G., & Semerari, A. (1999). Déficit de representación de objetivos. In A. Semerari (Ed.), *Psicoterapia cognitiva del paciente grave. Metacognición y relación terapéutica* (pp. 147–169). Desclée de Brouwer.

Carcione, A., Nicolò, G., Pedone, R., Popolo, R., Conti, L., Fiore, D., et al. (2011). Metacognitive mastery dysfunctions in personality disorder psychotherapy. *Psychiatry Research, 190*, 60–71.

Carleton, R. N. (2012). The intolerance of uncertainty construct in the context of anxiety disorders: Theoretical and practical perspectives. *Expert Review of Neurotherapeutics, 12*(8), 937–947. https://doi.org/10.1586/ern.12.82

Cartwright-Hatton, S., Mather, A., Illingworth, V., Brocki, J., Harrington, R., & Wells, A. (2004). Development and preliminary validation of the metacognitions questionnaire adolescent version. *Journal of Anxiety Disorder, 18*, 411–422.

Choi-Kain, L. W., & Gunderson, J. G. (2008). Mentalization: Ontogeny, assessment, and application in the treatment of borderline personality disorder. *The American Journal of Psychiatry, 165*(9), 1127–1135. https://doi.org/10.1176/appi.ajp.2008.07081360

Connor, D. R., & Callahan, J. L. (2015). Impact of psychotherapist expectations on client outcomes. *Psychotherapy, 52*(3), 351–362. https://doi.org/10.1037/a0038890

Constantino, M. J., Arnkoff, D. B., Glass, C. R., Ametrano, R. M., & Smith, J. Z. (2011). Expectations. *Journal of Clinical Psychology, 67*(2), 184–192. https://doi.org/10.1002/jclp.20754

Constantino, M. J., Aviram, A., Coyne, A. E., Newkirk, K., Greenberg, R. P., Westra, H. A., & Antony, M. M. (2020). Dyadic, longitudinal associations among outcome expectation and alliance, and their indirect effects on patient outcome. *Journal of Counseling Psychology, 67*(1), 40–50. https://doi.org/10.1037/cou0000364

Constantino, M. J., Coyne, A. E., Goodwin, B. J., Vîslă, A., Flückiger, C., Muir, H. J., & Gaines, A. N. (2021). Indirect effect of patient outcome expectation on improvement through alliance quality: A meta-analysis. *Psychotherapy Research, 31*(6), 711–725. https://doi.org/10.1080/10503307.2020.1851058

Corbett, B. A., Constantine, L. J., Hendren, R., Rocke, D., & Ozonoff, S. (2009). Examining executive functioning in children with autism spectrum disorder, attention deficit hyperactivity disorder and typical development. *Psychiatry Research, 166*(2–3), 210–222. https://doi.org/10.1016/j.psychres.2008.02.005

D'Argembeau, A., & Van der Linden, M. (2004). Phenomenal characteristics associated with projecting oneself back into the past and forward into the future: Influence of valence and temporal distance. *Consciousness and Cognition, 13*, 844–858.

Davey, G. C. L., Tallis, F., & Capuzzo, N. (1996). Beliefs about the consequences of worrying. *Cognitive Therapy and Research, 20*(5), 499–520. https://doi.org/10.1007/BF02227910

Dawson, P., & Guare, R. (2010). *Executive skills in children and adolescents: A practical guide to assessment and intervention* (2nd ed.). The Guilford Press.

Delis, D. C. (2012). *Delis rating of executive functions*. Pearson.

Diamond, A. (2000). Close interrelation of motor development and cognitive development and of the cerebellum and prefrontal cortex. *Child Development, 71*(1), 44–56. https://doi.org/10.1111/1467-8624.00117

Diamond, A. (2013). Executive functions. *Annual Review of Psychology, 64*, 135–168.

Dimaggio, G., & Lysaker, P. H. (Eds.). (2010). *Metacognition and severe adult mental disorders: From basic research to treatment*. Routledge.

Dimaggio, G., Procacci, A., & Semerari, A. (1999). Déficit de compartición y de pertenencia. In A. Semerari (Ed.), *Psicoterapia cognitiva del paciente grave. Metacognición y relación terapéutica* (pp. 235–280). Desclée de Brouwer.

Dimaggio, G., Semerari, A., Carcione, A., Nicolò, G., & Procacci, M. (2007). *Psychotherapy of personality disorders: Metacognition, states of mind and interpersonal cycles*. Routledge.

Dimaggio, G., Montano, A., Popolo, R., & Salvatore, G. (2015). *Metacognitive interpersonal therapy for personality disorders: A treatment manual*. Routledge.

Dugas, M. J., & Ladouceur, R. (2000). Treatment of GAD: Targeting intolerance of uncertainty in two types of worry. *Behavior Modification, 24*, 635–657.

Dugas, M. J., & Robichaud, M. (2007). A cognitive model of generalized anxiety disorder. In *Cognitive-behavioral treatment for generalized anxiety disorder* (1st ed., pp. 23–46). Routledge.

Dugas, M. J., Gagnon, F., Ladouceur, R., & Freeston, M. H. (1998). Generalized anxiety disorder: A preliminary test of a conceptual model. *Behaviour Research and Therapy, 36*(2), 215–226. https://doi.org/10.1016/s0005-7967(97)00070-3

Dugas, M. J., Gosselin, P., & Ladouceur, R. (2001). Intolerance of uncertainty and worry: Investigating specificity in a nonclinical sample. *Cognitive Therapy and Research, 25*(5), 551–558. https://doi.org/10.1023/A:1005553414688

Dugas, M. J., Hedayati, M., Karavidas, A., Buhr, K., Francis, K., & Phillips, N. A. (2005). Intolerance of uncertainty and information processing: Evidence of biased recall and interpretations. *Cognitive Therapy and Research, 29*(1), 57–70. https://doi.org/10.1007/s10608-005-1648-9

Ehring, T., & Watkins, E. (2008). Repetitive negative thinking as a transdiagnostic process. *International Journal of Cognitive Therapy, 1*(3), 192–205.

Eppinger, B., & Kray, J. (2011). To choose or to avoid: Age differences in learning from positive and negative feedback. *Journal of Cognitive Neuroscience, 23*(1), 41–52. https://doi.org/10.1162/jocn.2009.21364

Eysenck, M. W., & Derakshan, N. (2011). New perspectives in attentional control theory. *Personality and Individual Differences, 50*(7), 955–960. https://doi.org/10.1016/j.paid.2010.08.019

Eysenck, M. W., Payne, S., & Derakshan, N. (2005). Trait anxiety, visuospatial processing, and working memory. *Cognition and Emotion, 19*(8), 1214–1228.

Eysenck, M. W., Derakshan, N., Santos, R., & Calvo, M. (2007). Anxiety and cognitive performance: Attentional control theory. *Emotion, 7*(2), 336–353.

Falcone, M. (1999). Déficit de diferenciación. In A. Semerari (Ed.), *Psicoterapia cognitiva del paciente grave. Metacognición y relación terapéutica* (pp. 171–191). Desclée de Brouwer.

Falcone, M., Marraffa, M., & Carcione, A. (2003). Metarappresentazione e psicopatología. In A. Semerari e G. Dimaggio (a cura di), *I Disturbi di Personalità. Modelli e Trattamento* (pp. 43–76). Roma-Bari.

Fertuck, E. A., Lenzenweger, M. F., & Clarkin, J. F. (2005). The association between attentional and executive controls in the expression of borderline personality disorder features: A preliminary study. *Psychopathology, 38*(2), 75–81. https://doi.org/10.1159/000084814

Fisak, B., & Hammond, A. N. (2013). Are positive beliefs about post-event processing related to social anxiety? *Behaviour Change, 30*(1), 36–47.

Flavell, J. H. (1976). Metacognitive aspects of problem solving. In L. B. Resnik (Ed.), *The nature of intelligence* (pp. 231–235). Erlbaum.

Flavell, J. H. (1979). Metacognitive and cognitive monitoring: A new area of cognitive developmental inquiry. *American Psychologyst, 34*, 906–911.

Fleming, S. M., & Frith, C. D. (Eds.). (2014). *The cognitive neuroscience of metacognition.* Springer.

Fonagy, P., & Bateman, A. W. (2007). Teoría del apego y modelo orientado a la mentalización del trastorno límite de la personalidad. In J. Oldhan, A. Skodol, & D. Bender (Eds.), *Tratado de los Trastornos de Personalidad* (pp. 189–209). Elsevier Masson.

Fonagy, P., & Bateman, A. W. (2016). Adversity, attachment, and mentalizing. *Comprehensive Psychiatry, 64*, 59–66.

Fonagy, P., & Target, M. (2000). Playing with reality III: The persistence of dual psychic reality in borderline patients. *International Journal of Psycho-Analysis, 81*, 853–873.

Fonagy, P., Steele, M., Steele, H., Leigh, T., Kennedy, R., Mattoon, G., & Target, M. (1995). Attachment, the reflective self and borderline states: The predictive specificity of the adult attachment interview and pathological emotional development. In S. R. Muir & J. Kerr (Eds.), *Attachment theory: Social, developmental and clinical perspectives* (pp. 233–279). Analytic Press.

Frank, J. D. (1963). *Persuasión and healing: A comparative study of psychotherapy*. John Hopkins University Press.

Friedman, N. P., & Miyake, A. (2017). Unity and diversity of executive functions: Individual differences as a window on cognitive structure. *Cortex, 86*, 186–204. https://doi.org/10.1016/j.cortex.2016.04.023

Friston, K., & Kiebel, S. (2009). Predictive coding under the free-energy principle. *Philosophical Transactions of the Royal Society B: Biological Sciences, 364*, 1211–1221.

Fuster, J. M. (2008). *The prefrontal cortex* (4th ed.). Elsevier.

Garcia-Villamisar, D., Dattilo, J., & Garcia-Martinez, M. (2017). Executive functioning in people with personality disorders. *Current Opinion in Psychiatry, 30*(1), 36–44. https://doi.org/10.1097/YCO.0000000000000299

Gladstone, T. R., & Kaslow, N. J. (1995). Depression and attributions in children and adolescents: A meta-analytic review. *Journal of Abnormal Child Psychology, 23*, 597–606.

Goodman, L. A., Dutton, M. A., Weinfurt, K., & Cook, S. (2003). The intimate partner violence strategies index. *Violence Against Women, 9*(2), 163–186. https://doi.org/10.1177/1077801202239004

Greenberg, R. P., Constantino, M. J., & Bruce, N. (2006). Are patient expectations still relevant for psychotherapy process and outcome? *Clinical Psychology Review, 26*(6), 657–678. https://doi.org/10.1016/j.cpr.2005.03.002

Grieve, J., & Gnanasekaran, L. (2009). *Neuropsicología para terapeutas ocupacionales*. Editorial Panamericana.

Gumley, A. (2011). Metacognition, affect regulation and symptom expression: A transdiagnostic perspective. *Psychiatry Research, 190*(1), 72–78. https://doi.org/10.1016/j.psychres.2011.09.025

Haas, B. W., Omura, K., Constable, R. T., & Canli, T. (2007). Emotional conflict and neuroticism: Personality-dependent activation in the amygdala and subgenual anterior cingulate. *Behavioral Neuroscience, 121*(2), 249–256. https://doi.org/10.1037/0735-7044.121.2.249

Harvey, A. G., Watkins, E., Mansell, W., & Shafran, R. (2004). *Cognitive behavioural processes across psychological disorders: A transdiagnostic approach to research and treatment*. Oxford University Press.

Heider, F. (1944). Social perception and phenomenal causation. *Psychological Review, 51*, 358–374.

Hilt, L. M. (2004). Attribution retraining for therapeutic change: Theory, practice, and future directions. *Imagination, Cognition and Personality, 23*(4), 289–307.

Hobson, P. (2002). *The cradle of thought: The origins of thinking*. Macmillan.

Holm-Denoma, J. M., & Hankin, B. L. (2011). Perceived physical appearance mediates the rumination and bulimic symptom link in adolescent girls. *Journal of Clinical Child and Adolescent Psychology, 39*(4), 537–544.

Hu, T., Zhang, D., & Yang, Z. (2015). The relationship between attributional style for negative outcomes and depression: A meta-analysis. *Journal of Social and Clinical Psychology, 34*(4), 304–321.

James, W. (1890). *The principles of psychology*. Henry Holt.

Joiner, T. E. (2001). Negative attributional style, hopelessness depression and endogenous depression. *Behaviour Therapy and Research, 39*, 139–149.

Joiner, T. E., Jr., & Wagner, K. D. (1995). Attributional style and depression in children and adolescents: A meta-analytic review. *Clinical Psychology Review, 15*, 777–798.

Kalmbach, D. A., Pillai, V., & Ciesla, J. A. (2016). The correspondence of changes in depressive rumination and worry to weekly variations in affective symptoms: A test of the tripartite model of anxiety and depression in women. *Australian Journal of Psychology, 68*(1), 52–60.

Keilp, J. G., Gorlyn, M., Russell, M., Oquendo, M. A., Burke, A. K., Harkavy-Friedman, J., & Mann, J. J. (2013). Neuropsychological function and suicidal behavior: Attention control, memory and executive dysfunction in suicide attempt. *Psychological Medicine, 43*(3), 539–551. https://doi.org/10.1017/S0033291712001419

Kirsch, I. (1985). Response expectancy as a determinant of experience and behavior. *American Psychologist, 40*, 1189–1202.

Klein, T. A., Neumann, J., Reuter, M., Hennig, J., von Cramon, D. Y., & Ullsperger, M. (2007). Genetically determined differences in learning from errors. *Science, 318*, 1642–1645.

Kwon, P. (2002). Hope, defense mechanisms, and adjustment: Implications for false hope and defensive hopelessness. *Journal of Personality, 70*, 207–231.

Ladouceur, R., Gosselin, P., & Dugas, M. J. (2000). Experimental manipulation of intolerance of uncertainty: A study of a theoretical model of worry. *Behaviour Research and Therapy, 38*, 933–941.

Lench, H. C. (2011). Personality and health outcomes: Making positive expectations a reality. *Journal of Happiness Studies, 12*, 493–507.

Lezak, M. D. (1995). *Neuropsychological assessment* (3rd ed.). Oxford University Press.

Luu, P., Collins, P., & Tucker, D. M. (2000). Mood, personality, and self-monitoring: Negative affect and emotionality in relation to frontal lobe mechanisms of error monitoring. *Journal of Experimental Psychology: General, 129*, 43–60.

Lyubomirsky, S., Layous, K., Chancellor, J., & Nelson, S. K. (2015). Thinking about rumination: The scholarly contributions and intellectual legacy of Susan Nolen-Hoeksema. *Annual Review of Clinical Psychology, 11*, 1–22. https://doi.org/10.1146/annurev-clinpsy-032814-112733

McEvoy, P. M., & Brans, S. (2013). Common versus unique variance across measures of worry and rumination: Predictive utility and mediational models for anxiety and Depression. *Cognitive Therapy and Research, 37*(1), 183–196.

McEvoy, P. M., Watson, H., Watkins, E. R., & Nathan, P. (2013). The relationship between worry, rumination, and comorbidity: Evidence for repetitive negative thinking as a transdiagnostic construct. *Journal of Affective Disorders, 151*(1), 313–320. https://doi.org/10.1016/j.jad.2013.06.014

Metcalfe, J., & Shimamura, A. P. (Eds.). (1994). *Metacognition: Knowing about knowing*. The MIT Press. https://doi.org/10.7551/mitpress/4561.001.0001

Miyake, A., & Friedman, N. P. (2012). The nature and organization of individual differences in executive functions: Four general conclusions. *Current Directions in Psychological Science, 21*(1), 8–14.

Miyake, A., Friedman, N. P., Emerson, M. J., Witzki, A. H., Howerter, A., & Wager, T. D. (2000). The unity and diversity of executive functions and their contributions to complex "frontal lobe" tasks: A latent variable analysis. *Cognitive Psychology, 41*(1), 49–100. https://doi.org/10.1006/cogp.1999.0734

Moritz, S., & Lysaker, P. H. (2018). Metacognition – What did James H. Flavell really say and the implications for the conceptualization and design of metacognitive interventions. *Schizophrenia Research, 201*, 20–26.

Morrison, A. P., Wells, A., & Nothard, S. (2002). Cognitive and emotional predictors of predisposition to hallucinations in non-patients. *British Journal of Clinical Psychology, 41*(3), 259–270.

Nicolò, G. (1999). Déficit de descentramiento e ideación delirante. In A. Semerari (Ed.), *Psicoterapia cognitiva del paciente grave. Metacognición y relación terapéutica* (pp. 281–309). Desclée de Brouwer.

Nigro, G., & Neisser, U. (1983). Point of view in personal memories. *Cognitive Psychology, 15*(4), 467–482.

Nolen-Hoeksema, S., & Morrow, J. (1993). The effects of rumination and distraction on naturally-occurring depressed moods. *Cognition and Emotion, 7*(1), 561–570.

Nordahl, H., & Wells, A. (2018). Metacognitive therapy for social anxiety disorder: An A–B replication series across social anxiety subtypes. *Frontiers in Psychology, 9*, 540. https://doi.org/10.3389/fpsyg.2018.00540

Nordahl, H. M., Nordahl, H., & Wells, A. (2016). Metacognition and perspective taking predict negative self-evaluation of social performance in patients with social anxiety disorder. *Journal of Experimental Psychopathology, 7*, 601–607.

Olley, A., Malhi, G., & Sachdev, P. (2007). Memory and executive functioning in obsessive-compulsive disorder: A selective review. *Journal of Affective Disorders, 104*(1–3), 15–23. https://doi.org/10.1016/j.jad.2007.02.023

Onat, M., İnal Emiroğlu, N., Baykara, B., Özerdem, A., Özyurt, G., Öztürk, Y., Şahin, Ü., Ildız, A., Kaptancık Bilgiç, B., Hıdıroğlu Ongun, C., & Pekcanlar Akay, A. (2019). Executive functions and impulsivity in suicide attempter adolescents with major depressive disorder. *Psychiatry and Clinical Psychopharmacology, 29*(3), 332–339. https://doi.org/10.1080/24750573.2018.1541647

Papageorgiou, C., & Wells, A. (2001). Metacognitive beliefs about rumination in recurrent major depression. *Cognitive and Behavioral Practice, 8*(2), 160–164.

Pedroli, E., La Paglia, F., Cipresso, P., La Cascia, C., Riva, G., & La Barbera, D. (2019). A computational approach for the assessment of executive functions in patients with obsessive–compulsive disorder. *Journal of Clinical Medicine, 8*, 1975. https://doi.org/10.3390/jcm8111975

Petrovic, P., & Castellanos, F. X. (2016). Top-down dysregulation-from ADHD to emotional instability. *Frontiers in Behavioral Neuroscience, 10*, 70. https://doi.org/10.3389/fnbeh.2016.00070

Premack, D. (1986). *Gavagai*. The MIT Press.

Quinn, M. E., & Joormann, J. (2015). Control when it counts: Change in executive control under stress predicts depression symptoms. *Emotion (Washington, D.C.), 15*(4), 522–530. https://doi.org/10.1037/emo0000089

Reising, M. M., Bettis, A. H., Dunbar, J. P., Watson, K. H., Gruhn, M., Hoskinson, K. R., & Compas, B. E. (2018). Stress, coping, executive function, and brain activation in adolescent offspring of depressed and nondepressed mothers. *Child Neuropsychology, 24*(5), 638–656. https://doi.org/10.1080/09297049.2017.1307950

Richard-Devantoy, S., Gorwood, P., Annweiler, C., Olié, J. P., Le Gall, D., & Beauchet, O. (2012). Suicidal behaviours in affective disorders: A deficit of cognitive inhibition? *Canadian Journal of Psychiatry, 57*(4), 254–262. https://doi.org/10.1177/070674371205700409

Robinson, J. A., & Swanson, K. L. (1993). Field and observer modes of remembering. *Memory, 1*, 169–184.

Rock, I., & Gutman, D. (1981). The effects of inattention on form perception. *Journal of Experimental Psychology: Human Perception and Performance, 7*, 27–287.

Rock, P. L., Roiser, J. P., Riedel, W. J., & Blackwell, A. D. (2013). Cognitive impairment in depression: A systematic review and meta-analysis. *Psychological Medicine, 44*(10), 1–12.

Roselli, M., Jurado, M. B., & Matute, E. (2008). Las funciones ejecutivas a través de la vida. *Revista Neuropsicología, Neuropsiquiatría y Neurociencias, 8*(1), 23–46.

Sastre-Riba, S. (2006). Condiciones tempranas del desarrollo y el aprendizaje: el papel de las funciones ejecutivas. *Revista de Neurologia, 42*, 143–151.

Scheier, M. F., Matthews, K. A., Owens, J. F., Magovern, G. J., Lefebvre, R., Abbott, R. C., et al. (1989). Dispositional optimism and recovery from coronary artery bypass surgery: The beneficial effects on physical and psychological well-being. *Journal of Personality and Social Psychology, 57*, 1024–1040.

Schultz, W., Dayan, P., & Montague, P. R. (1997). A neural substrate of prediction and reward. *Science (New York, N.Y.), 275*(5306), 1593–1599. https://doi.org/10.1126/science.275.5306.1593

Semerari, A. (1999). *Psicoterapia cognitiva del paziente grave. Psicoterapia cognitiva del paziente grave. Metacognizione e relazione terapéutica*. Rafaello Cortina.

Semerari, A. (2000). *Storia, teorie e tecniche della psicoterapia cognitiva*. Gius Laterza.

Semerari, A., Carcione, A., Dimaggio, G., Nicolò, G., & Procacci, M. (2007). Understanding minds: Different functions and different disorders? The contribution of psychotherapy research. *Psychotherapy Research, 17*(1), 106–119.

Semerari, A., Colle, L., Pellecchia, G., Buccione, I., Carcione, A., & Dimaggio, G. (2014). Metacognition: Severity and styles in personality disorders. *Journal of Personality Disorders, 28*(6), 751–766.

Shannon, S. M., Kisleya, M. A., Hasker, P. D., Nathaniel, T. D., Campbell, A. M., & Davalosb, D. B. (2013). Cognitive function predicts neural activity associated with pre-attentive temporal processing. *Neuropsychologia, 51*, 211–219.

Snyder, H. R. (2013). Major depressive disorder is associated with broad impairments on neuropsychological measures of executive function: A meta-analysis and review. *Psychological Bulletin, 139*(1), 81–132.

Snyder, H. R., Kaiser, R. H., Whisman, M. A., Turner, A. E., Guild, R. M., & Munakata, Y. (2014). Opposite effects of anxiety and depressive symptoms on executive function: The case of selecting among competing options. *Cognition & Emotion, 28*(5), 893–902. https://doi.org/10.1080/02699931.2013.859568

Solem, S., Myers, S. G., Fisher, P. L., Vogel, P. A., & Wells, A. (2010). An empirical test of the metacognitive model of obsessive-compulsive symptoms: Replication and extension. *Journal of Anxiety Disorders, 24*(1), 79–86.

Spada, M. M., & Wells, A. (2010). Metacognitions across the continuum of drinking behaviour. *Personality and Individual Differences, 49*(5), 425–429.

Sternheim, L., Startup, H., Saeidi, S., Morgan, J., Hugo, P., Russell, A., et al. (2012). Understanding catastrophic worry in eating disorders: Process and content characteristics. *Journal of Behaviour Therapy and Experimental Psychiatry, 43*(4), 1095–1103.

Sweeney, P. D., Anderson, K., & Bailey, S. (1986). Attributional style in depression: A meta-analytic review. *Journal of Personality and Social Psychology, 50*, 974–991.

Tomasello, M. (1999). Having intentions, understanding intentions, and understanding communicative intentions. In J. W. Astington, D. R. Olson, & P. D. Zelazo (Eds.), *Developing theories of intention: Social understanding and self-control* (pp. 63–76). Erlbaum.

Tutty, L. M. (1996). Post-shelter services: The efficacy of follow-up programs for abused women. *Research on Social Work Practice, 6*, 425–441.

Ugarte, C. (2019). Obesidad y Trastornos de la conducta alimentaria: Un análisis desde las funciones ejecutivas. *Revista de Psicoterapia, 30*(112), 61–78.

Vassilopoulos, S. P., Brouzos, A., & Moberly, N. J. (2015). The relationships between metacognition, anticipatory processing, and social anxiety. *Behaviour Change, 32*(2), 114–126.

Vriezen, E. R., & Pigott, S. E. (2002). The relationship between parental report on the BRIEF and performance-based measures of executive function in children with moderate to severe traumatic brain injury. *Child Neuropsychology, 8*, 296–303.

Wagner, S., Doering, B., Helmreich, I., Lieb, K., & Tadić, A. (2012). A meta-analysis of executive dysfunctions in unipolar major depressive disorder without psychotic symptoms and their changes during antidepressant treatment. *Acta Psychiatrica Scandinavica, 125*(4), 281–292. https://doi.org/10.1111/j.1600-0447.2011.01762.x

Watkins, E. (2015). An alternative transdiagnostic mechanistic approach to affective disorders illustrated with research from clinical psychology. *Emotion Review, 7*, 250.

Watkins, E., Moulds, M., & Mackintosh, B. (2005). Comparisons between rumination and worry in a non-clinical population. *Behaviour Research and Therapy, 43*(12), 1577–1585. https://doi.org/10.1016/j.brat.2004.11.008

Weiner, B., & Graham, S. (1999). Attribution in personality psychology. In L. A. Pervin & O. P. John (Eds.), *Handbook of personality: Theory and research* (2nd ed., pp. 605–628). Guilford Press.

Wells, A. (1995). Meta-cognition and worry: A cognitive model of generalized anxiety disorder. *Behavioural and Cognitive Psychotherapy, 23*(3), 301–320. https://doi.org/10.1017/S1352465800015897

Wells, A. (1999). A metacognitive model and therapy for generalized anxiety disorder. *Clinical Psychology & Psychotherapy, 6*, 86–95.

Wells, A. (2000). *Emotional disorders and metacognition: Innovative cognitive therapy*. Wiley.

Wells, A. (2009). *Metacognitive therapy for anxiety and depression*. Guildford Press.

Wells, A. (2013). Advances in metacognitive therapy. *International Journal of Cognitive Therapy, 6*(2), 186–201.

Wells, A., & Matthews, G. (1994). *Attention and emotion: A clinical perspective*. Erlbaum.

Wendelken, C., Baym, C. L., Gazzaley, A., & Bunge, S. A. (2011). Neural indices of improved attentional modulation over middle childhood. *Developmental Cognitive Neuroscience, 1*(2), 175–186. https://doi.org/10.1016/j.dcn.2010.11.001

Wendelken, C., Munakata, Y., Baym, C., Souza, M., & Bunge, S. A. (2012). Flexible rule use: Common neural substrates in children and adults. *Developmental Cognitive Neuroscience, 2*(3), 329–339. https://doi.org/10.1016/j.dcn.2012.02.001

Williams, A. D., & Moulds, M. L. (2007). Cognitive avoidance of intrusive memories: Recall vantage perspective and associations with depression. *Behaviour Research and Therapy, 45*(6), 1141–1153. https://doi.org/10.1016/j.brat.2006.09.005

Williams, P. G., Suchy, Y., & Kraybill, M. L. (2010). Five-factor model personality traits and executive functioning among older adults. *Journal of Research in Personality, 44*(4), 485–491. https://doi.org/10.1016/j.jrp.2010.06.002

Wise, D., & Rosqvist, J. (2006). Explanatory style and well-being. In J. C. Thomas, D. L. Segal, & M. Hersen (Eds.), *Comprehensive handbook of personality and psychopathology* (*Personality and everyday functioning*) (Vol. 1, pp. 285–305). Wiley.

Wong, Q. J. J., & Moulds, M. L. (2010). Do socially anxious individuals hold positive metacognitive beliefs about rumination? *Behaviour Change, 27*(2), 69–83.

Zelazo, P. D. (2015). Executive function: Reflection, iterative reprocessing, complexity, and the developing brain. *Developmental Review, 38*, 55–68.

Zelazo, P., Muller, U., Frye, D., & y Marcovitch, S. (2003). The development of executive function: Cognitive complexity and control – Revised. *Monographs of the Society for Research in Child Development, 68*, 93–119.

Zelazo, P., Qu, L., & Muller, U. (2004). Hot and cool aspects of executive function: Relations in early development. In W. Schneider, R. Schumann, & B. Sodian (Eds.), *Young children's cognitive development: Interrelationships among executive Junctioning, working memory, verbal ability, and theory of mind* (pp. 71–93). Lawrence Eribaum Associates Publishers.

Chapter 6
Emotion

Emotions are a source for adaptation and well-being. We know that emotions involve a series of internal changes that result in external actions, which have proven to be advantageous for human beings throughout evolutionary history (Damasio, 1999; Lewis & Haviland-Jones, 2000). In this sense, emotions color all aspects of our lives, mobilize us and inform us of our environmental and intersubjective reality, and above all, are fundamental in the construction of individual/intersubjective meaning.

Emotional processing ("affective") has consequences, both in health (Kubzansky & Winning, 2016; Appleton & Kubzansky, 2014; Chida & Steptoe, 2009), psychopathology (Mu & Berenbaum, 2019; Kring & Mote, 2016; Espeset et al., 2012), psychotherapy (Smith & Ascough, 2016; Greenberg, 2016; Gilbert, 2015; Foa & Kozak, 1986; Guidano & Liotti, 1983; Frank, 1963), wellbeing (Gross et al., 2019; Fredrickson, 2001, 2016), contribution to logical thinking (Damasio, 2000), among other fields. Particularly, in the field of psychotherapy research, it is important not to forget, that there is not unanimously accepted understanding of how emotion and its processing lead to change (Hofman, 2016; Greenberg, 2016; Foa & Kozak, 1986).

In Case Formulation from an evolutionary perspective, the intersubjective knowledge domain "Emotion" is evaluated through two parsimonious distinctions: *alteration of emotional consciousness* and *emotional dysregulation* (Fig. 6.1), each one with indicators to evaluate and monitor in the psychotherapy process.

6.1 Alteration of Emotional Awareness

The first distinction is the ***Alteration of Emotional Awareness***, and the following possible alterations of emotional consciousness (indicators) are valued:

Á. Quiñones Bergeret, *Evolutionary Case Formulation*,
https://doi.org/10.1007/978-3-031-67412-9_6

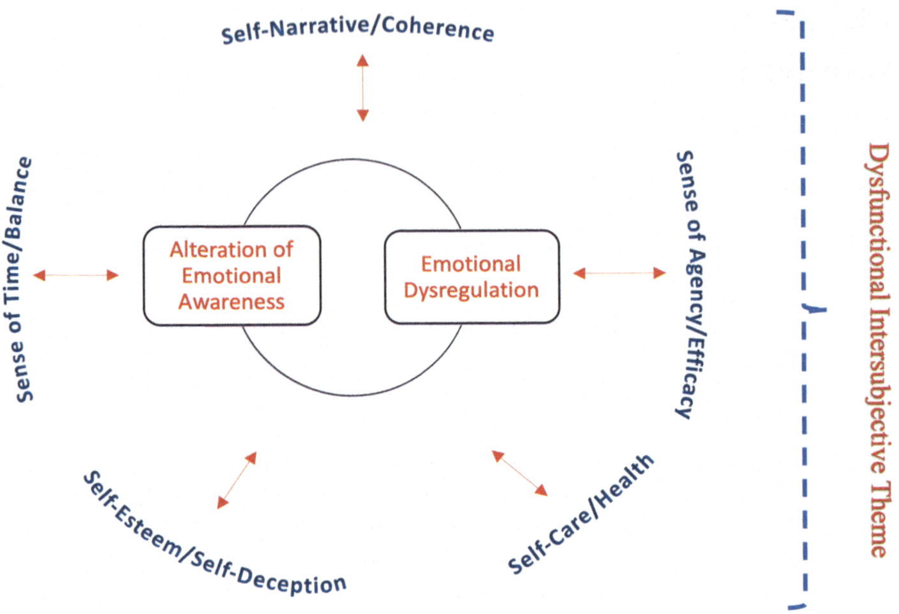

Fig. 6.1 Emotion

1. Emotional profile (examples: What emotions do you identify [anger, helplessness, anxiety, fear, anguish, envy, compassion, guilt, shame, pride, disgust, joy, jealousy, self-compassion]?; What emotional valence, intensity and amplitude appears as problematic?, etc.)
2. Emotional clarity (example: Are emotions useful to you to understand yourself and understand others?, etc.).
3. Emotional differentiation (example: Do you easily differentiate emotions in your daily life?, etc.).
4. Difficulty understanding emotions (example: When you feel emotions, do they serve as a useful guide in relationships with others?).
5. Difficulty using emotional assessment in decisions and problem solving (example: Do you find it difficult to use emotions in your decisions and problem solving?).
6. Dysfunctional mood (example: Do you feel that you cannot cope with the responsibilities of your daily life?).

In psychotherapy, self-understanding of emotions contributes to interpersonal psychological regulation. In this sense, it is useful to convey to patients directly and clearly, that it is worth achieving cognitively estimating their meaning in everyday life, for example, "Pay attention, tolerate, and understand what each emotion means in the interpersonal context, whether you feel it positive or negative, and use it to position yourself and solve problems, if that is the case."

We know from evidence that understanding emotions is not random. Having said that, we will focus on the construct *"cognitive appraisal" which has a long tradition that begins with Magda Arnold* (Lazarus, 1982, 1991, 1999, 2001; Frijda, 1986, 1988, 1993a; Scherer, 1984, 1999; Arnold, 1960) and currently there are different theories of appraisal. The key point is that the appraisal processes are considered as the "key" to understanding the different emotions in different individuals and in different circumstances.

In relation to "appraisal," there are different dimensions to consider according to the model being followed. In general, it is understood to be a calculation of the personal importance of an event. However, the dimensions proposed by Scherer (2001) of relevance, transcendence, coping potential, and normative meaning are useful:

1. How important is this event to me? Does it directly affect me or my social reference group? (Relevance).
2. What are the implications or consequences of this event and how do these affect my well-being and my immediate or long-term goals? (Transcendence).
3. How well can I cope with or adapt to these consequences? (Coping potential).
4. What is the meaning of this event in relation to my self-concept and social norms and values? (Normative meaning).

As a framework, Roseman and Smith (2001) hold the following common assumptions of different appraisal theories: (1) Emotions are differentiated by appraisals; (2) Differences in appraisal can explain individual and temporal differences in emotional response; (3) All situations assigned the same appraisal pattern will evoke the same emotion; (4) Appraisals precede and provoke emotions; (5) The appraisal process makes it likely that emotions are appropriate responses to the situations in which they occur; (6) Conflicting, involuntary or inappropriate appraisal can explain the irrational aspects of emotions; and (7) Changes in appraisal can explain clinically and developmentally induced emotional changes.

Richard Lazarus (1991, 1994, 2006) posits two types of appraisal (primary and secondary) that are part of a common process in which both actively combine and are dependent. The *primary appraisal* refers to the relevance of what is happening to the person in relation to their goals, values, commitments, and beliefs. Similarly, if the situation does not affect one's own well-being or goals, no stress or emotional reaction will occur.

Specifically, Lazarus (1999) posits that the *primary appraisal* consists of three evaluations: (1) the relevance of the goal; (2) the congruence/incongruence of the goal, and (3) the implication that the event has for the ego. Thus, it should be clarified that primary evaluations are not "primary" because they always go first in the temporal sequence, but they are primary because they confer personal relevance and signal that the situation has the potential to provoke emotional responses (Lazarus & Smith, 1988).

The *secondary appraisal* is a process of estimating what the person can do in that relevant situation to maintain or achieve well-being and good adaptation. This appraisal particularly refers to the evaluation of the coping resources that the person has to handle that relevant situation for their own well-being. In the end, Lazarus points out that the components of the secondary appraisal go through evaluating three basic aspects: (1) the responsibility in relation to the outcome of the situation, (2) the coping potential we have in the face of the event, and (3) future expectations.

In summary, the *primary* and *secondary* appraisals can be interdependent (Folkman & Lazarus, 1980). For example, primary evaluations may suggest a threatening situation with the potential to cause harm, like looking down a very steep and extensive skateboard slope. However, if secondary evaluations indicate that one can cope with the threat, both with the accumulated experience on such slopes and one's own expertise, the threat decreases.

In psychotherapy, the conceptualization of basic relational themes (Lazarus, 1991, 2001) for each emotion is optimal for working on the self-understanding of adult patients. For Lazarus (1991), the *central relational theme* of each emotion expresses a synthesis of the entire underlying relational meaning of each emotion, and it underscores such relevance by indicating that the appraisal process must be taken to a higher level of abstraction, that is, the central relational theme of each emotion. As an example, I highlight the emotion of anger in Table 6.1.

On another note, keeping in mind the distinction between *emotions* and *mood,* two related but distinct phenomena, is also necessary and useful.

Mood as an affective construct is usually defined by a comparison with emotion. Both affective constructs are the product of different mechanisms driven by appraisal. In the words of Lazarus:

Table 6.1 Central relational theme for the emotion of anger (Lazarus, 1991, 2001)

Emotions	Central relational theme	Primary appraisal components	Secondary appraisal components
Anger	Humiliating offense against me or mine	1. If the goal is relevant, then any emotion is possible, including anger. If not, there is no emotion 2. If there is incongruity in the goals, only negative emotions are possible, including anger 3. If the type of ego involvement at stake is to preserve or enhance the aspect of self-esteem or social self-esteem of one's own ego identity, then the emotional possibilities include anger, anxiety, and pride	4. If there is guilt, which is derived from the knowledge that someone is responsible for harmful actions, and that they could have been controlled, then anger occurs. If the guilt is from another, the anger is directed externally; if it is from oneself, the anger is directed internally 5. If the coping potential favors that the attack is viable, anger is facilitated 6. If the future expectation is positive about the environmental response to the attack, then anger is facilitated

> ...I am inclined to interpret *both* moods and acute emotions as reactions to the way one appraises relationships with the environment; moods refer to the larger, pervasive, existential issues of one's life, whereas acute emotions refer to an immediate piece of business, a specific and relatively narrow goal in an adaptational encounter with the environment. (1991, p.48)

Likewise, a definition that is also useful for understanding mood is the one held by Forgas, which says "...relatively low-intensity, diffuse, subconscious, and enduring affective states that have no salient antecedent cause and therefore little cognitive content" (2006, pp. 6–7).

It is important to keep in mind that the *moods interact reciprocally with emotions*, although it is not known precisely how this occurs. For example, a series of events that evoke negative emotions can induce a negative mood. Similarly, being in a particular mood can influence the valence or intensity of a sensory-evoked emotion (having a negative mood can reduce the strength of a positive emotional response to a favorite food, for example, pistachio ice cream). In extreme cases, moods can be very prolonged and pathological, such as depression or mania.

Nico Frijda (1993b) argued that moods can be considered as appraisal propensities. In his words:

> In a depressed mood, the world is felt to be barren, devoid of meaning and interest. Generalized appraisal along these dimensions is what distinguishes one unpleasant mood from another, or is among the major determinants of such distinction. Such a generalized propensity for a particular mode of appraisal can, like affect, be manifested as a generalized tuning to appraise any event whatever in a mood-consonant way, or as a decreased threshold for such appraisal when events ever so slightly lend themselves to it. (p. 384)

According to Frijda (1994), mood is a non-intentional affective state, that is, there does not have to be an object that elicits it as in the case of emotion (e.g., depression). It is also considered a specific form of affective state and differs from emotions based on three criteria: (1) having a longer duration, (2) less intensity, (3) having a global character (Morris, 1989). In particular, it is important to underline that moods are "diffuse and global"[1] and give rise to broad action tendencies, such as approach or withdrawal (Lang, 1995).

Morris (1992) makes a very relevant precision for psychotherapists and refers to the *informative value* of moods and emotions. Emotions provide information about the environment and the demands that environmental events impose on us, that is, emotions signal what is going wrong or right, what is approaching or moving away in terms of threatening or gratifying objects in our external environment. Mood, on the other hand, provides information about our internal state of affairs, about the resources we have available to face environmental threats and challenges.

---

[1] On the diffuse and global, an example is the pleasant mood has broad cognitive and social effects since it improves openness to social and non-social information, increases responsiveness and flexibility of response to such information and increases the feeling and prosocial behavior (see Isen, 2004). Another example is pleasure, which tends to facilitate a receptive and holistic attention mode, rather than active and analytical (Schwarz & Bless, 1991).

Pace-Schott et al. (2019) argue that mood and emotion are different in relation to introspection, and in particular, they point out that mood can be more strongly affected by interoception (i.e., sensory input from physiological responses or peripheral organs), as reflected in mood fluctuations due to inflammation, illness, etc.

Similarly, mood is mainly influenced by the following factors: a) exogenous (situational); b) endogenous (circadian rhythms, etc.), and c) personality traits and temperament (Watson & Clark, 1994).

In summary, we know that emotions have specific causes but moods do not necessarily. Therefore, an *effective emotion regulation strategy* can be to identify and reassess the cause, while an *effective mood regulation strategy* can be to moderate the resulting feelings, for example, by doing physical exercise, meditating, listening to music, etc.

To conclude, I mention that the *affect regulation process model* by James Gross (Gross et al., 2019; Gross, 2015) is a common framework for understanding how affect is generated[2] and how it can be regulated; it also shows how both processes contribute jointly to mental health. This framework conceives the generation of affections as a four-stage feedback cycle (situation, attention, appraisal, response) and the regulation of affections as a coordinated decision-making process of four families of regulation strategies (situational strategies, attentional strategies, cognitive strategies, and response modulation strategies). The adaptive functioning of each of these stages promotes mental health and well-being, while the maladaptive functioning of these stages can increase the risk of psychological problems and/or mental health difficulties. Similarly, it is noteworthy that the proposed model has four clinical implications (Gross et al., 2019), and they are as follows: (1) the framework suggests that problems with different affective states, such as emotions, stress responses, impulses, and mood states, can be analyzed in common terms; (2) unhealthy affect often arises from some combination of maladaptive affect generation and maladaptive affect regulation; (3) maladaptive affect regulation can arise from identification, selection, implementation, and monitoring decisions; (4) affective processes are equally relevant to mental illness and psychological well-being.

6.2 Emotional Dysregulation

The second distinction in the *emotion domain* is ***Emotional Dysregulation***. Evolutionarily, Homo Sapiens are highly skilled at regulating their emotions in order to adjust their behavior to the situational demands of different complexities.

[2] They understand "affect" as a general term to denote emotions such as anxiety or joy, stress responses such as feeling threatened or challenged, impulses such as the urge to flee or to drink, and moods such as depression or euphoria. They highlight that what these various processes have in common is that they all involve an appraisal (a distinction between good and bad for me) that can shape behavior (see Gross et al., 2019).

Such a feature is clearly different compared to the animal kingdom. This ability is evolutionarily adaptive (Izard, 1992; Lazarus, 1991) and is closely associated with the cognitive evaluation processes that distinguish humans from non-humans (Gross & John, 2003).

The first indicator is the *regulation strategies*. Emotions have many functions and range from preparing the body for action, directing our attention, facilitating social interactions, and more (Levenson, 1999), but we must be clear, that emotions can also hurt us if they occur at the wrong time or at the wrong intensity level. In fact, inappropriate emotional responses are involved in different mental health problems (Gross & Levenson, 1997; Bradley, 2000; Davidson, 2003), in physical illnesses (Boehm & Kubzansky, 2012; Appleton et al., 2013; Kiecolt-Glaser et al., 2002) and personality traits[3] (McCrae & Costa, 1986). Likewise, there is evidence that chronic stress is associated with cardiovascular risk in people with poor emotion regulation (Roy et al., 2018). After all, there is certainty that greater use of reappraisal protects against cardiovascular disease, while greater use of suppression implies a greater risk of various cardiovascular diseases (Appleton & Kubzansky, 2014; Gianaros et al., 2014).

In general, emotion regulation is a set of regulatory processes that can be used to redirect emotions in order to modify the magnitude, latency, and duration of affective responses (Miranda et al., 2012; Thompson, 1994). It includes the management of both positive and negative emotions that arise under a wide range of stressful and non-stressful situations (Compas et al., 2001).

Ross A. Thompson (1994) defined emotional regulation as "Emotion regulation consists of the extrinsic and intrinsic processes responsible for monitoring, evaluating and modifying emotional reactions, especially their intensive and temporal features, to accomplish one's goals" (pp. 27–28). This definition includes several characterizations of the processes of emotion regulation. It also has the particularity in considering the regulation of emotions as a broad and heterogeneous construction, rather than a unitary concept. More specifically, this definition suggests that (1) the regulation of emotions may involve maintaining, enhancing, and inhibiting emotions; (2) emotional regulation influences a range of aspects of emotional experience, including its valence, intensity, and temporal characteristics; (3) emotions are not only modified by self-regulation strategies but can also be regulated by others; and (4) emotion regulation involves a function (i.e., emotions are regulated for a reason and are directed towards a goal). It is noteworthy that based on this conceptualization, James Gross (1998b) defined *emotional regulation* "refers to the processes by which individuals influence which emotions they have, when they have them, and how they experience and express these emotions" (p. 275).

---

[3] More neurotic people (negative affectivity) tend to be more emotionally vulnerable and self-conscious than less neurotic people (McCrae & Costa, 1986). Likewise, they not only experience more negative emotions (Steel et al., 2008) but also have a strong tendency to ruminate on what went wrong (Nolen-Hoeksema et al., 2008). Even when reflecting on their past life, they continue to relive bitter and annoying experiences (Cappeliez & O'Rourke, 2002; Cully et al., 2001).

The existence of various forms of regulation strategies is recognized, but there are two that have been widely studied: *cognitive reappraisal* and *expressive suppression* (Gross, 1998a, 2014; Richards, & Gross, 1999; Goldin et al., 2008).

The first, *cognitive reappraisal* (an antecedent-focused strategy) is defined as the attempt to reinterpret an emotion-provoking situation in a way that alters its meaning and changes the emotional impact (Gross & John, 2003), and it particularly aims to reduce negative emotions by changing the interpretation or appraisal of affective stimuli. Moreover, it is used before an emotional response has been fully generated or activated (Gross & Thompson, 2007; Ochsner et al., 2004) and focuses on altering the effect of emotion-generating signals. For example, instead of thinking about her driving test (driver's license) as a matter of life or death, Perla could think of it as an opportunity to assess her progress in driving. It is relevant to note that cognitive reappraisal can make one feel better and has no cognitive or physiological costs (Gross, 1998a).

The second, *expressive suppression* (a response-focused strategy), is an attempt to hide, inhibit, or reduce ongoing emotional expressive behavior. It is a response-focused strategy that acts later in the emotion generation process and attempts to modify the behavioral expression of the emotion after having experienced it (Gross & John, 2003). For example, instead of bursting into tears over disappointing news, Juan bites his lip and clenches his hands.

While both strategies can decrease emotional behavior, *reappraisal* appears to be a more effective way of regulating emotions. In part, this is because someone who suppresses an emotional reaction may block the display of emotion, but does not make the feelings disappear (Gross & Levenson, 1997). In fact, physiologically, *suppression* leads to even greater activation of the sympathetic nervous system, presumably because the individual must strive to prevent their emotions from showing (Gross, 1998a). Similarly, there is a cognitive cost in suppression (Richards & Gross, 2000; Richards & Gross, 2006).

The regulation of emotions is also influenced by a number of individual skills. It is argued that there are three distinctions to assess individual differences in emotion regulation (Gross, 2015): (1) the frequency of emotion regulation, which refers to the frequency with which a particular form of emotion regulation is used; (2) the self-efficacy of emotional regulation, which refers to how capable a person believes they are of using a particular regulation strategy; and (3) the ability of emotion regulation, which refers to how successful a person is in the use of a particular form of emotion regulation. In other words, the ability to correctly identify an emotional state as something that needs to be regulated, select an appropriate strategy, and implement it effectively.

On the other hand, it has been reported by many researchers that emotional dysregulation underlies the etiological and maintenance mechanisms for a large number of mental health problems (Kring & Sloan, 2010). More specifically, literature reviews have shown that mood disorders, anxiety disorders, substance abuse disorders, eating disorders, personality disorders, schizophrenia, and psychotic disorders are directly related to emotional dysregulation (Livesley, 2016; Cisler et al., 2010;

Harrison et al., 2009; Thorberg et al., 2009; Kohler & Martin, 2006). As an example, deficiencies in emotion regulation in personality disorders have their peculiarities since they take at least two main forms: dysregulated and restricted. The *dysregulated pattern* involves reactive and unstable emotions associated with wavering relationships, which arise from a need for closeness that conflicts with the fear of rejection and abandonment. In contrast, the *restricted pattern* involves the restricted expression of feelings associated with socially evasive traits (Livesley, 2016).

The second indicator is the types of ***individual and dyadic coping***. Stress is considered a risk factor in mental and biological health. However, evidence tells us that the effects of stress can be negative or positive. Whether stress has positive or negative effects depends on its severity and temporal pattern, and particularly on how we cope with it.

The types of stressors that people experience in their life cycle change over time. Thus, problems with work and forming a family in early adulthood give way to dealing with health problems and caring for parents in middle age. Finally, the loss of loved ones through grief becomes much more common in old age.

It is well known that people differ widely in their response to stress.[4] For example, some react strongly to minor tensions while others are not even disturbed by major life tensions. That is, a situation that triggers fear and avoidance in one adult triggers energy and approach in another.

From a *transactional model* perspective, stress arises from an individual's experience with the environment. This implies that stress arises from a combination of environmental demands, vulnerabilities, and individual resources (Lazarus & Folkman, 1984). In this system, the *cognitive appraisal* is fundamental, and translates into an individual evaluating a situation in terms of whether it is benign (primary appraisal) or whether it involves a threat, harm, loss, or challenge (secondary appraisal).

It is worth noting that secondary appraisals and coping go hand in hand (Lazarus, 2001). These types of appraisals refer to an individual's perceived ability to handle a stressful event. These evaluations are key to identifying what could and can be done to face the stressor. In other words, under stressful circumstances (when people face circumstances that exceed their ability to handle them), self-regulation attempts become coping strategies.

In relation to the life cycle, coping is known differentially. We have better knowledge of developmental changes in coping knowledge in childhood and adolescence than in the adulthood (Skinner & Zimmer-Gembeck, 2016). Moreover, in old age there is little agreement on how coping changes (Aldwin et al., 2018).

Generally speaking, it can be argued that in childhood, emotion-focused coping seems to shift from behavior-oriented external strategies to cognition-based internal

---

[4] It is relevant to note that stress usually refers to stereotyped responses to negative situations, while emotion refers to more specific responses to both negative and positive situations (see Petrova & Gross, 2024).

strategies. Problem-focused coping becomes more differentiated and context-specific as coping repertoires increase with age (Skinner & Zimmer-Gembeck, 2016).

As adults,[5] it is expected that we learn to differentiate between problems that are essentially uncontrollable, those that will likely resolve themselves, and those for which effort is useful. In other words, we are expected to have learned which strategies work best in different situations. In this sense, it is expected that in middle age one is at the peak of coping ability. However, it is known that the strategies used by very old adults mainly aim to conserve energy, either through distancing, denial of responsibility for the problem, or dependence on others to help solve problems, either through the use of social support or through collaborative coping efforts (Aldwin, 2007).

Lazarus and Folkman (1984) define coping "as constantly changing cognitive and behavioral efforts to manage specific external and/or internal demands that are appraised as taxing or exceeding the resources of the person" (p. 141). Many distinctions have been made to categorize different coping responses (Skinner & Zimmer-Gembeck, 2016; Skinner et al., 2003). The most used coping distinctions (Lazarus, 1966, 1994, 1999, 2001, 2006; Lazarus & Folkman, 1984; Lazarus & Launier, 1978) are problem-focused coping versus emotion-focused coping. Both types of coping as a higher-order category do not turn out to be very useful for organizing forms of coping with respect to their adaptive functions (Skinner & Zimmer-Gembeck, 2016). Today, researchers have conceptualized and proposed hierarchical models that use higher-order families to organize multiple lower-order forms of coping (Connor-Smith et al. 2000; Skinner et al., 2003; Ryan-Wenger, 1992; Walker et al. 1997). It is relevant to note that conceptual and empirical analyses have converged on 12 families that can be used to classify most forms of coping. These families can be organized by their higher-order adaptive functions.

The 12 families are problem-solving, support-seeking, escape, rumination, helplessness, social isolation, emotional regulation, accommodation, information-seeking, negotiation, opposition, and delegation (for a review, see Skinner & Zimmer-Gembeck, 2016).

Lastly, it is relevant to note that *dyadic stress* represents a distinct form of social stress that should be assessed in individual psychotherapy. In the clinic, it is common to observe stress problems that involve the couple. Namely, Bodenmann (1995) expanded the concept of primary and secondary evaluations of the model of Lazarus and Folkman (1984) to include an interpersonal aspect, which focuses on different independent evaluations of both members of the couple, as well as their joint evaluation.

[5] More sophisticated coping responses, such as strategy development, decision making, planning, and reflection, may not fully emerge until late adolescence or early adulthood (Spear, 2000).

The *dyadic coping* according to Bodenmann (1995, 1997, 2005) is the way partners handle their daily stress as a couple. He defines dyadic stress as a stressful event or encounter that always concerns both members, either directly or indirectly. Essentially, dyadic stress can be grouped into three dimensions: (a) the way each partner is affected by the stressful event (i.e., directly or indirectly); (b) the origin of the stress (i.e., whether it originates within or outside the couple); and (c) the time sequence (at what point in the coping process each member gets involved).

Particularly, Bodenmann's model is known as "The model "systemic-transactional" and supports the fact that dyadic coping responses can be positive or negative. Positive responses involve responding with support to the other's stress signals, showing understanding and help, or engaging in joint problem-solving, etc. Put simply, "our" problem versus "his" or "my problem." In conclusion, negative dyadic coping can be of three types: *Hostile Dyadic Coping* involves distancing, mocking, showing disinterest or minimizing the severity of the situation; *Ambivalent Dyadic Coping* refers to offering support involuntarily or showing that support should not be necessary; *Superficial Dyadic Coping* refers to insincere efforts to support the stressed partner.

Another indicator is *adult attachment*. Attachment theory is a theory of human socio-emotional development (see John Bowlby) and there is also a group of researchers who understand it as a regulation theory (Thompson, 1994, 2011) which is the stance assumed in the case formulation from an evolutionary perspective. The scientific literature on this topic has a long way to go (Cassidy & Shaver, 2016; Crittenden & Landini, 2011) but not without debate, with disagreements and not minor controversies (examples: dimensional versus categorical, attachment prediction, what is the most appropriate way to evaluate attachment styles, temperament and attachment, etc.) and critics (Kagan, 2010; Field, 1996).

According to Slade (Slade, 2005; Slade et al., 2005), the various attachment styles tend to make differential use of cognitions and emotions. Thus, the *avoidant styles* usually use cognitions, but much less or do not use emotions ("they distrust emotions"), and the opposite in the case of ambivalent styles ("they distrust cognitions"). The *secure styles* tend to make integrated and balanced use of both types of information sources (Crittenden, 2002). It is argued that the *secure autonomous attachment* is related to high reflective function, the *preoccupied* with a confused reflective function, the *dismissing* with a disconnected reflective function, and the *unclassifiable*, with a low reflective function.

Indicators that inform us about how patients organize themselves in certain dimensions of emotionality linked to attachment, which I call "Adult Attachment" can be of great diversity: excessive concern for relationships, emotional self-sufficiency, defending oneself from affects, defending oneself from cognitions, difficulty in tolerating difficult feelings and/or emotions in session, etc.

Next, the second-order intersubjective knowledge domain "**EMOTION**" is shown in the case formulation protocol (the Case Formulation-Evaluation and the Case Formulation-Intervention are shown in Boxes 6.1 and 6.2).

Box 6.1: Case Formulation—Evaluation

[**EMOTION**] Indicate and weigh which processes contribute to psychological distress and/or dysregulation.: ....
....

(mark presence: x)

Alteration of emotional awareness:

Emotional profile ☐ Emotional clarity ☐ Emotional differentiation ☐

Understanding emotions ☐

Emotional appraisal in decision making and problem solving ☐

Dysfunctional mood ☐

Others: ____________________

Describe: ....
....

Emotional Dysregulation:

Regulation strategies ☐ Individual coping ☐ Dyadic coping ☐ Adult attachment ☐

Others: ____________________

Describe: ....
....

Psychological Distress						Psychological Well-Being
High	Moderate	Mild	Neutral	Mild	Moderate	High
-3	-2	-1	0	1	2	3
Psychological Dysregulation						**Psychological Regulation**
High	Moderate	Mild	Neutral	Mild	Moderate	High
-3	-2	-1	0	1	2	3

Box 6.2: Case Formulation—Intervention

EMOTION: Indicators of change

(mark presence: x)

Alteration of emotional awareness: Progress ☐ Regulation ☐

Describe: ……………………………………………………………………………………………

……………………………………………………………………………………………………

Emotional dysregulation: Progress ☐ Regulation ☐

Describe: ……………………………………………………………………………………………

……………………………………………………………………………………………………

- Functional Narrative Indicator: Integrates knowledge about emotion ☐

- Behavioral Change Indicator: Incorporates Changes ☐

Psychological Distress						Psychological Well-Being
High	Moderate	Mild	Neutral	Mild	Moderate	High
-3	-2	-1	0	1	2	3
Psychological Dysregulation						Psychological Regulation
High	Moderate	Mild	Neutral	Mild	Moderate	High
-3	-2	-1	0	1	2	3

Observations: ……………………………………………………………………………………………

……………………………………………………………………………………………………

References

Aldwin, C. M. (2007). *Stress, coping, and development: An integrative perspective* (2nd ed.). Guilford Press.

Aldwin, C. M., Igarashi, H., Gilmer, D. F., & Levenson, M. R. (2018). *Health, illness, and optimal aging: Biological and psychosocial perspectives* (3rd ed.). Springer.

Appleton, A., & Kubzansky, L. D. (2014). Emotion regulation and cardiovascular disease risk. In J. J. Gross (Ed.), *Handbook of emotion regulation* (pp. 596–612). Guildford Press.

Appleton, A. A., Buka, S. L., Loucks, E. B., Gilman, S. E., & Kubzansky, L. D. (2013). Divergent associations of adaptive and maladaptive emotion regulation strategies with inflammation. *Health Psychology, 13*, 748–756.

Arnold, M. B. (1960). *Emotion and personality*. Columbia University Press.

Bodenmann, G. (1995). A systemic-transactional view of stress and coping in couples. *Swiss Journal of Psychology, 54*, 34–49.

Bodenmann, G. (1997). Dyadic coping – A systemic-transactional view of stress and coping among couples: Theory and empirical findings. *European Review of Applied Psychology, 47*, 137–140.
Bodenmann, G. (2005). Dyadic coping and its significance for marital functioning. In T. Revenson, K. Kayser, & G. Bodenmann (Eds.), *Couples coping with stress: Emerging perspectives on dyadic coping* (pp. 33–50). American Psychological Association.
Boehm, J. K., & Kubzansky, L. D. (2012). The heart's content: The association between positive psychological well-being and cardiovascular health. *Psychological Bulletin, 138*(4), 655–691.
Bradley, S. (2000). *Affect regulation and the development of psychopathology*. Guilford Press.
Cappeliez, P., & O'Rourke, N. (2002). Personality traits and existential concerns as predictors of the functions of reminiscence in older adults. *The Journals of Gerontology, Series B: Psychological Sciences and Social Sciences, 57*, 116–123.
Cassidy, J., & Shaver, P. R. (Eds.). (2016). *Handbook of Attachment: theory, research, and clinical applications* (3rd ed.). Guilford Press.
Chida, Y., & Steptoe, A. (2009). The association of anger and hostility with future coronary heart disease: A meta-analytic review of prospective evidence. *Journal of the American College of Cardiology, 53*(11), 936–946.
Cisler, J. M., Olatunji, B. O., Feldner, M. T., & Forsyth, J. P. (2010). Emotion regulation and the anxiety disorders: An integrative review. *Journal of Psychopathology and Behavioral Assessment, 32*, 68–82.
Compas, B., O'Connor-Smith, J. K., Saltzman, S., Thomsen, A. H., & Wadsworth, M. E. (2001). Coping with stress during childhood and adolescence: Problems, progress, and potential in theory and research. *Psychological Bulletin, 127*, 87–127.
Connor-Smith, J. K., Compas, B. E., Wadsworth, M. E., Thomsen, A. H., & Saltzman, H. (2000). Responses to stress in adolescence: Measurement of coping and involuntary stress responses. *Journal of Counseling and Clinical Psychology, 68*, 976–992.
Crittenden, P. M. (2002). *Nuevas implicaciones clínicas de la teoría del apego*. Promolibro.
Crittenden, P. M., & Landini, A. (2011). *Assessing adult attachment: A dynamic-maturational approach to discourse analysis* (1st ed.). Norton.
Cully, J. A., LaVoie, D., & Gfeller, J. D. (2001). Reminiscence, personality, and psychological functioning in older adults. *The Gerontologist, 41*, 89–95.
Damasio, A. R. (1999). *The feeling of what happens: Body and emotion in the making of consciousness*. Harcourt.
Damasio, A. R. (2000). A second chance for emotion. In R. D. Lane & L. Nadel (Eds.), *Cognitive neuroscience of emotion* (pp. 12–23). Oxford University Press.
Davidson, R. J. (2003). Affective neuroscience and psycho physiology: Toward a synthesis. *Psychophysiology, 40*, 655–665.
Espeset, E. M. S., Gulliksen, K. S., Nordbø, R. H. S., Skårderud, F., & Holte, A. (2012). The link between negative emotions and eating disorder behaviour in patients with Anorexia Nervosa. *European Eating Disorders Review, 20*, 451–460.
Field, T. (1996). Attachment and separation in young children. *Annual Review of Psychology, 47*, 541–562.
Foa, E. B., & Kozak, M. J. (1986). Emotional processing of fear: Exposure to corrective information. *Psychological Bulletin, 99*, 20–35.
Folkman, S., & Lazarus, R. S. (1980). An analysis of coping in a middle-aged community sample. *Journal of Health and Social Behavior, 21*(3), 219–239.
Forgas, J. P. (Ed.). (2006). *Affect in social thinking and behavior*. Psychology Press.
Frank, J. D. (1963). *Persuasión and healing: A comparative study of psychotherapy*. John Hopkins University Press.
Fredrickson, B. L. (2001). The role of positive emotions in positive psychology: The broaden-and-build theory of positive emotions. *American Psychologist, 56*(3), 218–226.
Fredrickson, B. L. (2016). The eudaimonics of positive emotions. In J. Vittersø (Ed.), *Handbook of eudaimonic well-being* (pp. 183–190). Springer International.
Frijda, N. H. (1986). *The emotion*. Cambridge University Press.

Frijda, N. H. (1988). The laws of emotion. *American Psychologist, 43*(5), 349–358. https://doi.org/10.1037/0003-066X.43.5.349

Frijda, N. H. (1993a). The place of appraisal in emotion. *Cognition and Emotions, 7*, 357–382.

Frijda, N. H. (1993b). Moods, emotion episodes, and emotions. In M. Lewis & J. M. Haviland (Eds.), *Handbook of emotions* (pp. 381–403). Guilford Press.

Frijda, N. H. (1994). Varieties of affect: Emotions and episodes, mood, and sentiments. In P. Ekman & R. J. Davidson (Eds.), *The nature of emotion* (pp. 59–67). Oxford University Press.

Gianaros, P. J., Marsland, A. L., Kuan, D. C., Gidwitz, B. L., Jennings, J. R., Sheu, L. K., & Manuck, S. B. (2014). An inflammatory pathway links atherosclerotic cardiovascular disease to neural activity evoked by the cognitive regulation of emotion. *Biological Psychiatry, 75*, 738–745.

Gilbert, P. (2015). Self-disgust, self-hatred and compassion focused therapy. In P. A. Powell, P. G. Overton, & J. Simpson (Eds.), *The revolting self: Perspectives on the psychological, social, and clinical implications of self-directed disgust* (pp. 233–254). Karnac Books.

Goldin, P. R., McRae, K., Ramel, W., & Gross, J. J. (2008). The neural bases of emotion regulation: Reappraisal and suppression of negative emotion. *Biological Psychiatry, 63*(6), 577–586.

Greenberg, L. (2016). The clinical application of emotion in psychotherapy. In L. F. Barrett, M. Lewis, & J. M. Haviland-Jones (Eds.), *Handbook of emotions* (4th ed., pp. 670–684). Guilford Press.

Gross, J. J. (1998a). Antecedent-and response-focused emotion regulation: Divergent consequences for experience, expression, and physiology. *Journal of Personality and Social Psychology, 74*, 224–237.

Gross, J. J. (1998b). The emerging field of emotion regulation: An integrative review. *Review of General Psychology, 2*, 271–299.

Gross, J. J. (2014). Emotion regulation: Conceptual and empirical foundations. In J. J. Gross (Ed.), *Handbook of emotion regulation* (2nd ed., pp. 3–20). Guildford Press.

Gross, J. J. (2015). Emotion regulation: Current status and future prospects. *Psychological Inquiry, 26*(1), 1–26. https://doi.org/10.1080/1047840X.2014.940781

Gross, J. J., & John, O. P. (2003). Individual differences in two emotion regulation processes: Implications for affect, relationships, and well-being. *Journal of Personality and Social Psychology, 85*(2), 348–362. https://doi.org/10.1037/0022-3514.85.2.348

Gross, J. J., & Levenson, R. W. (1997). Hiding feelings: The acute effects of inhibiting negative and positive emotion. *Journal of Abnormal Psychology, 106*(1), 95–103.

Gross, J. J., & Thompson, R. A. (2007). Emotion regulation: Conceptual foundations. In J. J. Gross (Ed.), *Handbook of emotion regulation* (pp. 3–24). Guilford Press.

Gross, J. J., Uusberg, H., & Uusberg, A. (2019). Mental illness and well-being: An affect regulation perspective. *World Psychiatry, 18*(2), 130–139. https://doi.org/10.1002/wps.20618

Guidano, V., & Liotti, G. (1983). *Cognitive processes and emotional disorders*. Guilford Press.

Harrison, A., Sullivan, S., Tchanturia, K., & Treasure, J. (2009). Emotion recognition and regulation in anorexia nervosa. *Clinical Psychology & Psychotherapy, 16*(4), 348–356. https://doi.org/10.1002/cpp.628

Hofman, S. G. (2016). *Emotion in therapy: From science to practice*. Guilford Press.

Isen, A. M. (2004). Some perspectives on positive feelings and emotions: Positive affect facilitates thinking and problem solving. In A. R. S. Manstead, N. H. Frijda, & A. Fischer (Eds.), *Feelings and emotions: The Amsterdam symposium* (pp. 263–281). Cambridge University Press.

Izard, C. E. (1992). Basic emotions, relations among emotions, and emotion–cognition relations. *Psychological Review, 99*, 561–565.

Kagan, J. (2010). *El temperamento y su trama*. Katz.

Kiecolt-Glaser, J. K., McGuire, L., Robles, T. F., & Glaser, R. (2002). Emotions, morbidity, and mortality: New perspectives from psychoneuroimmunology. *Annual Review of Psychology, 53*, 83–107. https://doi.org/10.1146/annurev.psych.53.100901.135217

Kohler, C. G., & Martin, E. A. (2006). Emotional processing in schizophrenia. *Cognitive Neuropsychiatry, 11*(3), 250–271. https://doi.org/10.1080/13546800500188575

Kring, A. M., & Mote, J. (2016). Emotion disturbances as transdiagnostic processes in psychopathology. In L. F. Barrett, M. Lewis, & J. M. Haviland-Jones (Eds.), *Handbook of emotions* (4th ed., pp. 653–669). Guilford Press.

Kring, A. M., & Sloan, D. M. (2010). *Emotion regulation and psychopathology: A transdiagnostic approach to etiology and treatment*. Guilford Press.

Kubzansky, L. D., & Winning, A. (2016). Emotions and health. In L. F. Barrett, M. Lewis, & J. M. Haviland-Jones (Eds.), *Handbook of emotions* (4th ed., pp. 613–633). Guilford Press.

Lang, P. J. (1995). The emotion probe: Studies of motivation and attention. *American Psychologist, 50*, 372–385.

Lazarus, R. S. (1966). *Psychological stress and the coping process*. McGraw-Hill.

Lazarus, R. S. (1982). Thoughts on the relations between emotion and cognition. *American Psychologist, 37*, 1019–1024.

Lazarus, R. S. (1991). *Emotion and adaptation*. Oxford University Press.

Lazarus, R. S. (1994). Universal antecedents of the emotion. In P. Ekman & R. J. Davidson (Eds.), *The Nature of emotions: Fundamental questions* (pp. 146–149). Oxford University Press.

Lazarus, R. S. (1999). *Stress and emotion: A new synthesis*. Springer.

Lazarus, R. S. (2001). Relational meaning and discrete emotions. In K. R. Scherer, A. Schorr, & T. Johnstone (Eds.), *Appraisal processes in emotion: Theory, methods, research* (pp. 37–67). Oxford University Press.

Lazarus, R. S. (2006). Emotions and interpersonal relationships: Toward a person-centered conceptualization of emotions and coping. *Journal of Personality, 74*(1), 9–46. https://doi.org/10.1111/j.1467-6494.2005.00368.x

Lazarus, R. S., & Folkman, S. (1984). *Stress, appraisal, and coping*. Springer.

Lazarus, R. S., & Launier, R. (1978). Stress-related transactions between persons and environment. In L. A. Pervin & M. Lewis (Eds.), *Perspectives in interactional psychology* (pp. 287–327). Plenum.

Lazarus, R. S., & Smith, C. A. (1988). Knowledge and appraisal in the cognition–emotion relationship. *Cognition & Emotion, 2*(4), 281–300.

Levenson, R. W. (1999). The intrapersonal functions of emotion. *Cognition and Emotion, 13*, 481–504.

Lewis, M., & Haviland-Jones, J. M. (Eds.). (2000). *Handbook of emotions* (2nd ed.). The Guilford Press.

Livesley, W. J. (2016). A modular strategy for treating emotional dysregulation. In W. J. Livesley, G. Dimaggio, & J. F. Clarkin (Eds.), *Integrated treatment for personality disorder* (pp. 232–257). Guilford Press.

McCrae, R. R., & Costa, P. T. (1986). Personality, coping, and coping effectiveness in an adult sample. *Journal of Personality, 54*, 385–405.

Miranda, D., Gaudreau, P., Debrosse, R., Morizot, J., & Kirmayer, L. J. (2012). Variations on internalizing psychopathology. In R. MacDonald, G. Kreutz, & L. Mitchell (Eds.), *Music, health and wellbeing* (pp. 513–530). Oxford University Press.

Morris, W. N. (1989). *Mood: the frame of mind*. Springer-Verlag.

Morris, W. N. (1992). A functional analysis of the role of mood in affective systems. In M. S. Clark (Ed.), *Review of personality and social psychology, emotion* (pp. 256–293). Sage.

Mu, W., & Berenbaum, H. (2019). Negative self-conscious emotions: Appraisals, action tendencies, and labels. *Journal of Social and Clinical Psychology, 38*(2), 113–139.

Nolen-Hoeksema, S., Wisco, B. E., & Lyubomirsky, S. (2008). Rethinking Rumination. *Perspectives on Psychological Science, 3*(5), 400–424. https://doi.org/10.1111/j.1745-6924.2008.00088.x

Ochsner, K., Ray, R., Cooper, J., Robertson, E., Chopra, S., Gabrieli, J., & Gross, J. (2004). For better or for worse: Neural systems supporting the cognitive down- and up-regulation of negative emotion. *NeuroImage, 23*, 483–499.

Pace-Schott, E. F., Amole, M. C., Aue, T., Balconi, M., Bylsma, L. M., Critchley, H., Demaree, H. A., Friedman, B. H., Gooding, A. E. K., Gosseries, O., Jovanovic, T., Kirby, L. A. J., Kozlowska, K., Laureys, S., Lowe, L., Magee, K., Marin, M.-F., Merner, A. R., Robinson, J. L., et al. (2019). Physiological feelings. *Neuroscience and Biobehavioral Reviews, 103*, 267–304. https://doi.org/10.1016/j.neubiorev.2019.05.002

Petrova, K., & Gross, J. J. (2024). Emotion regulation in self and other. In I. Roskam, J. J. Gross, & M. Mikolajczak (Eds.), *Emotion regulation and parenting* (pp. 35–54). Cambridge University Press.

Richards, J. M., & Gross, J. J. (1999). Composure at any cost?: The cognitive consequences of emotion suppression. *Personality and Social Psychology Bulletin, 25*, 1033–1044.

Richards, J. M., & Gross, J. J. (2000). Emotion regulation and memory: The cognitive costs of keeping one's cool. *Journal of Personality and Social Psychology, 79*, 410–424.

Richards, J. M., & Gross, J. J. (2006). Personality and emotional memory: How regulating emotion impairs memory for emotional events. *Journal of Research in Personality, 40*, 631–651.

Roseman, I. J., & Smith, C. A. (2001). Appraisal theory: Overview, assumptions, varieties, controversies. In K. R. Scherer, A. Schorr, & T. Johnstone (Eds.), *Appraisal processes in emotion: Theory, methods, research* (pp. 3–19). Oxford University Press.

Roy, B., Riley, C., & Sinha, R. (2018). Emotion regulation moderates the association between chronic stress and cardiovascular disease risk in humans: A cross-sectional study. *Stress (Amsterdam, Netherlands), 21*(6), 548–555. https://doi.org/10.1080/10253890.2018.1490724

Ryan-Wenger, N. M. (1992). A taxonomy of children's coping strategies: A step toward theory development. *American Journal of Orthopsychiatry, 62*, 256–263.

Scherer, K. R. (1984). Emotion as a multicomponent process: A model and some cross-cultural data. In P. Shaver (Ed.), *Review of personality and social psychology* (Vol. 5, pp. 37–63). Sage.

Scherer, K. R. (1999). Appraisal theory. In T. Dalgleish & M. Power (Eds.), *Handbook of cognition and emotion* (pp. 337–363). Wiley.

Scherer, K. R. (2001). Appraisal considered as a process of multilevel sequential checking. In K. R. Scherer, A. Schorr, & T. Johnstone (Eds.), *Appraisal processes in emotion: Theory, methods, research* (pp. 92–120). Oxford University Press.

Schwarz, N., & Bless, H. (1991). Happy and mindless, but sad and smart? The impact of affective states on analytic reasoning. In J. P. Forgas (Ed.), *Emotion and social judgment* (pp. 55–71). Pergamon.

Skinner, E. A., & Zimmer-Gembeck, M. J. (2016). *The development of coping*. Springer.

Skinner, E. A., Edge, K., Altman, J., & Sherwood, H. (2003). Searching for the structure of coping: A review and critique of category systems for classifying ways of coping. *Psychological Bulletin, 129*, 216–269.

Slade, A. (2005). Parental reflective functioning: An introduction. *Attachment and Human Development, 7*(3), 269–281.

Slade, A., Grienenberger, J., Bernbach, E., Levy, D., & Locker, A. (2005). Maternal reflective functioning, attachment, and the transmission gap: A preliminary study. *Attachment & Human Development, 7*(3), 283–298.

Smith, R. E., & Ascough, J. C. (2016). *Promoting emotional resilience: Cognitive-affective stress management training*. Guilford Press.

Spear, L. P. (2000). The adolescent brain and age-related behavioral manifestations. *Neuroscience & Biobehavioral Reviews, 24*, 417–463.

Steel, P., Schmidt, J., & Shultz, J. (2008). Refining the relationship between personality and subjective well-being. *Psychological Bulletin, 134*, 138–161.

Thompson, R. A. (1994). Emotion regulation: A theme in search of definition. *Monographs of the Society for Research in Child Development, 59*, 25–52.

Thompson, R. A. (2011). Emotion and emotion regulation: Two sides of the developing coin. *Emotion Review, 3*, 53–61.

Thorberg, F. A., Young, R. M., Sullivan, K. A., & Lyvers, M. (2009). Alexithymia and alcohol use disorders: A critical review. *Addictive Behaviors, 34*(3), 237–245. https://doi.org/10.1016/j.addbeh.2008.10.016

Walker, L. S., Smith, C. A., Garber, J., & Van Slyke, D. A. (1997). Development and validation of the pain response inventory for children. *Psychological Assessment, 9*, 392–405.

Watson, D., & Clark, L. A. (1994). The vicissitudes of mood: A schematic model. In P. Ekman & R. J. Davidson (Eds.), *The nature of emotion* (pp. 400–4005). Oxford University Press.

Chapter 7
Interpersonal

Personal relationships "quality human connections" play an essential role in survival, physical health, mental health, and well-being throughout the life cycle (Waldinger & Shulz, 2023; Pezirkianidis et al., 2023; Holt-Lunstad et al., 2010). The alterations that occur in personal relationships, in many cases, are the main reasons why people seek psychotherapy.

Satisfactory personal relationships across the social matrix are a fundamental pillar of a full and healthy life trajectory. Indeed, relationships (family, friends, work relationships, neighbors, community, etc.) are part of the dynamics of meaning and purpose in individual and collective existence in human history.

We humans are a gregarious species, and proof of this is that we have always lived in groups according to the evidence we have. This condition has allowed us to survive, reproduce, protect ourselves from predators, develop in different social, cultural, and technological dimensions (examples: interactive virtual reality and robotics in the twenty-first century). We are social beings by nature, we solve problems together, we cooperate,[1] we respect each other, we love each other, we love each other and build meanings in relationships with other living beings and also with those already dead.

Tomasello (2009) emphasizes cooperation in our species, and states:

> To an unprecedented degree, *homo sapiens* are adapted for acting and thinking cooperatively in cultural groups, and indeed all of humans' most impressive cognitive achievements—from complex technologies to linguistic and mathematical symbols to intricate social institutions—are the products not of individuals acting alone, but of individuals interacting. As they grow, human children are equipped to participate in this cooperative groupthink through a special kind of cultural intelligence, comprising species-unique

[1] Tomasello and colleagues argue that evidence of our fundamentally cooperative nature in Homo Sapiens can also be seen in the whites of our eyes, which in contrast to the brown eyes of other apes, show the direction of our gaze. The fact that we announce the direction of our attention suggests that it is an advantage for us to convey our intentions to other members of our group (Tomasello et al., 2007).

Á. Quiñones Bergeret, *Evolutionary Case Formulation*,
https://doi.org/10.1007/978-3-031-67412-9_7

> social-cognitive skills and motivations for collaboration, communication, social learning, and other forms of shared intentionality. These special skills arose from processes of cultural niche construction and gene-culture coevolution; that is to say, they arose as adaptations that enabled humans to function effectively in any one of their many different self-built cultural worlds. (2009, XV–XVI)

Evolutionists agree that *Homo Sapiens* is superior to all species in its ability to cooperate. As a way in general, evolutionary psychology assumes that the human mind is endowed with a series of specific cognitive mechanisms, designed to solve the most frequent problems that our ancestors have encountered throughout the history of the species, for example: competing, cooperating, pairing, making friends, loving, raising children, managing time, transmitting information, etc. (Buss, 2005, 2007; Cosmides et al., 1992; Tooby & Cosmides, 1992, 2005).

As the safety and survival of human beings have depended for a long time on living in groups, researchers have suggested that human beings have a fundamental need to belong. Such a characteristic motivates them to avoid behaviors of different types that could lead to their expulsion from the group (Baumeister & Leary, 1995).

As a conceptualization of the intersubjective knowledge domain "Interpersonal," two parsimonious axes of analysis are proposed in the case formulation model and are called: **Alteration in personal relationships** (deficit of social skills, loneliness, lack of social support, discomfort with people, lack of friends, constant need for approval, dark triad of personality, conflictive work relationships) and **Alteration in romantic relationships** (decreased trust, decreased passion, decreased intimacy, decreased decision/commitment, insecurity, fear of abandonment, absence or low admiration, decreased cooperation, romantic friendship, violence in the couple, conflict).

Figure 7.1 shows the synergy especially with the Self System which is essential for formulating the patient's psychological problems in an idiographic way.

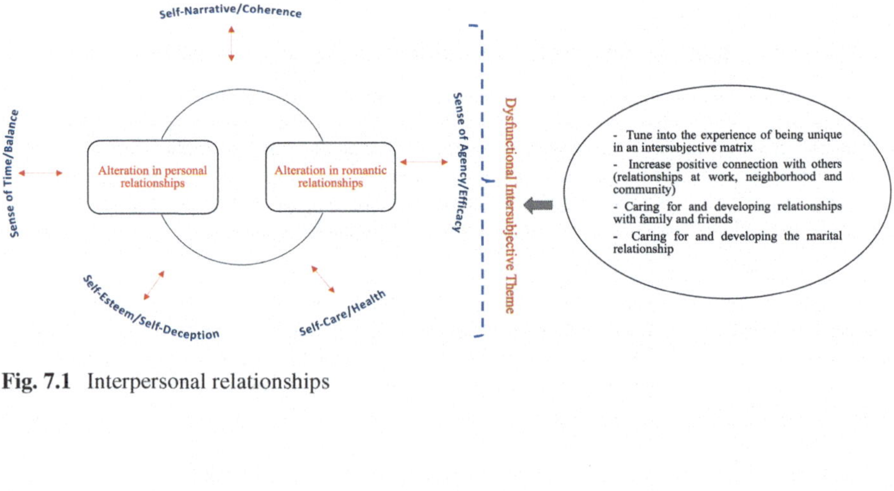

Fig. 7.1 Interpersonal relationships

7.1 Alteration in Personal Relationships

It should be noted that social skills are fundamental for adaptation and well-being. Social skills are a function of development and the complexity of increasing peer interaction. It is a complex construct that has abundant research over decades; however, it lacks a widely accepted definition. It should be noted that social skills have areas, for example, communication, cognition, emotion, and problem-solving skills (Grover et al., 2020). Also, social skills in the life cycle vary, for example in emerging, middle, and late adulthood, there are qualitative and quantitative changes that present their own differentiated complexities (for example, cognitive flexibility, etc.).

People develop social skills in their socialization and until the end of life. This process is fundamental for adaptation, social adjustment, and well-being. Decades of research indicate that deficient social skills are associated with different psychological disorders throughout life: eating disorders, anxiety, depression, personality disorders, neurocognitive disorders of old age, and others (see for an excellent review Kamper-DeMarco et al., 2020).

Assertiveness was the most evaluated domain in social skills; however, interest has now decreased. Regardless of trends, it is fundamental in all types of interpersonal, personal, and work relationships and has effects on mental health. In addition, assertiveness is a well-founded area of applied research. However, a challenge is that we do not have a consistent and precise definition of assertiveness after decades of research which has implications in drawing significant conclusions. In fact, St. Lawrence (1987) in the 1980s identified at least 20 clearly different definitions commonly used in research and assertiveness training. Tessa Pfafman defines assertiveness:

> Assertiveness involves appropriately expressing ideas, feelings, and boundaries while respecting other's rights, maintaining positive affect in the receiver, and considering potential consequences of the expression. It includes both positive and negative expressions and seeks to achieve personal and/or instrumental goals. (2017, p. 1)

For practical purposes in psychotherapy, assertiveness problems can be understood along a continuum from adaptive to maladaptive, that is, assertiveness problems are many and are observed in the clinic with high frequency, for example differentiating non-problematic kindness from excessive kindness (maladaptive example: submission).

We have evidence linking lack of assertiveness with clinical problems (Speed et al., 2018). In fact, meta-analyses comparing the outcomes of psychotherapy for depression and social anxiety have found that social skills training involving assertiveness was equally effective compared to other Cognitive Behavioral Therapy interventions (Barth et al., 2013; Cuijpers et al., 2008). Lastly, there is a high consensus that assertiveness training is a powerful transdiagnostic intervention.

We humans are social and friendly beings. Clearly we need each other. Studies indicate that having gratifying social and family relationships are the best predictors of overall life satisfaction compared to other domains of human activity, such as career and financial achievement (Waldinger & Shulz, 2023; Ryan & Willits, 2007).

In the clinical context, correlations between quality social relationships and psychological health are very well documented. In this sense, different types of social relationships are a consistent and often the main source of psychological health (Waldinger & Shulz, 2023; Berscheid & Reis, 1998). In the scientific literature on adult social relationships, friendships are described as an important source of social support that contributes to aspects of well-being ranging from happiness (Demir et al., 2007) to physical health and longevity (Mendes de Leon, 2005).

The American Psychological Association (APA) defines loneliness as the "distress or discomfort, affective and cognitive, from being or perceiving oneself as alone." Peplau and Perlman (1982) define loneliness:

> in our view loneliness is the unpleasant experience that occurs when a person's network of social relations is deficient in some important way, either quantitatively or qualitatively; and although loneliness may at times reach pathological proportions, we are mostly concerned with normal ranges of loneliness among the general public. (pp. 31–32)

Loneliness is a consequence of a deficient integration into the social network in a satisfactory way. About the quality of social relationships and well-being, there is ample evidence that loneliness is consistently negatively correlated with well-being (Helliwell & Putnam, 2004; VanderWeele et al., 2011).

There is abundant and consistent research that has extensively documented the associations between loneliness and physical and psychological health problems, as well as cognitive functioning deterioration and mortality risks (Deckx et al., 2018; Solmi et al., 2020; Lara et al., 2020). Likewise, we are learning from what happened in the COVID-19 pandemic in relation to mental health and the consequences of loneliness (Megalakaki & Kokou-Kpolou, 2022; Mayorga et al., 2022). Particularly, loneliness has been associated with adverse health outcomes, immune system suppression, less efficient sleep, and greater mortality in old age (Griffin et al., 2020; Holt-Lunstad et al., 2015; Hawkley & Cacioppo, 2010; Pressman et al., 2005).

Last but not least, being socially connected has significant and positive implications for psychological and physical well-being (Uchino, 2006) and for longevity (Shor et al., 2013). In this sense, understanding the conceptual distinction between loneliness and social isolation has implications for psychotherapy interventions. Essentially, loneliness represents the discrepancy between the desired and actual quality and quantity of a person's social relationships (Perlman & Peplau, 1981), in change, social isolation describes a lack of significant contact with the social network (Victor et al., 2000).

It is known that family and friendship relationships have an impact on physical and mental health (Waldinger & Shulz, 2023; Berkman et al., 2000; Baumeister & Leary, 1995). Regarding friends and their healthy effects, Waldinger and Shulz (2023) state:

> Friends diminish our perception of hardship—making us perceive adverse events as less stressful than we might otherwise see them—and even when we do experience extreme stress, friends can diminish its impact and duration. We feel the stress, but with the help of friends we're better able to manage it. Less stress and better stress management lead to less wear and tear on our bodies. (p. 310)

The research of Larson et al. (1986) is an excellent example of such knowledge. They examined in which company people between the ages of 18 and 85 were happiest and most enthusiastic. At all ages, respondents were happier and more excited when they were with friends. Although family can provide a stable and supportive environment, friends seem to offer more intense enjoyment, a conclusion that may explain the greater spread of happiness among friends than among family members (Fowler & Christakis, 2008). In short, we must not forget that true friends accompany us throughout life; in other words, they are with us in the "good times and the bad."

Adults differ significantly not only in terms of the quality of friendship, but also the number of friends one has and the hierarchy of friendships (Demir, 2015). Most people maintain small networks of close and long-term friends (Wrzus et al., 2017).

Mendelson and Aboud (1999) defined six components of friendship that delimit quality: stimulating companionship, help (social support), intimacy, reliable alliance, self-validation, and emotional security. It is noteworthy that this structure has been very useful for our understanding of friendship and research that has allowed us to better understand the association between friendship and well-being (see in particular the research by Pezirkianidis et al., 2023).

Ultimately, the quality of friendships and socializing with friends over time predict levels of wellbeing. In other words, human beings need to have and nurture friendships throughout their life cycle.

In relation to toxic relationships, a useful construct is the Dark Triad of personality. A well-established construct that has research and several measurement scales. It is a set of three socially undesirable and aversive personality traits: narcissism, Machiavellianism, and psychopathy (Paulhus & Williams, 2002; Furnham et al., 2013; Muris et al., 2017). People who score high on these personality dimensions can cause harm to the people they interact with, examples: mistreatment of coworkers, perpetration of partner violence, poor financial practices, aggressive behavior, antisocial behavior, social network addiction, problematic use of technologies, etc. In addition, a relevant marker to keep in mind is the insensitivity shown by people who present this triad (Furnham et al., 2013).

Work is fundamental in adult life because it offers a series of benefits such as financial stability, purposes, vitality, and relational achievements, among other possibilities (Waldinger & Shulz, 2023; Semmer & Zapf, 2019). The impact of interpersonal conflict in the workplace has negative consequences for health and well-being, for example, depression, psychosomatic complaints, dissatisfaction with life, negative emotional states, and stress (Meier et al., 2013, 2014; Dormann & Zapf, 2002; Frone, 2000; Spector et al., 1988). Therefore, therapists should assess work relationships, and in particular, conflictual relationships (at an individual level) and their impact on the experiential present.

It is relevant to keep in mind the research from the Harvard longitudinal study (Waldinger & Shulz, 2023) that indicates the importance of work in happiness:

> Sometimes we'd rather be doing anything other than working. But these hours are a major social opportunity. Many of the happiest men and women in the Harvard Study had positive relationships with their work and their workmates, whether they were selling tires or teaching kindergarten or performing surgery, and they were able to balance (often after much difficulty and negotiation) their work lives with their home lives. They understood it was all of a piece. (p. 197)

7.2 Alteration in Romantic Relationships

On another note, in the evolution and history of our species, the quality of life in a couple and its stability is fundamental to feel accompanied, maintain safe procreation, and provide greater possibilities for optimal psychological regulation. This is how interpersonal relationships that are called "love relationships or romantic relationships" are of the highest importance and therefore it is no coincidence that we like songs, movies, and novels about love so much.

Love in romantic relationships is a multifaceted and complex phenomenon that is omnipresent in our history as a species. In addition, we have clinical experience and research that indicates that romantic relationships are an essential component of people's development and are a powerful buffer of stress through social support, among other characteristics.

Current theories propose the decomposition of love into a certain number of dimensions, and without a doubt, a significant advance in the study of love was the innovative analysis by Zick Rubin (1973). Rubin defined love as an attitude that predisposes to think, feel, and act in a particular way towards the object of love. Along with this, he outlined three components of love: intimacy, need/attachment, and care.

In relation to the conceptualization of love, the Triangular Theory of Love by Robert J. Sternberg (1986, 1988, 2006, 2013) stands out. It is interesting because it clearly distinguishes the structure of love (the triangle is a metaphor) and the existence of a large number of possible triangles, and proposes from a narrative perspective a taxonomy of 26 love stories that are useful to help our patients understand how they conceptualize love: addiction, art, business, collection, horror, humor, religion, sacrifice, etc. (Sternberg, 2006; Sternberg et al., 2001). He asserts that intimacy, passion, and decision/commitment play a fundamental role in understanding love. Each component manifests a different aspect of love. Likewise, consummate love results from the complete combination of the three components and non-love refers to the absence of the three sustained components.

The first component of love is *Intimacy.* It refers to those feelings that occur in a human relationship and that foster proximity, bonding, and connection (Sternberg, 1998). Sternberg and Grajek (1984) argue that intimacy consists of at least ten elements: (1) desire to promote the well-being of the loved one, (2) feeling happy in the company of the loved one, (3) having high regard for the loved one, (4) being able to count on the loved one in difficult times, (5) understanding each other, (6) sharing everything with the loved one, (7) receiving emotional support from the loved one, (8) giving emotional support to the loved one, (9) communicating intimately with the loved one, and (10) valuing the loved one.

The second component of love is *Passion*. It refers to the impulses that lead to romance, physical attraction, sexual consummation, and related phenomena in love relationships, but it also goes beyond. The passion component includes those sources of motivation and other forms of arousal that lead to the experience of passion in a love relationship. Certainly, in a love relationship, sexual needs may predominate but are also present the needs for self-esteem, help, care, affiliation, dominance, submission, and self-realization (Sternberg, 2006). Sternberg on passion maintains:

> Passion refers to the drives that lead to romance, physical attraction, sexual consummation, and related phenomena in loving relationships. The passion component includes those sources of motivational and other forms of arousal that lead to the experience of passion in a loving relationship. (p. 185)

The third component of love is the *Decision/commitment*. It has two components: short-term and long-term. The short-term aspect consists of the decision that one loves a certain other, and in the long term, the commitment to preserve that love (Sternberg, 1998). As Sternberg (2006) maintains:

> These two aspects of the decision/commitment component do not necessarily go together, in that one can decide to love someone without being committed to the love in the long term, or one can be committed to a relationship without acknowledging that one loves the other person in the relationship. (p. 185)

In relation to the dynamics, it should always be valued, since the three components of love interact. Sternberg (2006) observes:

> … greater intimacy may lead to greater passion or commitment, just as greater commitment may lead to greater intimacy or, with lesser likelihood, greater passion. In general, then, the components are separable but interactive. Although all three components are important parts of loving relationships, their importance may differ from one relationship to another, or over time within a given relationship. Indeed, different kinds of love can be generated by limiting cases of different combinations of the components. (p. 186)

It is known that the ability to establish lasting romantic relationships is positively associated with happiness, positive affect, empathy, vitality, and satisfaction, among other healthy characteristics. From a nomothetic perspective, we know that people with personality disorders can experience the romantic experience with varying degrees of dysfunction (Lazarus et al., 2018; Gawda & Bochyńska, 2016; Selby et al., 2008). Specifically, data are reported on various personality disorder traits associated with dysfunctional romantic love experiences that vary depending on severity, for example, let's focus on borderline and antisocial personality disorders. Namely, individuals with antisocial personality disorder traits produce stories about love that contain more negative elements, ambivalence, and unclear perception of the partner or themselves. In particular, their love stories show excessive egocentrism and a lack of clarity regarding the valence of the love situation (Gawda, 2012, 2013). In the case of people who have a borderline personality disorder, they often present inconsistent behaviors, alternation between idealization and devaluation, ambivalence, mood swings, impulsivity, hostility, abandonment anxiety, frantic efforts to avoid abandonment, feelings of guilt, feelings of worthlessness, etc. (Hopwood et al., 2014; Selby et al., 2008).

Marriage is the long-term romantic relationship par excellence and plays a major role in people's quality of life. Today, we know that marriage can positively or negatively affect physical health and longevity (see meta-analysis conducted by Robles et al., 2014). In such a context of research and clinical experience, we know various types of difficulties that we must point out for an adequate case formulation. Special mention should be made of the presence of marital conflict, as there is extensive research indicating its negative effects on mental health (Yang et al., 2023). Specifically, Whisman et al. (2004) found that people's levels of depression and anxiety were significantly correlated with their marital satisfaction; however, the effect of depression was significantly greater than that of anxiety. Furthermore, in a meta-analysis of 26 cross-sectional studies, Whisman (2001) reported the magnitude of the effect of marital satisfaction on depression was −0.42 for women and −0.37 for men.

On the other hand, we have clear knowledge indicating that couples who exhibit more hostile behavior during marital discussions have elevated blood pressure and heart rates compared to less hostile couples (Robles & Kiecolt-Glaser, 2003). Similarly, the critical interaction in dyads is associated with greater dysregulation of immune functioning and unhealthy cardiovascular reactivity (Kiecolt-Glaser, 1999; Uchino et al., 2001). In addition, hostile conflict and negative emotionality in marriage is associated with an increase in death from coronary disease (Eaker et al., 2007). Lastly, the love bond and psychological well-being make it clear that quality is important and that there are potential risks to well-being inherent in such relationships. Potential costs, such as fears and experiences with rejection and abandonment, have well-documented negative associations with psychological health (Baron et al., 2007; Downey et al., 2000).

It is well known that members of the relationship, be they family, friends, and romantic partners, help mitigate the harmful effect that negative events and stress have on well-being (Hawkley et al., 2009; Randall & Bodenmann, 2009, 2017).

In the psychotherapeutic field, it is important to guide the therapist to observe some indicators of interpersonal relationships that we know contribute to psychological problems.

In the context of the proposed case formulation model, parsimoniously the intersubjective knowledge domain "Interpersonal" is valued in two dimensions: **alteration in personal relationships and alteration in romantic relationships.** It is worth remembering that the domains are synergistically related to other second-order domains (cognition, emotion, imagination, corporeality, sexuality, religiosity/spirituality) and first-order (Self System: agency/efficacy, self-narrative/coherence, time/balance; self-esteem/self-deception; self-care/health).

Next, the second-order intersubjective knowledge domain "**INTERPERSONAL**" is shown in the case formulation protocol (the Case Formulation-Evaluation and the Case Formulation-Intervention are shown in Boxes 7.1 and 7.2).

Box 7.1: Case Formulation—Evaluation

[INTERPERSONAL] Indicate and weigh what processes contribute to discomfort and/or psychological dysregulation: ....

....

(mark presence: x)

Alteration in personal relationships:

Social skills deficits ☐ Loneliness ☐
Deficit of social support ☐ Discomfort with people ☐
Lack of friends ☐ Constant need for approval ☐
Dark Triad personality ☐ Conflicting labor relations ☐

Others: ____________________

Describe: ....

....

Alteration in romantic relationships:

Decreased confidence ☐ Diminished passion ☐
Decreased intimacy ☐ Decreased decisiveness/commitment ☐
Insecurity ☐ Fear of abandonment ☐
Absence or low admiration ☐ Decreased cooperation ☐
Romantic friendship ☐ Intimate partner violence ☐
Conflict ☐
Others: ____________________

Describe: ....

....

Psychological Distress						Psychological Well-Being
High	Moderate	Mild	Neutral	Mild	Moderate	High
-3	-2	-1	0	1	2	3
Psychological Dysregulation						Psychological Regulation
High	Moderate	Mild	Neutral	Mild	Moderate	High
-3	-2	-1	0	1	2	3

Box 7.2: Case Formulation—Intervention

INTERPERSONAL: Indicators of change

(mark presence: x)

Alteration in personal relationships: Progress ☐ Regulation ☐

Describe: ....

....

Alteration in romantic relationships: Progress ☐ Regulation ☐

Describe: ....

....

- Functional Narrative Indicator:
  Integrates knowledge about interpersonal relationships ☐

- Behavioral Change Indicator: Incorporates changes ☐

Psychological Distress				Psychological Well-Being		
High	Moderate	Mild	Neutral	Mild	Moderate	High
-3	-2	-1	0	1	2	3
Psychological Dysregulation				Psychological Regulation		
High	Moderate	Mild	Neutral	Mild	Moderate	High
-3	-2	-1	0	1	2	3

References

Baron, K. G., Smith, T. W., Butner, J., Nealey-Moore, J., Hawkins, M. W., & Uchino, B. N. (2007). Hostility, anger, and marital adjustment: Concurrent and prospective associations with psychosocial vulnerability. *Journal of Behavioral Medicine, 30*(1), 1e10. https://doi.org/10.1007/s10865-006-9086

Barth, J., Munder, T., Gerger, H., Nuesch, E., Trelle, S., Znoj, H., et al. (2013). Comparative efficacy of seven psychotherapeutic interventions for patients with depression: A network meta-analysis. *PLoS Medicine, 10*, e1001454. https://doi.org/10.1371/journal.pmed.1001454

Baumeister, R. F., & Leary, M. R. (1995). The need to belong: Desire for interpersonal attachments as a fundamental human motivation. *Psychological Bulletin, 117*, 497–529.

Berkman, L. F., Glass, T., Brisette, I., & Seeman, T. E. (2000). From social integration to health: Durkheim in the new millennium. *Social Science and Medicine, 51*, 843–857.

Berscheid, E., & Reis, H. T. (1998). Attraction and close relationships. In D. T. Gilbert, S. T. Fiske, & G. Lindzey (Eds.), *The handbook of social psychology* (Vol. 1–2, pp. 193–281). McGraw-Hill.

Buss, D. M. (Ed.). (2005). *The handbook of evolutionary psychology*. Wiley.

Buss, D. M. (2007). *Evolutionary psychology: The new science of the mind* (3rd ed.). Allyn & Bacon.

Cosmides, L., Tooby, J., & Barkow, J. H. (1992). Introduction: Evolutionary psychology and conceptual integration. In J. H. Barkow, L. Cosmides, & J. Tooby (Eds.), *The adapted mind: Evolutionary psychology and the generation of culture* (pp. 3–15). Oxford University Press.

Cuijpers, P., van Straten, A., Andersson, G., & van Oppen, P. (2008). Psychotherapy for depression in adults: A meta- analysis of comparative outcome studies. *Journal of Consulting and Clinical Psychology, 76*, 909–922. https://doi.org/10.1037/a0013075

Deckx, L., van den Akker, M., Buntinx, F., & van Driel, M. (2018). A systematic literature review on the association between loneliness and coping strategies. *Psychology, Health & Medicine, 23*(8), 899–916. https://doi.org/10.1080/13548506.2018.1446096

Demir, M. (Ed.). (2015). *Friendship and happiness: Across the life-span and cultures*. Springer Science + Business Media. https://doi.org/10.1007/978-94-017-9603-3

Demir, M., Ozdemir, M., & Weitekamp, L. A. (2007). Looking to happy tomorrows with friends: Best and close friendships as they predict happiness. *Journal of Happiness Studies, 8*, 243–271.

Dormann, C., & Zapf, D. (2002). Social stressors at work, irritation, and depressive symptoms: Accounting for unmeasured third variables in a multi-wave study. *Journal of Occupational and Organizational Psychology, 75*, 33–58.

Downey, G., Feldman, S., & Ayduk, O. (2000). Rejection sensitivity and male violence in romantic relationships. *Personal Relationships, 7*(1), 45–61.

Eaker, E. D., Sullivan, L. M., Kelly-Hayes, M., D'Agostino, R. B., Sr., & Benjamin, E. J. (2007). Marital status, marital strain, and risk of coronary heart disease or total mortality: The Framingham offspring study. *Psychosomatic Medicine, 69*(6), 509–513.

Fowler, J. H., & Christakis, N. A. (2008). The dynamic spread of happiness in a large social network. *British Medical Journal, 337*, a2338. https://doi.org/10.1136/bmj.a2338

Frone, M. R. (2000). Interpersonal conflict at work and psychological outcomes: Testing a model among young workers. *Journal of Occupational Health Psychology, 5*, 246–255.

Furnham, A., Richards, S. C., & Paulhus, D. L. (2013). The dark triad of personality: A 10 year review. *Social and Personality Psychology Compass, 7*(3), 199–216. https://doi.org/10.1111/spc3.12018

Gawda, B. (2012). Dysfunctional love in psychopathic criminals – The neural basis. *NeuroQuantology, 10*(4), 725–732.

Gawda, B. (2013). The emotional lexicon of individuals diagnosed with antisocial personality disorder. *Journal of Psycholinguistic Research, 42*(6), 571–580.

Gawda, B., & Bochyńska, K. (2016). Love in the multicultural world. *The Social Studies, 2*, 5–13.

Griffin, S. C., Williams, A. B., Ravyts, S. G., Mladen, S. N., & Rybarczyk, B. D. (2020). Loneliness and sleep: A systematic review and meta-analysis. *Health Psychology Open, 7*(1), 2055102920913235.

Grover, R. L., Nangle, D. W., Buffie, M., & Andrews, L. A. (2020). Defining social skills. In D. W. Nangle, C. A. Erdley, & R. A. Schwartz-Mette (Eds.), *Social skills across the life span: Theory, assessment, and intervention* (pp. 3–24). Elsevier Academic Press. https://doi.org/10.1016/B978-0-12-817752-5.00001-9

Hawkley, L. C., & Cacioppo, J. T. (2010). Loneliness matters: A theoretical and empirical review of consequences and mechanisms. *Annals of Behavioral Medicine, 40*, 218–227.

Hawkley, L. C., Thisted, R. A., & Cacioppo, J. T. (2009). Loneliness predicts reduced physical activity: Cross-sectional & longitudinal analyses. *Health Psychology, 28*(3), 354.

Helliwell, J. F., & Putnam, R. D. (2004). The social context of well-being. *Philosophical Transactions-Royal Society of London Series B Biological Sciences, 359*(1449), 1435–1446.

Holt-Lunstad, J., Smith, T. B., & Layton, J. B. (2010). Social relationships and mortality risk: A meta-analytic review. *PLoS Medicine, 7*, e1000316.

Holt-Lunstad, J., Smith, T. B., Baker, M., Harris, T., & Stephenson, D. (2015). Loneliness and social isolation as risk factors for mortality: A meta-analytic review. *Perspectives on Psychological Science, 10*(2), 227–237. https://doi.org/10.1177/1745691614568352

Hopwood, C. J., Schade, N., & Pincus, A. L. (2014). A contemporary interpersonal model of borderline personality development. In *Handbook of borderline personality disorder in children and adolescents* (pp. 293–310). Springer.

Kamper-DeMarco, K. E., Shankman, J., Fearey, E., Lawrence, H. R., & Schwartz-Mette, R. A. (2020). Linking social skills and adjustment. In D. W. Nangle, C. A. Erdley, & R. A. Schwartz-Mette (Eds.), *Social skills across the life span: Theory, assessment, and intervention* (pp. 47–66). Elsevier Academic Press. https://doi.org/10.1016/B978-0-12-817752-5.00003-2

Kiecolt-Glaser, J. K. (1999). Stress, personal relationships, and immune function: Health implications. *Brain, Behavior and Immunity, 13*(1), 61–72.

Lara, E., Moreno-Agostino, D., Martín-María, N., Miret, M., Rico-Uribe, L. A., Olaya, B., Cabello, M., Haro, J. M., & Ayuso-Mateos, J. L. (2020). Exploring the effect of loneliness on all-cause mortality: Are there differences between older adults and younger and middle-aged adults? *Social Science & Medicine, 258*(1982), 258., 113087. https://doi.org/10.1016/j.socscimed.2020.113087

Larson, R., Mannell, R., & Zuzanek, J. (1986). The daily experience of older adults with family and friends. *Psychology and Aging, 1*, 117–126.

Lazarus, S. A., Scott, L. N., Beeney, J. E., Wright, A. G. C., Stepp, S. D., & Pilkonis, P. A. (2018). Borderline personality disorder symptoms and affective responding to perceptions of rejection and acceptance from romantic versus nonromantic partners. *Personality Disorders: Theory, Research, and Treatment, 9*(3), 197–206.

Mayorga, N. A., Smit, T., Garey, L., Gold, A. K., Otto, M. W., & Zvolensky, M. J. (2022). Evaluating the interactive effect of COVID-19 worry and loneliness on mental health among young adults. *Cognitive Therapy and Research, 46*(1), 11–19. https://doi.org/10.1007/s10608-021-10252-2

Megalakaki, O., & Kokou-Kpolou, C. K. (2022). Effects of biopsychosocial factors on the association between loneliness and mental health risks during the COVID-19 lockdown. *Current Psychology, 41*(11), 8224–8235.

Meier, L. L., Gross, S., Spector, P. E., & Semmer, N. K. (2013). Task and relationship conflict at work: Interactive short-term effects on angry mood and somatic complaints. *Journal of Occupational Health Psychology, 18*, 144–156.

Meier, L. L., Semmer, N. K., & Gross, S. (2014). The effect of conflict at work on well-being: Depressive symptoms as a vulnerability factor. *Work & Stress, 28*(1), 31–48. https://doi.org/10.1080/02678373.2013.876691

Mendelson, M. J., & Aboud, F. E. (1999). Measuring friendship quality in late adolescents and young adults: McGill friendship questionnaires. *Canadian Journal of Behavioural Science, 31*, 130–132. https://doi.org/10.1037/h0087080

Mendes de Leon, C. F. (2005). Why do friendships matter for survival? *Journal of Epidemiology and Community Health, 59*(7), 538–539. https://doi.org/10.1136/jech.2004.031542

Muris, P., Merckelbach, H., Otgaar, H., & Meijer, E. (2017). The malevolent side of human nature: A meta-analysis and critical review of the literature on the dark triad (narcissism, Machiavellianism, and psychopathy). *Perspectives on Psychological Science, 12*(2), 183–204. https://doi.org/10.1177/1745691616666070

Paulhus, D. L., & Williams, K. M. (2002). The dark triad of personality: Narcissism, machiavellianism, and psychopathy. *Journal of Research in Personality, 36*(6), 556–563. https://doi.org/10.1016/S0092-6566(02)00505-6

Peplau, L. A., & Pelman, D. (1982). *Loneliness: A sourcebook of current theory, research, and therapy*. Wiley.

Perlman, D., & Peplau, L. A. (1981). Toward a social psychology of loneliness. *Personal Relationships, 3*, 31–56.

Pezirkianidis, C., Galanaki, E., Raftopoulou, G., Moraitou, D., & Stalikas, A. (2023). Adult friendship and wellbeing: A systematic review with practical implications. *Frontiers in Psychology, 14*, 1059057. https://doi.org/10.3389/fpsyg.2023.1059057

Pfafman, T. (2017). Assertiveness. In V. Zeigler-Hill & T. K. Shackelford (Eds.), *Encyclopedia of personality and individual differences*. Springer Cham.

Pressman, S. D., Cohen, S., Miller, G. E., Barkin, A., Rabin, B. S., & Treanor, J. J. (2005). Loneliness, social network size, and immune response to influenza vaccination in college freshman. *Health Psychology, 24*(4), 348.

Randall, A. K., & Bodenmann, G. (2009). The role of stress on close relationships and marital satisfaction. *Clinical Psychology Review, 29*, 105–115.

Randall, A. K., & Bodenmann, G. (2017). Stress and its associations with relationship satisfaction. *Current Opinion in Psychology, 13*, 96–106.

Robles, T. F., & Kiecolt-Glaser, J. K. (2003). The physiology of marriage: Pathways to health. *Physiology & Behavior, 79*(3), 409–416.

Robles, T. F., Slatcher, R. B., Trombello, J. M., & McGinn, M. M. (2014). Marital quality and health: A meta-analytic review. *Psychological Bulletin, 140*(1), 140–187. https://doi.org/10.1037/a0031859

Rubin, Z. (1973). *Liking and loving: An invitation to social psychology*. Holt, Rinehart and Winston.

Ryan, A. K., & Willits, F. K. (2007). Family ties, physical health, and psychological well-being. *Journal of Aging and Health, 19*, 907–920.

Selby, E. A., Braithwaite, S. R., Joiner, T. E., Jr., & Fincham, F. D. (2008). Features of borderline personality disorder, perceived childhood emotional invalidation, and dysfunction within current romantic relationships. *Journal of Family Psychology, 22*(6), 885–893.

Semmer, N. K., & Zapf, D. (2019). The meaning of demands, stressors, and resources at work. In T. W. Taris, M. C. W. Peeters, & H. De Witte (Eds.), *The fun and frustration of modern working life. Contributions from an occupational health psychology perspective. Festschrift for prof. Dr. Wilmar Schaufeli* (pp. 80–93). Pelckmans Pro.

Shor, E., Roelfs, D. J., & Yogev, T. (2013). The strength of family ties: A meta-analysis and meta-regression of self-reported social support and mortality. *Social Networks, 35*, 626–638. https://doi.org/10.1016/j.socnet.2013.08.004

Solmi, M., Veronese, N., Galvano, D., Favaro, A., Ostinelli, E. G., Noventa, V., Favaretto, E., Tudor, F., Finessi, M., Shin, J. I., Smith, L., Koyanagi, A., Cester, A., Bolzetta, F., Cotroneo, A., Maggi, S., Demurtas, J., De Leo, D., & Trabucchi, M. (2020). Factors associated with loneliness: An umbrella review of observational studies. *Journal of Affective Disorders, 271*, 131–138. https://doi.org/10.1016/j.jad.2020.03.075

Spector, P. E., Dwyer, D. J., & Jex, S. M. (1988). Relation of job stressors to affective, health, and performance outcomes: A comparison of multiple data sources. *Journal of Applied Psychology, 73*, 11–19.

Speed, B. C., Goldstein, B. L., & Goldfried, M. R. (2018). Assertiveness training: A forgotten evidence-based treatment. *Clinical Psychology: Science and Practice, 25*, e12216. https://doi.org/10.1111/cpsp.12216

St Lawrence, J. S. (1987). Assessment of assertion. *Progress in Behavior Modification, 21*, 152–190.

Sternberg, R. J. (1986). A triangular theory of love. *Psychological Review, 93*, 119–135.

Sternberg, R. J. (1988). *The triangle of love*. Basic Books.

Sternberg, R. J. (1998). *Cupid's arrow*. Cambridge University Press.

Sternberg, R. J. (2006). A duplex theory of love. In R. J. Sternberg & K. Weis (Eds.), *The new psychology of love* (pp. 184–199). Yale University Press.

Sternberg, R. J. (2013). Searching for love. *The Psychologist, 26*(2), 98–101.

Sternberg, R. J., & Grajek, S. (1984). The nature of love. *Journal of Personality and Social Psychology, 47*, 312–329.

Sternberg, R. J., Hojjat, M., & Barnes, M. L. (2001). Empirical aspects of a theory of love as a story. *European Journal of Personality, 15*, 1–20.

Tomasello, M. (2009). *Why we cooperate*. MIT Press.

Tomasello, M., Hare, B., Lehmann, H., & Call, J. (2007). Reliance on head versus eyes in the gaze following of great apes and human infants: The cooperative eye hypothesis. *Journal of Human Evolution, 52*, 314–320.

Tooby, J., & Cosmides, L. (1992). The psychological foundations of culture. In J. H. Barkow, L. Cosmides, & J. Tooby (Eds.), *The adapted mind: Evolutionary psychology and the generation of culture* (pp. 19–139). Oxford University Press.

Tooby, J., & Cosmides, L. (2005). Conceptual foundations of evolutionary psychology. In D. M. Buss (Ed.), *The handbook of evolutionary psychology* (pp. 5–67). Wiley.

Uchino, B. N. (2006). Social support and health: A review of physiological processes potentially underlying links to disease outcomes. *Journal of Behavioral Medicine, 29*, 377–387. https://doi.org/10.1007/s10865-006-9056-5

Uchino, B. N., Holt-Lunstad, J., Uno, D., & Flinders, J. B. (2001). Heterogeneity in the social networks of young and older adults: Prediction of mental health and cardiovascular reactivity during acute stress. *Journal of Behavioral Medicine, 24*(4), 361–382.

VanderWeele, T. J., Hawkley, L. C., Thisted, R. A., & Cacioppo, J. T. (2011). A marginal structural model analysis for loneliness: Implications for intervention trials and clinical practice. *Journal of Consulting and Clinical Psychology, 79*(2), 225–235.

Victor, C., Scambler, S., Bond, J., & Bowling, A. (2000). Being alone in later life: Loneliness, social isolation and living alone. *Reviews in Clinical Gerontology, 10*(4), 407–417. https://doi.org/10.1017/S0959259800104101

Waldinger, R., & Schulz, M. (2023). *The good life. Lessons from the world's longest scientific study of happiness*. Simon and Shuster.

Whisman, M. A. (2001). The association between depression and marital dissatisfaction. In S. R. H. Beach (Ed.), *Marital and family processes in depression: A scientific foundation for clinical practice* (pp. 3–24). American Psychological Association. https://doi.org/10.1037/10350-001

Whisman, M. A., Uebelacker, L. A., & Weinstock, L. M. (2004). Psychopathology and marital satisfaction: The importance of evaluating both partners. *Journal of Consulting and Clinical Psychology, 72*(5), 830–838. https://doi.org/10.1037/0022-006X.72.5.830

Wrzus, C., Zimmermann, J., Mund, M., & Neyer, F. J. (2017). Friendships in young and middle adulthood: Normative patterns and personality differences. In M. Hojat & A. Moyer (Eds.), *Psychology of friendship* (pp. 21–38). Oxford University Press. https://doi.org/10.1093/acprof:oso/9780190222024.003. 0002.

Yang, L., Yang, Z., & Yang, J. (2023). The effect of marital satisfaction on the self-assessed depression of husbands and wives: Investigating the moderating effects of the number of children and neurotic personality. *BMC Psychology, 11*(1), 163. https://doi.org/10.1186/s40359-023-01200-8

Chapter 8
Imagination

Imagination is a domain of human knowledge of immense complexity and with a great tradition of research in different disciplines that seek to understand its scope for human life (Nanay, 2023; Abraham, 2020; Irish, 2020). Likewise, it is necessary to clarify that we do not have a comprehensive theory of imagination.

Arne Dietrich and Sandra Zakka (2020) very sharply capture the complexity of the state of the art and the challenge that imagination implies:

> The human imagination is vast and unknown. It is vast in its scope and unknown in its structure. What's more, we have little understanding of its purpose or the brain mechanisms involved. Efforts to capture it, whole or in part, have been either brave or foolhardy, depending on your point of view. But in our quest to understand the human condition, psychologists, neuroscientists, and philosophers, among many others, must embrace this challenge. We spend a great deal of time "in our heads" and it is certainly true that no theory or general framework of the mind is complete without the imagination occupying a central role. (p. 132)

A starting point that introduces us to this powerful human capacity and that is fundamental to generate change in psychotherapy through case formulation is that we keep in mind that it provides us with different possible scenarios imagined privately without having to rehearse in interpersonal reality. In this sense, it is a powerful domain of knowledge that is a source of counterfactual reasoning, hypothesis generation, mental time travel, mental problem-solving rehearsal, among other possibilities, that accompanies us in the life cycle.

Imagination (including images[1]) in the processing of information and construction of intersubjective meaning in Homo Sapiens is ubiquitous and unique. Imagination has been a fundamental capacity in the evolution of our species, as it has allowed us to simulate "possible scenarios" and deal with various possible

[1] It is pointed out that we can have mental images without imagination, for example, the case of Flashbacks (see Nanay, 2021; Kind, 2001) and "Earworm" in patients with musical obsessions (Nanay, 2023).

Á. Quiñones Bergeret, *Evolutionary Case Formulation*,
https://doi.org/10.1007/978-3-031-67412-9_8

difficulties (examples: interpersonal conflicts, climate changes, agricultural damage, etc.) and anticipate and plan viable, creative, and adaptive solutions.

We know that imagination is an alternative to present perception and includes the following: mental images of things that may or may not exist, counterfactual conjectures, alternative pasts, daydreaming, fantasizing, problem simulation ("what would happen if") and solutions, mental simulation of other minds, mental rehearsal (Markman et al., 2009).

Mental images Kosslyn et al. (2001) define as:

> Mental imagery occurs when perceptual information is accessed from memory, giving rise to the experience of 'seeing with the mind's eye', 'hearing with the mind's ear' and so on. By contrast, perception occurs when information is registered directly from the senses. Mental images need not result simply from the recall of previously perceived objects or events; they can also be created by combining and modifying stored perceptual information in novel ways. (p. 635)

It is to emphasize in this definition, that mental imagination is the simulation or recreation of the perceptual experience through sensory modalities, and therefore they describe mental images as the experience of "seeing with the eyes of the mind," "listening with the ear of the mind." In addition, it is understood as the experience of perception in the absence of coincident sensory information and can be from the past or hypothetical future and can be voluntary (deliberately generated) or involuntary (that comes to mind spontaneously) (Kosslyn et al., 2006).

Our *mental life* is unthinkable without the possibilities of imagination because it allows us the "mental journey" in time ("what could happen in the imagined future") and imagination and narrative are linked since any narrative experience requires imagination. In fact, mental images are essential for our mental life, because they allow us to remember the past, simulate and experience the future, and make decisions (Schacter et al., 2012).

Images can be used to access autobiographical memories and their associated emotions. It has been shown that people with episodic memory deficits have difficulties in imagining specific events that could happen in their personal future (Addis et al., 2008, 2009; D'Argembeau et al., 2008; Tulving, 1985; Williams et al., 1996). In this sense, the imaging[2] is essential for our mental life and narrative identity, as they allow us to hypothetically flow in time, simulate multiple existential scenarios, and anticipate possible conflict resolutions.

One aspect to highlight is the evidence that informs us about the difference in properties of the images. A property that stands out is that visual images compared to verbal thoughts of similar content, it is clear that visual mental images are classified as more "real" by people and have a greater impact on behavior (Mathews et al., 2013).

And finally, mental images with their imaginative combination and their possible maladaptive dynamics occur in different psychological disorders (Depression,

[2]The relationship between autonoetic consciousness, episodic memory, and imagination is not developed as it is not the purpose of this book, but I do highlight the relationship and increasing understanding that is being developed thanks to research.

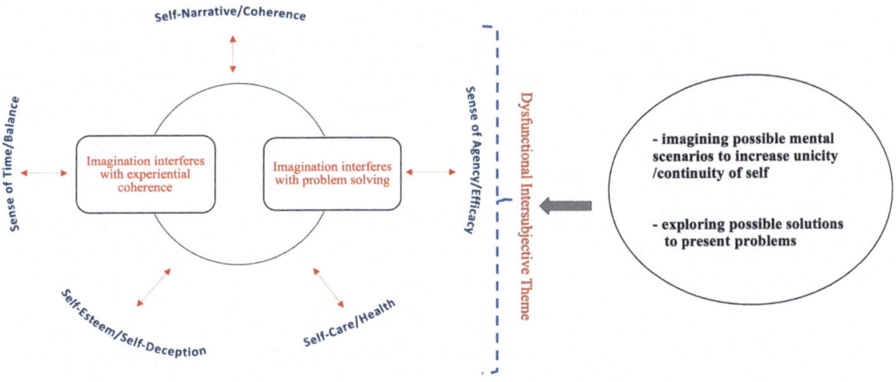

Fig. 8.1 Imagination

Post-traumatic Stress, Social Phobia, Agoraphobia, Obsessive Compulsive Disorder, Bipolar Disorder, Body Dysmorphic Disorder, Addictions, Schizophrenia, etc.) as indicated by the scientific literature (Holmes et al., 2005, 2008a, b, 2019; Clark et al., 2006; Day et al., 2004; Kilts et al., 2001; Osman et al., 2004; Ehlers & Clark, 2000).

The exploration of imagination in psychotherapy is fundamental because it plays a very relevant role for adaptation (example: contribute to effective planning in time management to prepare the doctoral thesis) or maladaptation (example: terrifying images after a traumatic event).

As a conceptualization of the intersubjective knowledge domain "Imagination," two parsimonious axes of analysis are proposed in the case formulation model and are called *Imagination interferes with experiential coherence* (Intrusive images, Flash-backs, Hotspots, Suicidal Flashforwards, Images as emotional amplification) and *Imagination interferes with problem solving* (alteration in mental simulation, deficit of imagination directed at personal goals, imagination is a source of self-sabotage).

In Fig. 8.1 the synergy is observed especially with the Self System which is essential to formulate the patient's psychological problems in an idiographic way.

8.1 Imagination Interferes with Experiential Coherence

The ***intrusive mental images*** are a transdiagnostic process (Brewin et al., 2010) and the perspective from which patients experience intrusions varies according to disorders. In psychopathology, mental images have various impacts on verbal cognitions and emotions (Holmes & Mathews, 2005). Similarly, intrusive images often appear associated with negative emotions and are a focus of observation in the information processing and construction of meaning in various psychological problems.

The origin of intrusive images is a sort of continuum, that is, it can originate from memories of past adverse experiences or even entirely or partially from the imagination. A prototypical example of severe adverse experiences is post-traumatic stress disorder (Grey & Holmes, 2008) which is often associated with traumatic experiences. At the other extreme, in depression and bipolarity, the present images can be a flash-forward of imagined future suicide attempts (Holmes et al., 2008a, b, 2019).

Obsessive Images Obsessive images are formed against one's own will and being egodystonic is a common characteristic in obsessive compulsive disorder. Rachman and de Silva states:

> An obsession is a recurrent, unwanted, intrusive, unacceptable, and persistent thought, image, or impulse. Obsessions are not voluntarily produced, but are experienced as events that interrupt one's attention. The affected person recognizes that these thoughts are his own, and are not introduced or controlled by some outer force or other person. (2009, p. 3)

Padmal de Silva (1986) and Stanley Rachman (1997, 2007) synthesized the clinical evidence that obsessive images[3] often encapsulate fears of aggressive violence, illness and death, sexual perversion, blasphemy, disaster, and madness.

For therapists, it is interesting to know that obsessive images usually involve seeing scenes from a "field" perspective, that is, from one's own point of view (Speckens et al., 2007b). In contrast, patients with social phobia or agoraphobia tend to see scenes from an observer's perspective (Hackmann et al., 1998, 2000; Wells & Papageorgiou, 1999).

Flashbacks Images can "hijack" attention strongly through their highly absorbing nature and figure in "the now." The distinctive and essential feature of post-traumatic stress disorder is the recurrent sensory images of a past trauma, known as "flashbacks" (Brewin & Holmes, 2003; Ehlers & Clark, 2000; Speckens et al., 2007a). Flashbacks are vivid, threatening memories that repeat with intense emotion and a sense of "now," as if the event were happening in the "here and now," against the person's will. In addition, there is agreement on the importance of "hotspots" in the memory of traumatic events (Foa & Rothbaum, 1998; Ehlers & Clark, 2000). The term ***hotspot*** is used to refer to the specific parts of the trauma memory that cause higher levels of emotional distress and are associated with intense re-experiencing of aspects of the trauma (Grey & Holmes, 2008). Holmes et al. (2005) have defined hotspots as "moments of peak emotional distress during the event" (p. 3).

Suicidal Flash-Forwards Images play a role in suicide attempts[4] and such mental images related to suicide are called suicidal flash-forwards. It is known that the act of imagining future events is causal in predicting behavior (Libby et al., 2007) and

---

[3] The word "obsession" is derived from the Latin "*obsidere*," to be besieged.

[4] Most suicidal behaviors occur in depressive states. We know that once a person has experienced a suicidal ideation or behavior during a depressive episode, it is more likely to experience it again if the depression recurs (see Williams et al., 2006).

imagined events are also rated as more likely than those that have not been imagined (Pham & Taylor, 1999). Therefore, images increase the likelihood of completing a suicidal act "planning a future suicide attempt" (Holmes et al., 2008a, b; Crane et al., 2012).

In line with the assumption that mental images drive behavior, it is relevant for therapists to ask about images associated with distress and suicide explicitly and not just stay with verbal thoughts. In other words, suicidal flash-forwards should always be evaluated as the scientific literature establishes them as a possible marker of suicide risk (Ng et al., 2016).

Holmes et al. (2008a, b) have shown that broader consideration of mental images about suicide can provide benefits for patients. Today, the characteristics of these images and their possible modifications through different modalities are considered, for example relating in a different way to the images (example: mindfulness) or incorporating new meanings (examples: slow-motion technique, rescript the image, etc.). Therefore, suicide prevention should explore suicidal flash-forward images and modify their meaning and reduce their appeal. When applicable (Hales et al., 2011).

Emotional Amplification Experimental research suggests that images more easily elicit an emotional response than verbal information of the same content (Holmes & Mathews, 2005).

Mental images can contribute to emotional dysfunction in a variety of psychological disorders (Holmes et al., 2016, 2019; Holmes and Mathews, 2010). In this sense, it is relevant to point out that images have perceptual correspondence with sensory experience, "as if" it were actually happening. That is, it is possible that images directly provoke emotion in a way similar to real perception. Namely, Sirigu and Duhamed (2001) show that the neural representation of visual images is similar to that produced by real visual performance.

Research on mental images has shown that it has a powerful effect on increasing both negative and positive emotions and is considered an "**emotional amplifier**" of mood, particularly exacerbating manic and depressive states, as well as anxiety in bipolar disorder (Holmes et al., 2008a, b). In bipolarity, it has been proposed that intrusive vivid mental images can act as an "emotional amplifier" that drives both anxiety and mood escalation in bipolar disorder (Holmes et al., 2019; Ng et al., 2016). For example, people with bipolar disorder who experience intrusive mental images of "vivid, negative, and future-related" characteristics, provoke anxiety. Such negative mental images, in a number of cases, amplify the expectation of a future threat, causing anxiety or low mood and thus contributing to mood instability. Finally, there is experimental evidence that mental images can act as an amplifier of positive mood in the bipolar-manic spectrum (O'Donnell et al., 2018).

8.2 Imagination Interferes with Problem-Solving

The ***mental simulation*** is the ability to construct mental models to imagine what could happen (Johnson-Laird, 2012) and it is considered essential in human cognition as very sharply established by Kenneth Craik[5] in the mid-twentieth century (Craik, 1943). In addition, research indicates that it is involved in physical reasoning (Battaglia et al., 2013), counterfactual reasoning (Harris, 2000), memory (Schacter et al., 2012), "scene construction" (Hassabis et al., 2007), language (Zwaan, 1999), among others.

Imagination as ***mental simulation*** ("sequence of images", "movie") is a dimension of our adaptive mental processing that allows us to anticipate possible scenarios and have various possibilities of adaptive anticipation, contextual adjustments, and problem-solving (example: coping, emotional intensity, interpersonal problems, etc.).

Holmes et al. (2008b) have shown that people with high dysphoria content have a poorer ability to imagine positive future events compared to people with low dysphoria content. Likewise, depression has been associated with the elevated occurrence of emotionally distressing mental images and the reduced occurrence of positive mental images (Holmes et al., 2016). In contrast, patients with bipolar disorder also have very vivid negative future images, and it is known that vividness is greater in those with a more unstable course of the disorder (Hales et al., 2011). Unlike major depression, bipolar disorder is associated with the presence of vivid positive images at times of high positive affect (Ivins et al., 2014), and in the case of hypomania, it is associated with intrusive positive images about future events and a greater tendency to use images in everyday life (Gregory et al., 2010; Meyer et al., 2011).

Maladaptive mental simulation can take many forms. For illustration, people with depression are more likely to have a negative bias and make a negative interpretation (example: a friend does not return their phone call in the day and they suspect that they are being intentionally ignored). One of the ways used to resolve the ambiguity inherent in all kinds of everyday situations is to imagine the outcome, which allows us to mentally simulate the resolution of the situation. Given the powerful effect that images have on emotion, this strategy will be especially harmful ("toxic") when accompanied by a negative interpretation (Holmes & Mathews, 2005). That is, it is argued that by imagining a negative outcome and then mentally simulating it (for example, seeing oneself alone, abandoned and rejected, after a friend did not return the morning phone call), it is likely to exacerbate the depressed mood to a greater degree than if the person were to think verbally about the same event.

Deficit of Imagination Directed at Personal Goals Imagination plays a relevant role in the establishment and achievement of personal goals since it is an important

[5] Kenneth Craik (1943) argued that the brain constructs mental models that support inference through mental simulations in a way analogous to how engineers use simulations for the prediction and manipulation of complex physical systems (for example: analyzing the stability and failure modes of a bridge design before construction).

component of different personal narratives (Quiñones, 2024). Likewise, it is noteworthy that imagination plays a relevant role in Jonathan Evans' decision-making theory (2007), which states:

> … many decisions are made automatically, perhaps in response to past learning. Consequential decision making, however, requires hypothetical thinking about future events. We need somehow to imagine the world (in relevant respects) as it might be following a particular choice or action under our control and decide how much we would like to be living in it. Moreover, we need to conduct a set of thought experiments for each possible action and compare their evaluations. (p. 12)

Clinical experience and research tell us that it is important to explore personal goals and all the possible aspects that it implies for people in their life cycle (Watkins, 2011). In the field of research, the work done by Gamble et al. (2021) stands out. They conducted the first detailed evaluation of goal-directed imagination and its links with mental health with an idiographic approach, making the 153 adult participants imagine scenes related to their own goals, among other particularities. They state in their conclusion:

> …when it comes to the *simulation* mode of prospection, depression seems to feature not only a deficit in positive future imagery but also an increase in negative future imagery (…). Emotional valence of simulations also appears to be particularly important in the context of predicting mental health over time, given that the Negativity factor was a strong predictor of later well-being even after covarying for baseline mental health. That imagining a more negative (and less positive) future actually predicts later decreased well-being underscores this process as a potential intervention target. (p. 15)

This research is relevant as it clearly shows that little is known about individual differences in goal-directed imagination.

Imagination as a source of ***self-sabotage***. This dimension of interference from less to more is observed in various clinical cases and is not always investigated (example: social phobia) by psychotherapists who prioritize verbal communication. Self-sabotage can take many forms and generate all kinds of intersubjective tensions (example: not taking timely measures because we imagine that we will make mistakes or not going to the doctor for fear of having bad news about our health, etc.).

As psychotherapists, we know from experience and research that there are individual differences in people's information processing, that is, "visualizers versus verbalizers" (Kozhevnikov et al., 2002; Dadds et al., 2004), as well as differences in how they mentally imagine the past (Sheldon et al., 2017) and in the richness and types of images that they use to represent visual information (Pearson & Kosslyn, 2015). Therefore, it is relevant that psychotherapists explore and clearly ask about mental images in the psychotherapeutic process (sensory qualities: visual, olfactory, taste, tactile, movement; and descriptions in terms of content, vividness, clarity, color, shapes, etc.) since our conscious cognition can occur in mental images or in verbal-linguistic formats. In other words, problematic images may be much more frequent than is often assumed and may go unnoticed and, therefore, inviting patients to report on whether their cognition involves mental images can provide essential information about the nature of the experience of distress psychological and psychological dysregulation and provide information for a proper intervention.

To conclude, I will pause for a moment on imagination and its importance for narrative scaling. The following is a transcript of a brief dialogue that shows its relevance:

Patient	Sometimes I feel like a stone in a beautiful garden.
Therapist	Can you tell me a little more about what the image of that stone might represent?
Patient	It represents that I feel "on the margins of people".
Therapist	Can you say something more?
Patient	I am destined to remain alone... without true companionship.
Therapist	Does the stone represent you in these last months?
Patient	Yes.
Therapist	And particularly your depressed mood?
Patient	Yes, and now I care about being alone. And I don't know if I will get out of this state of great pain...

Next, the second-order intersubjective knowledge domain "**IMAGINATION**" is shown in the case formulation protocol (the Case Formulation-Assessment and the Case Formulation-Intervention are shown in Boxes 8.1 and 8.2).

Box 8.1: Case Formulation—Assessment

[IMAGINATION] Indicate and weigh what processes contribute to distress and/or psychological dysregulation: ....

....

(mark presence: x)

Imagination interferes with experiential coherence:

Intrusive mental images ☐ Flashbacks ☐ Hotspots ☐

Suicidal flashforwards ☐ Images as an emotional amplifier ☐

Others: ____________________

Describe: ....

....

Imagination interferes with problem solving:

Alteration in mental simulation ☐

Deficit of imagination directed to personal goals ☐

Imagination is a source of self-sabotage ☐

Others: ____________________

Describe: ....

....

Psychological Distress						Psychological Well-Being
High	Moderate	Mild	Neutral	Mild	Moderate	High
-3	-2	-1	0	1	2	3
Psychological Dysregulation						Psychological Regulation
High	Moderate	Mild	Neutral	Mild	Moderate	High
-3	-2	-1	0	1	2	3

Box 8.2: Case Formulation—Intervention

IMAGINATION: Change indicators

(mark presence: x)

Interferes with experiential coherence: Progress ☐ Regulation ☐

Describe: ....

....

Interferes with troubleshooting: Progress ☐ Regulation ☐

Describe: ....

....

- Functional Narrative Indicator: Integrates knowledge about imagination ☐
- Behavioral Change Indicator: Incorporates changes ☐

Psychological Distress						Psychological Well-Being
High	Moderate	Mild	Neutral	Mild	Moderate	High
-3	-2	-1	0	1	2	3
Psychological Dysregulation						Psychological Regulation
High	Moderate	Mild	Neutral	Mild	Moderate	High
-3	-2	-1	0	1	2	3

Observations:

....

....

References

Abraham, A. (2020). Surveying the imagination landscape. In A. Abraham (Ed.), *The Cambridge handbook of the imagination* (pp. 1–10). Cambridge University Press. https://doi.org/10.1017/9781108580298.001

Addis, D. R., Wong, A. T., & Schacter, D. L. (2008). Age-related changes in the episodic simulation of future events. *Psychological Science, 19*(1), 33–41. https://doi.org/10.1111/j.1467-9280.2008.02043.x

Addis, D. R., Pan, L., Vu, M. A., Laiser, N., & Schacter, D. L. (2009). Constructive episodic simulation of the future and the past: Distinct subsystems of a core brain network mediate imagining and remembering. *Neuropsychologia, 47*(11), 2222–2238. https://doi.org/10.1016/j.neuropsychologia.2008.10.026

Battaglia, P. W., Hamrick, J. B., & Tenenbaum, J. B. (2013). Simulation as an engine of physical scene understanding. *PANAS, 110*, 18327–18332.

Brewin, C. R., & Holmes, E. A. (2003). Psychological theories of posttraumatic stress disorder. *Clinical Psychology Review, 23*(3), 339–376. https://doi.org/10.1016/s0272-7358(03)00033-3

Brewin, C. R., Gregory, J. D., Lipton, M., & Burgess, N. (2010). Intrusive images in psychological disorders: Characteristics, neural mechanisms, and treatment implications. *Psychological Review, 117*(1), 210–232. https://doi.org/10.1037/a0018113

Clark, D. M., Ehlers, A., Hackmann, A., McManus, F., Fennell, M., Grey, N., Waddington, L., & Wild, J. (2006). Cognitive therapy versus exposure and applied relaxation in social phobia: A randomized controlled trial. *Journal of Consulting and Clinical Psychology, 74*(3), 568–578.

Craik, K. (1943). *The nature of explanation*. Cambridge University Press.

Crane, C., Shah, D., Barnhofer, T., & Holmes, E. A. (2012). Suicidal imagery in a previously depressed community sample. *Clinical Psychology & Psychotherapy, 19*(1), 57–69. https://doi.org/10.1002/cpp.741

Dadds, M. R., Hawes, D., Schaefer, B., & Vaka, K. (2004). Individual differences in imagery and reports of aversions. *Memory, 12*(4), 462–466.

D'Argembeau, A., Raffard, S., & Van der Linden, M. (2008). Remembering the past and imagining the future in schizophrenia. *Journal of Abnormal Psychology, 117*(1), 247–251. https://doi.org/10.1037/0021-843X.117.1.247

Day, S. J., Holmes, E. A., & Hackmann, A. (2004). Occurrence of imagery and its link with early memories in agoraphobia. *Memory (Hove, England), 12*(4), 416–427. https://doi.org/10.1080/09658210444000034

de Silva, P. (1986). Obsessional–compulsive imagery. *Behaviour Research and Therapy, 24*(3), 333–350. https://doi.org/10.1016/0005-7967(86)90193-2

Dietrich, A., & Zakka, S. (2020). Capturing the imagination. In A. Abraham (Ed.), *The Cambridge handbook of the imagination* (pp. 132–142). Cambridge University Press.

Ehlers, A., & Clark, D. M. (2000). A cognitive model of posttraumatic stress disorder. *Behaviour Research and Therapy, 38*(4), 319–345. https://doi.org/10.1016/s0005-7967(99)00123-0

Evans, J. S. B. T. (2007). *Hypothetical thinking: Dual processes in reasoning and judgement*. Psychology Press.

Foa, E. B., & Rothbaum, B. O. (1998). *Treating the trauma of rape*. Guilford Press.

Gamble, B., Tippett, L. J., Moreau, D., & Addis, D. R. (2021). The futures we want: How goal-directed imagination relates to mental health. *Clinical Psychological Science, 9*(4), 732–751. https://doi.org/10.1177/2167702620986096

Gregory, J. D., Brewin, C. R., Mansell, W., & Donaldson, C. (2010). Intrusive memories and images in bipolar disorder. *Behaviour Research and Therapy, 48*(7), 698–703.

Grey, N., & Holmes, E. A. (2008). "Hotspots" in trauma memories in the treatment of post-traumatic stress disorder: a replication. *Memory (Hove, England), 16*(7), 788–796. https://doi.org/10.1080/09658210802266446

Hackmann, A., Surawy, C., & Clark, D. M. (1998). Seeing yourself through others' eyes: A study of spontaneously occurring images in social phobia. *Behavioural and Cognitive Psychotherapy, 26*, 3–12.

Hackmann, A., Clark, D. M., & McManus, F. (2000). Recurrent images and early memories in social phobia. *Behaviour Research and Therapy, 38*(6), 601–610. https://doi.org/10.1016/s0005-7967(99)00161-8

Hales, S. A., Deeprose, C., Goodwin, G. M., & Holmes, E. A. (2011). Cognitions in bipolar affective disorder and unipolar depression: Imagining suicide. *Bipolar Disorders, 13*(7–8), 651–661.

Harris, P. L. (2000). *The work of the imagination*. Blackwell Publishing.

Hassabis, D., Kumaran, D., & Maguire, E. A. (2007). Using imagination to understand the neural basis of episodic memory. *The Journal of Neuroscience: The Official Journal of the Society for Neuroscience, 27*(52), 14365–14374. https://doi.org/10.1523/JNEUROSCI.4549-07.2007

Holmes, E. A., & Mathews, A. (2005). Mental imagery and emotion: A special relationship? *Emotion (Washington, D.C.), 5*(4), 489–497. https://doi.org/10.1037/1528-3542.5.4.489

Holmes, E. A., & Mathews, A. (2010). Mental imagery in emotion and emotional disorders. *Clinical Psychology Review, 30*(3), 349–362. https://doi.org/10.1016/j.cpr.2010.01.001

Holmes, E. A., Grey, N., & Young, K. A. (2005). Intrusive images and "hot- spots" of trauma memories in posttraumatic stress disorder: An exploratory investigation of emotions and cognitive themes. *Journal of Behavior Therapy and Experimental Psychiatry, 36*(1), 3–17. https://doi.org/10.1016/j.jbtep.2004.11

Holmes, E. A., Geddes, J. R., Colom, F., & Goodwin, G. M. (2008a). Mental imagery as an emotional amplifier: Application to bipolar disorder. *Behaviour Research and Therapy, 46*(12), 1251–1258. https://doi.org/10.1016/j.brat.2008.09.005

Holmes, E. A., Lang, T. J., Moulds, M. L., & Steele, A. M. (2008b). Prospective and positive mental imagery deficits in dysphoria. *Behaviour Research and Therapy, 46*(8), 976–981. https://doi.org/10.1016/j.brat.2008.04.009

Holmes, E. A., Blackwell, S. E., Burnett Heyes, S., Renner, F., & Raes, F. (2016). Mental imagery in depression: Phenomenology, potential mechanisms, and treatment implications. *Annual Review of Clinical Psychology., 12*, 249.

Holmes, E. A., Hales, S. A., Young, K., & Di Simplicio, M. (2019). *Imagery-based cognitive therapy for bipolar disorder and mood instability*. The Guilford Press.

Irish, M. (2020). On the interaction between episodic and semantic representations – Constructing a unified account of imagination. In A. Abraham (Ed.), *The Cambridge handbook of the imagination* (pp. 447–465). Cambridge University Press. https://doi.org/10.1017/9781108580298.027

Ivins, A., Di Simplicio, M., Close, H., Goodwin, G. M., & Holmes, E. (2014). Mental imagery in bipolar affective disorder versus unipolar depression: Investigating cognitions at times of 'positive' mood. *Journal of Affective Disorders, 166*(100), 234–242. https://doi.org/10.1016/j.jad.2014.05.007

Johnson-Laird, P. N. (2012). Inference with mental models. In K. J. Holyoak & R. G. Morrison (Eds.), *The Oxford Handbook of thinking and reasoning* (pp. 134–145). Oxford University Press.

Kilts, C. D., Schweitzer, J. B., Quinn, C. K., Gross, R. E., Faber, T. L., Muhammad, F., Ely, T. D., Hoffman, J. M., & Drexler, K. P. (2001). Neural activity related to drug craving in cocaine addiction. *Archives of General Psychiatry, 58*(4), 334–341.

Kind, A. (2001). Putting the image back in imagination. *Philosophy and Phenomenological Research, 62*(1), 85–110.

Kosslyn, S. M., Ganis, G., & Thompson, W. L. (2001). Neural foundations of imagery. *Nature Reviews: Neuroscience, 2*(9), 635–642.

Kosslyn, S. M., Thompson, W. L., & Ganis, G. (2006). *The case for mental imagery*. Oxford University Press.

Kozhevnikov, M., Hegarty, M., & Mayer, R. E. (2002). Revising the visualizer/verbalizer dimension: Evidence for two types of visualizers. *Cognition and Instruction, 20*, 47–77.

Libby, L. K., Shaeffer, E. M., Eibach, R. P., & Slemmer, J. A. (2007). Picture yourself at the polls: Visual perspective in mental imagery affects self-perception and behavior. *Psychological Science, 18*(3), 199–203. https://doi.org/10.1111/j.1467-9280.2007.01872.x

Markman, K. D., Klein, W. M., & Suhr, J. A. (2009). Overview. In K. D. Markman, W. M. Klein, & J. A. Suhr (Eds.), *Handbook of imagination and mental simulation* (pp. vii–xvi). Taylor & Francis.

Mathews, A., Ridgeway, V., & Holmes, E. A. (2013). Feels like the real thing: Imagery is both more realistic and emotional than verbal thought. *Cognition and Emotion, 27*(2), 217–229. https://doi.org/10.1080/02699931.2012.698252

Meyer, T. D., Finucane, L., & Jordan, G. (2011). Is risk for mania associated with increased daydreaming as a form of mental imagery? *Journal of Affective Disorders, 135*(1–3), 380–383. https://doi.org/10.1016/j.jad.2011.06.002

Nanay, B. (2021). Imagining one experience to be another. *Synthese, 199*(5–6), 13977–13991. https://doi.org/10.1007/s11229-021-03406-y

Nanay, B. (2023). *Mental imagery: Philosophy, psychology, neuroscience*. Oxford University Press.

Ng, R. M., Di Simplicio, M., & Holmes, E. A. (2016). Mental imagery and bipolar disorders: Introducing scope for psychological treatment development? *International Journal of Social Psychiatry, 62*(2), 110e113. https://doi.org/10.1177/0020764015615905

O'Donnell, C., Di Simplicio, M., Brown, R., Holmes, E. A., & Burnett Heyes, S. (2018). The role of mental imagery in mood amplification: An investigation across subclinical features of bipolar disorders. *Cortex, 105*, 104–117. https://doi.org/10.1016/j.cortex.2017.08.010

Osman, S., Cooper, M., Hackmann, A., & Veale, D. (2004). Spontaneously occurring images and early memories in people with body dysmorphic disorder. *Memory, 12*(4), 428–436.

Pearson, J., & Kosslyn, S. M. (2015). The heterogeneity of mental representation: Ending the imagery debate. *Proceedings of the National Academy of Sciences of the United States of America, 112*(33), 10089–10092. https://doi.org/10.1073/pnas.1504933112

Pham, L. B., & Taylor, S. E. (1999). From thought to action: Effects if process – Versus outcome based mental simulations on performance. *Personality and Social Psychology Bulletin, 25*, 250–260.

Quiñones, A. (2024). Perspectiva evolucionista para la formulación de caso: Un sistema abierto. In Á. Quiñones & C. Caro (Eds.), *Formulación de Caso: Hacia una Psicoterapia de precisión* (pp. 107–135). UNED editorial.

Rachman, S. (1997). A cognitive theory of obsessions. *Behaviour Research and Therapy, 35*, 793–802.

Rachman, S. (2007). Unwanted intrusive images in obsessive compulsive disorders. *Journal of Behavior Therapy and Experimental Psychiatry, 38*(4), 402–410. https://doi.org/10.1016/j.jbtep.2007.10.008

Rachman, S., & de Silva, P. (2009). *Obsessive – Compulsive disorder: the facts* (4th ed.). Oxford University Press.

Schacter, D. L., Addis, D. R., Hassabis, D., Martin, V. C., Spreng, R. N., & Szpunar, K. K. (2012). The future of memory: Remembering, imagining, and the brain. *Neuron, 76*(4), 677–694. https://doi.org/10.1016/j.neuron.2012.11.001

Sheldon, S., Amaral, R., & Levine, B. (2017). Individual differences in visual imagery determine how event information is remembered. *Memory (Hove, England), 25*(3), 360–369. https://doi.org/10.1080/09658211.2016.1178777

Sirigu, A., & Duhamel, J. R. (2001). Motor and visual imagery as two complementary but neurally dissociable mental processes. *Journal of Cognitive Neuroscience, 13*(7), 910–919. https://doi.org/10.1162/089892901753165827

Speckens, A. E., Ehlers, A., Hackmann, A., Ruths, F. A., & Clark, D. M. (2007a). Intrusive memories and rumination in patients with post-traumatic stress disorder: A phenomenological comparison. *Memory (Hove, England), 15*(3), 249–257. https://doi.org/10.1080/09658210701256449

Speckens, A. E., Hackmann, A., Ehlers, A., & Cuthbert, B. (2007b). Imagery special issue: Intrusive images and memories of earlier adverse events in patients with obsessive compulsive disorder. *Journal of Behavior Therapy and Experimental Psychiatry, 38*(4), 411–422. https://doi.org/10.1016/j.jbtep.2007.09.004

Tulving, E. (1985). Memory and consciousness. *Canadian Psychology, 26*, 1–12.

Watkins, E. (2011). Dysregulation in level of goal and action identification across psychological disorders. *Clinical Psychology Review, 31*(2), 260–278. https://doi.org/10.1016/j.cpr.2010.05.004

Wells, A., & Papageorgiou, C. (1999). The observer perspective: Biased imagery in social phobia, agoraphobia, and blood injury phobia. *Behaviour Research and Therapy, 37*, 653–658.

Williams, J. M. G., Ellis, N. C., Tyers, C., Healy, H., Rose, G., & MacLeod, A. K. (1996). The specificity of autobiographical memory and imageability of the future. *Memory & Cognition, 24*, 116–125.

Williams, J. M., Crane, C., Barnhofer, T., Van der Does, A. J., & Segal, Z. V. (2006). Recurrence of suicidal ideation across depressive episodes. *Journal of Affective Disorders, 91*(2–3), 189–194. https://doi.org/10.1016/j.jad.2006.01.002

Zwaan, R. A. (1999). Situation models: The mental leap into imagined worlds. *Current Direction in Psychological Science, 8*, 15–18.

Chapter 9
Corporeality

The bodily sense[1] in Homo Sapiens is omnipresent, intersubjective, and always active. In this sense, the body is fundamental to human existence from birth to death as it enables the processing of contextually situated information and the active generation of intersubjective meaning. In other words, "we are body in action" and only this dynamic of action ends at the moment we die.

There are many interesting questions, and some are as follows: What does the body imply for our mind? What does the body imply for our identity? What does it really mean to experience one's own body as the origin of contextually situated knowledge? How do we explain that the sense of corporeality is altered? How relevant are interoceptive skills for mental health? etc.

From the tradition of *embodied cognition*, cognitive processes are understood to be anchored in the perception and actions of the body. That is, the body is the medium for the elaboration of perceptions, cognitions, and affects, and for constructing the sense of the Self (the sensation that my body belongs to me). Particularly the "body in the mind" is part of the structure of the cognitive system that allows us to understand the world as an ordered and meaningful whole.

From anthropology, what Clifford Geertz maintained is instructive:

> We live, as one writer has neatly put it, in an "information gap." Between what our body tells us and what we have to know in order to function, there is a vacuum we must fill ourselves, and we fill it with information (or misinformation) provided by our culture. The boundary between what is innately controlled and what is culturally controlled in human behavior is an ill-defined and wavering one. Some things are, for all intents and purposes, entirely controlled intrinsically: we need no more cultural guidance to learn how to breathe than a fish needs to learn how to swim. (1973, p. 51)

We cannot continue to leave the human body out of our vision of the human being, and therefore, a psychopathology without considering what makes it possible is a

[1] Corporeality and the dimension of the Self System "Self-Care/Health" have a close relationship (see Self-Care/Health).

Á. Quiñones Bergeret, *Evolutionary Case Formulation*,
https://doi.org/10.1007/978-3-031-67412-9_9

paradox. A typical example is the conception of rationality in the West that Mark Johnson (1991, 1993, 2007) criticizes. He asserts that rationality is a fundamental concept of Western philosophy, and it cannot be understood as a property of a mind isolated from the conditions of our corporeality. Paraphrasing Johnson (2007), there would not be a separate and independent body and mind, but two aspects of the same bodily process (motor program, sensation, emotion, action, thought, language, meaning, culture). The mind is not only shaped by the body, but it is born from it, as a conceptual structure that shapes human reality in the sense that it makes it meaningful.

The concept of "Embodied Cognition" represents not only an extension of the concept of cognition so far, but also opens the possibility for the development of new forms of intervention in psychotherapy.

Our body is what allows us to live and gradually build our representations and integrations of information at different levels of complexity. Thus, the primary place of self-awareness is the body itself. As Thomas Fuchs maintains "... basal consciousness or the 'feeling of being alive' emerges deep inside the organism, only to then direct itself, on higher levels of integration, towards the environment" (Fuchs, 2018, p. vi).

Gallagher concludes in his book "How the Body Shapes the Mind" maintaining that embodiment affects not only perception, emotion, and action, but also higher mental processes:

> I hope that I have furthered the realization that nothing about human experience remains untouched by human embodiment: from the basic perceptual and emotional processes that are already at work in infancy, to a sophisticated interaction with other people; from the acquisition and creative use of language, to higher cognitive faculties involving judgment and metaphor; from the exercise of free will in intentional action, to the creation of cultural artifacts that provide for further human affordances. (2005, p. 247)

In relation to narrative and embodiment, the dominant idea that the self has an "abstract" narrative base without embodiment has recently generated much controversy, and many therapists know from the practice of working with the body, that an excess of narrative is not useful since not everything is narratable (e.g., an epileptic seizure, etc.). There are researchers who tend to reduce the importance of the narrative (Lamarque, 2004; Tammi, 2006) or reject it completely (Strawson, 2004). It is argued that there is a certain degree of consensus that individuality cannot be understood as a purely abstract narrative construction, but that the narrative must be based on a more fundamental notion of an embodied self. Lastly, I highlight what Zahavi (2007) argues about the narrative individuality presupposing an embodied level of the pre-reflective individuality as a condition for the narrative to be attributed to a subject of experience.

On the other hand, perceiving, feeling, and representing oneself bodily in intersubjectivity with acceptance give us a sense of possibility and healthy limit. The intersubjective knowledge domain that I call "Corporeality" refers to the bodily sense in the structuring of the continuity of experience in an intersubjective/cultural matrix.

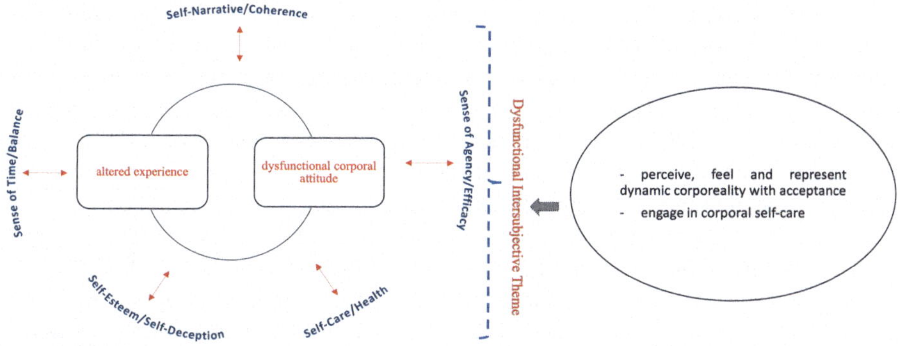

Fig. 9.1 Corporeality

Now, alterations of corporeality inform us of problems in the continuity of the "construction of experience." I will only briefly touch on research on body image, interoceptive skills, and somatic symptoms that are common in patient care, but it is understood that there are many types of deregulations in the field of corporeality.

As a conceptualization of the intersubjective knowledge domain "corporeality," two parsimonious axes of analysis are proposed in the case formulation model and are called: *altered experience* (lack of energy/fatigue, somatosensory amplification, Alterations of interoception, alteration of mental representation of the body) and *dysfunctional body attitude* (inadequate body self-care, sleep deficiency).

In Fig. 9.1 the synergy is observed especially with the *Self System* which is essential to formulate in an idiographic way the psychological problems of the patient.

9.1 Altered Experience

First, the **"lack of energy/fatigue"** stands out. It is also known as asthenia. It is very present in both psychiatric and psychological clinics.

Fatigue is defined as a physiological state of reduced mental or physical capacity, which can develop as a result of sleep loss or prolonged wakefulness, circadian rhythm disruption, or increased workload (Van Dongen et al., 2003).

Within the general population, women experience fatigue more frequently than men and highlight life events such as childbirth, menopause, and socially imposed roles can grant a unique vulnerability (Cahill, 1999).

Fatigue is an omnipresent symptom that is experienced in a wide range of physical and psychiatric diseases (Robinson et al., 2015). It is well known that fatigue is particularly prominent in Major Depressive Disorder, where it has been reported in 95% of patients (McIntyre et al., 2002) and is associated with a negative impact on daily functioning, health, and quality of life (Duncan, 1996; Lock et al., 2018; Tylee, 2000).

Secondly, body image. In this regard, it is evaluated whether there is a **deficit in clear and real mental representation of the body**. Cash (2004) maintains body image refers to the multifaceted psychological experience of representation especially but not exclusively of physical appearance. The aspect of diversity is relevant and is also observed in the statement: "Body image is body images" (Cash & Pruzinsky, 1990, pp. xi). In summary, it encompasses self-perceptions and personal attitudes related to the body, including thoughts, beliefs, feelings, and behaviors.

To illustrate, the theoretical conceptualization of positive body image has been extensively researched since the late twentieth century (Cash, 2004, 2011; Cash & Pruzinsky, 1990). Various facets of positive body image include maintaining favorable opinions of the body, respecting the body, feeling gratitude towards the body, rejecting society's ideals of attractiveness, the internal positivity that influences external behavior, and a broad conceptualization of beauty. Likewise, theoretical models of positive body image show that body appreciation is positively associated with different indicators of well-being that include self-esteem, proactive coping, optimism, positive affect, self-compassion, life satisfaction, and subjective happiness. Body appreciation is also positively associated with intuitive eating, sexual functioning, and physical activity when the motive for exercise is not based on appearance (See Halliwell, 2015).

Thirdly, the development and presentation of somatic symptoms is a complex and diverse phenomenon observed in the clinic. The scientific literature indicates that it is unlikely to be fully explained by any individual cognitive or perceptual characteristic. Likewise, research to date suggests a role for somatosensory amplification and attribution styles, and it is likely that other factors such as emotional state, alexithymia, culture, and neuroticism/negative affectivity also have an impact (Barsky, 1992; Barsky et al., 1988; Duddu et al., 2006; Nakao & Barsky, 2007).

As an example, I mention a construct that has been well studied and is known as ***somatosensory amplification***. It is a useful construct in the evaluation of somatization and in the conceptualization of psychosomatic illness (Nakao & Takeuchi, 2018; Taycan et al., 2017; Nakao et al., 2002; Nakao & Barsky, 2007). Barsky uses this term to refer to the tendency to experience somatic sensations as intense, harmful, and disruptive (Barsky et al., 1988). It includes the individual's disposition to focus on unpleasant physiological and psychological sensations, and to consider them as pathological rather than normal (Barsky et al., 1988; Barsky, 1992). The three components of somatosensory amplification have been described as follows: (1) body hyper-vigilance that involves increased self-control and greater attention to unpleasant body sensations, (2) tendency to select and focus on certain relatively weak or infrequent sensations, and (3) tendency to value visceral and somatic sensations as abnormal and symptomatic of some disease. Finally, it should be added that somatosensory amplification is observed in hypochondria in particular (Jones et al., 2004; Nakao et al., 2002) and, at the same time, constitutes a nonspecific symptom of other mental disorders that present with physical symptoms (example: depressive spectrum) and is also observed in the exposure to transient stressful life events, among others.

From the history of the development of cognitive-behavioral therapies, third-wave procedures stand out, which have already integrated concepts such as mindfulness, acceptance, and emotional work, and all of them can be developed and complemented with embodiment techniques (see Hauke et al., 2016) that focus on the processes of *bottom-up* that refer to:

1. Placing the focus on sensory perceptions, physical perceptions and impulses, movements of the whole body and parts of the body in space.
2. Observing this to gain access to the roots of emotional experience, to automatic impulses and prelinguistic processes.
3. Inducing sensory-motor input (examples: tension, movement, conscious breathing, etc.) so that automated processes and categorizations become conscious.
4. Focusing on the here and now (time perspective) provides the possibility to escape from the "memory trance," resist automatisms and try alternatives.

Fourthly, the ***interoception***. Interoceptive processing occurs in all major biological systems involved in maintaining body homeostasis, including cardiovascular, pulmonary, gastrointestinal, genitourinary, nociceptive, chemosensory, osmotic, thermoregulatory, visceral, immune, and autonomic (see Khalsa et al., 2018). We know from research that interoception is not a simple process, but has several facets since the act of detecting, interpreting, and integrating information about the state of the body's internal systems can be related to different elements such as interoceptive attention, detection, discrimination, accuracy, insight, sensitivity, and self-report. In addition, most of the interoceptive processes occur outside the realm of consciousness (Khalsa et al., 2018; Vaitl, 1996).

Interoception has been defined in various ways since Sherrington introduced the term in his fundamental work (Khalsa & Lapidus, 2016; Ceunen et al., 2016; Sherrington, 1906). For example, it has been defined by Vaitl (1996) as a general concept, which includes two different forms of perception: proprioception and visceroception. Garfinkel et al. (2015) define it as the detection and representation of signals related to the internal state of the body. Khalsa and Lapidus (2016) argue that interoception refers to the process of how the brain detects and integrates signals that originate inside the body, providing a moment-to-moment mapping of the body's internal landscape. Couto et al. (2013), the processing of body signals from the viscera and somatic tissues. In summary, the important thing is to highlight that interoceptive skills are relevant both for constituting our sense of self, and for adequate mental and physical health.

On the other hand, Garfinkel and Critchley (2013) propose three facets of interoceptive processing, namely:

1. The *interoceptive accuracy* can be defined as the ability to detect signals from within the body, such as heartbeats, hunger, or thirst.
2. The *interoceptive sensitivity* is the ability to report on body states such as muscle tension, hunger, and dry mouth. Examples are "my mouth is dry," "I feel muscle tension in my arms," or "how strong is my heart beating," etc.

3. The *interoceptive awareness* is the awareness of the body states, but more than that, it is a measure of the confidence in the accuracy of interoceptive states.

Other researchers (Herbert et al., 2012; Pollatos et al., 2016) propose a fourth dimension, which is the *emotional evaluation of interoceptive signals*. Examples are "How anxious have you been feeling your heartbeats?", How anxious have you been feeling your stomach bloated?, etc.

In particular, we are interested in *interoceptive regulation*. Farb et al. (2015) define it *as how well a person can match an interoceptive signal with their desired state*. Research studies in cognitive and affective neuroscience indicate that depression, anxiety, post-traumatic stress disorder, substance abuse disorders, eating disorders, and psychosomatic pain often go hand in hand with a lack of ability to detect, evaluate, or respond to interoceptive signals (Goodkind et al., 2015). Similarly, there is a growing body of evidence supporting the importance of such interoceptive dysregulation in these disorders (Farb et al., 2015; Barret & Simmons, 2015; Harshaw, 2015; Paulus & Stewart, 2014; Domschke et al., 2010).

9.2 Dysfunctional Body Attitude

First, the *body care that every person presents* implies a dimension that can be visualized from adequate to inadequate. The *self-care* is relevant for a healthy, vital, and psychologically regulated life. Practicing healthy lifestyle habits is essential to maintain a healthy body, cultivate well-being, and prevent all kinds of health problems. In this sense, there are several key aspects to consider: healthy eating, hygiene, exercise, hydration, avoiding sedentary lifestyle, self-awareness of the physical condition (examples: knowing your body mass index -BMI-, cholesterol level, blood pressure, and getting health check-ups timely, etc.).

Second, sleep is essential for the optimal functioning of the human being (Cirelli & Tononi, 2008). We know that poor sleep quality (sleep and body deficiency) affects people in many ways (example: the brain does not function optimally), but an essential aspect is that our body does not fully recover and has consequences for daytime performance. Negative consequences of poor sleep are many. Some examples are the following: it can produce a higher than normal blood sugar concentration, chronic pain, difficulty maintaining a healthy balance between the hormones that make you feel hungry (ghrelin) and full (leptin), high blood pressure, etc.

I will only briefly focus on fatigue to clarify the complexity of this possibility of psychological dysregulation that is observed in clinical cases. In this sense, what Pastier et al. (2022) point out in a study with 495 adults who completed an online survey about energy and fatigue traits, as well as sleep quality, is relevant:

> …that participants who reported poor sleep quality also reported higher trait physical and mental fatigue but not lower trait mental and physical energy. Similarly, state fatigue (i.e., current mood) was associated with worse sleep quality, but state energy was not. (p. 378)

The point is that therapists should be attentive to many consequences of sleep quality and its relationship with body dynamics. Similarly, the possible synergistic contributions of the interaction of sleep and body dynamics to the dysfunctional intersubjective issues that patients idiosyncratically present.

Next, the second-order intersubjective knowledge domain "**CORPOREALITY**" is shown in the case formulation protocol (the Case Formulation-Evaluation and the Case Formulation-Intervention are shown in Boxes 9.1 and 9.2).

Box 9.1: Case Formulation—Evaluation

[**CORPOREALITY**] Indicate and weigh what processes contribute to discomfort and/or psychological dysregulation: ……………………………………………………………………………

……………………………………………………………………………………………………

(mark presence: x)

Altered experience:

Lack of energy/fatigue ☐ Somatosensory amplification ☐

Interoception disturbances ☐ Alteration of mental representation of the body ☐

Others: ____________________

Describe: ……………………………………………………………………………………

……………………………………………………………………………………………………

Dysfunctional body attitude:

Insufficient body self-care ☐ Consequences of sleep on the body ☐

Others: ____________________

Describe: ……………………………………………………………………………………

……………………………………………………………………………………………………

Psychological Distress						Psychological Well-Being
High	Moderate	Mild	Neutral	Mild	Moderate	High
-3	-2	-1	0	1	2	3
Psychological Dysregulation						Psychological Regulation
High	Moderate	Mild	Neutral	Mild	Moderate	High
-3	-2	-1	0	1	2	3

Box 9.2: Case Formulation—Intervention

CORPOREALITY: Indicators of change

(mark presence: x)

Altered experience: Progress ☐ Regulation ☐

Describe: ....

....

Dysfunctional body attitude: Progress ☐ Regulation ☐

Describe: ....

....

- Functional Narrative Indicator: Integrates knowledge about corporeality ☐

- Behavioral Change Indicator: Incorporates changes ☐

Psychological Distress						Psychological Well-Being
High	Moderate	Mild	Neutral	Mild	Moderate	High
-3	-2	-1	0	1	2	3
Psychological Dysregulation						Psychological Regulation
High	Moderate	Mild	Neutral	Mild	Moderate	High
-3	-2	-1	0	1	2	3

Observations: ....

....

References

Barrett, L. F., & Simmons, W. K. (2015). Interoceptive predictions in the brain. *Nature Reviews. Neuroscience, 16*(7), 419–429. https://doi.org/10.1038/nrn3950

Barsky, A. J. (1992). Amplification, somatization, and the somatoform disorders. *Psychosomatics, 33*(1), 28–34. https://doi.org/10.1016/S0033-3182(92)72018-0

Barsky, A. J., Goodson, J. D., Lane, R. S., & Cleary, P. D. (1988). The amplification of somatic symptoms. *Psychosomatic Medicine, 50*(5), 510–519. https://doi.org/10.1097/00006842-198809000-00007

Cahill, C. A. (1999). Differential diagnosis of fatigue in women. *Journal of Obstetric, Gynecologic, and Neonatal Nursing: JOGNN, 28*(1), 81–86. https://doi.org/10.1111/j.1552-6909.1999.tb01968.x

Cash, T. F. (2004). Body image: Past, present, and future. *Body Image, 1*(1), 1–5. https://doi.org/10.1016/S1740-1445(03)00011-1

Cash, T. F. (2011). Crucial considerations in the assessment of body image. In T. F. Cash & L. Smolak (Eds.), *Body image: A handbook of science, practice, and prevention* (pp. 129–137). Guilford Press.

Cash, T. F., & Pruzinsky, T. (Eds.). (1990). *Body images: Development, deviance, and change*. The Guilford Press.

Ceunen, E., Vlaeyen, J. W. S., & Van Diest, I. (2016). On the origin of interoception. *Frontiers in Psychology, 7*, 743. https://doi.org/10.3389/fpsyg.2016.00743

Cirelli, C., & Tononi, G. (2008). Is sleep essential? *PLoS Biology, 6*(8), e216. https://doi.org/10.1371/journal.pbio.0060216

Couto, B., Salles, A., Sedeno, L., Peradejordi, M., Barttfeld, P., Canales-Johnson, A., et al. (2013). The man who feels two hearts: The different pathways of interoception. *Social Cognitive Affect Neuroscience, 9*, 1253–1260.

Domschke, K., Stevens, S., Pfleiderer, B., & Gerlach, A. L. (2010). Interoceptive sensitivity in anxiety and anxiety disorders: An overview and integration of neurobiological findings. *Clinical Psychology Review, 30*(1), 1–11. https://doi.org/10.1016/j.cpr.2009.08.008

Duddu, V., Isaac, M. K., & Chaturvedi, S. K. (2006). Somatization, somatosensory amplification, attribution styles and illness behaviour: A review. *International Review of Psychiatry (Abingdon, England), 18*(1), 25–33. https://doi.org/10.1080/09540260500466790

Duncan, K. D. (1996). Fatigue: The predictors relevant to depression. *Dissertation Abstracts International. Section B Sciences and Engineering, 56*(10-B), 5763.

Farb, N., Daubenmier, J., Price, C. J., Gard, T., Kerr, C., Dunn, B. D., Klein, A. C., Paulus, M. P., & Mehling, W. E. (2015). Interoception, contemplative practice, and health. *Frontiers in Psychology, 6*, 763. https://doi.org/10.3389/fpsyg.2015.00763

Fuchs, T. (2018). *Ecology of the brain. The phenomenology and biology of the embodied mind*. Oxford University Press.

Gallagher, S. (2005). *How the body shapes the mind*. Oxford University Press.

Garfinkel, S. N., & Critchley, H. D. (2013). Interoception, emotion and brain: New insights link internal physiology to social behaviour. Commentary on: "Anterior insular cortex mediates bodily sensibility and social anxiety" by Terasawa et al. (2012). *Social Cognitive and Affective Neuroscience, 8*(3), 231–234. https://doi.org/10.1093/scan/nss140

Garfinkel, S. N., Critchley, H. D., & Pollatos, O. (2015). The interoceptive system: Implications for cognition, emotion, and health. In J. T. Cacioppo, L. G. Tassinary, & G. G. Berntson (Eds.), *Handbook of psychophysiology* (4th ed.). Cambridge University Press.

Geertz, C. (1973). *The interpretation of cultures: Selected essays*. Basic Books.

Goodkind, M., Eickhoff, S. B., Oathes, D. J., Jiang, Y., Chang, A., Jones-Hagata, L. B., Ortega, B. N., Zaiko, Y. V., Roach, E. L., Korgaonkar, M. S., Grieve, S. M., Galatzer-Levy, I., Fox, P. T., & Etkin, A. (2015). Identification of a common neurobiological substrate for mental illness. *JAMA Psychiatry, 72*(4), 305–315. https://doi.org/10.1001/jamapsychiatry.2014.2206

Halliwell, E. (2015). Future directions for positive body image research. *Body Image*. https://doi.org/10.1016/j.bodyim.2015.03.003

Harshaw, C. (2015). Interoceptive dysfunction: Toward an integrated framework for understanding somatic and affective disturbance in depression. *Psychological Bulletin, 141*(2), 311–363. https://doi.org/10.1037/a0038101

Hauke, G., Lohr, C., & Pietrzak, T. (2016). Moving the mind: Embodied cognition in cognitive behavioral therapy (CBT). *European Psychotherapy, 13*, 154–178.

Herbert, B. M., Herbert, C., Pollatos, O., Weimer, K., Enck, P., Sauer, H., & Zipfel, S. (2012). Effects of short-term food deprivation on interoceptive awareness, feelings and autonomic cardiac activity. *Biological Psychology, 89*(1), 71–79. https://doi.org/10.1016/j.biopsycho.2011.09.004

Johnson, M. (1991). *El cuerpo en la mente. Fundamentos corporales del significado, la imaginación y la razón*. Debate.

Johnson, M. (1993). *Moral imagination. Implications of cognitive science for ethics*. The University of Chicago Press.

Johnson, M. (2007). *The meaning of the body: Aesthetics of human understanding*. The University of Chicago Press.
Jones, M. P., Schettler, A., Olden, K., & Crowell, M. D. (2004). Alexithymia and somatosensory amplification in functional dyspepsia. *Psychosomatics, 45*, 508–516.
Khalsa, S. S., & Lapidus, R. C. (2016). Can Interoception improve the pragmatic search for biomarkers in psychiatry? *Frontiers in Psychiatry, 7*, 121. https://doi.org/10.3389/fpsyt.2016.00121
Khalsa, S. S., Adolphs, R., Cameron, O. G., Critchley, H. D., Davenport, P. W., Feinstein, J. S., Feusner, J. D., Garfinkel, S. N., Lane, R. D., Mehling, W. E., Meuret, A. E., Nemeroff, C. B., Oppenheimer, S., Petzschner, F. H., Pollatos, O., Rhudy, J. L., Schramm, L. P., Simmons, W. K., Stein, M. B., Stephan, K. E., et al. (2018). Interoception and mental health: A roadmap. *Biological Psychiatry, 3*(6), 501–513. https://doi.org/10.1016/j.bpsc.2017.12.004
Lamarque, P. (2004). On not expecting too much from narrative. *Mind & Language, 19*(4), 393–408. https://doi.org/10.1111/j.0268-1064.2004.00265.x
Lock, A. M., Bonetti, D. L., & Campbell, A. D. K. (2018). The psychological and physiological health effects of fatigue. *Occupational Medicine (Oxford, England), 68*(8), 502–511. https://doi.org/10.1093/occmed/kqy109
McIntyre, R., Kennedy, S., Bagby, R. M., & Bakish, D. (2002). Assessing full remission. *Journal of Psychiatry & Neuroscience, 27*(4), 235–239.
Nakao, M., & Barsky, A. J. (2007). Clinical application of somatosensory amplification in psychosomatic medicine. *BioPsychoSocial Medicine, 1*, 17. https://doi.org/10.1186/1751-0759-1-17
Nakao, M., & Takeuchi, T. (2018). Alexithymia and somatosensory amplification link perceived psychosocial stress and somatic symptoms in outpatients with psychosomatic illness. *Journal of Clinical Medicine, 7*(5), 112. https://doi.org/10.3390/jcm7050112
Nakao, M., Barsky, A. J., Kumano, H., & Kuboki, T. (2002). Relationship between somatosensory amplification and alexithymia in a Japanese psychosomatic clinic. *Psychosomatics, 43*(1), 55–60. https://doi.org/10.1176/appi.psy.43.1.55
Pastier, N., Jansen, E., & Boolani, A. (2022). Sleep quality in relation to trait energy and fatigue: An exploratory study of healthy young adults. *Sleep Science (Sao Paulo, Brazil), 15*(Spec 2), 375–379. https://doi.org/10.5935/1984-0063.20210002
Paulus, M. P., & Stewart, J. L. (2014). Interoception and drug addiction. *Neuropharmacology, 76*, 342–350. https://doi.org/10.1016/j.neuropharm.2013.07.002
Pollatos, O., Herbert, B. M., Mai, S., & Kammer, T. (2016). Changes in interoceptive processes following brain stimulation. *Philosophical Transactions of the Royal Society B: Biological Sciences, 371*, 20160016. https://doi.org/10.1098/rstb.2016.0016
Robinson, R. L., Stephenson, J. J., Dennehy, E. B., Grabner, M., Faries, D., Palli, S. R., & Swindle, R. W. (2015). The importance of unresolved fatigue in depression: Costs and comorbidities. *Psychosomatics, 56*(3), 274–285. https://doi.org/10.1016/j.psym.2014.08.003
Sherrington, C. S. (1906). *The integrative action of the nervous system*. Yale University Press.
Strawson, G. (2004). Against narrativity. *Ratio, 17*, 428–452. https://doi.org/10.1111/j.1467-9329.2004.00264.x
Tammi, P. (2006). Against narrative ("a boring story"). Partial answers. *Journal of Literature and the History of Ideas, 4*(2), 19–40. https://doi.org/10.1353/pan.0.0113
Taycan, O., Özdemir, A., & Erdoğan Taycan, S. (2017). Alexithymia and somatization in depressed patients: The role of the type of somatic symptom attribution. *Noro Psikiyatri Arsivi, 54*(2), 99–104. https://doi.org/10.5152/npa.2016.12385
Tylee, A. (2000). Depression in Europe: Experience from the DEPRES II survey. Depression research in European society. *European Neuropsychopharmacology, 10*(Suppl 4), S445–S448. https://doi.org/10.1016/s0924-977x(00)00112-7
Vaitl, D. (1996). Interoception. *Biological Psychology, 42*(1–2), 1–27. https://doi.org/10.1016/0301-0511(95)05144-9

Van Dongen, H. P., Maislin, G., Mullington, J. M., & Dinges, D. F. (2003). The cumulative cost of additional wakefulness: Dose-response effects on neurobehavioral functions and sleep physiology from chronic sleep restriction and total sleep deprivation. *Sleep, 26*(2), 117–129. https://doi.org/10.1093/sleep/26.2.117

Zahavi, D. (2007). Self and other: The limits of narrative understanding. *Royal Institute of Philosophy Supplement, 60*, 179–202.

Chapter 10
Sexuality

Sexuality and sex are among the main determinants of people's health and well-being. As a framework, the World Health Organization (WHO) defines *sexuality*:

> Sexuality is a central aspect of being human throughout life and encompasses sex, gender identities and roles, sexual orientation, eroticism, pleasure, intimacy, and reproduction. Sexuality is experienced and expressed in thoughts, fantasies, desires, beliefs, attitudes, values, behaviors, practices, roles, and relationships. While sexuality can include all of these dimensions, not all of them are always experienced or expressed. Sexuality is influenced by the interaction of biological, psychological, social, economic, political, cultural, ethical, legal, historical, religious, and spiritual factors. (WHO, 2017, p. 3)

And it defines sexual health:

> Sexual health is a state of physical, emotional, mental, and social well-being in relation to sexuality; it is not merely the absence of disease, dysfunction, or infirmity. Sexual health requires a positive and respectful approach to sexuality and sexual relationships, as well as the possibility of having pleasurable and safe sexual experiences, free of coercion, discrimination, and violence. For sexual health to be attained and maintained, the sexual rights of all persons must be respected, protected, and fulfilled. (WHO, 2017, p. 3)

Evolution shows that our sexual dimension is ubiquitous. In other words, "sexual desire is always present"[1] and it could not be otherwise, as we are wired for it.

Sex is a driving force that brings two people into intimate contact. Both people may have nothing in common, except mutual sexual interest, and nothing more. Similarly, sex is related to erotic feelings, experiences, desires, fantasies, sexual thoughts, sexual impulses, feelings of attraction, etc., but there is also the possibility that it can be the main topic of the relationship in their lives and, often, can lead to the formation of a stable relationship and a family. It is important to highlight the importance of marriage in people's quality of life, as we know that when marriages

[1] Jaak Panksepp proposes that one of the seven affective systems is sexual desire. The one that presents brain areas and neurotransmitter systems involved (see Panksepp, 1998, 2004, 2005).

Á. Quiñones Bergeret, *Evolutionary Case Formulation*,
https://doi.org/10.1007/978-3-031-67412-9_10

are stable and satisfying, spouses are healthier (Robles et al., 2014), happier (Be et al., 2013) and live more time (Whisman et al., 2018).

The functions of sexual behavior,[2] in addition to the basic function of reproduction, have others: affirmation of masculinity or femininity, reinforcement or maintenance of self-esteem, exercise of power or dominance, uniting dyadic relationships and fostering intimacy, source of pleasure, reduction of tension, expression of hostility, risk-taking as a source of excitement and material gain (Bancroft, 2009).

As a context, we know from the scientific literature that the majority of empirical research studies on the sexual activities and relationships of men and women in adulthood have tended to focus on the negative dimensions of sexual activity, for example, physical deterioration, sexual dysfunction, and dissatisfaction (Sahithya & Kashyap, 2022; Karraker et al., 2011; Domoney 2009; Robles & Kingsberg, 2002). Similarly, sexual health and sexuality also require a greater positive focus (WHO, 2017) of research.

As a conceptualization of the intersubjective knowledge domain "sexuality," two parsimonious axes of analysis are proposed in the case formulation model and are called: *Sexual disconnection with partner* (absence of sexual interest, anxiety about sexual performance, deficient sexual communication, sexual dysfunction, sexual stress, unsatisfactory sexuality) and *Disconnection with others* (pornography abuse, sexual addiction, excessive masturbation).

In Fig. 10.1 the synergy is observed especially with the *Self System* which is essential to formulate in an idiographic way the psychological problems of the patient.

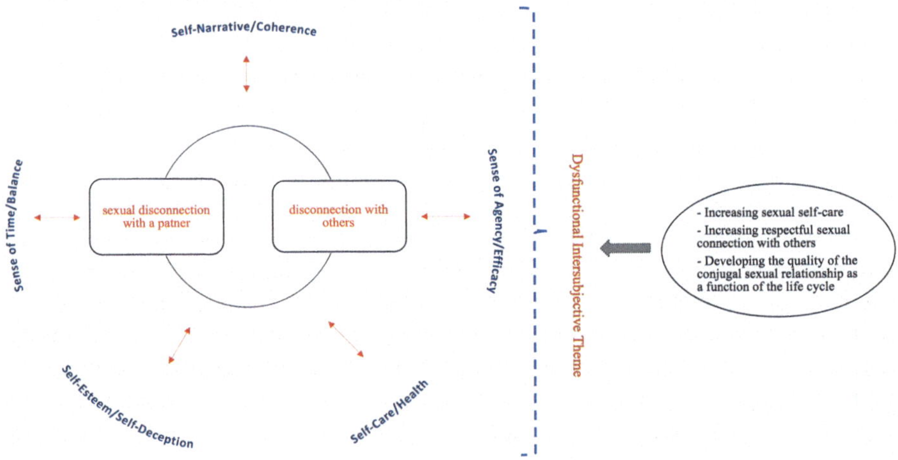

Fig. 10.1 Sexuality

[2] Many of the functions indicated are not peculiarly human and can be observed in the behavior of non-human primates.

10.1 Sexual Disconnection with the Partner

Couples have a common development that can be understood as a dimension from connection to disconnection. In this sense, there are many possibilities of behaviors of sexual disconnection with the partner that manifest in various ways.

In relation to *sexual dysfunction*, gender is fundamental. Firstly, the *female sexual dysfunction* is defined as a disorder in desire, arousal, orgasm, and/or pain during sexual intercourse, which generates personal stress and has an impact on quality of life and interpersonal relationships (Walton & Thorton, 2003). Secondly, the *male sexual dysfunction* in general terms includes erectile dysfunction, ejaculatory dysfunction, hypogonadism and low sexual desire, Peyronie's disease and other morphological alterations of the penis, and urinary incontinence associated with sexual function (Tal, 2017).

The *sexual satisfaction* is "as an affective response arising from one's subjective evaluation of the positive and negative dimensions associated with one's sexual relationship" (Lawrance & Byers, 1995, p. 268). It encompasses aspects of sexuality, such as the frequency of sexual intercourse (Schmiedeberg et al., 2017), sexual variety, and communication about sexuality (Frederick et al., 2017).

As therapists, we know that one aspect that is very relevant for a relationship to be healthy is the *sexual communication* about what each member of the heterosexual or homosexual couple likes and dislikes. In addition, the passage of time must be included, since progression through the life cycle generates different variations and changes (Tetley et al., 2016). Consequently, a conversation about tastes and changes/adjustments over the course of the life cycle is a fundamental requirement for a good sexual relationship to be maintained over time.

Today, the *sexual satisfaction* is positively associated with the quality and in some cases with the stability of the marital relationship in young adults, middle age, and the elderly (Bagherinia et al., 2024; Rausch & Rettenberger, 2021; Edwards & Booth, 1994; Yeh, et al., 2006; Delamater et al., 2008; Delamater & Moorman, 2007; Young et al., 1998). Regarding sexual satisfaction, it is worth briefly commenting on the research by Delamater et al. (2008). They used data on sexuality among men (n = 2156) and women (n = 1955) in the United States, with an age range of 62–67 years. The respondents reported having sex 1.7 times a month. Regression analyses were used to identify variables associated with sexual behavior and satisfaction. Measures of physical health, sexual functioning, psychological distress, and relationship satisfaction were included. The frequency of sexual activity was significantly predicted by reports that the partner lost interest in sex. Satisfaction with the sexual relationship was predicted by marital/relationship satisfaction and the frequency of sexual activity. The relevant point is that sexual expression remains a significant aspect of intimate relationships in the seventh decade of life. These findings are consistent with other research on sexuality among young and middle-aged adults, which also indicates that sexual frequency and sexual satisfaction are closely related (Young et al., 1998).

Problems with sexual satisfaction are considered an indicator of sexual health and are associated with individual well-being (WHO, 2010). The evidence shows that the majority of couples consider that their sexual satisfaction and that of their partners is an important aspect of their relationship (Byers, 2005; Byers & Rehman, 2014). In fact, the association of sexual satisfaction with overall relationship satisfaction and well-being is so strong that sexual satisfaction has been identified as the barometer of marital quality of life (See Sprecher et al., 2006). This suggests that sexual satisfaction can be best assessed from a dyadic perspective, that is, taking into account the experiences of both partners.

Studies also show that stress within the dyad, in the form of marital tension and conflict, covaries with lower sexual satisfaction and a higher likelihood of sexual dysfunction (Hurlbert et al., 2000). In this sense, the literature on coping points out that the *dyadic coping* perceived as support is related in Western couples with sexuality, romance, and passion, constructive conflict resolution and communication, shared meaning, and relationship stability (Bodenmann & Cina, 2005; Ledermann, et al., 2010; Vedes et al., 2013, 2016).

Predictors of sexual satisfaction include the state of the relationship, sexual activity, and mental health, among others.

First, being in a romantic relationship has been associated with sexual satisfaction in several studies (Byers & Rehman, 2014; Pedersen & Blekesaune, 2003). Pedersen and Blekesaune (2003) found that young adults who were married or in committed relationships reported greater sexual satisfaction compared to a group of uncommitted young people.

Second, the frequency of sexual activity. There is solid evidence of a relationship between a higher frequency of sexual intercourse and sexual satisfaction for both men and women (Costa & Brody, 2012). Sexual intercourse is more frequent in couple relationships, and sexual intercourse, in some cases, has been seen as a proxy for relationship satisfaction (McNulty et al., 2016). Interestingly, there is research by Trapnell et al. (1997) that showed that body dissatisfaction predicted a lower frequency of sexual intercourse, but research on sexual activity in relation to body image is still small.

Thirdly, mental health can be a significant confounding factor in the relationship between the body and sexual satisfaction. Research has consistently shown that mental health problems, such as depression and anxiety, are related to reduced sexual functioning and relationship factors that are detrimental to sexual satisfaction (del Mar Sánchez-Fuentes et al., 2014).

Considering a person's life cycle is essential for assessing sexuality. Numerous studies have identified a decrease in sexual interest and sexual activity in old age (Araujo et al., 2004; Dennerstein & Lehert, 2004; Hayes & Dennerstein, 2005; Laumann et al., 2005; Lindau et al., 2007; Nicolosi et al., 2006). This transition has been explained by biological factors, psychological factors, diseases, mental conditions, boredom with the relationship, and widowhood (DeLamater & Sill, 2005; Thienhaus, 1988). Currently, we consistently know that as we age, there are difficulties (Hinchliff et al., 2017) and decline in both men and women (Mitchell et al., 2013). In men, as a group, the relationship with age is relatively linear, although there is considerable individual variability, with some men showing an early decline, others later. In contrast, in women, the pattern is less linear, showing a more marked decrease in middle age and, subsequently, more gradual, and considerable variation among women (Bancroft, 2009). There is evidence that when one partner loses interest in sexual activity, both genders experience a decrease in sexual frequency, but women experience a greater decrease than men (DeLamater et al., 2008).

It is relevant to consider that most older adults report that sex is an integral part of their quality of life and a significant component of a satisfying relationship (Fisher et al., 2010). Therefore, therapists must value aging, as chronic disorders such as cardiovascular diseases, hypertension, diabetes, arthritis, and prostate disease have a negative effect on sexual functioning and response (DeLamater & Sill, 2005).

The *sexual dysfunction* is a very present problem and increasingly studied in the twenty-first century. Population research informs us that between 40% and 45% of adult women and between 20% and 30% of adult men worldwide suffer from at least one sexual dysfunction (Lewis et al., 2004). Sexual dysfunctions, a group of heterogeneous disorders, included in the DSM-V are: delayed ejaculation, erectile disorder, female orgasmic disorder, female sexual interest/arousal disorder, genito-pelvic pain/penetration disorder, male hypoactive sexual desire disorder, premature (early) ejaculation, substance/medication-induced sexual dysfunction, etc.

It is very interesting what Laurent and Simon (2009) show us in their review about abundant evidence of a relationship between worse mental health, in the case of depression and anxiety, and greater sexual dysfunction, particularly the loss of libido for both men and women.

Laurent and Simons (2009) point out "...the relationship between sexual dysfunction, depression, and anxiety is multifactorial, complex, and often bidirectional, implying that the causal path is not clear, with sexual and depressive or anxious symptoms often manifesting at the same time" (p.575).

For therapists, it is important to be aware that there is a lack of knowledge about the specific mechanisms that produce these types of disorders, for example, if one considers the religious values that can produce psychological adaptation and maladaptation. For many people, religion and sexuality are intimately intertwined, as virtually all religions try to regulate sexual behavior and promote values related to sexuality. In this sense, religious systems have been considered as powerful contexts for the formation of sexual identity, contexts with the potential to both affirm (Love et al., 2005) as to oppress (Jeffries et al., 2008; Rosario et al., 2006).

It has been reported that religious rigidity is associated with a deteriorated marital sexual functioning, which includes guilt, inhibition and lower levels of sexual interest, sexual activity, and responsiveness (Purcell, 1984). Positive associations have also been found between religiosity and marital satisfaction in different religious groups, such as Christians, Jews, Mormons, and Muslims (Marks, 2005); however, studies on sexuality and religion are scarce. For example, Kennedy and Whitlock (1997) surveyed 31 pastors of conservative evangelical denominations and found that although these pastors had conservative moral principles, they affirmed and promoted sexuality within marriage. According to these pastors, religion and sexuality were totally compatible in the marital relationship.

The *anxiety about sexual performance* is a frequent complaint, both in men and women. Prevalence data in the United States and Europe are high (Pyke, 2020). Relevant to this chapter is mentioning that there is a great debate, there are no proven psychotherapeutic treatments and no agreements on specific psychological mechanisms, but the generality that anxiety (evaluative component) is involved (Dèttore et al., 2013). In generic terms, the most used psychotherapeutic approaches for anxiety about sexual performance are cognitive, mindfulness, emotion-focused, behavioral, and couple approaches (Rowland et al., 2021).

10.2 Disconnection with Others

People have a sexual development with various possible trajectories, adaptive versus maladaptive.

The *Masturbation can be understood as a dimension*—adaptive sense as sexual self-knowledge and improvement of sexual functioning[3]—and in a maladaptive sense—when it becomes deregulation. Research tells us that the frequency of masturbation decreases somewhat in stable relationships and continues to be part of sexual expression (Hurlbert & Whittaker, 1991). Both for men and women, masturbation has been associated with sexual satisfaction by functioning as a complement to sex in a relationship (Coleman, 2002; Das, 2007) or as compensation for the lack of sex or satisfaction with sex in a couple (Das, 2007).

For women, masturbation has been related to body satisfaction by suggesting that it can be a way to explore the body and increase comfort, which gives women the possibility of learning what is sexually pleasurable (Bowman, 2013; Coleman, 2002). Deserves special attention, the work of Shulman and Horne (2003) found an association between a higher frequency of masturbation and body satisfaction in European and non-African American women. It is clear that there is still a lack of research on the association between the frequency of masturbation and body satisfaction in women.

In the case of men, masturbation has been widely studied, but many questions remain unanswered. An aspect that deserves special attention is the little research on masturbation in the context of lack of sexual desire (Gerressu et al., 2008; Kaestle & Allen, 2011; Lipsith et al., 2003). It has often been thought that masturbation is a product of sexual desire. However, a qualitative study indicates that men did not consider masturbation as necessarily sexual but described that it occurred when they were "bored" or "alone at home without a partner" (Janssen et al., 2008). This

[3] See especially: Kılıç Onar et al. (2020) and Kaestle and Allen (2011).

makes it possible to consider that masturbation sometimes can serve as a method of reducing anxiety and/or inhibiting sexual desire, it can be specific to the current partner and not be associated with a decrease in autoerotic activity as already argued (Nutter & Condron, 1985). It is worth noting that masturbation is a sexual behavior that is contemplated for to treat sexual dysfunctions, for example premature ejaculation (Ma et al., 2019).

Nowadays, the use of *pornography* is increasing in the digitalized society. Recent representative surveys show that in developed countries with unlimited access to the Internet, such as the United States and Australia, the majority of men (64–70%) and approximately a quarter/third (23–33%) of women use pornography (Grubbs et al., 2019; Rissel et al., 2017) and it is gradually being researched and understood (Miller et al., 2019; Dwulit & Rzymski, 2019).

In fact, a recent line of research is the impact of *pornography* on romantic relationships. The review conducted by Wright et al. (2017) highlights some common claims to many of the theoretical explanations on how pornography can negatively affect relationships: (a) pornography creates certain expectations of sexual relationships, shaping what is considered normative and desirable; (b) these expectations are not met by the sexual partners of the "real world"; (c) this incongruity between what is expected and what actually occurs within sexual relationships leads to sexual dissatisfaction; and (d) this sexual dissatisfaction negatively affects relationship satisfaction.

The *sex addiction* (also called hypersexuality or compulsive sexual behavior) is increasingly observed in psychotherapy consultations. It occurs when sexual behaviors become compulsive, intrusive sexual thoughts, uncontrollable presence to self-control sexuality and deterioration of relational life, among other characteristics. A significant prevalence study in the United States shows a general prevalence of 8.6% general and gender differences were 10.3% for men and 7.0% for women (Dickenson et al., 2018).

From a nomothetic point of view, it is known as sexual addiction disorder (ICD-11) and often presents with comorbid disorders such as mood disorders, substance use disorders, attention deficit hyperactivity disorder, and anxiety spectrum disorders. It is relevant that we do not have clarity about the mechanisms that produce this type of psychological problem and there are several proposed intervention models and it is not clear if sexual addiction is an addiction, an impulse control disorder or a compulsive disorder (Sahithya & Kashyap, 2022).

In the case formulation model, sexuality is an evolutionary domain of knowledge. Therefore, both the *sexual disconnection with the partner* and the *disconnection with others* must be understood in synergy with the second-order intersubjective knowledge domains and with the Self System.

Next, the second-order intersubjective knowledge domain "Sexuality" is shown in the case formulation protocol (the Case Formulation-Evaluation and the Case Formulation-Intervention are shown in Boxes 10.1 and 10.2).

Box 10.1: Case Formulation—Evaluation

[SEXUALITY] Indicate and weigh what processes contribute to discomfort and/or psychological deregulation: ....

....

(mark presence: x)

Sexual disconnection with a partner:

Absence of sexual interest ☐ Sexual performance anxiety ☐

Poor sexual communication ☐ Sexual dysfunction ☐

Sexual stress ☐ Unsatisfactory sexuality ☐

Others: ______________________________

Describe: ....

....

Disconnection with others:

Pornography abuse ☐ Sexual addiction ☐

Excessive masturbation ☐

Others: ______________________________

Describe: ....

....

Psychological Distress						Psychological Well-Being
High	Moderate	Mild	Neutral	Mild	Moderate	High
-3	-2	-1	0	1	2	3
Psychological Dysregulation						**Psychological Regulation**
High	Moderate	Mild	Neutral	Mild	Moderate	High
-3	-2	-1	0	1	2	3

Box 10.2: Case Formulation—Intervention

SEXUALITY: Indicators of change

(mark presence: X)

Sexual disconnection with a partner: Progress ☐ Regulation ☐

Describe: ....

....

Sexual disconnection with others: Progress ☐ Regulation ☐

Describe: ....

....

- Functional Narrative Indicator: Integrates knowledge about sexuality ☐

- Behavioral Change Indicator: Incorporates changes ☐

Psychological Distress				Psychological Well-Being		
High	Moderate	Mild	Neutral	Mild	Moderate	High
-3	-2	-1	0	1	2	3
Psychological Dysregulation				Psychological Regulation		
High	Moderate	Mild	Neutral	Mild	Moderate	High
-3	-2	-1	0	1	2	3

Observations: ....

....

References

Araujo, A. B., Mohr, B. A., & McKinlay, J. B. (2004). Changes in sexual function in middle-aged and older men: Longitudinal data from the Massachusetts male aging study. *Journal of the American Geriatrics Society, 52*(9), 1502–1509. https://doi.org/10.1111/j.0002-8614.2004.52413.x

Bagherinia, M., Dolatian, M., Mahmoodi, Z., Ozgoli, G., & Alavi Majd, H. (2024). Predictors of social intermediate factors associated with sexual quality of life of women: Systematic review and meta-analysis. *BMC Women's Health, 24*(1), 64. https://doi.org/10.1186/s12905-024-02899-2

Bancroft, J. (2009). *Human sexuality and its problems* (3rd ed.). Elsevier.

Be, D., Whisman, M. A., & Uebelacker, L. A. (2013). Prospective associations between marital adjustment and life satisfaction. *Personal Relationships, 20*(4), 728–739. https://doi.org/10.1111/pere.12011

Bodenmann, G., & Cina, A. (2005). Stress and coping among stable-satisfied, stable-distressed, and separated/divorced Swiss couples: A 5-year prospective longitudinal study. *Journal of Divorce & Remarriage, 44*(1–2), 71–89. https://doi.org/10.1300/J087v44n01_04

Bowman, C. P. (2013). Women's masturbation: Experiences of sexual empowerment in a primarily sex-positive sample. *Psychology of Women Quarterly, 38*, 363–378.

Byers, E. S. (2005). Relationship satisfaction and sexual satisfaction: A longitudinal study of individuals in long-term relationships. *Journal of Sex Research, 42*(2), 113–118. https://doi.org/10.1080/00224490509552264

Byers, E. S., & Rehman, U. S. (2014). Sexual well-being. In D. L. Tolman, L. M. Diamond, J. A. Bauermeister, W. H. George, J. G. Pfaus, & L. M. Ward (Eds.), *APA handbook of sexuality and psychology* (*Person-based approaches*) (Vol. 1, pp. 317–337). American Psychological Association.

Coleman, E. (2002). Masturbation as a means of achieving sexual health. *Journal of Psychology & Human Sexuality, 14*(2–3), 5–16. https://doi.org/10.1300/J056v14n02_02

Costa, R. M., & Brody, S. (2012). Sexual satisfaction, relationship satisfaction, and health are associated with greater frequency of penile-vaginal intercourse. *Archives of Sexual Behavior, 41*(1), 9–10. https://doi.org/10.1007/s10508-011-9847-9

Das, A. (2007). Masturbation in the United States. *Journal of Sex & Marital Therapy, 33*, 301–317.

del Mar Sánchez-Fuentes, M., Santos-Iglesias, P., & Sierra, J. C. (2014). A systematic review of sexual satisfaction. *International Journal of Clinical and Health Psychology, 14*(1), 67–75. https://doi.org/10.1016/S1697-2600(14)70038-9

DeLamater, J. D., & Moorman, S. M. (2007). Sexual behavior in later life. *Journal of Aging and Health, 19*, 921–945.

DeLamater, J. D., & Sill, M. (2005). Sexual desire in later life. *Journal of Sex Research, 42*(2), 138–149. https://doi.org/10.1080/00224490509552267

DeLamater, J., Hyde, J. S., & Fong, M. C. (2008). Sexual satisfaction in the seventh decade of life. *Journal of Sex & Marital Therapy, 34*(5), 439–454. https://doi.org/10.1080/00926230802156251

Dennerstein, L., & Lehert, P. (2004). Women's sexual functioning, life-style, mid-age, and menopause in 12 European countries. *Menopause, 11*, 778–785.

Dèttore, D., Pucciarelli, M., & Santarnecchi, E. (2013). Anxiety and female sexual functioning: An empirical study. *Journal of Sex & Marital Therapy, 39*(3), 216–240. https://doi.org/10.1080/0092623X.2011.606879

Dickenson, J. A., Gleason, N., Coleman, E., & Miner, M. H. (2018). Prevalence of distress associated with difficulty controlling sexual urges, feelings, and behaviors in the United States. *JAMA Network Open, 1*(7), e184468. https://doi.org/10.1001/jamanetworkopen.2018.4468

Domoney, C. (2009). Sexual function in women: What is normal? *International Urogynecology Journal and Pelvic Floor Dysfunction, 20*(Suppl 1), S9–S17. https://doi.org/10.1007/s00192-009-0841-x

Dwulit, A. D., & Rzymski, P. (2019). The potential associations of pornography use with sexual dysfunctions: An integrative literature review of observational studies. *Journal of Clinical Medicine, 8*, 914. https://doi.org/10.3390/jcm8070914

Edwards, J. N., & Booth, A. (1994). Sexuality, marriage, and Well-being: The middle years. In A. S. Rossi (Ed.), *The John D. And Catherine T. MacArthur Foundation series on mental health and development: Studies on successful midlife development. Sexuality across the life course* (pp. 233–259). University of Chicago Press.

Fisher, L., Anderson, G. O., Chapagain, M., Mentenegro, X., Smoot, J., & Takalkar, A. (2010). *Sex, romance, and relationships: AARP survey of midlife and older adults*. AARP Research. https://doi.org/10.26419/res.00063.001

Frederick, D. A., Lever, J., Gillespie, B. J., & Garcia, J. R. (2017). What keeps passion alive? Sexual satisfaction is associated with sexual communication, mood setting, sexual variety, oral sex, orgasm, and sex frequency in a National U.S. study. *Journal of Sex Research, 54*(2), 186–201. https://doi.org/10.1080/00224499.2015.1137854

Gerressu, M., Mercer, C. H., Graham, C. A., Wellings, K., & Johnson, A. M. (2008). Prevalence of masturbation and associated factors in a British national probability survey. *Archives of Sexual Behavior, 37*(2), 266–278. https://doi.org/10.1007/s10508-006-9123-6

Grubbs, J. B., Kraus, S. W., & Perry, S. L. (2019). Self-reported addiction to pornography in a nationally representative sample: The roles of use habits, religiousness, and moral incongruence. *Journal of Behavioral Addictions, 8*(1), 88–93. https://doi.org/10.1556/2006.7.2018.134

Hayes, R., & Dennerstein, L. (2005). The impact of aging on sexual function and sexual dysfunction in women: A review of population-based studies. *The Journal of Sexual Medicine, 2*(3), 317–330. https://doi.org/10.1111/j.1743-6109.2005.20356.x

Hinchliff, S., Tetley, J., Lee, D., & Nazroo, J. (2017). Older adults' experiences of sexual difficulties: Qualitative findings from the English longitudinal study on ageing (ELSA). *The Journal of Sex Research, 55*, 152. https://doi.org/10.1080/00224499.2016.1269308

Hurlbert, D. F., & Whittaker, K. E. (1991). The role of masturbation in marital and sexual satisfaction: A comparative study of female masturbators and nonmasturbators. *Journal of Sex Education and Therapy, 17*, 272–282.

Hurlbert, D. F., Apt, C., Hurlbert, M. K., & Pierce, A. P. (2000). Sexual compatibility and the sexual desire-motivation relation in females with hypoactive sexual desire disorder. *Behavior Modification, 24*(3), 325–347. https://doi.org/10.1177/0145445500243002

Janssen, E., McBride, K. R., Yarber, W., Hill, B. J., & Butler, S. M. (2008). Factors that influence sexual arousal in men: A focus group study. *Archives of Sexual Behavior, 37*(2), 252–265. https://doi.org/10.1007/s10508-007-9245-5

Jeffries, W. L., Dodge, B., & Sandfort, T. G. (2008). Religion and spirituality among bisexual black men in the USA. *Culture, Health & Sexuality, 10*(5), 463–477. https://doi.org/10.1080/13691050701877526

Kaestle, C. E., & Allen, K. R. (2011). The role of masturbation in healthy sexual development: Perception s of Young adults. *Archives of Sexual Behavior, 40*, 983–994. https://doi.org/10.1007/s10508-010-9722-0

Karraker, A., DeLamater, J., & Schwartz, C. R. (2011). Sexual frequency decline from midlife to later life. *The Journals of Gerontology: Series B: Psychological Sciences and Social Sciences, 66B*(4), 502–512. https://doi.org/10.1093/geronb/gbr058

Kennedy, P., & Whitlock, M. L. (1997). Therapeutic implications of conservative clergy views on sexuality: An empirical analysis. *Journal of Sex & Marital Therapy, 23*(2), 140–153.

Kılıç Onar, D., Armstrong, H., & Graham, C. A. (2020). What does research tell us about women's experiences, motives and perceptions of masturbation within a relationship context? A systematic review of qualitative studies. *Journal of Sex & Marital Therapy, 46*(7), 683–716. https://doi.org/10.1080/0092623X.2020.1781722

Laumann, E. O., Nicolosi, A., Glasser, D. B., Paik, A., Gingell, C., Moreira, E., Wang, T., & GSSAB Investigators' Group. (2005). Sexual problems among women and men aged 40-80 y: Prevalence and correlates identified in the global study of sexual attitudes and behaviors. *International Journal of Impotence Research, 17*(1), 39–57. https://doi.org/10.1038/sj.ijir.3901250

Laurent, S. M., & Simons, A. D. (2009). Sexual dysfunction in depression and anxiety: Conceptualizing sexual dysfunction as part of an internalizing dimension. *Clinical Psychology Review, 29*(7), 573–585. https://doi.org/10.1016/j.cpr.2009.06.007

Lawrance, K. A., & Byers, E. S. (1995). Sexual satisfaction in long-term heterosexual relationships: The interpersonal exchange model of sexual satisfaction. *Personal Relationships, 2*, 267–285.

Ledermann, T., Bodenmann, G., Gagliardi, S., Charvoz, L., Verardi, S., Rossier, J., et al. (2010). Psychometrics of the dyadic coping inventory in three language groups. *Swiss Journal of Psychology, 69*, 201–212.

Lewis, R. W., Fugl-Meyer, K. S., Bosch, R., Fugl-Meyer, A. R., Laumann, E. O., Lizza, E., & Martin-Morales, A. (2004). Epidemiology/risk factors of sexual dysfunction. *The Journal of Sexual Medicine, 1*(1), 35–39. https://doi.org/10.1111/j.1743-6109.2004.10106.x

Lindau, S. T., Schumm, L. P., Laumann, E. O., Levinson, W., O'Muircheartaigh, C. A., & Waite, L. J. (2007). A study of sexuality and health among older adults in the United States. *The New England Journal of Medicine, 357*(8), 762–774. https://doi.org/10.1056/NEJMoa067423

Lipsith, J., McCann, D., & Goldmeier, D. (2003). Male psychogenic sexual dysfunction: The role of masturbation. *Sex & Relationship Therapy, 18*, 447–471.

Love, P. G., Bock, M., Jannarone, A., & Richardson, P. (2005). Identity interaction: Exploring the spiritual experiences of lesbian and gay college students. *Journal of College Student Development, 46*(2), 193–209. https://doi.org/10.1353/csd.2005.0019

Ma, G. C., Zou, Z. J., Lai, Y. F., Zhang, X., & Zhang, Y. (2019). Regular penis-root masturbation, a novel behavioral therapy in the treatment of primary premature ejaculation. *Asian Journal of Andrology, 21*(6), 631–634. https://doi.org/10.4103/aja.aja_34_19

Marks, L. (2005). How does religion influence marriage? Christian, Jewish, Mormon, and Muslim perspectives. *Marriage & Family Review, 38*(1), 85–111. https://doi.org/10.1300/J002v38n01_07

McNulty, J. K., Wenner, C. A., & Fisher, T. D. (2016). Longitudinal associations among relationship satisfaction, sexual satisfaction, and frequency of sex in early marriage. *Archives of Sexual Behavior, 45*(1), 85–97. https://doi.org/10.1007/s10508-014-0444-6

Miller, D. J., McBain, K. A., Wendy, W. L., & Raggat, P. T. F. (2019). Pornography, preference for porn-like sex, masturbation, and men's sexual and relationship satisfaction. *Personal Relationship, 26*, 93–113.

Mitchell, K. R., Mercer, C. H., Ploubidis, G. B., Jones, K. G., Datta, J., Field, N., Copas, A. J., Tanton, C., Erens, B., Sonnenberg, P., Clifton, S., Macdowall, W., Phelps, A., Johnson, A. M., & Wellings, K. (2013). Sexual function in Britain: Findings from the third National Survey of sexual attitudes and lifestyles (Natsal-3). *Lancet (London, England), 382*(9907), 1817–1829. https://doi.org/10.1016/S0140-6736(13)62366-1

Nicolosi, A., Buvat, J., Glasser, D. B., Hartmann, U., Laumann, E. O., Gingell, C., & GSSAB Investigators' Group. (2006). Sexual behaviour, sexual dysfunctions and related help seeking patterns in middle-aged and elderly Europeans: The global study of sexual attitudes and behaviors. *World Journal of Urology, 24*(4), 423–428. https://doi.org/10.1007/s00345-006-0088-9

Nutter, D., & Condron, M. (1985). Sexual fantasy and activity patterns of males with inhibited sexual desire and males with erectile dysfunction versus normal controls. *Journal of Sex & Marital Therapy, 11*, 91–98.

Panksepp, J. (1998). *Affective neuroscience*. Oxford University Press.

Panksepp, J. (2004). *Textbook of biological psychiatry*. Wiley-Liss.

Panksepp, J. (2005). Affective consciousness: Core emotional feelings in animals and humans. *Consciousness and Cognition, 14*(1), 30–80. https://doi.org/10.1016/j.concog.2004.10.004

Pedersen, W., & Blekesaune, M. (2003). Sexual satisfaction in young adulthood: Cohabitation, committed dating or unattached life? *Acta Sociologica, 46*(3), 179–193. https://doi.org/10.1177/00016993030463001

Purcell, S. L. (1984). An empirical study of the relationship between religious orthodoxy (defined as religious rigidity and religious closed-mindedness) and marital sexual functioning (doctoral dissertation, Andrews University, 1984). *Dissertation Abstracts International, 45*, 1695A.

Pyke, R. E. (2020). Sexual performance anxiety. *Sexual Medicine Reviews, 8*(2), 183–190. https://doi.org/10.1016/j.sxmr.2019.07.001

Rausch, D., & Rettenberger, M. (2021). Predictors of sexual satisfaction in women: A systematic review. *Sexual Medicine Reviews, 9*(3), 365–380. https://doi.org/10.1016/j.sxmr.2021.01.001

Rissel, C., Richters, J., de Visser, R. O., McKee, A., Yeung, A., & Caruana, T. (2017). A profile of pornography users in Australia: Findings from the second Australian study of health and relationships. *Journal of Sex Research, 54*(2), 227–240. https://doi.org/10.1080/00224499.2016.1191597

Robles, T. F., & Kingsberg, S. A. (2002). The impact of aging on sexual function in women and their partners. *Archives of Sexual Behavior, 31*(5), 431–437. https://doi.org/10.1023/a:1019844209233

Robles, T. F., Slatcher, R. B., Trombello, J. M., & McGinn, M. M. (2014). Marital quality and health: A meta-analytic review. *Psychological Bulletin, 140*(1), 140–187. https://doi.org/10.1037/a0031859

Rosario, M., Yali, A. M., Hunter, J., & Gwadz, M. V. (2006). Religion and health among lesbian, gay, and bisexual youths: An empirical investigation and theoretical explanation. In A. M. Omoto & H. S. Kurtzman (Eds.), *Sexual orientation and mental health: Examining identity and development in lesbian, gay, and bisexual people* (pp. 117–140). American Psychological Association.

Rowland, D. L., Moyle, G., & Cooper, S. E. (2021). Remediation strategies for performance anxiety across sex, sport and stage: Identifying common approaches and a unified cognitive model. *International Journal of Environmental Research and Public Health, 18*(19), 10160. https://doi.org/10.3390/ijerph181910160

Sahithya, B. R., & Kashyap, R. S. (2022). Sexual addiction disorder- a review with recent updates. *Journal of Psychosexual Health, 4*(2), 95–101. https://doi.org/10.1177/26318318221081080

Schmiedeberg, C., Huyer-May, B., Castiglioni, L., & Johnson, M. D. (2017). The more or the better? How sex contributes to life satisfaction. *Archives of Sexual Behavior, 46*(2), 465–473. https://doi.org/10.1007/s10508-016-0843-y

Shulman, J. L., & Horne, S. G. (2003). The use of self-pleasure: Masturbation and body image among African American and European American women. *Psychology of Women Quarterly, 27*, 262–269.

Sprecher, S., Christopher, F. S., Cate, R., Vangelisti, A. L., & Perlman, D. (2006). Sexuality in close relationships. In A. L. Vangelisti & D. Perlman (Eds.), *The Cambridge handbook of personal relationships* (pp. 463–482). Cambridge University Press.

Tal, R. (2017). Epidemiology of male sexual dysfunction. In S. Minhas & J. Mulhall (Eds.), *Male sexual dysfunction: A clinical guide* (pp. 1–7). Wiley.

Tetley, J., Lee, D., Nazroo, J., & Hinchliff, S. (2016). Let's talk about sex: What do older men and women say about their sexual relations and sexual activities? A qualitative analysis of ELSA wave 6 data. *Ageing and Society, 38*, 497. https://doi.org/10.1017/S0144686X16001203

Thienhaus, O. J. (1988). Practical overview of sexual function and advancing age. *Geriatrics, 43*, 63–67.

Trapnell, P. D., Meston, C. M., & Gorzalka, B. B. (1997). Spectatoring and the relationship between body image and sexual experience: Self-focus or self-valence? *Journal of Sex Research, 34*, 267–278.

Vedes, A., Nussbeck, F. W., Bodenmann, G., Lind, W., & Ferreira, A. (2013). Psychometric properties and validity of the dyadic coping inventory in Portuguese. *Swiss Journal of Psychology, 72*(3), 149–157. https://doi.org/10.1024/1421-0185/a000108

Vedes, A., Hilpert, P., Nussbeck, F. W., Randall, A. K., Bodenmann, G., & Lind, W. R. (2016). Love styles, coping, and relationship satisfaction: A dyadic approach. *Personal Relationships, 23*(1), 84–97. https://doi.org/10.1111/pere.12112

Walton, B., & Thorton, T. (2003). Female sexual dysfunction. *Current Women's Health Reports, 3*(4), 319–326.

Whisman, M. A., Gilmour, A. L., & Salinger, J. M. (2018). Marital satisfaction and mortality in the United States adult population. *Health Psychology, 37*(11), 1041–1044. https://doi.org/10.1037/hea0000677

World Health Organization. (2010). *Measuring sexual health: Conceptual and practical considerations and related indicators*. Retrieved from http://whqlibdoc.who.int/hq/2010/who_rhr_10.12_eng.pdf

World Health Organization. (2017). *Sexual health and its linkages to reproductive health: An operational approach*. World Health Organization.

Wright, P. J., Tokunaga, R. S., Kraus, A., & Klann, E. (2017). Pornography consumption and satisfaction: A meta-analysis. *Human Communication Research, 43*, 315–343.

Yeh, H. C., Lorenz, F. O., Wickrama, K. A., Conger, R. D., & Elder, G. H., Jr. (2006). Relationships among sexual satisfaction, marital quality, and marital instability at midlife. *Journal of Family Psychology, 20*(2), 339–343. https://doi.org/10.1037/0893-3200.20.2.339

Young, M., Luquis, R., Denny, G., & Young, T. (1998). Correlates of sexual satisfaction in marriage. *The Canadian Journal of Human Sexuality, 7*, 1–12.

Chapter 11
Religiosity and Spirituality

Religiosity and spirituality[1] are phenomena that are inherently intertwined (Hill et al., 2000) and have been part of the collective human experience throughout the history of humanity. They permeate every category of human endeavor and intersubjective meaning, and are observed expressed in ethics, art, architecture, literature, music, poetry, culture, war, inspiration, aspiration, sacrifice, death, illness, morality, conflict, and multitudes of other human activities. In other words, people's search for and participation in religion and spirituality is ubiquitous and dynamic in the history of our species.

It is important to know that there are no consensus operational definitions for the constructs of religiosity and spirituality[2] and the debate remains open. In this sense, Hill et al. (2000) point out:

> Spirituality can and often does occur within the context of religion, but it also may not. By the same token, the practice of spirituality can lead people to become religious and to become part of an organized or emerging religion, but it also may not. Additionally, to the extent that spirituality is defined as a more or less coherent picture of what is sacred and a lifestyle that incorporates beliefs, attitudes, values, or actions in response to this picture of the sacred, then religion can be understood as, among other things, a repository for one or more spiritualities. Individual religions (particularly those that are large, culturally heterogeneous, and have a long chronological record) might have adherents who endorse some spiritual core (e.g., Christians ostensibly reverence Jesus Christ and view God as one entity incorporated in three persons), even though the religion itself is broad enough to

[1] Historically, to understand the growing interest of psychologists in this topic, it is necessary to mention the January 2003 edition of American Psychologist dedicated to the relationship between religiosity, spirituality, and health.

[2] See the excellent article by Hill et al. (2000) that points out the debate on the conceptualization of the two constructs "religiosity" and "spirituality," and it highlights possible negative implications for research and applications in psychotherapy, among other problems. Also see the excellent Chap. 1, titled "Envisioning an Integrative Paradigm for the Psychology of Religion and Spirituality" by Pargament et al. (2013), in which useful guidelines are pointed out in a context of an integrative paradigm for the psychology of religion and spirituality.

Á. Quiñones Bergeret, *Evolutionary Case Formulation*,
https://doi.org/10.1007/978-3-031-67412-9_11

> accommodate people who also endorse distinctive spiritualities (e.g., desert spiritualities, evangelical spiritualities, feminist spiritualities, nature spiritualities, etc.). (pp. 70–71)

From a perspective of the history of psychology, it is worth mentioning that the American Psychological Association (APA) created a special group (Division 36) that is now called the Society for the Psychology of Religion and Spirituality,[3] holds annual meetings and conducts regular international events. In addition, it has the journal "Psychology of Religion and Spirituality" which started in 2009, and has been running for 14 years to date.

It is important to note that religiosity (religion) and spirituality can be both positive and negative factors in predicting mental health. They can also promote greater social belonging, community practices, connection, hope, personal growth, gratitude, and interpersonal support, etc. Similarly, it allows various adjustments and accommodations to stressors through the creation of meaning, coping, and resistance (see Paloutzian & Park, 2014).

Kenneth Pargament on spirituality in relation to psychotherapy, argues:

> When people walk into the therapist's office, they don't leave their spirituality behind in the waiting room. They bring their spiritual beliefs, practices, experiences, values, relationships, and struggles along with them. Implicitly or explicitly, this complex of spiritual factors often enters the process of psychotherapy. And yet many therapists are unaware of or unprepared to deal with this dimension in treatment. How does the therapist understand spirituality? How does the therapist address the spiritual dimension in psychotherapy? (2007, p. 4)

In the third decade of the twenty-first century, religiosity and spirituality still do not appear in the curricula of psychology schools or in postgraduate programs in clinical psychology. Added to this, it is rarely evaluated in psychotherapy but we know that its utility is irrefutable in certain cases of religious, spiritual, and even atheist patients.

Other authors such as Mytko and Knight (1999) argue that a broad definition of spirituality should include feelings of connection with oneself, with nature, with the community, with the purpose and meaning of life. Pargament (2007), a renowned researcher in the area, in the introduction of his book "Spiritually integrated psychotherapy: Understanding and addressing the sacred," points out what he understands by the dimension of spirituality:

> Spirituality is an extraordinary part of the ordinary lives of people. From birth to death, spirituality is manifest in life's turning points, revealing mystery and depth during these pivotal moments in time. In crisis and catastrophe, spirituality is often intertwined in the struggle to comprehend the seemingly incomprehensible and to manage the seemingly unmanageable. But this isn't the full story. Spirituality is not reserved exclusively for times of crisis and transition. It is interwoven into the fabric of the everyday. We can find the spiritual in a piece of music, the smile of a passing stranger, the color of the sky at dusk, or a daily prayer of gratitude upon awakening. Spirituality can reveal itself in the ways we think, the ways we feel, the ways we act, and the ways we relate to each other. Paradoxically, the presence of the spiritual dimension can also be felt through its absence, in feelings of loss and emptiness, in questions about meaning and purpose, in a sense of alienation and abandonment, and in cries about injustice and unfairness. Spirituality is, in short, another dimen-

[3] Originally established in 1949 as the American Association of Catholic Psychology.

> sion of life. An extraordinary dimension, yes, but one that is a vital part of ordinary life and what it means to be human. We are more than psychological, social, and physical beings; we are also spiritual beings. (pp. 3–4)

There has been an increase in attention to religion and spirituality among psychologists at the beginning of the twenty-first century (Łowicki et al., 2018; Lucchetti & Lucchetti, 2014; Hill et al., 2000; Emmons & Paloutzian, 2003; Shafranske, 2002). It deserves special attention, the interest in investigating the relationship between religiosity, spirituality, mental health, and health in general (Permana, 2018; Saroglou & Muñoz-García, 2008; Hill & Pargament, 2003; Miller & Thoresen, 2003). Continuing in coherence with the above, religiosity and spirituality have progressively captured the attention of researchers and we know more about the positive impact for certain types of patients and psychological problems such as depression and anxiety (Koenig et al., 2012; James & Wells, 2003).

As a conceptualization of the intersubjective knowledge domain "religiosity/spirituality" two parsimonious axes of analysis are proposed in the case formulation model and are named *Existential Tension* (negative religious and spiritual coping, religious and/or spiritual beliefs interfere re-signify events) and *Dysfunctional Religious Attachment* (anxious /ambivalent attachment, avoidant attachment).

In Fig. 11.1, the synergy is observed especially with the *Self System* which is essential to formulate in an idiographic way the psychological problems of the patient.

11.1 Existential Tension

Religion and spirituality from a psychological point of view have positive effects on adaptation to different stressful situations. Also, religion and spirituality can have negative effects on the lives of religious and spiritual people.

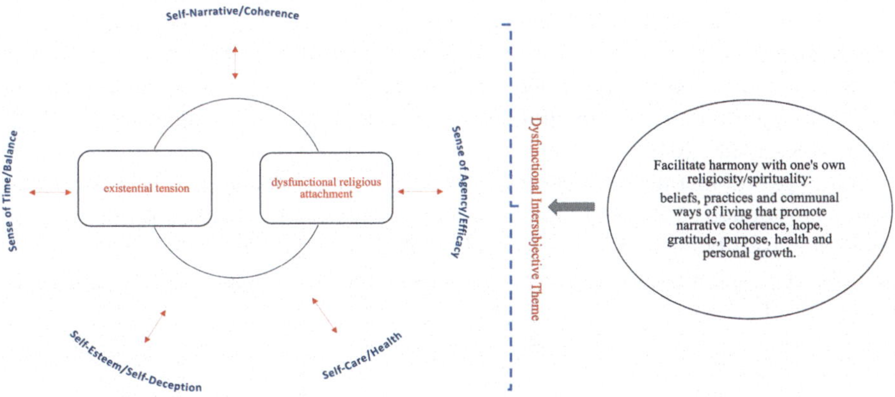

Fig. 11.1 Religiosity/spirituality

Religion/spirituality plays an essential role in people's meaning and is also related to coping with difficult situations and various demands of life.

Pargament et al., on religious coping, maintain:

> Religious coping represents a rich phenomenon in and of itself. Although religious coping could be defined and measured in terms of the degree to which religion is a part of the process of understanding and dealing with critical life events, it is important to consider not only *how much* religion is involved in coping, but also *how* religion is involved in coping: specifically, the *who* 's (e.g., clergy, congregation members, God), *what* 's (e.g., prayer, Bible reading, ritual), *when* 's (e.g., acute stressors, chronic stressors), *where* 's (e.g., within a congregation, privately), and *why* 's (e.g., to find meaning, to gain control) of coping. (2005, p. 482)

The psychotherapeutic interest is in negative religious/spiritual coping (also called spiritual struggles[4]) which is expressed in multiple ways: feeling discontent with God and the religious community, different events perceived as God's punishment, perceiving God as a punisher, experiencing the abandonment of God, experiences of spiritual desert, etc. In addition, negative religious/spiritual coping has been related to worse physical and social functioning, vitality and mental health problems, and emotional distress (Pargament et al., 2001; Scandrett & Mitchell, 2009; Taheri-Kharameh et al., 2016; Exline, 2013).

A very relevant research in the field of the mediating role of negative and positive coping between resilience and mental well-being is the one carried out by Surzykiewicz et al. (2022). They point out:

> Our findings offer indications for the development of resilience- and coping-based interventions to protect the mental health and well-being of individuals. The results of this study generally indicate that the development of psychological resources is able to help protect mental health from negative coping. (p. 10–11)

Finally, in relation to *religious and/or spiritual beliefs interfere re-signify events* are fundamental to research for therapists. In addition, we know that beliefs of different types can positively or negatively affect mental health (beliefs about oneself, the world, and the future). In such logic, basic beliefs also explicitly involve religious and/or spiritual themes for the non-clinical population and for the clinical population. Therefore, researching the possible religious and/or spiritual beliefs that interfere with psychological well-being is essential in any case formulation to increase effectiveness.

Research has been conducted in the field of intervention incorporating religiosity/spirituality as a constitutive aspect of intervention (Rosmarin et al., 2010, 2011; Hook et al., 2010).

In the psychotherapeutic field, there are different models in psychotherapy that have incorporated strategies to facilitate a religiosity/spirituality that promotes psychological well-being and psychological regulation, and there are also proposals for models of psychotherapy specifically focused on the subject (see Pargament & Exline, 2021).

---

[4] In this chapter, the terms "negative religious coping" and "spiritual struggles" are used interchangeably. For the approach that differentiates both terms, see the extraordinary work of Pargament and Exline (2021).

11.2 Dysfunctional Religious Attachment

Attachment theory has had many impacts on understanding how we bond with the living and also with the not present (symbolic). The field of research is complex, has significant limitations, and is in growing development. Granqvist and Kirkpatrick point out "...attachment theory has been of heuristic value in spurring empirical research on why and how people relate to God and why they embrace some less conventional forms of spirituality" (2013, p. 151).

One of the fundamental articles in the field of attachment and its relationship with the religious is the one written by Lee Kirkpatrick written in the early 1990s. He points out:

> No understanding of attachment, personal relationships, stress and coping, self-esteem, loneliness, or related topics will be complete unless religious beliefs are explicitly considered. For many individuals, any account of their social-support and interpersonal-relationship networks that fails to include God would be incomplete. Moreover, beliefs about God may reveal important insights concerning issues such as (a) hierarchies of attachment figures, (b) substitute attachment figures, (c) the process of relinquishing parents as attachment figures, and (d) the various provisions offered by different types of close relationships. (1992, p. 23)

From a clinical point of view, the measurement of individual differences proposed by Kirkpatrick and Shaver (1992) which is categorical has been very useful in the complex field of research on the style of attachment to God and mental health, among other dimensions of analysis (Rowatt & Kirkpatrick, 2002; Granqvist & Kirkpatrick; 2013; Mikulincer & Shaver, 2016). Similarly, it guides therapists to help religious patients with psychological distress.

Kirkpatrick and Shaver (1992) asked respondents to answer the question "Which of the following statements best describes your beliefs about God and your relationship with God?" and they had to choose one of the following response alternatives:

(a) *Secure*: God is generally warm and responsive to me; He always seems to know when to be supportive and protective of me, and when to let me make my own mistakes. My relationship with God is always comfortable, and I am very happy and satisfied with it.
(b) *Avoidant*: God is generally impersonal, distant, and often seems to have little or no interest in my personal affairs and problems. I frequently have the feeling that He doesn't care very much about me, or that he might not like me.
(c) *Anxious-Ambivalent*: God seems to be inconsistent in His reactions to me; He sometimes seems very warm and responsive to my needs, but sometimes not. I'm sure that He loves me and cares about me, but sometimes He seems to show it in ways I don't really understand. (1992, p. 270).

In conclusion, Kirkpatrick (2005) described how secure attachments with God (God—warm and receptive) can provide the individual with a safe haven of protection and direction in life when feeling psychological distress. On the other hand, he also described the complex dynamics of insecure attachments [(anxious/ambivalent—God as inconsistent) and (avoidant—God as distant and rejecting)] with predisposition to anxiety and avoidance that take various forms in stressful situations involving various intensities of psychological distress and dissatisfaction with life.

In the case formulation model presented, "religiosity/spirituality" is proposed as a domain of intersubjective knowledge to be considered in understanding and possible interventions. Because it can be an essential part of the solution to various psychological problems that the scientific literature points out. Therefore, "religios ity/spirituality" is a powerful source of knowledge that translates into motivation, clarification, creation of meaning, and strength for people to face the multiple adversities of life. In such a context, therapists should study the psychology of religion and spirituality, to increase effectiveness with their patients, and finally, to have great respect and humility with cultural sensitivity when it comes to listening to and understanding the religious/spiritual views and practices of their patients.

Next, the second-order intersubjective knowledge domain "**RELIGIOSITY/ SPIRITUALITY**" is shown in the case formulation protocol (the Case Formulation-Evaluation and the Case Formulation-Intervention are shown in Boxes 11.1 and 11.2).

Box 11.1: Case Formulation—Evaluation

[RELIGIOSITY/SPIRITUALITY] Indicate and weigh what processes contribute to discomfort and/or psychological dysregulation: ....

....

(mark presence: x)

Existential tension:

Negative religious and spiritual coping ☐

Religious and/or spiritual beliefs interfere with re-signifying events ☐

Others: ______________________

Describe: ....

....

Dysfunctional religious attachment:

Anxious/ambivalent attachment ☐

Avoidant attachment ☐

Others: ______________________

Describe: ....

....

Psychological Distress						Psychological Well-Being
High	Moderate	Mild	Neutral	Mild	Moderate	High
-3	-2	-1	0	1	2	3
Psychological Dysregulation						Psychological Regulation
High	Moderate	Mild	Neutral	Mild	Moderate	High
-3	-2	-1	0	1	2	3

Box 11.2: Case Formulation—Intervention

RELIGIOSITY/SPIRITUALITY: Change indicators

(mark presence: x)

Existential tension: Progress ☐ Regulation ☐

Describe: ....

....

Dysfunctional religious attachment: Progress ☐ Regulation ☐

Describe: ....

....

- Functional Narrative Indicator: Integrates knowledge about religiosity/spirituality ☐

- Behavioral Change Indicator: Incorporates changes ☐

Psychological Distress				Psychological Well-Being		
High	Moderate	Mild	Neutral	Mild	Moderate	High
-3	-2	-1	0	1	2	3
Psychological Dysregulation				Psychological Regulation		
High	Moderate	Mild	Neutral	Mild	Moderate	High
-3	-2	-1	0	1	2	3

Observations: ....

....

References

Emmons, R. A., & Paloutzian, R. F. (2003). The psychology of religion. *Annual Review of Psychology, 54*, 377–402. https://doi.org/10.1146/annurev.psych.54.101601.145024

Exline, J. J. (Ed.). (2013). Religious and spiritual struggles. In K. I. Pargament, J. J. Exline, & J. W. Jones (Eds.), *APA handbook of psychology, religion, and spirituality* (*Context, theory, and research*) (Vol. 1, pp. 459–475). American Psychological Association. https://doi.org/10.1037/14045-025.

Granqvist, P., & Kirkpatrick, L. A. (2013). Religion, spirituality, and attachment. In K. I. Pargament, J. J. Exline, & J. W. Jones (Eds.), *APA handbook of psychology, religion, and spirituality* (*Context, theory, and research*) (Vol. 1, pp. 139–155). American Psychological Association. https://doi.org/10.1037/14045-007.

Hill, P. C., & Pargament, K. I. (2003). Advances in the conceptualization and measurement of religion and spirituality. Implications for physical and mental health research. *The American Psychologist, 58*(1), 64–74. https://doi.org/10.1037/0003-066x.58.1.64

Hill, P. C., Pargament, K. I., Hood, R. W., McCullough, M. E., Swyers, J. P., Larson, D. B., & Zinnbauer, B. J. (2000). Conceptualizing religion and spirituality: Points of commonality, points of departure. *Journal for the Theory of Social Behavior, 30*(1), 51–77.

Hook, J. N., Worthington, E. L., Jr., Davis, D. E., Jennings, D. J., 2nd, Gartner, A. L., & Hook, J. P. (2010). Empirically supported religious and spiritual therapies. *Journal of Clinical Psychology, 66*(1), 46–72. https://doi.org/10.1002/jclp.20626

James, A., & Wells, A. (2003). Religion and mental health. Towards a cognitive behavioural framework. *British Journal of Mental Health Psychology, 8*(3), 359–376.

Kirkpatrick, L. A. (1992). An attachment -theory approach to the psychology of religion. *Journal for the Psychology of Religion, 2*(1), 3–28.

Kirkpatrick, L. A. (2005). *Attachment, evolution, and the psychology of religion*. Guilford Press.

Kirkpatrick, L. A., & Shaver, P. R. (1992). An attachment-theoretical approach to romantic love and religious belief. *Personality and Social Psychology Bulletin, 18*, 266–275. https://doi.org/10.1177/0146167292183002

Koenig, H. G., King, D., & Carson, V. B. (2012). *Handbook of religion and health* (2nd ed.). Oxford University Press.

Łowicki, P., Witowska, J., Zajenkowski, M., & Stolarski, M. (2018). Time to believe: Disentangling the complex associations between time perspective and religiosity. *Personality and Individual Differences, 134*, 97–106. https://doi.org/10.1016/j.paid.2018.06.001

Lucchetti, G., & Lucchetti, A. L. (2014). Spirituality, religion, and health: Over the last 15 years of field research (1999–2013). *International Journal of Psychiatry in Medicine, 48*(3), 199–215.

Mikulincer, M., & Shaver, P. R. (2016). *Attachment in adulthood, second edition structure, dynamics, and change* (2nd ed.). Guilford Press.

Miller, W. R., & Thoresen, C. E. (2003). Spirituality, religion, and health: An emerging research field. *American Psychologist, 58*(1), 24–35. https://doi.org/10.1037/0003-066X.58.1.24

Mytko, J. J., & Knight, S. J. (1999). Body, mind and spirit: Towards the integration of religiosity and spirituality in cancer quality of life research. *Psycho-Oncology, 8*(5), 439–450.

Paloutzian, R. F., & Park, C. L. (Eds.). (2014). *Handbook of the psychology of religion and spirituality* (2nd ed.). Guilford Press.

Pargament, K. I. (2007). *Spiritually integrated psychotherapy: Understanding and addressing the sacred*. Guilford Press.

Pargament, K. I., & Exline, J. J. (2021). *Working with spiritual struggles in psychotherapy: From research to practice*. Guilford Press.

Pargament, K. I., Koenig, H. G., Tarakeshwar, N., & Hahn, J. (2001). Religious struggle as a predictor of mortality among medically ill elderly patients: A 2-year longitudinal study. *Archives of Internal Medicine, 161*(15), 1881–1885. https://doi.org/10.1001/archinte.161.15.1881

Pargament, K. I., Ano, G. G., & Wachholtz, A. B. (2005). The religious dimension of coping: Advances in theory, research, and practice. In R. F. Paloutzian & C. L. Park (Eds.), *Handbook of the psychology of religion and spirituality* (pp. 479–495). The Guilford Press.

Pargament, K. I., Mahoney, A., Exline, J. J., Jones, J. W., & Shafranske, E. P. (2013). Envisioning an integrative paradigm for the psychology of religion and spirituality. In K. I. Pargament, J. J. Exline, & J. W. Jones (Eds.), *APA handbook of psychology, religion, and spirituality* (*Context, theory, and research*) (Vol. 1, pp. 3–19). American Psychological Association. https://doi.org/10.1037/14045-001.

Permana, I. (2018). How religosity and/or spirituality might influence self-care in diabetes management: A structured review. *Bangladesh Journal of Medical Science, 17*(2), 185–193.

Rosmarin, D. H., Pargament, K. I., & Robb, H. B. (2010). Spiritual and religious issues in behavior change: Introduction. *Cognitive and Behavioral Practice, 17*(4), 343–347. https://doi.org/10.1016/j.cbpra.2009.02.007

Rosmarin, D. H., Auerbach, R. P., Bigda-Peyton, J. S., Björgvinsson, T., & Levendusky, P. G. (2011). Integrating spirituality into cognitive behavioral therapy in an acute psychiatric setting: A pilot study. *Journal of Cognitive Psychotherapy: An International Quarterly, 25*(4), 287–303.

Rowatt, W. C., & Kirkpatrick, L. A. (2002). Two dimensions of attachment to god and their subsequent attachment to affect, religiosity, and personality constructs. *Journal for the Scientific Study of Religion, 41*, 637–651. https://doi.org/10.1111/1468-5906.00143

Saroglou, V., & Muñoz-García, A. (2008). Individual differences in religion and spirituality: An issue of personality traits and/or values. *Journal for the Scientific Study of Religion, 47*(1), 83–101. https://doi.org/10.1111/j.1468-5906.2008.00393.x

Scandrett, K. G., & Mitchell, S. L. (2009). Religiousness, religious coping, and psychological well-being in nursing home residents. *Journal of the American Medical Directors Association, 10*(8), 581–586. https://doi.org/10.1016/j.jamda.2009.06.001

Shafranske, E. P. (2002). The necessary and sufficient conditions for an applied psychology of religion. *Psychology of Religion Newsletter, 27*, 1–12.

Surzykiewicz, J., Skalski, S. B., Niesiobędzka, M., & Konaszewski, K. (2022). Exploring the mediating effects of negative and positive religious coping between resilience and mental well-being. *Frontiers in Behavioral Neuroscience, 16*, 954382. https://doi.org/10.3389/fnbeh.2022.954382

Taheri-Kharameh, Z., Abdi, M., Omidi Koopaei, R., Alizadeh, M., Vahidabi, V., & Mirhoseini, H. (2016). Investigating the relationship between communication and collaboration of nurses with physicians from Nurses' point of view in Neyshabur hospitals. *Health, Spirituality and Medical Ethics, 3*(1), 30–35.

Part II
Psychotherapy Process

Chapter 12
Overview of the Psychotherapy Process Trajectory

Four assumptions need to be explicitly stated to the reader to facilitate the understanding of the complete psychotherapeutic process that will be presented in Chap. 13.

First, starting with a theme communicated by the therapist about the patient's suffering and psychological dysregulation facilitates an initial self-understanding that provides possibilities for new psychological regulation.

Second, it is advantageous for a better understanding of the psychological analysis to be able to describe and explain a therapeutic process session by session according to a guide for psychological formulation.

Third, evaluating and investigating the indicators of change that are jointly discovered (refute or confirm) between therapist and patient is beneficial for the intense intersubjective attunement in the particular existential encounter for a "time delimited by therapeutic objectives."

Fourth, hypothetically knowing and being able to represent where one is "Locating the patient psychologically" (quadrants: I, II, III, or IV; see Chap. 1, Fig. 1.3) in the psychotherapy process is very useful for reviewing with the patient and co-correcting timely what is required, in order to advance more efficiently towards the *dimensional psychological regulation and the adaptive intersubjective sense of reality*.

The Case Formulation protocol from an evolutionary perspective (ECF) has three complementary sections to conceptualize, intervene, and monitor the psychotherapeutic process (see Appendix: Evolutionary Case Formulation Protocol). They are described below.

Á. Quiñones Bergeret, *Evolutionary Case Formulation*,
https://doi.org/10.1007/978-3-031-67412-9_12

12.1 Evolutionary Case Formulation-Evaluation (ECF-E)

The Evolutionary Case Formulation-Evaluation (ECF-E) section (see Appendix: Evolutionary Case Formulation Protocol—Section 1) has the following purposes:

To delimit a dysfunctional intersubjective theme with understandable language, dimensionally evaluate the dysfunctional domains involved (profile), represent the domains according to the axes of analysis (Discomfort-Wellbeing/Dysregulation-Regulation), make explicit the therapeutic objectives, point out the main psychological reformulations, and communicate a psychological clinical hypothesis.

Specifically from a process point of view, the ECF-E is used for psychological evaluation and psychological feedback. In other words, it is to open a possibility to the "generation of scaffolding for change" through narrative scaling.

One last practical aspect to point out is that the experience with psychotherapists who use the Evolutionary Case Formulation indicates that two or three sessions are enough to achieve an optimal psychological formulation of the patient's problem (ECF-E). Case formulation is progressively adjusted and enriched in the psychotherapy process through Evolutionary Case Formulation-Intervention (ECF-I) and Psychotherapy Process Assessment Interview (PPAI).

12.2 Evolutionary Case Formulation-Intervention (ECF-I)

The Evolutionary Case Formulation-Intervention (ECF-I) section (see Appendix: Evolutionary Case Formulation Protocol—Section 2) guides the systematic work of reconstructing the patient's psychological experience in various situations where they experience psychological discomfort and/or dysregulation (Thematization).

It facilitates the systematic work of monitoring and assessing progress in modifying the *Dysfunctional Intersubjective Theme* (TID). In addition, it presents different indicators of change at different levels of complexity that allow for the sequential assessment of the gradual achievement of objectives (Fig. 12.1) and psychological change achieved (Fig. 12.2).

It should be clarified that the indicated change indicators should all be present when the patient is in quadrant I (see Chap. 1, Table 1.3).

Assessment of compliance with therapeutic objectives [mark presence: x]

Significant change valued by the patient	
Significant change assessed by the therapist	
Significant change assessed by the therapist	

Fig. 12.1 Assessment of therapeutic objectives

Indicators of change [mark presence: x]	
Behavioral changes	
Dimensional psychological regulation (quadrant I)	
Functional narrative	

Fig. 12.2 Change indicators

The indicators of Fig. 12.1 are defined below:

- *Significant change valued by the patient* refers to changes that the patient considers important and stable after the start of psychotherapy.
- *Significant change valued by the therapist* refers to changes valued by the therapist with nomothetic and idiographic criteria.
- *There is agreement on achievement of objectives between therapist and patient* refers to explicitly agreed upon significant objectives achieved by both patient and therapist.

The indicators of Fig. 12.2 are defined below:

- *Behavioral changes* refers to changes valued by the therapist and that include emerging and consolidated changes.
- *Dimensional psychological regulation* (quadrant I) refers to various possibilities of psychological well-being and individual psychological regulation (such results are identified with various possibilities depending on the profile of second-order intersubjective knowledge domains in quadrant I, see Table 1.3 in Chap. 1). In other words, it is what is understood as psychological health in the case formulation model from an evolutionary perspective.
- *Functional narrative refers to when in the* patient the psychological conflict is not observed parsimoniously expressed in what is called *Dysfunctional Intersubjective Theme.*[1] It is a consequence of a dialectic of *descriptive and reflective narratives "strengthened in quantity and progressively quality" that are observed in the change indicators for first and second order domains (FCE-Intervention)*, which emerge and consolidate in regulation and in the indicators of "Integrates acquired knowledge about the evaluated second order domain"[2] and "Incorporates changes." This implies, for example, new causal connections, stable sense of agency, positive self-deception, adaptive cognitions, adequate emotional decoding, interpersonal awareness, temporal awareness, body awareness, narrative coherence, etc.

[1] Therapists should ensure that in each session the patients feel that they were able to work on the agreed objectives and topics they wanted to work on.

[2] For example, integrate knowledge acquired about cognition.

12.3 Psychotherapy Process Assessment Interview (PPAI)

The Psychotherapy Process Assessment Interview (PPAI) (see Appendix: Evolutionary Case Formulation Protocol—Section 3) is a qualitative interview of 14 questions that seeks to assess the therapeutic process from the perspective and experience of the patient in the therapeutic process (see Box 12.1). It is a directed, open, and reflective dialogue with the patient about various aspects of the psychotherapeutic process carried out.

Box 12.1: Characteristics of the Psychotherapy Process Assessment Interview (PPAI)

1. Qualitative interview of 14 questions.
2. Understandable language.
3. It is applied at different moments of the psychotherapeutic process.
4. Allows and facilitates process monitoring through thematic analysis.
5. Facilitates patient curiosity.
6. Encourages self-observation, self-examination, reflection and metacognition.
7. Helps the therapist focus on the patient's learnings and resources.
8. It generates a space of special intersubjective care in the therapeutic process, which implies the "active listening of the therapist".
9. The patient gives feedback to the therapist.

The PPAI is very useful for increasing knowledge about the process therapeutic experienced by the patient through making explicit aspects partially communicated or unknown to the therapist.

In the relational aspect, it seeks to reinforce the "feeling of being listened to and co-participant in the direction of his psychotherapeutic process" through assessments, feedback, information on difficulties, and adjustment requests (from his "lived experience in therapy") to achieve the agreed objectives.

Regarding the application of the PPAI, it is applied at the same time as the ECF-Intervention is conceptualized. The relevant thing is that it is applied together with the ECF-I at different moments of the psychotherapeutic process.

Below is a figure that aims to show a process psychotherapeutic guided by the Evolutionary Case Formulation Protocol (see Fig. 12.3).

In summary, the psychotherapeutic process is oriented through the three sections of the Case Formulation Model according to an Evolutionary perspective that are applied synergistically (see Fig. 12.4).[3]

---

[3]The clinical experience of psychotherapists who use the case formulation model from an evolutionary perspective indicates that every four or five sessions, they consider it appropriate to carry out the ECF-I.

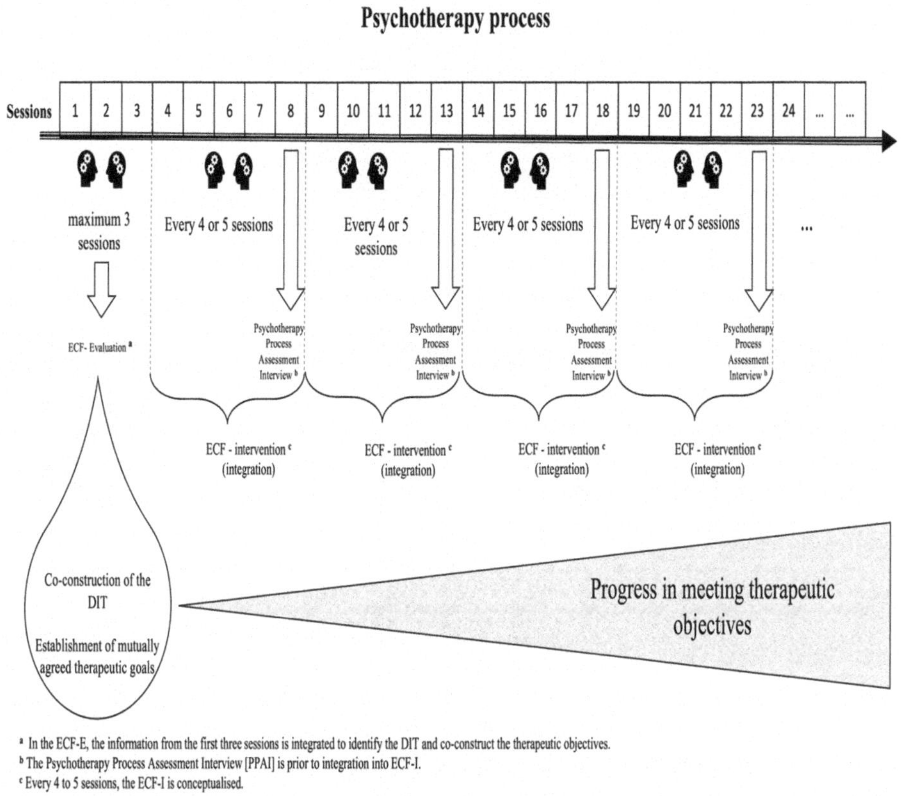

Fig. 12.3 Psychotherapeutic process guided by case formulation protocol from an evolutionary perspective (ECF). (Adapted from Quiñones, 2024)

The therapist in the dyad is a helper, who co-constructs and co-regulates to facilitate a "curious and active" self-observation by the patient, focused experiential monitoring, guided reconstruction of the experience and shared reflection and testing of new behaviors. In this way, a gradual Functional Narrative is expected to emerge (with a sense of agency/effectiveness, self-care/health, self-narrative/coherence, sense of time/balance and self-esteem/self-deception) that implies behavioral changes with dimensional psychological regulation and adaptive intersubjective sense of reality.

Before starting with the case that illustrates the application of the case formulation protocol from an evolutionary perspective in this book (see Meg's case, Chap. 13), I will briefly stop at the therapeutic relationship. As a frame of reference, I quote Edward Bordin:

> The goals set and collaboration specified appear intimately linked to the nature of the human relationship between therapist and patient. For example, two persons will be more concerned about liking or disliking each other if they are proposing to settle into a working relationship of several years duration, meeting three or more times a week, than if their

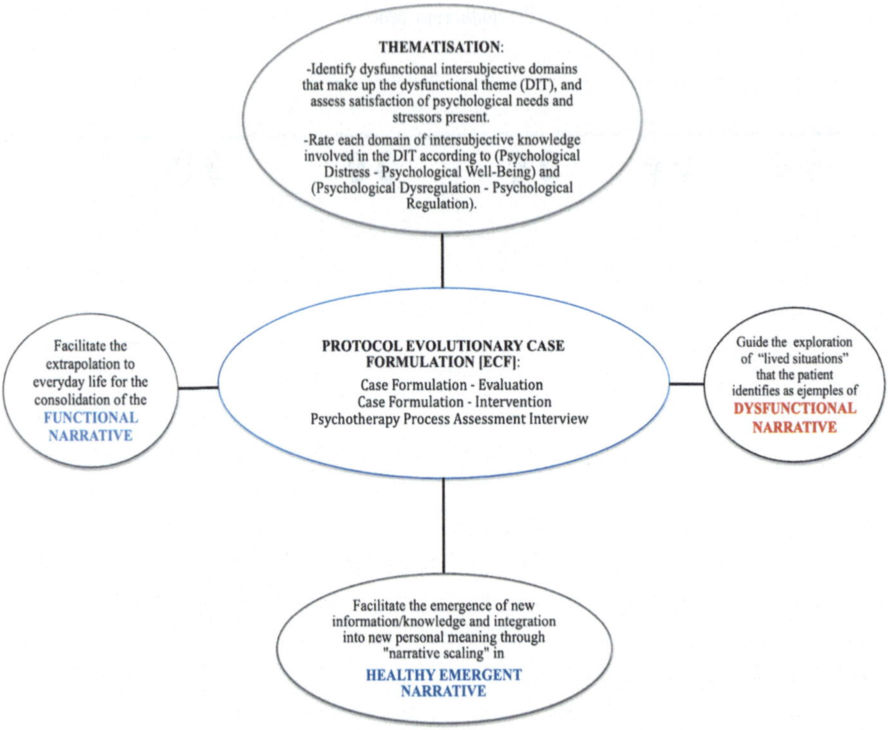

Fig. 12.4 Conceptual scheme of the psychotherapy process

> relationship is expected to terminate in three months or less. Some basic level of trust surely marks all varieties of therapeutic relationships, but when attention is directed toward the more protected recesses of inner experience, deeper bonds of trust and attachment are required and developed. Our examinations of such features of therapeutic work need to be more pointed. For example, the kind of bond developed when a therapist gives a patient a form and asks him to make a daily record of his submissive and assertive acts and of the circumstances surrounding them, appears quite different from the bond developed when a therapist shares his or her feelings with a patient, in order to provide a model, or to provide feedback on the patient's impact on others. One bond may not necessarily be stronger than the other, but they do differ in kind. Another nuance in the therapeutic bond might be defined by the difference between a caretaker and a consultant. Some modes of psychotherapy have much more of a take-charge element built into them. (1979, p. 254–255)

The *quality of the therapeutic relationship* is an active ingredient in promoting psychological change that must be gradually achieved, reinforced, monitored, and adjusted. There are four aspects to consider:

In *first place*, part of the beginning of building an *optimal therapeutic alliance* is to achieve therapeutic objectives that are understandable, have existential meaning, are manageable and with the expectation of being achievable by the patient. For this, it is fundamental that *they are agreed between the patient and the therapist.* Clearly stated, it is to make the patient feel understood by the therapist.

In *second place*, it is essential to involve the patient in a guided collaborative relationship to "investigate their private intersubjective world." Such a process has the particularity of being self-centered and requires triggering curiosity in exploring "their being in the world with others" with the purpose of discovering the best possible ways to achieve a new healthy psychological regulation. In this sense, it is necessary to be very clear and direct with the patient, that gradual psychological change is possible, but it implies "taking care" through an active commitment "self-responsibility" and permanent "persistence" in the investigation of their psychological discomfort and/or psychological Dysregulation.

In *third place*, evaluate the initial expectations and during the course of the therapeutic process. For this purpose, it is relevant to ask the patient: How do you imagine/expect/feel/think a change in aspects of your existence will be?, What are the aspects that you would like to change about yourself?, What are the relational situations that you would like to be different?, What fears do you have about changing?, What has the change achieved in the psychotherapy process implied experientially?, etcetera. In other words, the *expectations in the therapeutic process* must be known and reflected upon ("meditated") in the therapeutic dyad, as they are fundamental ingredients in the outcome of the co-construction and co-regulation process led by the therapist.

Namely, sometimes patients' expectations regarding their issues are not in line with what can be expected from a therapeutic process based on the patient's characteristics (evolutionary moment, relational context, etc.). Therefore, the psychotherapist must take care of *probabilistically delimiting* with frankness, clarity, and assertiveness what are the possibilities and limitations of the therapeutic process at the present moment of the evaluation. To this end, it is mainly relevant in the evaluation sessions to ask and give nomothetic (paradigmatic) information to adjust expectations so that they are viable. Then, in the intervention process, explore and adapt possibilities based on the idiographic (narrative).

One type of expectation that is fundamental in every therapeutic process is hope. It is mandatory to monitor hope at all times of the psychotherapeutic process, as it is central to generate and maintain the motivation to discover, try, choose, and gradually change towards a *being in existential process* with greater sense, coherence, and purpose (Functional Narrative). Consequently, the therapist must strive to reassuringly and explicitly convey to patients that he has experience with people who have presented similar problems and that he has been able to help them. Also, "inform bluntly" that in his professional experience, what makes the difference in contributing to achieve success or failure is that patients have consented to be helped and have put all their intelligence, intuition, honesty, reflection, and creativity in their own self-observation. Such a position of "entry" with the patient strongly helps to generate hope that the "therapist in front of him" will be able to help him, but making it very clear that the positive results of psychotherapy will be significantly dependent on his own commitment to his process of investigation on how he generates and maintains his psychological discomfort and/or psychological dysregulation. In short, ensuring that hope is present and maintained at an optimal level is a "laborious" task for the therapist.

In *fourth place*, the therapist must be very attentive to the indicators of tension and/or rupture that as a *participant observer* he may detect and/or that the *patient* reveals, or that both discover at times in the therapeutic process. Therefore, having a hypothesis of the *patient's relational style with the therapist* is essential to direct, adjust, and manage the *relational framework* with the purpose of facilitating him to explore and reconstruct intersubjective situations that generate tension and/or dysregulation.

References

Bordin, E. S. (1979). The generalizability of the psychoanalytic concept of the working alliance. *Psychotherapy: Theory, Research & Practice, 16*(3), 252–260. https://doi.org/10.1037/h0085885

Quiñones, A. (2024). Perspectiva evolucionista para la formulación de caso: Un sistema abierto. In A. Quiñones & C. Caro (Eds.), *Formulación de Caso: Hacia una Psicoterapia de precisión* (pp. 107–135). UNED editorial.

Chapter 13
Psychotherapy Process

This didactic case has 29 sessions and includes two follow-up sessions (F).

The frequency of the sessions over the 13 months had different periodicities. In the first month, the frequency was once a week, and from the second to the eighth month, the frequency was three sessions per month. Two sessions were held in the ninth and tenth months, and it went down to one session in the eleventh month. The process concluded with two follow-up sessions, held in the twelfth and thirteenth months (see Fig. 13.1).

Information on psychopharmacology and other topics were omitted in consideration that the essential objective was to describe in a didactic way a psychotherapeutic process using the Case Formulation Model from an evolutionary perspective (ECF-E, ECF-I and PPAI).

To conclude, in the therapeutic process that will be detailed below, a variety of techniques were used: Socratic dialogue, narrative tasks, behavioral exercises, moviola, full awareness, empty chair, various records (record of thoughts, emotions and activity), psychoeducation and directed readings, etc.

13.1 Anamnesis and Description of the First Sessions

- Meg[1] (pseudonym) is 58 years old.
- Only child. Born in a single-parent family.
- Marital status: Divorced.
- Currently living with Jordi (current partner).

[1] The present therapeutic process is based on a real case. The information and sociodemographic data exposed have been modified to safeguard anonymity. Similarly, the information has been modified and adjusted for academic and didactic purposes with the sole purpose of showing the conceptualization of case from an evolutionary perspective.

Á. Quiñones Bergeret, *Evolutionary Case Formulation*,
https://doi.org/10.1007/978-3-031-67412-9_13

month	1º month				2º month				3º month				4º month				5º month				6º month			
Weeks	1	2	3	4	1	2	3	4	1	2	3	4	1	2	3	4	1	2	3	4	1	2	3	4
Session conducted	x	x	x	x		x	x	x		x	x	x		x	x	x		x	x	x	Holiday			

month	7º month				8º month				9º month				10º month				11º month				12º month				13º month			
Weeks	1	2	3	4	1	2	3	4	1	2	3	4	1	2	3	4	1	2	3	4	1	2	3	4	1	2	3	4
Session conducted		x	x	x		x	x	x		x		x		x		x		x				F						F

Fig. 13.1 Session chronology

- She weighs 84 kilos and has a BMI: 32.4 (Obesity type 1) and is insulin resistant.
- Chronic sedentary lifestyle.
- No history of mental illnesses in her family.
- No history of substance abuse.
- Consumes alcohol only in social situations.
- She is a professional engineer.
- No periods of unemployment in her work history.

In general:

She attends a psychotherapist (psychologist) referred from her treating psychiatrist. She dresses elegantly and formally. In addition, she shows a very polite and kind treatment. It should be noted that she appears to have low vitality.

Her pharmacological treatment started 5 weeks ago. The diagnosis made by the psychiatrist is Major Depressive Disorder (first episode). She has a depressive mood, loss of interest, loss of energy, feelings of worthlessness and guilt, decreased ability to concentrate, and sleep disturbance (insomnia, mainly with interruption and waking up early in the morning). She was prescribed antidepressants (selective serotonin reuptake inhibitors). She has not experienced negative effects from taking the drugs and adheres to taking them as prescribed. About this, she says: "*I have felt a little better, a bit more energy on some days. That's right, I sleep much better for about 10 days now. However, my problems continue.*"

At the time of consultation, she has had two sessions with her psychiatrist and is on medical leave for 21 days (first leave). The leave started 15 days ago as she was having energy and concentration difficulties at work. Also, it is noted that she has no history of psychological or psychiatric treatment prior to the consultation with the psychiatrist.

Finally, suicidal ideation was explored and ruled out. No indicator was found present or past in the story told by Meg.

13.1.1 Fragments from the First Sessions

The beginning of the session after asking general information is transcribed below:

Therapist What brings you to consult?

Meg The psychiatrist told me to come see you. Anyway, I feel "strange," "deceptive" with my partner Jordi... and in the last month and a bit more, I sometimes wish the earth would "swallow me up"... Anyway, I also frequently think about having asked for a divorce from my husband more than 4 years ago. And I don't understand "why I feel this way."

Therapist When did you start feeling this way?

Meg Several months ago.

Therapist How many months approximately?

Meg Maybe 5 months and something.

Therapist Has your discomfort intensified in these months?

Meg Yes... it has increased in the last month.

Therapist I understand.

Meg I haven't told you. I clarify that I am legally divorced from my ex-husband. I don't miss him or anything, but it happens that I don't feel well and I remember the divorce.

Therapist Are you referring to your ex-husband?

Meg Yes.

Therapist What's his name?

Meg His name is Antonio.

Therapist You have been divorced for a while.

Meg Sure, two and a half years legally.

Therapist How long have you been in your new relationship with Jordi?

Meg We will complete 2 years in 1 month. Imagine, after many years of disagreement and boredom with my ex-husband, now I am with a man who loves me, strives to take care of me, please me and give me security... but I feel "strange"... it's as if I can't tolerate him being so close to me... I don't understand myself, I feel bad... with little desire for everything. I don't know what I feel for him and no matter how much I think, I don't solve anything…

Therapist I understand. Your relationship will be 2 years soon. And in these 14 months that you have been living together, when did this "I don't know what I feel for him" start?

Meg It started little by little...

Therapist And when did it become a problem for you?

Meg Maybe about 6 months ago, his physical closeness started to be unpleasant.

Therapist "His physical closeness started to be unpleasant," has it remained or fluctuated?

Meg It has remained and I am very worried. And I don't know if I want to continue in the relationship with Jordi, I am doubtful. Also, I am on medical leave as I told you and I want to go back to work as soon as possible, but I don't feel capable.

Therapist Is the doubt about whether to continue in the relationship or not, your biggest concern now?

Meg It's what has my head in chaos, yes.

Therapist Can't you resolve it?

Meg I can't.

Therapist	I understand… We will return to the issue of not being able to resolve your doubt. When did you start the medical leave?
Meg	Two weeks ago.
Therapist	Ok. Could you tell me about times when you are sharing with Jordi?
Meg	With Jordi, I feel very distant and I don't understand the reasons. In my marriage, I also felt somewhat similar, but it was different and I got through it alone... as it has always been in my life, but now, I can't...
Therapist	How long ago did that happen in your marriage?
Meg	About 15 years ago. At that time, I was quite unwell.
Therapist	And in what sense was it "similar"?
Meg	Downcast.
Therapist	Only in being downcast?
Meg	I think so...
Therapist	If I do the math correctly, you were 43 years old at that time.
Meg	That's right.
Therapist	What happened 15 years ago?
Meg	My husband had work problems... his salary was significantly reduced.
Therapist	Was it an unexpected situation?
Meg	He had been having problems at the company for a while... it wasn't so unexpected for him, but I thought it wouldn't happen so soon.
Therapist	So, did you also feel downcast then?
Meg	A little, but it made me more distant from him for quite some time.
Therapist	And did you also feel a lack of energy and motivation?
Meg	I didn't feel a lack of energy or motivation. Only somewhat downcast.
Therapist	Can you explain the difference a bit more?
Meg	My job was fine, I woke up with energy and did my work well. My downfall was when I had to go home and be at my house. It didn't happen at work.
Therapist	I see. And what did you do with your downcast feeling?
Meg	My job was very important, I focused a lot on the projects.
Therapist	So your downcast feeling didn't affect your work performance like now?
Meg	It didn't affect it.
Therapist	If I understand correctly what you're telling me, the downcast feeling was exclusively outside of your work. Is that correct?
Meg	Yes, when I got home I felt downcast.
Therapist	And how did it resolve?
Meg	I would go to my room.
Therapist	Did you have separate rooms?
Meg	Yes, for some time now.
Therapist	Did you talk when you got home?
Meg	Sometimes, if we ran into each other.
Therapist	And how did your downcast feeling pass?
Meg	I stopped feeling downcast a couple of weeks later. But I don't know if our greater distance was resolved... We stopped sharing a bedroom and then it became a habit.

Therapist	How was that "habit"?
Meg	He snored and it was hard for me to sleep... we left it like that.
Therapist	Didn't your husband complain?
Meg	Not at all.
Therapist	What did you think about it?
Meg	It didn't bother me in the slightest.
Therapist	Being with someone and not feeling close to them, how would you describe it?
Meg	Sought solitude...
Therapist	Solitude that didn't bother you.
Meg	Something like that...
Therapist	To understand more specifically what it means to you, could you give me an example from your life?
Meg	I've always felt somewhat distant from people. Loneliness doesn't bother me.
Therapist	Do you have friends?
Meg	In school, I had two great friends. One went abroad and I lost track of her. The second friend lives at the other end of the country and we occasionally talk for the end-of-year holidays and birthdays. I see her from afar.
Therapist	And with your two friends, did you feel distant?
Meg	No.
Therapist	Let's go back to "distant from people." What is this distance that you feel and perceive in yourself?
Meg	I don't feel interested... it's like not dancing to the same music. And it happens to me frequently, for example with the people at my work.
Therapist	Is it as if "the other" is dancing milonga and you are dancing cumbia?
Meg	Yes.
Therapist	And does "the other" realize the dissonance?
Meg	Sometimes. I think they see me as uninterested.
Therapist	I see. And has this been happening for a long time or is it recent?
Meg	Since university, I think... I like solitude and I prefer it to company.
Therapist	Since when did solitude become your preference?
Meg	In my marriage, I think, but already in university it didn't bother me at all.
Therapist	I see. We will look at this in more detail at another time.
Meg	Sure.

At another moment in the first session, the therapist explores the similarities of both romantic relationships:

Meg	It's the feeling of being alone and accompanied... it's strange... something like that... I couldn't specify anything more...
Therapist	A 24-year marriage is different from your relationship of almost 2 years... not only in time obviously...

Meg	Yes, of course they are very different, but I have this thing of comparing... it's strange, I don't usually compare people.
Therapist	But going back to "alone and accompanied," do you have any explanation?
Meg	I don't understand it, no. I just feel bad... anxious, sad, I cry sometimes... that's all I can say.
Therapist	If I understood correctly, it seems that with Antonio you didn't feel uncomfortable with the distance after the problem occurred at your work.
Meg	Sure.
Therapist	But on the other hand, with the affectionate closeness that Jordi expresses to you daily, you feel that the distance towards him is inexplicable.
Meg	Yes...
Therapist	You have been living with Jordi for a little over a year.
Meg	That's right.
Therapist	Did you feel uncomfortable before living with him?
Meg	No, not at all. It was very pleasant and I was happy.
Therapist	When did you start feeling uncomfortable with him?
Meg	About 6 months ago, more or less.
Therapist	Do you have any idea of the reasons for your discomfort?
Meg	I'm not clear on the reasons, but I do agree with you that they are two different relationships.
Therapist	We will clarify the reasons little by little. But it is clear that they are two very different relationships that you compare. With Antonio you were she felt alone and particularly unaccompanied for the past 15 years; in contrast, with Jordi, you feel uncomfortable with his warm company.
Meg	Yes... it's inexplicable to me.
Therapist	Gradually, we will work to clarify this transition aspect with Jordi more. We lack more details and context information to better understand the transition situation in your relationship with Jordi towards discomfort...
Meg	Agreed.
Therapist	In my view, I can tell you that the comparison of Antonio and Jordi is not absurd, but in a certain sense it helps you to position yourself in the face of the novelty experience... It's being with someone warm and feeling accompanied... Does what I'm saying make sense to you?
Meg	It makes me think... I hadn't seen it that way...
Therapist	But at this moment you are reflecting with me.
Meg	That's right. It makes sense.
Therapist	We will continue with this.

13.1.2 Work Situation

Meg has been working for 33 years in the area of programming and IT support to large companies. She has been in charge of a department for 10 years in a multinational. In addition, academically she has a doctorate in computer science obtained at a prestigious foreign university. She has been evaluated as outstanding by her superiors in her 10 years of trajectory. Before her current job, she worked in two companies in the same area, and also held relevant positions. It is noteworthy that in all her working years, she has never had a period of unemployment and has never taken sick leave.

She says she really likes her job and reiterates that she wants to return as soon as possible. Her job is a source of gratification and she says she is very proud of her professional career in the three companies where she has worked. Similarly, she emphasizes that in her working life she has always been very professional with the people she has had to work with in her more than three decades. In this sense, she emphasizes that she understands "professional relationships" to solve problems and that she does not like the "culture of meetings to get together and not solve anything." And she says: "*I have never had a coffee with anyone from my office to chat about life, except in the meetings I have to attend. I only interact to obtain information, evaluate and solve problems when it concerns me.*"

Also, she describes herself as very goal-oriented and a person of much analysis, reflection, and problem solving. She adds with a proud expression: "I have had a working life without periods of unemployment, I have intensely collaborated in achieving the proposed objectives in the companies where I have worked. And I have achieved it. In addition, I have always felt obligated to pay the family expenses; and in all these years, I have never failed financially."

Next, her work situation at the present time is explored; part of the dialogue is transcribed:

Meg	Now, I am on medical leave for the first time in my professional career. My job is not the same anymore. It was hard for me to go and I was low on energy and had little problem-solving capacity... my head was elsewhere, I had never had my job become "uphill," but it happened to me and I don't know how I got to this state.
Therapist	I understand that it has been an experience that you had not experienced.
Meg	Yes.
Therapist	Was there any change in how you organized your time, particularly, in the moments when work became "uphill"?
Meg	Before I organized my time very well. Since I started with this unpleasant state, time passes me by and I can't organize myself as before, and now I solve very little... it's not usual for me... I can't explain it.

Therapist	Could you give me an example of when what you're telling me happened so I can get a more precise picture?
Meg	I remember one Monday, I arrived late to my work and had to resolve several issues and didn't know how to start... and I couldn't organize myself... it was very unpleasant for me... I didn't do my job well and had to postpone urgent matters...
Therapist	I understand. And how long did it take you to resolve those issues?
Meg	By the afternoon of the next day.
Therapist	Had you experienced similar problems before?
Meg	Of course, but it took me much longer than expected. It had never happened to me before.
Therapist	Did you solve the problems?
Meg	Yes, but late.
Therapist	And how did you feel?
Meg	Worried about myself...
Therapist	I see. On the other hand, when you got home from your work, did you feel like you had energy?
Meg	Lately, I would arrive and go to bed exhausted.
Therapist	Since when?
Meg	A month and a bit more, maybe... it could be a little more.
Therapist	Aha. Had it happened to you before, arriving home so worn out for so many weeks?
Meg	Not that I remember.

Next, the therapist explores any potential work-related stress situation:

Therapist	When did you start feeling that your job was different?
Meg	I'm not sure.
Therapist	Did anything happen with a colleague, a change in the management, a new company policy, etcetera?
Meg	The company offered early retirement to some employees.
Therapist	When was the offer made?
Meg	A little over 5 months ago.
Therapist	And was this possibility offered to you?
Meg	Yes, my area manager called me to a personal meeting and offered me the benefit. He was enthusiastic about the benefit which consisted of a financial bonus.
Therapist	Is your boss a man or a woman?
Meg	Man.
Therapist	Aha.
Meg	I work in a company where 80% of the employees are men. And all my superiors are men.
Therapist	I see. So, he offered you the benefit.
Meg	Yes.

Therapist	And did you like that possibility?
Meg	I didn't like it. I told him I wasn't interested in principle.
Therapist	And what did your boss say to you?
Meg	He told me to think it over...
Therapist	And seeing him insist, how did you take it?
Meg	I didn't like it, but I didn't express anything. I told him I would think about it.
Therapist	If I understand correctly, besides being unpleasant it was surprising.
Meg	Yes, I didn't expect it at all.
Therapist	After the meeting, how did you feel?
Meg	Somewhat uncomfortable.
Therapist	And did you talk to Jordi about it that afternoon?
Meg	I didn't tell him anything.
Therapist	And during the week?
Meg	No.
Therapist	Does he know?
Meg	I haven't told him.

13.1.3 Marriage

Meg got married at 30 and was married for 24 years to Antonio. Just over 4 years ago, she filed for divorce, she has been living separately for 4 years and has been legally divorced for 2 and a half years. It was a mutual agreement with her husband. She says: "*During that period, I moved to an apartment. It was a pleasant transition. Frankly, I got rid of a very heavy "backpack." I felt liberated and at the same time I was more productive at work. I was very happy.*"

The two and a half years she has been divorced from Antonio she describes as a "real relief." According to her, she maintains a cordial relationship with her ex-husband (e.g., she greets him for his birthday and holidays, and talks occasionally on the phone, etc.). She describes her 24-year marital relationship as essentially boring, emotionally distant, and with almost no sexual activity for many years.

The therapist asks her if there was admiration for her husband. Meg says: "I've never thought about it... I don't think so. He was a nice man and that's it."

The following describes part of the therapeutic dialogue about the marriage:

Meg	We didn't entertain each other, we also didn't have a social life with other couples. He read all the time and I watched series on Netflix and also read a lot. We talked very little, particularly the last 2 years. We slept in separate rooms for almost 9 years and a bit more at the time of separation. He snored and I couldn't sleep.
Therapist	I see. Meg, you told me that you had left home and then filed for divorce, when did you realize that the relationship "wasn't going anywhere"?

Meg	Just before I left home. I was bored and didn't want to come home... that's what made me understand that it was enough and 1 day I decided to come home earlier. I called him on the phone, and told him "Antonio, I'll be home at 3:30 and I need to talk to you." I arrived, made myself a tea and offered him a soda. He was very calm and with his usual face. I told him I was bored, that I would divorce him and that I would leave that same night.
Therapist	And how did he take it?
Meg	He understood.
Therapist	And?
Meg	I told him I was going to my apartment which was close to the office. That later my lawyer would contact him.
Therapist	And he agreed?
Meg	Yes.
Therapist	How do you explain that after 24 years of history together, you simply informed him that you were leaving?
Meg	I got completely bored.
Therapist	I see... And what could happen to him with what you told him?
Meg	I don't know... I was very bored.
Therapist	But, did you think about it? Did you weigh it?
Meg	I didn't think about it or weigh it.
Therapist	It seems to me that the disconnection went beyond what was tolerable and the "us" ceased to exist. And as a result, the pleasure of being together was not felt.
Meg	It's very possible... I wasn't interested in sharing with him.
Therapist	I see... Meg, at that time, did you feel energy in your day to day?
Meg	I don't know, but my job was going very well. But coming to my home, it was uncomfortable and I would go to my room and think about what I would have to do the next day.

From her marriage to Antonio, their daughter, "Marcia," was born. Her pregnancy was normal and Meg did not have any problems during the pregnancy or after giving birth. Both her husband's and her relationship with Marcia is primarily defined by obligations. "*From a young age, she was a loving, responsible child, helpful with chores, and did not give us any major problems*." On the other hand, Marcia's relationship with her father is defined as loving and attached from the beginning. She says: "*They had and still have a very close relationship. Moreover, his period of unemployment coincided with Marcia's most important years. Antonio was always concerned about her. To this day, they visit each other frequently*." Marcia would always go on vacation for 2 weeks to stay with her paternal grandparents, with whom she got along very well, in another city. Lastly, she points out that the daughter's relationship with her maternal grandmother was acceptable but is now distant. Marcia never got along with her grandmother.

Marcia is 23 years old, a professional, married for 2 years, and does not have children. Meg describes her relationship with her daughter as "close but not so much... we had and still have many differences," and for the past 3 years, they see each other once a year because her daughter lives in another city and comes for work to the city where Meg lives. She adds that they talk on the phone once a month. Also, she points out that since her daughter left home, they have not had conflicts, which were frequent before and always ended in verbal fights of mutual disqualification; they would not talk for several days and then the situation would be resolved "as if nothing had happened." The therapist asks her to specify, what kind of disqualifications? "You're a robot, Marcia would tell me." And you Meg, what would you say? "Focus on your studies so you can become someone in life... the way you're going, you won't get anywhere."

She highlights that today, her relationship with Marcia is not a concern and adds: "*I fulfilled my duty with Marcia, I gave her an excellent education in the best schools and paid for her university until she graduated. She never lacked anything. Even until recently, I was concerned about whether she needed money and I have always told her that she can count on me.*"

The therapist asks about Marcia's birthday celebrations. Meg says: "*In general, we would get together to eat a cake and give her a book or some course she wanted to take on her vacations. In fact, my husband and I gave her language courses on several occasions and any other course she wanted to do. When she turned 15, we gave her permission to have a party. We rented a place and she had her party.*"Did you go to the party with your husband? "Well, I was there for 2 hours and then I left. I gave her a pen, ate cake, and went home alone. My husband stayed all afternoon."

At another point in the session, part of the dialogue about the reason for her divorce is transcribed:

When asked about the reason for the divorce, she refers to her 24 years of marriage as very boring and lonely "alone in company," and with some minor financial difficulties at certain periods that she resolved. Her ex-husband had many periods of unemployment (he was unemployed for at least 5 years and months in total) and she always took care of the finances. The therapist explores how she experienced this difficulty; part of the dialogue is transcribed:

Meg	His periods of unemployment were a problem since we had quite a few expenses, but Marcia was small, and I didn't demand much from him... For me, the important thing was that the girl was protected and cared for by her father and the housekeeper. Something like that...
Therapist	Aha... but for you, in summary, what did your husband's unemployment mean?
Meg	That he was incompetent and lacked the strength to move forward.
Therapist	And this image of your husband, did you have it before these periods of unemployment?
Meg	No.
Therapist	What image or images did you have before?
Meg	Working man.

Therapist	And the incompetent part?
Meg	No.
Therapist	What if you put yourself in the moment when you decide to divorce?
Meg	Boring, lonely, without challenges or drive to “reinvent” himself.
Therapist	And now?
Meg	It remains the same. He has no challenges.

She describes her ex-husband as a working and lonely person at first. Later, his lack of energy, enthusiasm, and low motivation to look for work would appear. He didn’t care about not having enough money, as long as he could read his favorite novels, the newspaper, and watch news during the day. In addition, she says that social life was non-existent for at least the last 10 years and their intimate sexual life had not existed for many years. She says: “To be honest with you, the sexual aspect with Antonio never mattered much to me.”

13.1.4 Love Story

Meg reveals that her only boyfriend was her husband Antonio. She met him in the university library when she was finishing her doctoral thesis. In that last year, they started dating. Two years later, they got married.

Regarding her current boyfriend “Jordi.” She says that she met him at a conference 2 years and 2 months ago. They started dating months later and 14 months ago she moved in with him. He is 61 years old and has a consolidated and relaxed economic situation.

She describes Jordi as a friendly person, enthusiastic about his work, and very sociable. She adds that she admires him in a certain way for being very hardworking, competent, responsible, friendly, and affectionate. And she adds: “He admires my career and is interested in what I do.”

On the other hand, she describes her relationship with Jordi as “strange” and “tricky” for some time now. In the second session, the therapist explores more about what she means by “strange.” The following is a fragment of the session:

Therapist	Let’s clarify a bit more this thing you already mentioned in the first session, about feeling “strange.”
Meg	I feel “strange but close” I would say.
Therapist	And how do you realize you’re “strange but close”?
Meg	Most of the time in these months I don’t know what I feel and I think a lot about this. And sometimes I can’t stop thinking... it’s silly... many hours and I don’t come to any conclusion, why do I feel this way? Jordi, I don’t like feeling him so attentive to me... sometimes his closeness

and concern bother me... it sounds strange, but that's how I feel. I'm always thinking about the relationship and I have doubts about whether to continue with him.

Therapist Do you think thinking for many hours will help you solve your problem?

Meg Of course. For me, worrying and thinking about the causes of feeling this way will surely help me organize my mind and solve the problem.

Therapist But that hasn't happened so far.

Meg No.

Therapist Okay. Let's go slowly Meg, what does "closeness" mean to you?

Meg It's sometimes a fun relationship for me, as he has a lot of sense of humor... he makes me laugh... and he asks me, how are you? how was work? how was your day? and things like that... that's what I mean by closeness.

Therapist And the "concern"?

Meg That he is constantly attentive.

Therapist I partially understand. To understand you accurately, could you give me a real example?

Meg I come home from work and he hugs me, offers me something to drink. He asks me what I want for dinner, jokes around, etcetera. He seems interested, in a good mood, and very attentive to me.

Therapist Is that uncomfortable?

Meg Yes.

Therapist I understand. Was it different with your ex-husband?

Meg Absolutely. My marriage was always boring, we didn't talk... sometimes we didn't see each other on weekdays, we also didn't sleep together... it's a huge difference. I don't remember coming home from work and my husband offering me something or anything like that... He wasn't a courteous man, he was very distant at times, he hardly spoke.

Therapist Both relationships are very different in emotional closeness.

Meg Yes, a lot.

Therapist Do you always sleep with Jordi?

Meg Yes.

Therapist Is it pleasant to share the bedroom?

Meg Yes, it's pleasant.

Therapist And your sex life?

Meg With Jordi we have a satisfying sex life, but in recent months the frequency has decreased because I don't feel like it.

Therapist Since when?

Meg About 3 months.

Therapist And how does Jordi handle that?

Meg He worries about me... he's always happy and affectionate.

At another point in the session, the therapist explores if there is any aspect that makes her uncomfortable in relation to the future:

Therapist	If we visualize the near future, is there anything that worries you?
Meg	Yes, there is an issue I need to decide. Jordi proposed with great enthusiasm that we move to another city in about a year and a half. This is because he will be promoted to a high position in the company. It will be in the coming months and then he will have to move.
Therapist	When did he tell you about moving?
Meg	About 7 months ago.
Therapist	And what did you think of the proposal?
Meg	It surprised me.
Therapist	That "it surprised me," is it pleasant, indefinable or unpleasant?
Meg	I don't know... more unpleasant I think...
Therapist	Did you consider it possible?
Meg	I don't know.
Therapist	Could you imagine it at that time?
Meg	Not at all.
Therapist	And now, after 7 months, can you imagine it?
Meg	I haven't been able to.
Therapist	I understand. If we look at it from reflection, how do you assess the possibility of moving to another city?
Meg	I have doubts. Frankly, I don't know.
Therapist	That "I don't know," does it refer only to "Meg" or to "Meg with Jordi"?
Meg	I think more to me... it's me who doesn't know, I hadn't felt like this.
Therapist	How so?
Meg	That I have no direction... a bit lost... something like that.
Therapist	Can you visualize in images your future in the city that Jordi will move to?
Meg	I can't.
Therapist	And if we focus on your sensation of yourself, of Meg, with respect to that possibility of living in another city with Jordi
Meg	I struggle... lost... something like that.
Therapist	Less control perhaps?
Meg	Clearly, I don't feel or have any control.
Therapist	Without control.
Meg	Yes.
Therapist	It seems to me that the impact is more emotional... I feel fear here... am I correct?
Meg	Yes.
Therapist	It's loss of control wrapped in fear... and I understand that you haven't felt this way with anyone in love.
Meg	Yes, it scares me... yes.
Therapist	It's a relationship of warmth and security that you haven't experienced as far as I understand.

Meg	Yes, nothing like this happened in my marriage.
Therapist	A man who takes care of you, confident in himself and who cares about your well-being.
Meg	I have no experience in this.
Therapist	This that you reflect and communicate to me, in my view, partly explains the comparison between Antonio and Jordi...
Meg	In what sense?
Therapist	In that they are two relationships that differ robustly. You avoided Antonio and were not bothered by the situation. In contrast with Jordi, you are uncomfortable with his kindness, affection, and concern for many months and do not isolate yourself from Jordi. Am I correct?
Meg	Yes, I don't avoid him. Only sometimes.
Therapist	That's what I observe in what you tell me. So, comparing the two relationships allows for more parameters to better understand the present moment which is somewhat confusing for you.
Meg	I understand... It would be a way to understand what I don't understand...
Therapist	I would specify, start to gradually understand what you don't understand at a sufficient level to have adequate psychological regulation. In other words, fear is a way to alert one's own attention... it's like saying "More attention Meg on this matter!"
Meg	Yes.
Therapist	Also, if I understand correctly, if you were to move to another city and all that implies, it would reflect a greater emotional commitment, am I right?
Meg	I think so... and I don't know if I could tolerate it...
Therapist	I understand that he, despite his state of decline, continues to support you and does not alter his plans to move to another city with you.
Meg	That's right. I didn't expect that...
Therapist	He is a man who is committed to you.
Meg	I'm not used to it...
Therapist	And could that be related to what you told me about feeling "deceptive"?
Meg	Of course. I feel like I'm not being honest with Jordi... I have a mess in my head.
Therapist	Haven't you told Jordi anything about your doubts?
Meg	I haven't said anything.
Therapist	Meg, I understand the situation you are going through, and asking for psychological help is a way to take care of yourself and the people around you.
Meg	Asking for help... hard for me, but it's true.
Therapist	I reiterate that it is a way to take care of your psychological health and your relationship with Jordi. And I must tell you, I also observe a genuine interest on your part in taking care of your romantic relationship with Jordi.
Meg	Maybe. And my doubts?

Therapist	They are legitimate in a situation of greater commitment in the short term. It's not terrible, it's a way to reflect, but you remain in the relationship.
Meg	I see…
Therapist	Look Meg, depression can also be generally understood as a way of partially or totally withdrawing from the social to have more time to reflect on the importance of the present moment and the near future, in a context of change and possible threats. In other words, it can be understood as a pattern adaptive that is activated in particular situations that are threatening to people for various reasons. And essentially it is to capture, decipher and resolve.
Meg	I like that way of understanding it…
Therapist	It can happen to all of us.
Meg	I understand.
Therapist	We will work together to better understand this crucial dilemma in your life.
Meg	Agreed.

13.1.5 Family of Origin

Meg was the only child of a single mother, whom she describes as a very hardworking, distant and hypercritical woman. Her mother has been insulin-dependent since she was 41 years old. She has had morbid obesity since she was 33 years old and remains in the same condition at present.

Meg studied at a girls' school, from her start in childhood until her adolescence. Her mother always supported her in her academic development. In fact, the only conversations she remembers are about her grades. She notes that her adolescence was difficult and she had many difficulties with her mother. She says "*On many occasions we argued and did not speak for several days*." When asked what she means by "difficult," she points out: "*We argued because I stayed up very late every day doing puzzles*."

Currently, her mother lives in another city, is 77 years old, and continues working in her company. The relationship, today, is quite distant. They only call each other by phone from afar.

Regarding her father, she did not know him. And all she knows is that he is alive, is a merchant marine and has lived abroad for decades. She has never been interested in knowing about him. She says "*My biological father has never been interested in me*." It is noteworthy that when she referred to her biological father, her facial expression was cold, her eye contact decreased and a certain degree of displeasure was observed on her face.

When asked about extended family (grandparents, uncles, etc.), she refers that she has vague memories of her grandparents. Her maternal grandparents died when she was very young, she practically has no memories, and her mother is an only child.

The emotional climate in her house was quite cold and distant according to her description. She went to school and at night, her mother came home and asked her about her homework and little else. They rarely had dinner together. There was always food prepared in the fridge and Meg heated up the dinner when she got home. Her mother, only highlighted the importance of the duty to be a good student and to give her best effort to achieve her purposes.

She has few memories of emotional warmth, affection, and celebrations of birthdays and Christmases. Before turning 18, she went to study at the university, in another city.

Next, a fragment of the session is transcribed:

Meg	It was a very happy period for me from the moment I left home.
Therapist	Do you have any explanation for that happiness you highlight?
Meg	Of course, my mother could no longer keep asking me if I had done my homework, because I simply controlled whether I answered the landline.
Therapist	She had no control over you.
Meg	Of course, she no longer controlled me or saw me every day. It was an absolute liberation.

13.1.6 University Life

Meg was an excellent student. She loved her career from the first day. She describes her undergraduate study years as very happy. She says "*My passion was the computer lab and I loved the classes.*"

She had no friends at university, only study partners in certain subjects. Later, a few months after graduating as an engineer, she obtained a scholarship to pursue a doctorate at a prestigious university. She completed her doctorate in 5 years.

When asked about leisure and recreation during her university period, she says "*Not much... I think I only went to the graduation ceremony... I don't remember attending any parties. I often went to the cinema alone. And also to theater performances at the university.*"

13.1.7 General Health

Meg has type I obesity and has been insulin resistant for over a decade. She is 1.61 meters tall and noticeably overweight (weighs 84 kilos). She indicates that although she tries to lose weight very sporadically, she finds it difficult and sometimes impossible, as she constantly "snacks" and at times, when she doesn't feel very well, or remembers her separation or her doubt about continuing with Jordi, she "raids the refrigerator for sweets and ice cream." She has never done any physical activity and explicitly states that she is not interested. Part of the conversation is reproduced:

Meg	I have gained weight in these months, but I couldn't tell you precisely. I prefer not to weigh myself.
Therapist	You informed me that you are insulin resistant.
Meg	Yes. I feel tired and uncomfortable... I feel heavy and I don't like myself at all.
Therapist	Has your sedentary lifestyle increased in these months?
Meg	Yes.
Therapist	Sedentary lifestyle is not good for your condition of insulin resistance. You need to exercise more.
Meg	Exercise is not productive... we all have to die of something (laughs)
Therapist	You are laughing now, do you realize that? (kindly reflects).
Meg	Yes, I can be a bit ironic sometimes.
Therapist	I see. Now, maintaining weight and exercising is very necessary for people who are insulin resistant.
Meg	Yes, I know... I find it hard to take responsibility.
Therapist	Don't you feel the same way about your job?
Meg	Until recently, no. I'm on leave.
Therapist	I see. We will continue to talk about the importance of exercise and self-care for health at another time.
Meg	Okay.

The following are transcriptions of different moments from the second session. At the beginning of the second session, Meg tells the therapist:

Meg	There is an aspect that I want to discuss with you and it may be helpful. From a very young age, I couldn't tell you exactly when, maybe a little before I got married... I started having stomach discomfort and I vomited several times and got scared. I even went to the doctor and after several tests I was diagnosed with an ulcer. I took medication for a long time and avoided certain foods and spices like chili peppers. And since then I have always had these discomforts and annoyances that vary over time. In fact, for about 6 months now the discomfort has returned.
Therapist	How has that discomfort been in the last month?
Meg	I have felt "fires" in my stomach and discomfort. I will go to the doctor as soon as possible.
Therapist	Could it be related to how you feel?
Meg	It could be... I don't know.
Therapist	I understand. It's important that you check your health status with your doctor. When was your last medical check-up?
Meg	About 2 years ago and a bit more. I'll make an appointment when I'm at home. The psychiatrist told me the same thing.
Therapist	Taking care of one's health is very important and especially smart.
Meg	It's something that's hard for me...
Therapist	You mentioned it in the last session.
Meg	That's right.

At another moment in the second session, the therapist explores more about the offer of early retirement at the company:

Therapist	Let's go back to the issue of the early retirement benefit and additional bonus you mentioned in the first session. What expectations do you have for your career?
Meg	Money doesn't worry me today, I have enough money since I've worked all my life, I have no debts, and I've saved for my pension. I have expectations of making innovations in high complexity management and I've been working on it in my free time.
Therapist	And how long have you been working on it?
Meg	For about 4 years and a bit, on my weekends... my experience has allowed me to make some initial sketches. In the end, it's no longer an expectation, I'm close to finishing and testing how much it works.
Therapist	I see and feel you're excited about your project.
Meg	Yes, it's something longed for and I feel like it's the crowning of my ideas.
Therapist	Of course. And how do you value this offer of optional early retirement in relation to your project?
Meg	It's an obstacle, I don't like it at all.
Therapist	A feeling of obstacle to finish the project and continue developing your career, if you accepted?
Meg	Yes, that's right... everything will become uphill.
Therapist	Is "uphill" a thought or image?
Meg	It's an image of a rocky mountain that I can't climb.
Therapist	Are you alone or accompanied?
Meg	Alone.
Therapist	I feel you're distressed now, am I correct?
Meg	Yes.
Therapist	And does this image appear frequently in your mind?
Meg	Quite a bit, for weeks, maybe months... It's unpleasant because they appear...
Therapist	They're called intrusive images.
Meg	I didn't know. It's very distressing.
Therapist	It seems there's also helplessness?
Meg	Of course... I don't know how to climb, something like that.

At another moment in the session, they return to the issue of her project and offer of early retirement:

Therapist	I understand the issue of the obstacle to continue with your project more or less. Couldn't you do that in another organization for example?
Meg	I haven't thought about it...
Therapist	It's a good time to start...
Meg	I think in a world where women are treated differently than men, it gets quite complicated.

Therapist	I agree with you on that point.
Meg	That's why I think it would be harder in another company.
Therapist	It's possible, but not impossible. Good ideas have no gender, there are several examples.
Meg	That's true. It could be…
Therapist	Good ideas and their executions are not subject to any company that I know of... You can look for a job in another company, you have an excellent resume... if you set your mind to it, I don't see insurmountable difficulties.
Meg	That's true, but it gets complicated being a woman.
Therapist	It's a point to consider, but it also depends on the quality of the company... "Sowing and reaping a good seed also depends on the quality of the soil."
Meg	That's true. I like the metaphor.
Therapist	Okay (both laugh). Focusing on your project and setting aside the fact that you are a woman, an aspect that I agree with you on regarding treatment differences, in what way does the offer of early retirement complicate things for you?
Meg	I was surprised by this offer... it's not the right time.
Therapist	It seems that the surprise disconcerted you... as if you hadn't anticipated it as a possibility, and at the same time, it adds that you feel it breaks and stops a near future plan.
Meg	My performance has been very good and I didn't imagine it as a possibility. Frankly, I didn't see it coming.
Therapist	Of course, but it's an optional benefit. It's not an obligation to accept it. Am I correct?
Meg	True.
Therapist	Also, in general, a good performance from an employee is not immunity for a company not to offer retirement incentives or dismiss an employee... I mean changing workers for innovation plans for different reasons.
Meg	That's right. I know it very well because I had to dismiss employees at different times.
Therapist	Of course. Meg, I feel like it's as if you couldn't carry out your project if you accept the benefit... and frankly, I don't see that impossibility, do you understand me?
Meg	I understand what you're saying, but I feel down and without a clear direction. I know, I can say no, but I feel uncomfortable.
Therapist	I see, but you haven't lost control of your work life, Meg.
Meg	I feel like I have quite a bit.
Therapist	I understand... It affected you since you didn't expect it and that project of yours is a significant advancement in your career of achievements that you have embraced and expected to present at the company.
Meg	It was a contribution I had been working on quietly... yes, I was hoping to do that.

Therapist	Now you're speaking in the past tense, Meg.
Meg	True... (5 s)
Therapist	You're still at the company, Meg.
Meg	Yes.
Therapist	Your work at the company hasn't ended, nor has your project that you're about to finish.
Meg	Yes.
Therapist	Your project is present and near future... It's up to you to make that achievement you've been working on for years come true.
Meg	I find it hard to see it that way.
Therapist	But it's up to you... it's your contribution and it doesn't depend on the company you work for... do you see it?
Meg	I see it as linked.
Therapist	But it's not necessarily like that... First of all, they haven't informed you that you have to accept early retirement; and, secondly, there are many companies that value and are receptive to good technological innovations regardless of whether the author is a man or a woman.
Meg	That's true, but I'm also 58 years old... changes will come in the company with or without me, and it's harder. If I stay, it will be harder and if I leave, it will also be.
Therapist	It will be different in any of the options, but I don't know if it will be harder.
Meg	It might be.
Therapist	Age and good ideas that end in technological innovation are not tied to any particular company. And even more so, considering that it has been carried out as your own project, it is your authorship... you have great freedom and opportunities.
Meg	That's right... I struggle to feel it that way.
Therapist	Before we finish this point, it seems to me that working with predominantly men challenges you, am I correct?
Meg	Yes,
Therapist	In what sense?
Meg	In that I always have to be alert that my work is very good.
Therapist	Only in that it is very good?
Meg	Now that you ask me, I don't know.
Therapist	That it is of equal quality?
Meg	No, it has to be superior. Being of equal quality is negative for me.
Therapist	And how do you feel about the question?
Meg	I don't understand what you mean.
Therapist	I observe you tense facially.
Meg	Yes. I'm uncomfortable
Therapist	I see. Is the question pleasant or unpleasant?
Meg	Unpleasant.
Therapist	I understand Meg. We will continue talking about this at another time.
Meg	Yes, it's important to me.

At the end of the second session, the therapist asks Meg to describe how she is psychologically and what is the most urgent. Part of the session is reproduced:

Meg	I'm distant from my partner and from myself... I've never felt like this before.
Therapist	And how do you realize that now?
Meg	Before I was calm, I was proud of my plans and very sure of what I was doing... now I'm without energy and lost... I don't feel interested or challenged by anything... I don't feel like working and I feel uncomfortable and distanced from Jordi... and I don't understand what's happening to me... I feel horrible.
Therapist	Trapped? Tangled? Stuck?
Meg	Stuck... without direction in my life, I don't understand why it's happening to me... I feel horrible.
Therapist	By the way, at any point in these months have you had ideas or images of harming yourself?
Meg	No, not at all. I've felt very bad at times, but it's never crossed my mind to harm myself.
Therapist	I understand. Meg, now I observe you and feel scared and fearful mainly with Jordi, am I wrong?
Meg	You're not wrong. I've never felt so scared.
Therapist	Is it only with Jordi or does it also happen with your work?
Meg	It worries and scares me too.
Therapist	Aha. And what is the main focus of the fear?
Meg	My partner. I'm 58 years old and I feel like I don't have a compass... something like that.
Therapist	Do you think about it?
Meg	Yes.
Therapist	Do you also have images?
Meg	Sometimes images of me being alone appear...
Therapist	Give me an example of one of those images that appeared in your consciousness.
Meg	Alone and sad.
Therapist	Don't you see anyone around you?
Meg	No.
Therapist	Does the image repeat and interfere with what you're doing?
Meg	Yes, it's quite frequent.
Therapist	We will look at those images in the next sessions.
Meg	Okay.
Therapist	In my view, you feel emotionally distant from your partner because you live with fear and anguish in "an unknown territory" called warmth, affection, and intimacy, that is, being with someone caring, secure, concerned about your well-being and happiness.
Meg	It's true that I'm not used to it and I feel distant. It's so true that Jordi is now in the waiting room of your office.

Therapist	I understand.
Meg	He insisted on accompanying me and postponed a work meeting.
Therapist	And you, how do you feel about his waiting?
Meg	I feel "strange"...
Therapist	"Cared for" by Jordi?
Meg	Possibly.
Therapist	I see you're sad now.
Meg	Yes, I feel sorry for myself. Imagine... I'm a woman of a certain age and I feel like I don't know what I want... "I wish the earth would swallow me up."
Therapist	You're very hard on yourself, Meg.
Meg	Maybe.
Therapist	To me, it seems excessively harsh. Now, it seems to me that you don't feel up to your personal image, that is, "a woman of your age should know what she wants."
Meg	I don't like myself.
Therapist	Can you be more specific about what you don't like?
Meg	My doubts... I don't know if I want to continue in the relationship and I'm ambiguous... and even more so, he wants us to move together to another city in a while...
Therapist	I perceive that you also censor yourself. Meg, we can all have doubts...
Meg	Yes, but it's not fair.
Therapist	What's not fair?
Meg	I don't tell him anything and he puts up with me. He doesn't know what's going on with me.
Therapist	But you look worried and uneasy... and that informs that he is very present in your conscience. It speaks well of you as far as I'm concerned.
Meg	I don't know... He's a caring and kind person, he doesn't deserve to be in a situation like this, where he doesn't know what's going on with me.
Therapist	I understand your point of view, but he is an adult who knows how to take care of himself.
Meg	Maybe.
Therapist	And what is the most urgent thing to resolve now?
Meg	To clarify my doubts about whether to continue with Jordi or not. That's what I need, he doesn't deserve it.
Therapist	Haven't you been able to clarify by thinking about it?
Meg	I think a lot and I can't clarify and it frustrates me not to get anywhere.
Therapist	We will work on it, Meg.
Meg	That's what I need... I can't solve this alone and it causes me a lot of distress.
Therapist	I understand, Meg. We will work on this issue.
Meg	Thank you!

At the end of the second session, Meg asks the therapist if it would be possible for him to speak with Jordi for a few minutes:

Therapist	If you consider it appropriate, then of course, but it must be in his presence to avoid any misunderstanding.
Meg	Sure, I'll stay. Yes, it's appropriate for us all to talk because sometimes I get overwhelmed and I don't know what to say. You'll surely feel more at ease.
Therapist	Well, we will notify him immediately.
Meg	Thank you very much!

Essentially, Jordi communicates to the therapist a lot of concern about Meg's state since she was given medical leave, and he highlights that she is very down, sometimes distant, somewhat moody and sad, and he wants to know how he can help her in her recovery.

In addition, he emphasizes that he feels worried because Meg doesn't say anything about what's happening to her or very little, which worries him even more. It is noteworthy that Meg listens attentively to what Jordi says to the therapist, and nods her head, but says nothing.

Lastly, the therapist generally explains Meg's psychological condition of depression and informs him that they have agreed with Meg to undergo a process of psychotherapy. And that, if necessary, the three of them will meet again.

13.2 Protocol Application: Case Formulation from an Evolutionary Perspective

13.2.1 Case Formulation from an Evolutionary Perspective: Assessment

Name: Meg.
Evaluation conducted in session 3. It includes the integration of the two previous sessions conducted over a period of 2 weeks.

Reason for consultation (in patient's own words): "To clarify my doubts about whether to continue with Jordi or not. That's what I need, he doesn't deserve this."

13.2.1.1 Thematic Conceptualization

Dysfunctional Intersubjective Theme (co-construction): Trapped by not feeling emotionally in tune with her partner.

(mark presence: **x**)

Specify thematic axis(es):

Psychological intimacy ☒ Death/Finitude of existence ☐ Surrender ☐ Greatness ☐ Inferiority ☐ Avenger ☐ Power ☐ Failure ☐ Loss ☐ Complacent ☐ Inauthenticity ☐ Freedom ☐ Uncontrollability ☐ Certainty ☐ Mistrust ☐ Perfectionism ☐ Betrayal ☐ Opposition ☐ Loneliness ☐ Limitation ☐ Sabotage ☐ Transcend ☐ Contempt ☐ Hypercontrol ☐ Hypercriticism ☐ Discrimination ☐ Jealousy ☐ Compete ☐ Postponement ☐ Uprooting ☐ Self-sacrifice ☐ Sexualization ☐ Unworthy ☐ Abandonment ☐ Incompetence ☐ Moral superiority ☐
Fear of aging ☐ Paternal absence ☐ Maternal deficiency ☐
Technological addiction ☐ Others: ________________

Dysfunctional Narrative:

Example: "Before I was calm, I felt proud of my plans and very sure of what I was doing… now I'm without energy and lost… I don't feel interested or challenged by anything… I don't feel like working and I feel uncomfortable and distanced from Jordi… and I don't understand what's happening to me… I feel horrible."

Beginning of the Topic(s)? Course?

It starts in full bloom 6 months ago according to Meg.

Are there relevant life events and/or precipitating stressors?

There are 2 relevant events according to what Meg communicates:
1st: Her current partner has proposed moving to another city in 1 and a half years. He will be promoted to a high position at his job in the coming months and then he will have to move.
2nd: The company offered her early retirement and she did not like the offer.

Is there frustration of basic psychological needs: competence, autonomy, relationship?

The psychological need for relationship is observed to be altered. chronically. It should be noted that the new couple cares about her well-being, values her, and has future plans with her.

What strengths do you identify in the person?

Meg is a person with superior intelligence.

Observations: The focus is on the unknown of experiencing a warm loving relationship.

SELF SYSTEM: Clinical Assessment

(mark presence: **x**)

SENSE OF AGENCY/EFFICIENCY: Alteration ☒

Describe: The sense of agency is observed with alterations in motivation, purposes, and self-confidence. It is noteworthy that there is a deficit in expectations of efficacy and outcome. For example: "With Jordi, I feel very distant and I don't understand the reasons."

SELF-NARRATIVE/COHERENCE: Alteration ☒

Describe: The self-narrative about the development of her "relationship with Jordi" is a source of discontinuity for her identity, for example: "Stuck... aimless in my life, I don't understand why it happens to me... I feel horrible."

SENSE OF TIMING/BALANCE: Alteration ☒

Describe: The psychological temporal dynamic is not fluid. She perceives herself with a problematic present and does not visualize futures. For example: "Before, I organized my time very well. Since I started with this unpleasant state, time passes me by and I do not manage to organize myself as before, and now I solve very little... it is not usual for me... I can't explain it."

SELF-ESTEEM/SELF-DECEPTION: Alteration ☒

Describe: She describes herself as "weird" and "deceptive" in her love relationship. Basically, "weird" refers to not having experience with feeling cared for and loved. And " deceptive" is the self-assessment of feeling guilty for not telling Jordi her doubts about whether to continue in the relationship.

SELF-CARE/HEALTH: Alteration ☒

Describe: She has insomnia. Also, she has type 1 obesity, insulin resistance, chronic problems with food, and a history of ulcers. She does not value physical activity; she says: "Exercise is not productive... we all have to die of something."

Observations: The crux of her sense of narrative discontinuity is a meaning of being "trapped." She perceives herself as lost, dishonest with Jordi and added to this, the feeling of "professional invalidation" due to the offer of early retirement.

13.2.1.2 Evaluation of Dysfunctional Intersubjective Knowledge Domains

[COGNITION] Indicate and weigh which processes contribute to discomfort and/or psychological dysregulation: Meg presents high psychological discomfort and moderate psychological dysregulation.

(mark presence: **x**)

Cognitive alterations:
Rumination ☒ Worry ☒ Intolerance to uncertainty ☐ Selective attention ☒
Problematic attributional profile ☒ Absence of realistic expectations ☐
Deficit in problem solving ☐ Others: ______________________

Describe: First, there is presence of rumination and worry. The rumination is about "whether or not to continue with Jordi" (confused). On the other hand, the worry is about what to do in the face of Jordi's move ("I have doubts. Frankly, I don't know"). Second, she presents selective attention to negative aspects that feed the "doubt" and problematic attribution: She values loneliness and avoidance as beneficial.

Alterations in metacognition:

Representation ☐ Differentiation ☐ Decentering ☐ Sharing ☐ Belonging ☐
Integration ☐ Positive metacognitive beliefs ☒ Negative metacognitive beliefs ☒
Others: ______________________

Describe: The alteration of the sense of belonging is observed, example: "I have always felt somewhat distant from people. Loneliness does not bother me."
In addition, she presents positive and negative metacognitive beliefs about rumination:
a) Positive metacognitive belief, for example: " For me worrying and thinking about the causes of feeling this way will surely help me to organize my mind and solve the problem".
b) Negative metacognitive belief (uncontrollability and worry), example: "I think a lot and I can't clarify and it despairs me not to get anywhere".

Alterations in executive functions:

Cognitive flexibility ☒ Attentional control ☒ Inhibition ☐ Self-monitoring ☐
Planning ☐ Others: ______________________

Describe: Cognitive rigidity, difficulties in attentional control and concentration are observed.

Psychological Distress						Psychological Well-Being
High	Moderate	Mild	Neutral	Mild	Moderate	High
-3	-2	-1	0	1	2	3
Psychological Dysregulation						Psychological Regulation
High	Moderate	Mild	Neutral	Mild	Moderate	High
-3	**-2**	-1	0	1	2	3

[**EMOTION**] Indicate and weigh which processes contribute to psychological distress and/or dysregulation: Meg presents high psychological distress and moderate psychological dysregulation.

(mark presence: **x**)

Alteration of emotional awareness:
Emotional profile ☒ Emotional clarity ☒ Emotional differentiation ☐
Understanding emotions ☒ Emotional appraisal in decision making and problem solving ☒ Dysfunctional mood ☒ Others: ____________________

Describe: An emotional profile is observed in which guilt, anger, fear, sadness, and anxiety stand out. In addition, there is a decreased emotional clarity, difficulty in understanding emotions in their context, and absence of assessment in decision making and problem solving. Finally, presence of depressive mood.

Emotional Dysregulation:
Regulatory strategies ☒ Individual Coping ☒ Dyadic Coping ☒ Adult attachment ☒
Others: ____________________

Describe: There is emotional suppression and deficit of individual and dyadic coping. In addition, presence of avoidant adult attachment, eg: "To Jordi, I don't like feeling him so attentive to me, sometimes his closeness and concern bother me... it sounds strange, but that's how I feel. I'm thinking about the relationship all the time and I have doubts about whether to continue with him."

Psychological Distress						Psychological Well-Being
High	Moderate	Mild	Neutral	Mild	Moderate	High
-3	-2	-1	0	1	2	3
Psychological Dysregulation						Psychological Regulation
High	Moderate	Mild	Neutral	Mild	Moderate	High
-3	**-2**	-1	0	1	2	3

[INTERPERSONAL] Indicate and weigh what processes contribute to discomfort and/or psychological dysregulation:_Meg presents mild psychological discomfort and mild psychological dysregulation.

(mark presence: **x**)

Alteration in personal relationships:

Social skills deficits ☐
Deficit of social support ☐
Lack of friends ☐
Dark Triad personality ☐
Loneliness ☒
Discomfort with people ☒
Constant need for approval ☐
Conflicting labor relations ☐
Others: Low motivation to meet people is observed.

Describe: The most notable thing is the loneliness that she experiences as comfortable and has become excessive in her life trajectory: "I have always felt somewhat distant from people. Loneliness does not bother me". And she is aware of discomfort with people but it is not a problem that is observed in her work role. Low motivation to meet people in her past and present history is also observed.

Alteration in romantic relationships:

Decreased confidence ☐
Decreased intimacy ☒
Insecurity ☐
Absence or low admiration ☐
Romantic friendship ☐
Conflict ☐
Diminished passion ☐
Decreased decisiveness/commitment ☐
Fear of abandonment ☐
Decreased cooperation ☐
Intimate partner violence ☐
Others: ________________________

Describe: In her marriage, the harmony ("us") and intimacy was very little present and became non-existent before her divorce. In her love relationship, tolerating intimacy is observed to be diminished.

Psychological Distress						Psychological Well-Being
High	Moderate	Mild	Neutral	Mild	Moderate	High
-3	-2	**-1**	0	1	2	3
Psychological Dysregulation						Psychological Regulation
High	Moderate	Mild	Neutral	Mild	Moderate	High
-3	-2	**-1**	0	1	2	3

[IMAGINATION] Indicate and weigh what processes contribute to distress and/or psychological dysregulation: Meg Presents mild psychological discomfort and moderate psychological deregulation.

(mark presence: **x**)

Imagination interferes with experiential coherence:
Intrusive mental images ☒ Flashbacks ☐ Hotspots ☐ Suicidal flashforwards ☐
Images as an emotional amplifier ☐ Others: ____________________

Describe: Communicates that he has intrusive images of loneliness (e.g., he sees himself without company Jordi).

Imagination interferes with problem solving:
Alteration in mental simulation ☒ Deficit of imagination directed to personal goals ☐
Imagination is a source of self-sabotage ☒ Others: ____________________

Describe: There are images of self-sabotage "rocky mountain" (impotence) that begin after she was informed of the offer of early retirement. In addition, the absence of imagination to simulate possible mental scenarios impoverishes the representation of possibilities to consider a new scenario of relationship and change of city.

Psychological Distress						Psychological Well-Being
High	Moderate	Mild	Neutral	Mild	Moderate	High
-3	-2	**-1**	0	1	2	3
Psychological Dysregulation						Psychological Regulation
High	Moderate	Mild	Neutral	Mild	Moderate	High
-3	**-2**	-1	0	1	2	3

[CORPOREALITY] Indicate and weigh what processes contribute to discomfort and/or psychological dysregulation: Meg presents mild psychological discomfort and moderate psychological dysregulation.

(mark presence: **x**)

Altered experience:

Lack of energy/fatigue ☒ Somatosensory amplification ☐

Interoception disturbances ☐ Alteration of mental representation of the body ☐

Others: ________________________

Describe: The lack of energy is observed to be present, example: "Recently, I would come home and go to bed exhausted".

Dysfunctional body attitude:

Insufficient body self-care ☒ Consequences of sleep on the body ☐

Others: ________________________

Describe: For Meg, her physical condition and body have been neglected, example: "I feel tired and I don't feel comfortable... I feel heavy and I don't like myself at all". Also, she has gained weight in recent months.

Psychological Distress						Psychological Well-Being
High	Moderate	Mild	Neutral	Mild	Moderate	High
-3	-2	**-1**	0	1	2	3
Psychological Dysregulation						**Psychological Regulation**
High	Moderate	Mild	Neutral	Mild	Moderate	High
-3	**-2**	-1	0	1	2	3

[SEXUALITY] Indicate and weigh what processes contribute to discomfort and/or psychological deregulation: Meg presents mild psychological discomfort and mild psychological dysregulation.

(mark presence: **x**)

Sexual disconnection with a partner:

Absence of sexual interest ☒ Sexual performance anxiety ☐

Poor sexual communication ☐

Sexual dysfunction ☐

Sexual stress ☐ Unsatisfactory sexuality ☒

Others: ______________________

Describe: Has not felt sexual interest for approximately 3 months but maintains sexual life less frequently. Experiences their sexuality, which they describe as unsatisfactory, as unpleasant (and with anxiety) and fears it may be progressive.

Disconnection with others:

Pornography abuse ☐ Sexual addiction ☐

Excessive masturbation ☐ Others: ______________

Describe: Nothing to comment.

Psychological Distress						Psychological Well-Being
High	Moderate	Mild	Neutral	Mild	Moderate	High
-3	-2	**-1**	0	1	2	3
Psychological Dysregulation						Psychological Regulation
High	Moderate	Mild	Neutral	Mild	Moderate	High
-3	-2	**-1**	0	1	2	3

13.2.1.3 Representation of the Domains of Dysfunctional Intersubjective Knowledge

a.1 Indicate the evaluations in the boxes for the domains of dysfunctional intersubjective knowledge according to Psychological Distress-Well-being (D-W) and Psychological Dysregulation-Regulation (D-R). Also, represent the second order intersubjective knowledge domains in the quadrants for psychological evaluation (see Table 13.1 and Fig. 13.2).

Table 13.1 Domains of dysfunctional intersubjective knowledge (session 3)

	Distress- well-being	Dysregulation- regulation
Cognition [C]	−3	−2
Emotion [E]	−3	−2
Interpersonal [I]	−1	−1
Imagination [Im]	−1	−2
Corporeality [Cor]	−1	−2
Sexuality [sex]	−1	−1

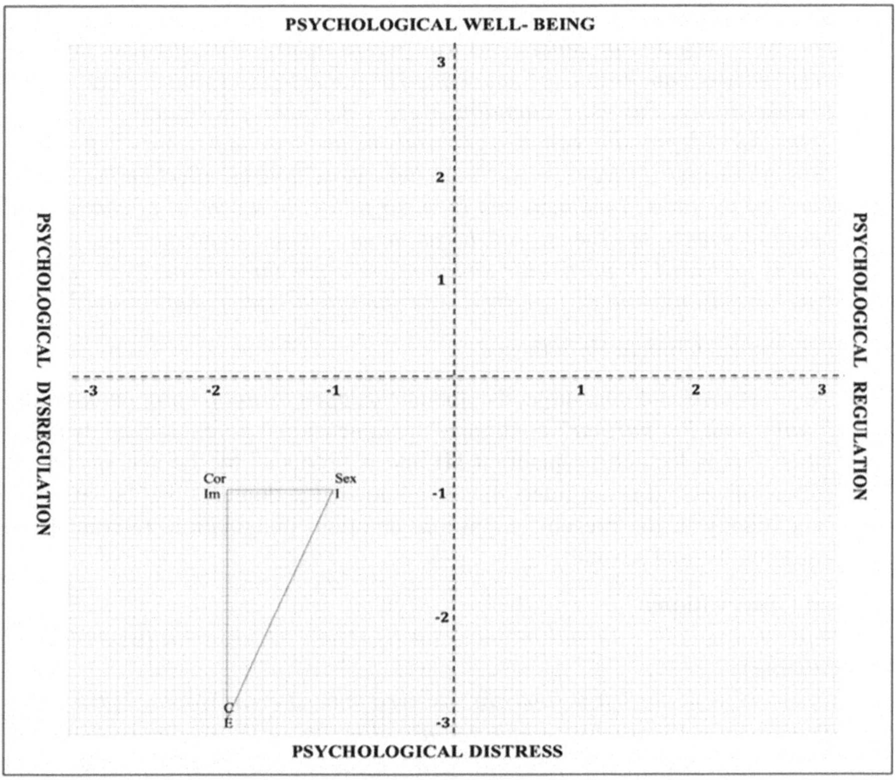

Fig. 13.2 Domains of dysfunctional intersubjective knowledge (session 3)

a.2 Indicate the agreed Therapeutic Objectives:

1. *Remission of depressive symptoms*
2. *Clarify and resolve doubts about her romantic relationship*

a.3 Main psychological reformulations communicated to the patient:

> "*We will clarify the reasons little by little. But it is clear that these are two very different relationships that you are comparing. With Antonio, you felt alone and not accompanied, particularly for the last 15 years; in contrast, with Jordi, you feel uncomfortable with his warm company.*"
> "*In my view, you feel emotionally distant from your partner because you live with fear and anguish of "an unknown territory for you called warmth, affection, and intimacy," that is, being with someone caring, secure, concerned about your well-being and happiness.*"
> "*You would need to gradually start understanding what you cannot fully decipher yet... you do not understand well yet. In other words, the fear that you acknowledge can initially be understood as a way to alert your own attention. It's like saying: Pay more attention, Meg, to decipher this matter!*"
> "*Look Meg, depression can also generally be understood as a way to partially or totally withdraw from the social to have more time to reflect on the importance of the present moment and the near future, in a context of change and possible threats. In other words, it can be understood as an adaptive pattern that is activated in particular situations that are threatening to people for various reasons. And essentially it is to capture, decipher, and resolve.*"

a.4 Psychological Clinical Hypothesis:

> The dysfunctional intersubjective theme ***"trapped by not feeling emotionally in tune with her partner"*** configures the dimensional psychological dysregulation that is located in quadrant **III** and is produced by the synergy of the following second-order intersubjective knowledge domains that behave dysfunctionally in the present: cognition, emotion, imagination, interpersonal, corporeality, and sexuality.

General Observations

Meg is psychologically situated in quadrant III (High dimensional psychological dysregulation).

All dimensions of the Self System are observed to be altered. Moreover, the greatest difficulties in psychological regulation are observed in the secondary intersubjective knowledge domains: "cognitive" and "affective" (see D-W and D-R).

It should be noted that the second-order intersubjective knowledge domain "Religiosity/Spirituality" is not part of Meg's processing because she is neither religious nor spiritual. She defines herself as an atheist and clarifies that she is not spiritual, and it is not observed that this intersubjective knowledge domain participates in the Dysfunctional Intersubjective Theme.

It is noteworthy that in the two evaluation sessions, Meg has been kind and collaborative, and her intelligence stands out as a great strength. To conclude, including her partner in the second session is valued as an indicator of good prognosis for an emerging dyadic coping.

13.2.1.4 Psychometric Tests: First Application (Baseline)

The results of the two psychometric tests applied before the third session are presented in Table 13.2.

Table 13.2 BDI-II results[a] OQ-45 area results[b] (first application)

Instrument	Total score	OQ-45 areas	Score
BDI–II	32	Symptoms and subjective discomfort	72
		Interpersonal relationships	27
		Social role	20
		OQ-45 global scale	119

[a]The cut-off points suggested for the BDI-II by the authors are 0–13 = minimum; 14–19 = mild; 20–28 = moderate and 29–63 = severe (Beck et al., 1996). On the other hand, Dozois et al. (1998) set the cut-off point of the BDI–II at 19 to discriminate the presence of clinically significant depressive symptoms

[b]The population cut-off points are Symptomatology Scale = 43; Interpersonal Relationships = 16; Social Role = 14; OQ-45 total = 73 (Von Bergen & De La Parra, 2002)

- The BDI-II indicates, from a psychometric point of view, depression.
- The OQ-45 shows discomfort in all areas: symptoms, interpersonal relationships and social role. This is consistent with various dimensions of the clinical diagnosis of Major Depression.

In summary, the results of the BDI-II and OQ-45 are consistent with the Clinical diagnosis of Major Depression, the clinical judgment of the psychotherapist, and the case formulation. Finally, psychometric evidence does not refute the clinical diagnosis.

13.2.2 Case Formulation from an Evolutionary Perspective: Intervention (Session 9)

13.2.2.1 Thematic Conceptualization

Name: Meg.

Conceptualization of the sessions: 4th, 5th, 6th, 7th and eighth (see Box 13.9).

SELF SYSTEM: Clinical Assessment.

(mark presence: **x**)

SENSE OF AGENCY/EFFICIENCY: Alteration ☒ Progress ☐ Regulation ☐

Describe: Meg has felt for the past two sessions that she has more control over herself and that her will is beginning to emerge again. Example: "Writing about my life with my two partners has allowed me to realize that my discomfort and avoidance that occurs now has a lot to do with my way of being." (Narrative task discussed in 7 th session).

SELF-NARRATIVE/COHERENCE: Alteration ☒ Progress ☐ Regulation ☐

Describe: The auto-narrative about her "relationship with Jordi". In the reconstruction "Having Tea with Jordi" (6 th session), Meg experiences a certain degree of discontinuity in her narrative identity that she identifies with her way of being and makes new causal connections with aspects of her love history. The emotions of anger and fear, step by step, she begins to connect thematically with her personal difficulties to tolerate company, closeness, and affection.

SENSE OF TIME/BALANCE: Alteration ☒ Progress ☐ Regulation ☐

Describe: Less rigid sense of time: "I was not fully in the present because I was not interested in what Jordi was saying, although I did not show my disinterest. I was not fully in the present." (see "Having tea with Jordi").

SELF-ESTEEM/SELF-DECEPTION: Alteration ☐ Progress ☒ Regulation ☐

Describe: In the 8 th session she shares a deferred reflection on what was reconstructed in "Having tea with Jordi" based on another similar situation, which consisted of a dinner that Jordi prepared as a surprise one weekday. She says: "Unlike the previous time, now I could tolerate my discomfort with Jordi's closeness and stay. And after a moment I was able to re-center my attention and the discomfort decreased to a mild degree. I realized that my distance from Jordi is defensive." In addition, it is noteworthy that the feeling of being "cheating" has decreased and she attributes it to starting to talk with Jordi.

SELF-CARE/HEALTH: Alteration ☐ Progress ☒ Regulation ☐

Describe: Insomnia has significantly decreased. Also, she now recognizes that her neglect of herself has been detrimental to her health. Her doctor ruled out an ulcer.

Observations: Progress is beginning to be observed in Self-esteem/Self-deception and Self-care/Health. In general, I observe her to be more reflective in the sessions that have taken place and less defensive.

13.2.2.2 Assessment of Dysfunctional Intersubjective Knowledge Domains

Cognition: Change Indicators.

(mark presence: **x**)

Cognitive alterations: Progress ☐ Regulation ☐

Describe: There is less rumination, less selective attention to negative stimuli and greater attentional control. Also, the attribution "loneliness is beneficial" has begun to be questioned.

Metacognition alterations: Progress ☐ Regulation ☐

Describe: She has begun to monitor the positive and negative metacognitive beliefs. She is able to observe her mental states a little better. The alteration in the sense of belonging (family) continues.

Alterations in executive functions: Progress ☐ Regulation ☐

Describe: Decreased cognitive flexibility and difficulties with attentional control. She has now managed to reduce a little the attention to negative stimuli and an effort to control her attention is observed, which sometimes works, but it is not significant yet. Similarly, less frequency of repetitive thoughts (e.g: To continue or not to continue with Jordi?).

- Functional Narrative Indicator: Integrates knowledge ab out cognition ☐
- Behavioral Change Indicator: Incorporates changes ☐

Psychological Distress						Psychological Well-Being
High	Moderate	Mild	Neutral	Mild	Moderate	High
-3	**-2**	-1	0	1	2	3
Psychological Dysregulation						Psychological Regulation
High	Moderate	Mild	Neutral	Mild	Moderate	High
-3	**-2**	-1	0	1	2	3

Observations: She realizes that her attention automatically focuses on her doubts about her relationship with Jordi at times when she is not focused on her work.

Emotion: Indicators of Change.

(mark presence: **x**)

Alteration of emotional awareness: Progress ☐ Regulation ☐

<u>Describe:</u> She tolerates fear, guilt, anger, sadness, and anxiety emotions a bit better, strives to pay attention to her emotions that emerge in her interpersonal relationships. And she realizes her difficulties in emotional clarity and understanding and in the absence of emotional valuation in decision making and problem solving. Finally, the depressive mood is still present.

Emotional dysregulation: Progress ☐ Regulation ☐

<u>Describe:</u> First, there is less intensity of the emotions.
Second, suppression still predominates.
Third, avoidant coping is still present although she has managed to talk to Jordi about what is happening to her on a couple of occasions.

- Functional Narrative Indicator: Integrates knowledge about emotion ☐
- Behavioral Change Indicator: Incorporates Changes ☐

Psychological Distress						Psychological Well-Being
High	Moderate	Mild	Neutral	Mild	Moderate	High
-3	**-2**	-1	0	1	2	3
Psychological Dysregulation						Psychological Regulation
High	Moderate	Mild	Neutral	Mild	Moderate	High
-3	**-2**	-1	0	1	2	3

Observations: Less alteration and attitude of dealing with what happens to him.

Interpersonal: Indicators of Change.

(mark presence: **x**)

Alteration in personal relationships: Progress ☐ Regulation ☐

<u>Describe</u>: No modification for the moment.

Alteration in romantic relationships: Progress ☐ Regulation ☐

<u>Describe</u>: No modification for the moment.

- Functional Narrative Indicator:
Integrates knowledge about interpersonal relationships ☐

- Behavioral Change Indicator: Incorporates changes ☐

Psychological Distress						Psychological Well-Being
High	Moderate	Mild	Neutral	Mild	Moderate	High
-3	-2	**-1**	0	1	2	3
Psychological Dysregulation						Psychological Regulation
High	Moderate	Mild	Neutral	Mild	Moderate	High
-3	-2	**-1**	0	1	2	3

Observations: Slight minor alteration. Interprets her interpersonal history as "poor" and highlights a constant avoidance of interpersonal relationships.

Imagination: Indicators of Change.

(mark presence: **x**)

Interferes with experiential coherence: Progress ☐ Regulation ☐

Describe: No progress.

Interferes with troubleshooting: Progress ☐ Regulation ☐

Describe: Gradually begin to explore the imagination to mentally simulate future situations.

- Functional Narrative Indicator: Integrates knowledge about imagination ☐

- Behavioral Change Indicator: Incorporates changes ☐

Psychological Distress						Psychological Well-Being
High	Moderate	Mild	Neutral	Mild	Moderate	High
-3	-2	**-1**	0	1	2	3
Psychological Dysregulation						Psychological Regulation
High	Moderate	Mild	Neutral	Mild	Moderate	High
-3	-2	**-1**	0	1	2	3

Observations: Pays attention to imagination, an aspect that was not present before.

Corporeality: Change indicators.

(mark presence: **x**)

Altered experience: Progress ☐ Regulation ☐

Describe: There are no changes about her lack of energy/fatigue.

Dysfunctional body attitude: Progress ☒ Regulation ☐

Describe: In relation to her insufficient body self-care, Meg recognizes that she has neglected her body, and at different times in her life, she has been negligent.

- Functional Narrative Indicator: Integrates knowledge about corporeality ☐
- Behavioral Change Indicator: Incorporates changes ☐

Psychological Distress						Psychological Well-Being
High	Moderate	Mild	Neutral	Mild	Moderate	High
-3	-2	**-1**	0	1	2	3
Psychological Dysregulation						Psychological Regulation
High	Moderate	Mild	Neutral	Mild	Moderate	High
-3	-2	**-1**	0	1	2	3

Observations: Emerging awareness of their body and physical condition is observed.

Sexuality: Change indicators.

(mark presence: **x**)

Sexual disconnection with a partner: Progress ☒ Regulation ☐

Describe: There is no change in what they feel about their sexual interest and sexuality, which they consider unsatisfactory. However, they continue to have sexual relations (low frequency). What stands out is that they are now actively involved in better understanding their low interest (e.g., they read about depression and sexuality and ask questions to the therapist).

- Functional Narrative Indicator: Integrates knowledge about sexuality ☐
- Behavioral Change Indicator: Incorporates changes ☐

Psychological Distress						Psychological Well-Being
High	Moderate	Mild	Neutral	Mild	Moderate	High
-3	-2	**-1**	0	1	2	3
Psychological Dysregulation						Psychological Regulation
High	Moderate	Mild	Neutral	Mild	Moderate	High
-3	-2	-1	**0**	1	2	3

Observations: She shows awareness and proactivity to change the situation regarding her low sexual interest and unsatisfactory sexuality. It is noteworthy that for Meg her change of attitude is a progress and she feels more in control.

13.2.2.3 Monitoring of the Psychotherapeutic Process

A. Assessment of sessions:

a.1 What changes are observed in the Dysfunctional Narrative?

The dysfunctional narrative has taken the form: "I continue with fewer doubts about whether I want to continue sharing my life with Jordi. It is less frequent and intense. My marital problem is part of a bigger problem." There are new causal relationships ("My problem with Jordi is part of a bigger problem"). In addition, she assumes that the loneliness in her life is due to not feeling comfortable with people. Similarly, she realizes that her "style of escaping from emotional closeness" has been the way of "being" with others. Added to this, academic achievement and later work make her feel different and protected.

a.2 What characteristics does the Functional Narrative have?

Absent: ☐ Emerging: ☒ Stable: ☐

A very gradually emerging narrative begins to be observed, for example: "I realized that my distancing from Jordi is defensive."

The emotional intensity has begun to decrease and this has allowed her to better self-observe in her daily life.

The attribution "loneliness is beneficial" has begun to significantly question due to the negative consequences.

She presents a new awareness that the possible "early retirement" (in her company) that is offered to her produces discomfort, which she begins to identify as anxiety and fear.

In relation to their self-care, they acknowledge that they have neglected their body and have been negligent at many moments in their life.

a.3 Represent the second-order intersubjective knowledge domains in quadrants for psychological evaluation. Indicate the assessments in the boxes (see Table 13.3 and Fig. 13.3.).

Table 13.3 Intersubjective knowledge domains (session 9)

ECF evaluation			ECF intervention	
Discomfort—well-being	Dysregulation—regulation		Discomfort—well-being	Dysregulation—regulation
−3	−2	Cognitive [C]	−2	−2
−3	−2	Emotion [E]	−2	−2
−1	−1	Interpersonal [I]	−1	−1
−1	−2	Imagination [Im]	−1	−1
−1	−2	Corporeality [Cor]	−1	−1
−1	−1	Sexuality [sex]	−1	0

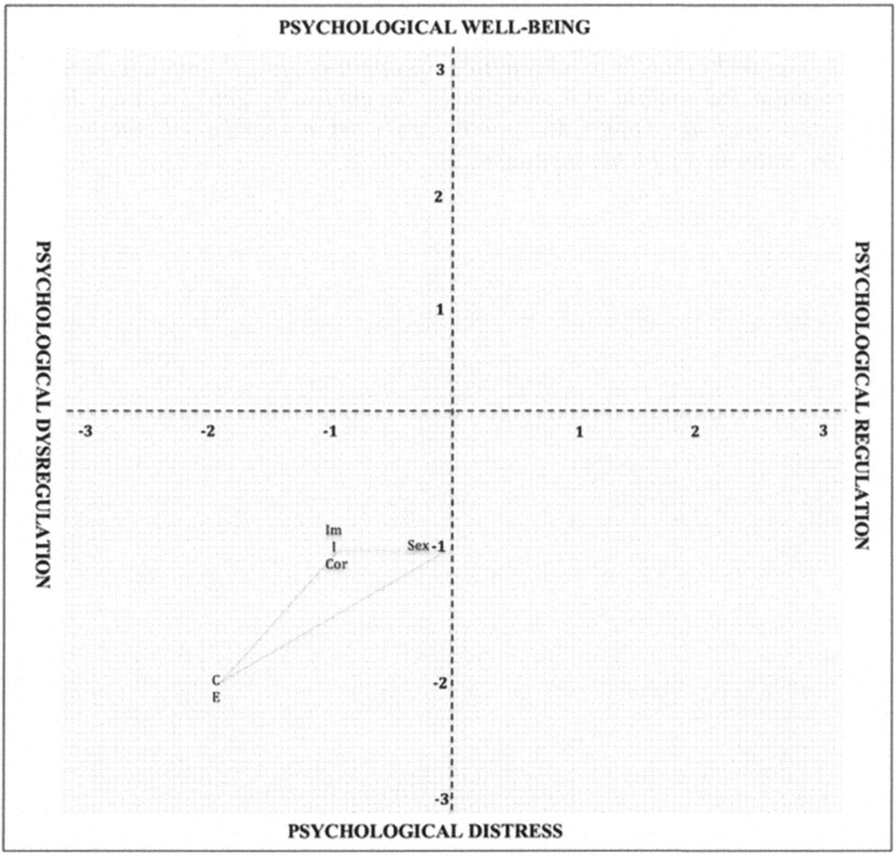

Fig. 13.3 Intersubjective knowledge domains (session 9)

a.4 Assessment of therapeutic objectives fulfillment [mark presence: **x**]:

Significant change valued by the patient	
Significant change valued by the therapist	
There is agreement on the achievement of objectives between therapist and patient	

a.5 Indicators of change [mark presence: **x**]:

Behavioral changes	x
Dimensional psychological regulation (quadrant I)	
Functional narrative	

General Observations

Meg remains psychologically in quadrant III (High dimensional psychological dysregulation).

She returned to her job once the second medical leave was over after the sixth session. Initially, she will start with half a day and in 2 weeks she will resume the full day.

Self-deception has begun to transition from maladaptive to meaning decodings. An example of her progress is that she now shows awareness that the possible "early retirement" causes her anxiety and fear.

There are behavioral changes, particularly her commitment to psychoeducation and her committed self-observation stands out.

It is noteworthy that the psychometric tests applied before the ninth session indicate progress and confirm psychometrically the clinical judgment that the depressive picture continues. Finally, Meg continues to work in a committed, collaborative, and very active way with her therapist.

13.2.2.4 Psychotherapy Process Assessment Interview [PPAI] (Session 9)

Name: Meg Conducted in session: 9

1. We have had **8** sessions so far, in terms of usefulness for your well-being, how has the psychotherapy process been for you? *Beneficial, but it has sometimes been exhausting because I don't like to talk about myself. I have realized that asking for help is very complicated, but receiving help is even more complicated.*

Now I no longer feel that horrible discomfort that I had at the beginning of psychotherapy.

Please, score:

0	1	2	**3**
No utility	Slight utility	Moderate utility	**High utility**

2. Of the topic we agreed to work on, how much has changed in your opinion? **If the answer is Yes**) Could you please detail it for me?

The most important thing is that the doubts "to continue or not with Jordi" have decreased. Mainly, I don't feel deceitful. I also realize that I don't feel comfortable with people. Also, my communication difficulties with Jordi have decreased a bit and we can talk more about the differences, although it is quite hard for me. For now, I have told him that I will not make any decision to move to another city.

Please, rate:

0	1	**2**	3
None	Mild	**Moderate**	High

3. For you, what progress has been made in the agreed therapeutic objectives? In the patient's words:

I am less depressed and I talk a little about what happens to me with Jordi. I avoid less talking about what I don't like.

(**If the answer is Yes**), rate how much progress you have experienced according to the following scale:

0	1	**2**	3
No progress	Mild progress	**Moderate progress**	High progress

4. In general, what changes have you noticed in yourself since you started psychotherapy?

I have realized my loneliness and distance from people.

(**If the answer is YES**), Rate change according to the following scale:

0	1	**2**	3
None	Mild	**Moderate**	High

5. Do you remember having had an experience of novelty in any session?

Before, every time I had problems, I did not go to anyone because I did not trust and my loneliness increased. My philosophy was "I solve everything alone." Now, with the help of a psychologist and psychiatrist, it has been different but useful.

(**If the answer is YES**), rate how much according to the following scale:

0	1	2	**3**
None	Mild	Moderate	**High**

6. What do you believe (according to your personal theory) has caused the changes you have experienced? Specify if there are external life situations.

I have resumed my work and it has not been so hard. With Jordi, I do not feel "so strange" as when I started psychotherapy. There have also been tense moments, but they have not been intense.

Please, rate if you have had responsibility in the changes according to the following scale:

0	1	2	**3**
None	Mild	Moderate	**High**

7. What psychological explanations (reformulations), that I have conveyed to you in the sessions, have been most helpful? Why? (in patient's words):

Psychological reformulation made by the therapist:

"The news about the possibility of early retirement and of moving to another city due to Jordi's transfer... I underline that these are possibilities and not facts. The offer of retirement is not an obligation and the change of city is not something decided yet. Apparently, the first possibility you have lived as "not efficiently fulfilling your job." It is a kind of invalidation of your image of well-done work according to your evaluations in the last 10 years. And the second possibility, you have lived it as a loss of control in your love relationship."

Psychological reformulation remembered by the patient (in patient's words):

Feeling unrecognized by the retirement offer and feeling with little control in my relationship with Jordi.

Why? (in patient's words):

Both situations I did not expect, I think.

Please, rate on the following scale how much they have helped you:

0	1	2	**3**
No benefit	Mild	Moderate	**High**

8. Reflecting on the time you have been in psychotherapy, have there been setbacks in your psychotherapeutic process? Yes: ☐ No: ☒

If the answer is Yes, please specify (in the patient's words): *None.*

Please rate on the following scale how much of a setback:

0	1	2	3
None	Mild	Moderate	High

9. Of the homework tasks we have agreed upon, is there any that has been impossible, difficult, or uncomfortable for you to perform? Yes: ☒ No: ☐

If the answer is Yes, in the patient's words, why? *Paying attention to my discomfort with Jordi. Before, I would just withdraw and often tell him that I had a headache and he believed it. Now I can tolerate and stay in the situation.*

Please rate on the following scale how difficult/uncomfortable it has been:

0	1	2	**3**
None	Mild	Moderate	**High**

10. What learnings do you believe are due to psychotherapy?

Recognizing and relating anxiety, fear, sadness, guilt, and anger to my personal issues has allowed me to better understand my current situation.

Please rate the learnings according to the following scale:

0	1	2	**3**
None	Mild	Moderate	**High**

11. What expectations do you now have about the psychotherapeutic process? (in the patient's words):

Now I believe it is useful to allocate time and money to psychotherapy. I no longer have doubts about whether it will be helpful because it has been helpful. I am working with you on myself, that is, talking about myself and I am starting to feel comfortable. I confess that I am surprised at myself saying: "The therapist has helped me."

Please rate the amount of expectations according to the following scale:

0	1	2	**3**
None	Mild	Moderate	**High**

12. We have been working for 8 sessions now, do you have any suggestions for me to be able to help you better?

If the answer is Yes, in the patient's words, what suggestion(s)? *Talk to Jordi. He still has doubts about how to help me and you know, I find it hard to talk about myself.*

Please rate the number of suggestions according to the following scale:

0	**1**	2	3
None	**Minimum**	Some	Many

13. In relation to your awareness of internal time, in the last 2 weeks, is your behavior generally influenced by your current circumstances, by what happened in the past or by the possible future consequences?

- **If the answer is one or more of the temporal dimensions, Which one(s)?** *The present and future.*

Could you describe what you indicate in an example? *Until recently, I was frozen in the present and lost in a certain way because I didn't know what decision to make. Now I see a future and I'm not stuck in the now.*

Please rate on the following scale if your internal time causes you discomfort:

0	**1**	2	3
None	**Mild**	Moderate	High

14. Rate according to the following scale, how have you been in the last 2 weeks?

Psychological distress						Psychological well-being
High	Moderate	Mild	Neutral	Mild	Moderate	High
-3	−2	−1	0	**+1**	+2	+3

13.2.2.5 Psychometric Tests: Second Application

BDI-II and OQ-45 were applied before the ninth session. See results in Table 13.4 and Figs. 13.4 and 13.5.

Table 13.4 BDI-II results OQ-45 area results (second application)

Instrument	Score	OQ-45 areas	Score
BDI–II	22	Symptoms and subjective discomfort	50
		Interpersonal relationships	21
		Social role	15
		OQ-45 global scale	86

In summary, the results of the two psychometric instruments (BDI-II and OQ-45) indicate the maintenance of depressive symptoms.

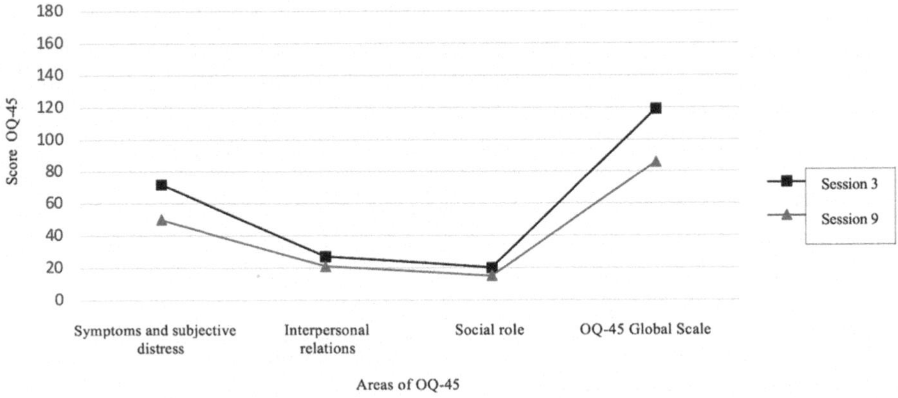

Fig. 13.4 Evolution of the overall OQ-45 score from the first to the second application

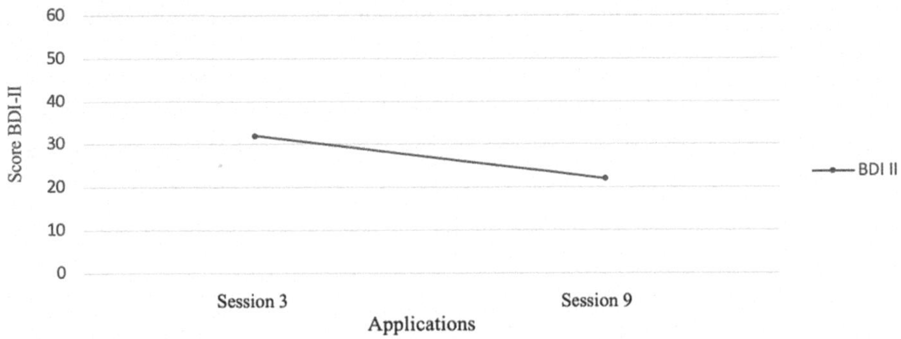

Fig. 13.5 Evolution of BDI-II scores from the first to the second application

13.2.3 Narrative Reconstruction (Session 6)

Below is a situation reconstructed in the sixth session of the Meg case.

Form for Narrative Reconstruction.

RECONSTRUCTED SITUATION [Dysfunctional Narrative] **Session:** 6th

We will call the situation: "**Having tea with Jordi**"

Descriptive Narrative:

What happened? I was on the terrace having tea with Jordi and suddenly I felt enraged, I held back and went to the bedroom.

Who were present? Only Jordi and me.

Where did it happen? On the terrace of our house. We were having tea with Jordi.

How did it start? It was very quick. We were sitting and I was quiet without expressing anything. Jordi was talking about the garden and how beautiful the day was.

How did it unfold? Jordi was talking about the new plants in the garden and the colors. And a little later about the beautiful day. I didn't say anything, I just looked at the tea. And I went from discomfort to anger.

How did it end? I held back and told him I had a bit of a headache. That he should excuse me. I got up from the chair and went to the bedroom. A few minutes later he came to the bedroom, I pretended to be asleep, and he left me a glass of water and a pill for the headache.

How long did it last? Not long, 7 minutes or a little more.

Reflective Narrative:

What were your intentions? I wanted to be in the garden.

What were the intentions of those present? Jordi, I think he wanted to chat and enjoy the company.

What bodily sensations did you experience? Some heaviness and tension.

What emotions do you identify in yourself? In me, I observe mild discomfort that quickly turns into anger.

What emotions do you identify in those present? Jordi seems happy all the time.

Do you have an explanation for why what happened occurred? I don't feel comfortable with everyday topics that don't have to do with work, I mean projects, goals, and achievements.

In what happened, are you focused on the present or are you thinking about your past or future? I was not in the present because I was not interested in what Jordi was saying, although I did not show my disinterest. Clearly, I was thinking about my past.

Did you feel comfortable afterwards? No, not at all. I didn't understand why I got angry and I felt stupid.

What does what happened mean to you? I don't know how to enjoy being with another person who cares about my comfort and who I know cares about me.

What does it mean to the others present? For Jordi... he was concerned because he believed I had a headache. Even, a moment later he brought me a pill to the bedroom.

What do you realize if you observe the panorama of what happened? The moment I take the second sip of tea, the moment when Jordi talks about the garden, I felt strange.

And if you look at the moment when you move to "feel strange"? His closeness and interest make me uncomfortable. I try not to let him notice and I succeed.
Has something similar happened to you before? With my ex-husband something similar but different, but I don't remember a specific moment. But yes, I felt a lot of discomfort before my separation, I was annoyed when he talked to me after he came back from work and I avoided him. And I didn't I cared if he noticed. It's different but similar at the same time.
What consequences do you observe now upon reflecting with me? I avoided an unpleasant moment for Jordi, but I also missed a pleasant moment. What happens to me has to do with my way of being.

Effects of the reconstruction according to therapist and patient (deferred):

What changes are observed in the Dysfunctional Narrative? There are new causal connections about his sense of strangeness. And it relates to his way of being. The question "Why do I feel this way?" becomes "What do I do to feel this way?".
Does a Functional Narrative emerge? Yes: ☒ No: ☐
What characteristics does the emerging Functional Narrative have?
Caring for Jordi.
Are there behavioral changes associated with Functional Narrative emerging in everyday life? Yes: ☒ No: ☐
It's subtle, but he makes sure not to make Jordi feel uncomfortable.

Observations: Unlike before, Meg currently inhibits and prevents Jordi from feeling uncomfortable. It is an indicator of the emergence of functional narrative.

13.2.4 *Case Formulation from an Evolutionary Perspective: Intervention (Session 15)*

13.2.4.1 Thematic Conceptualization

Name: Meg.

Conceptualization of sessions No.: 10th, 11th, 12th, 13th and 14th.

Self System: Clinical Assessment.

(mark presence: **x**)

SENSE OF AGENCY/EFFICIENCY: Alteration ☐ Progress ☒ Regulation ☐

Describe: The sense of agency is gradually strengthening. Her self-control continues to progress. Meg feels in control of herself and reflects better, for example: "Now I can decide without having to think so much.... before it was as if my thinking ruled my will". In addition to this, there are advances in efficacy and outcome expectations.

SELF-NARRATIVE/COHERENCE: Alteration ☐ Progress ☒ Regulation ☐

Describe: The self-narrative about her "relationship with Jordi" has more continuity due to new causal connections (more benign) and more dynamic temporality. At present, greater understanding and new associations are observed in order to value human contact more.

The self-narrative about her "professional invalidation" is not present as invalidation, but rather what she will do in the future. Her sense of competence and dignity is developing not only in terms of her performance but in learning to value collaboration more and more.

SENSE OF TIME/BALANCE: Alteration ☐ Progress ☒ Regulation ☐

Describe: Her temporal profile shows a better balance. She now attends to her past as information and learning for her present and visualizes possible futures.

SELF-ESTEEM/SELF-DECEPTION: Alteration ☐ Progress ☒ Regulation ☐

Describe: Meg is increasingly identifying her way of self-deception. She doesn't feel weird, deceitful, or stuck. Moreover, she acknowledges that the distance from others has aspects of not being let down and abandoned. She now doesn't avoid people and pays attention to relationships. It stands out that at work she strives to establish a cordial and friendly conversation with her colleagues and no defensive attitude is observed. Also with Marcia, there has been a more existential approach from Meg, not focused on financial aid. Lastly, her self-esteem appears more balanced.

SELF-CARE/HEALTH: Alteration ☐ Progress ☒ Regulation ☐

Describe: Insomnia is not present. She has also made healthy behavioral changes, for example: Medical check-up with a nutritionist.

Observations: *The five dimensions of the Self System are seen in progress.*

13.2.4.2 Assessment of Dysfunctional Intersubjective Knowledge Domains

Cognition: Change Indicators.

(mark presence: **x**)

Cognitive alterations: Progress ☐ Regulation ☒

Describe: There is regulation of rumination, worry, and attentional control. Selective attention or attribution about the benefit of solitude is not observed.

Metacognition alterations: Progress ☐ Regulation ☒

Describe: There are observed progresses in re-articulating the sense of belonging. Also, presence of control and decrease of positive and negative metacognitive beliefs about rumination and avoidance. Moreover, she reflects on the possible mental states of Jordi.

Alterations in executive functions: Progress ☒ Regulation ☐

Describe: There are progresses in attentional control and presence of cognitive flexibility. Also, she better monitors and controls her ongoing mental states.

- Functional Narrative Indicator: Integrates knowledge about cognition ☒
- Behavioral Change Indicator: Incorporates changes ☐

Psychological Distress						Psychological Well-Being
High	Moderate	Mild	Neutral	Mild	Moderate	High
-3	-2	-1	0	**1**	2	3
Psychological Dysregulation						Psychological Regulation
High	Moderate	Mild	Neutral	Mild	Moderate	High
-3	-2	-1	0	**1**	2	3

Observations: The regulation of cognitive alterations and metacognitive alterations has been decisive in their progress. In addition, it incorporates knowledge into the emerging functional narrative.

Emotion: Indicators of Change.

(mark presence: **x**)

Alteration of emotional awareness: Progress ☒ Regulation ☐

Describe: Depressive mood is still present but less intense. In addition, there are advances in being able to identify, express, and verbalize feelings of guilt, fear, anxiety, sadness, and anger. He also manages to better decode the meaning that emotions give to his experience (emotional clarity and understanding).
He carefully considers the emotions that emerge in his interpersonal relationships. And he realizes his difficulties in using emotional assessment in decision-making and problem-solving in interpersonal relationships.

Emotional dysregulation: Progress ☒ Regulation ☐

Describe: First, there are advances in that the intensity of negative emotions are less frequent, intense, and interfering. Second: He no longer applies suppression automatically, and increasingly, he uses cognitive reevaluation. Third: There is the presence of adaptive coping, for example: he has sometimes managed to control avoidance with Jordi. However, there is an absence of dyadic coping.

- Functional Narrative Indicator: Integrates knowledge about emotion ☐
- Behavioral Change Indicator: Incorporates Changes ☐

Psychological Distress						Psychological Well-Being
High	Moderate	Mild	Neutral	Mild	Moderate	High
-3	-2	**-1**	0	1	2	3
Psychological Dysregulation						**Psychological Regulation**
High	Moderate	Mild	Neutral	Mild	Moderate	High
-3	-2	**-1**	0	1	2	3

Observations: It is noteworthy that their mood is still depressive but less intense.

Interpersonal: Indicators of Change.

(mark presence: **x**)

Alteration in personal relationships: Progress ☒ Regulation ☐

Describe: There are noticeable improvements in starting to value interpersonal relationships. Notably with Marcia a more existential approach. They have also made healthy behavioral changes at work, for example: having coffee with their colleagues outside of meetings and talking about non-work related topics.

Alteration in romantic relationships: Progress ☒ Regulation ☐

Describe: There are improvements in valuing leisure time with Jordi. They have made healthy behavioral changes: walking with Jordi, attending events and preparing dinners for Jordi.

- Functional Narrative Indicator:
Integrates knowledge about interpersonal relationships ☐

- Behavioral Change Indicator: Incorporates changes ☐

Psychological Distress						Psychological Well-Being
High	Moderate	Mild	Neutral	Mild	Moderate	High
-3	-2	**-1**	0	1	2	3
Psychological Dysregulation						Psychological Regulation
High	Moderate	Mild	Neutral	Mild	Moderate	High
-3	-2	-1	**0**	1	2	3

Observations: Marital reciprocity and assertive conversation support better psychological balance. In addition, Meg now values interpersonal relationships more.

Imagination: Indicators of Change.

(mark presence: **x**)

Interferes with experiential coherence: Progress ☐ Regulation ☒

Describe: Start using your imagination to try to understand situations beyond the present.

Interferes with troubleshooting: Progress ☐ Regulation ☒

Describe: Uses imagination to mentally simulate and creatively solve situations.

- Functional Narrative Indicator: Integrates knowledge about imagination ☒

- Behavioral Change Indicator: Incorporates changes ☐

Psychological Distress				Psychological Well-Being		
High	Moderate	Mild	Neutral	Mild	Moderate	High
-3	-2	-1	0	**1**	2	3
Psychological Dysregulation				Psychological Regulation		
High	Moderate	Mild	Neutral	Mild	Moderate	High
-3	-2	-1	**0**	1	2	3

Observations: There is regulation. She uses imagination to simulate possible situations and it is useful to her. In addition, she incorporates knowledge into the emerging functional narrative.

Corporeality: Change indicators.

(mark presence: **x**)

Altered experience: Progress ☒ Regulation ☐

Describe: Meg comments that her energy is better, but there is still a way to go to be as before her depression.

Dysfunctional body attitude: Progress ☒ Regulation ☐

Describe: She shows an attitude of starting to take care of her body. She recently went to a nutritionist. She emphasizes that she does not "attack the refrigerator" but it has not been easy.

- Functional Narrative Indicator: Integrates knowledge about corporeality ☐
- Behavioral Change Indicator: Incorporates changes ☐

Psychological Distress						Psychological Well-Being
High	Moderate	Mild	Neutral	Mild	Moderate	High
-3	-2	-1	**0**	1	2	3
Psychological Dysregulation						Psychological Regulation
High	Moderate	Mild	Neutral	Mild	Moderate	High
-3	-2	**-1**	0	1	2	3

Observations: Meg started a diet a few days ago supported by a nutritionist. In addition, there are advances on the importance of her corporeality.

Sexuality: Change indicators.

(mark presence: **x**)

Sexual disconnection with a partner: Progress ☒ Regulation ☐

Describe: There is no change in what they feel about their sexual interest and sexuality, which they consider unsatisfactory. However, they continue to have sexual relations (low frequency). What stands out is that they are now actively involved in better understanding their low interest (e.g., they read about depression and sexuality and ask questions to the therapist).

- Functional Narrative Indicator: Integrates knowledge about sexuality ☒
- Behavioral Change Indicator: Incorporates changes ☐

Psychological Distress						Psychological Well-Being
High	Moderate	Mild	Neutral	Mild	Moderate	High
-3	-2	-1	**0**	1	2	3
Psychological Dysregulation						Psychological Regulation
High	Moderate	Mild	Neutral	Mild	Moderate	High
-3	-2	-1	**0**	1	2	3

Observations: Share readings about sexuality and depression with Jordi. Also, discussing sexuality and clarifying doubts with the therapist has been very useful for her well-being. In addition, she begins to incorporate knowledge into the emerging functional narrative.

13.2.4.3 Monitoring of the Psychotherapeutic Process

A. Evaluation of sessions:

a.1 What changes are observed in the Dysfunctional Narrative?

1. The dysfunctional narrative is still present, but quite weakened.
2. She does not feel "strange," "deceptive," or "stagnant."
3. The rumination about "whether or not to continue in her marital relationship" has decreased in frequency, intensity, and scope. About such discomfort, there are no "black—white" thoughts and Meg distinguishes "grays."
4. Such discomfort has transformed into a motivation to pay attention to the "being attentive to what happens to others" as an indicator of her avoidance of psychological proximity.

a.2 What characteristics does Functional Narrative have?

Absent: ☐ Emerging: ☒ Stable: ☐

The essential thing is that Meg begins to value the importance of the closeness of interpersonal relationships. She has incorporated knowledge that she has acquired through experience and reflection into her functional narrative.

a.3 Represent the domains of second-order intersubjective knowledge in quadrants for psychological evaluation. Indicate the assessments in the boxes (see Table 13.5 and Fig. 13.6).

Table 13.5 Domains of second-order intersubjective knowledge (session 15)

ECF evaluation			ECF intervention	
Distress—well-being	Dysregulation—regulation		Distress—well-being	Dysregulation—regulation
−3	−2	Cognitive [C]	1	1
−3	−2	Emotion [E]	−1	−1
−1	−1	Interpersonal [I]	−1	0
−1	−2	Imagination [Im]	1	0
−1	−2	Corporeality [Cor]	0	−1
−1	−1	Sexuality [sex]	0	0

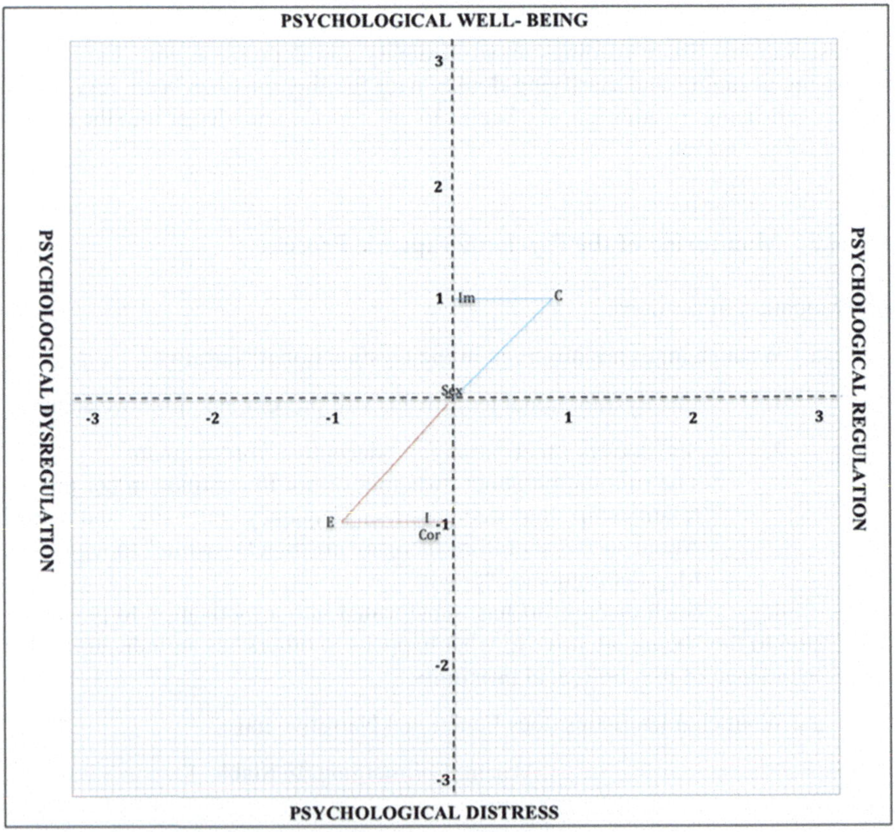

Fig. 13.6 Domains of second-order intersubjective knowledge (session 15)

a.4 Assessment of therapeutic objectives fulfillment [mark presence: **x**]:

Significant change valued by the patient	
Significant change valued by the therapist	
There is agreement on the achievement of objectives between therapist and patient	

a.5 Change indicators [mark presence: **x**]:

Behavioral changes	x
Dimensional psychological regulation (quadrant I)	
Functional narrative	x

General Observations

The 14 sessions with Meg show a gradual advancement and tendency towards quadrant I.

Therapeutic objectives show progress:

1. *Decrease in depressive symptoms. Clinical judgment coincides with psychometric tests.*
2. *Progress is observed in all intersubjective domains involved in the profile detected in the conceptualization of the sessions: 10th, 11th, 12th, 13th, and 14th.*
3. *There are benefits of better communication with Jordi and her work environment.*

The second-order intersubjective knowledge domains "cognitive" and "imagination" are functioning with regulation and are observed in Quadrant I (Dysfunctional Psychological Regulation). Also progress in "Sexuality" since she does not show discomfort or dysregulation. Finally, the three domains "Corporeality, Interpersonal and Emotion" are functioning in quadrant III but present advances in both dimensions (D-W and D-R).

Meg has performed without difficulties in her job, and smoothly transitioned from part-time to full-time. Her sense of competence and dignity is developing not only based on her performance but in learning to increasingly value collaboration. It is noteworthy that she is experiencing and cultivating a more human contact and not focused solely on achievement and duty.

In relation to progress, the highlights are:

1. *New way of integrating information and using it to represent her current situation and in perspective (future). Progress is observed in the dimensions of the Self System.*
2. *Behavioral changes continue to be added:*

- *Assertive conversation with Jordi.*
- *Taking care of her interpersonal relationships.*
- *She uses imagination to simulate situations.*
- *Started a diet regime supported by a nutritionist.*
- *Sharing readings about sexuality with Jordi.*
- *Clarify doubts about sexuality with the therapist.*

3rd Functional Narrative is emerging. New synergistic associations have arisen between different domains of intersubjective knowledge. In particular, Meg shows awareness that her marital problem is related to the avoidance of close and affectionate relationships.

In relation to psychological tests, both the BDI-II (=13) and the OQ-45 applied before session 15th show indicators of a trend towards psychological recovery (see Psychometric Tests: 3rd application, Figs. 13.7 and 13.8*) compared to the second application of psychometric tests.*

The total OQ-45 scale (=76) continues to show less dysfunction. Similarly, the Symptomatology, Interpersonal Relationships scales continue to indicate dysfunction but it is less than the 2nd application. It stands out that the Social Role scale (=14) ceased to be dysfunctional.

Finally, with the therapist, she continues to show a stable profile and consists of being kind, active, and collaborative.

13.2.4.4 Psychotherapy Process Assessment Interview [PPAI] (Session 15)

Name: Meg Conducted in session: 15

1. We have had **14** sessions so far, in terms of usefulness for your well-being, how has the psychotherapy process been for you? *It continues to be beneficial and it's a little less difficult for me to talk about myself.*

Please, rate:

0	1	2	**3**
No use	Slight use	Moderate use	**High use**

2. Of the Topic we agreed to work on, how much has changed in your opinion? (**If the answer is Yes**) Could you please detail for me?

The doubts about whether to continue with Jordi or not have decreased to almost disappear. Now, my question is whether it is the right time to move to another city or continue the long-distance relationship. I have also decided to accept early retirement.

Please, rate:

0	1	**2**	3
None	Slight	**Moderate**	High

3. For you, what progress has been made in the agreed therapeutic objectives? In the patient's words: "*I don't feel depressed"; "I regained my sense of humor," "Jordi and I communicate better"; "We have gradually regained having fun together."*

(**If the answer is Yes**), score how much progress has been experienced according to the following scale:

0	1	**2**	3
No progress	Slight progress	**Moderate progress**	High progress

4. In general, what changes have you noticed in yourself since you started psychotherapy?

At times I have been arrogant with people at my job and it was negative for me and for others. Realizing that I have behaved for decades distant and indifferent with many people motivates me to make an effort to behave differently. Also, I have benefited from paying attention to my emotions and taking better care of my body and health.

(**If the answer is YES**), score how much change according to the following scale:

0	1	**2**	3
None	Slight	**Moderate**	High

5. Do you remember having a novel experience in any session?

Recognizing the fear and anxiety I feel in moments of affectionate closeness with my partner.

(**If the answer is YES**), score according to the following scale:

0	1	2	**3**
None	Slight	Moderate	**High**

6. What do you believe (according to your personal theory) has caused the changes you have experienced? Specify if there are external life situations.

First: Recognizing my emotions and in particular my fear.

Second: I have changed my belief about "people." I realize that I need them and they need me. There is an issue about this with my mother, which I had not in mind.

Please, rate if you have had responsibility in the changes according to the following scale:

0	1	2	**3**
None	Mild	Moderate	**High**

7. What psychological explanations (reformulations), that I have conveyed to you in the sessions, have been most helpful? Why? (in patient's words):

Psychological reformulation made by the therapist: "I think your recurring doubts accompanied by fear, of whether to continue or not with Jordi, is a way of defending yourself from human warmth and genuine affection."

Psychological reformulation remembered by the patient (in patient's words): "Of defending myself from affection through fear."

Why? (in patient's words):

Realizing that I have felt very little human warmth and genuine affection. And relating my fear with difficulties to tolerate human warmth and affection, has been difficult.

Please, rate on the following scale how much it has helped you:

0	1	2	**3**
No use	Mild	Moderate	**High**

8. f you reflect on the time you have been in psychotherapy, have there been setbacks in your psychotherapeutic process? Yes: ☐ No: ☒

If the answer is Yes, specify (in patient's words): *None.*

Please, rate on the following scale how much of a setback:

0	1	2	3
None	Mild	Moderate	High

9. Of the household tasks we have agreed upon, is there any that has been impossible, difficult, or uncomfortable for you to perform? Yes: ☒ No: ☐

If the answer is Yes, in the patient's words, why? *Observing my discomfort with people has been difficult. And I think it's because I was defending myself from people.*

Please rate on the following scale how difficult/uncomfortable it has been:

0	1	2	**3**
None	Mild	Moderate	**High**

10. What learnings do you consider are due to psychotherapy? *Recognizing and relating my fear with my difficulties in tolerating human warmth and affection.*

Please rate the learnings according to the following scale:

0	1	2	**3**
None	Mild	Moderate	**High**

11. What expectations do you now have about the psychotherapeutic process? (in the patient's words):

That it allows me to learn more about how to take care of my close relationships.

Please rate the amount of expectations according to the following scale:

0	1	2	**3**
None	Mild	Moderate	**High**

12. We have been working for 14 sessions now, do you have any suggestions for how I can help you better?

If the answer is Yes, in the patient's words, what suggestion(s)? *Not at the moment.*

Please, rate the number of suggestions according to the following scale:

0	1	2	3
None	Minimum	Some	Many

13. In relation to your awareness of internal time, in the last 2 weeks, is your behavior generally influenced by your current circumstances, by what happened in the past, or by the possible future consequences?

   - **If the answer is one or more of the temporal dimensions, which one(s)?** *The present, past, and future.*

Could you describe what you indicate in an example? *Now I see the future and my present is no longer frozen. My past no longer weighs me down.*

Please, rate on the following scale if your internal time causes you discomfort:

0	1	2	3
None	Mild	Moderate	High

14. Rate according to the following scale, how have you been in the last 2 weeks?

Psychological distress				Psychological well-being		
High	Moderate	Mild	Neutral	Mild	Moderate	High
-3	−2	−1	0	**+1**	+2	+3

13.2.4.5 Psychometric Tests: Third Application

BDI-II and OQ-45 were applied before the 15th session (see results in Table 13.6 and Figs. 13.7 and 13.8).

Table 13.6 BDI-II results and OQ-45 area results (third application)

Instrument	Score	OQ-45 areas	Score
BDI–II	13	Symptoms and subjective discomfort	44
		Interpersonal relationships	18
		Social role	14
		OQ-45 global scale	76

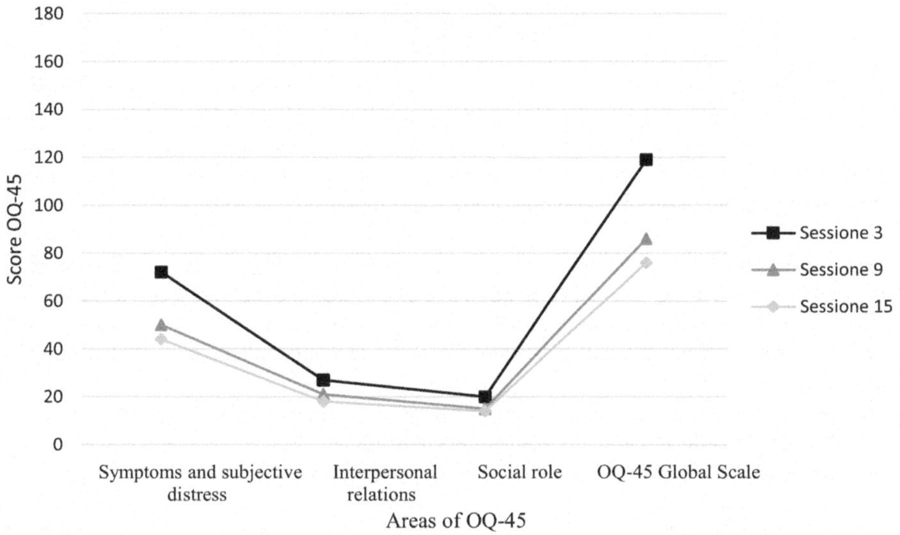

Fig. 13.7 Evolution of the overall OQ-45 score from the first to the third application

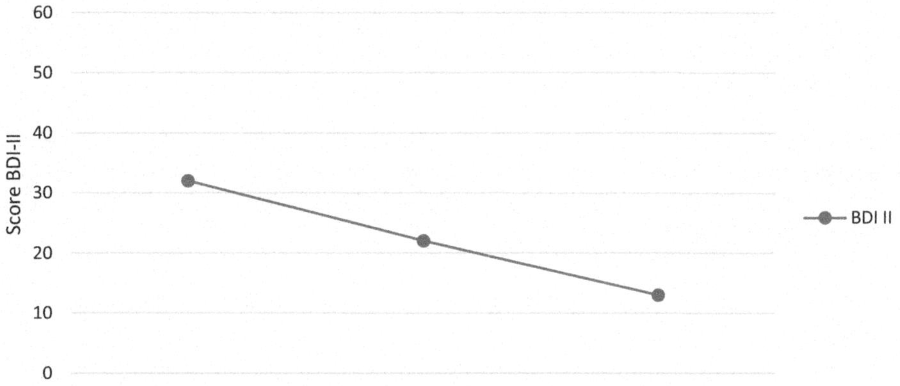

Fig. 13.8 Evolution of the BDI-II score from the first to the third application

13.2.5 Case Formulation from an Evolutionary Perspective: Intervention (Session 21)

13.2.5.1 Thematic Conceptualization

Name: Meg.
Conceptualization of sessions No.: 16th, 17th, 18th, 19th, and 20th.
Self System: Clinical Assessment.

(mark presence: **x**)

SENSE OF AGENCY/EFFICIENCY: Alteration ☐ Progress ☐ Regulation ☒
Describe: The sense of agency has consolidated and now she can relate to her problems differently and visualize alternatives and options that are under her control. She feels in control and confident about what she decides to do and can do. In addition to the above, there is regulation of efficacy and outcome expectations.

SELF-NARRATIVE/COHERENCE: Alteration ☐ Progress ☐ Regulation ☒
Describe: The narrative about her relationship with Jordi is observed to be articulated and provides continuity to her identity since it presents optimal contextualization, agency, better temporal balance, emotional understanding, self-care, and absence of intersubjective tension.
The narrative about her father's supposed disinterest has been refuted. At present, she is getting to know details and integrating information.
The narrative about her professional invalidation is not present.

SENSE OF TIME/BALANCE: Alteration ☐ Progress ☐ Regulation ☒
Describe: Her temporal profile has reached regulation. Now her present is energized by her future possibilities.

SELF-ESTEEM/SELF-DECEPTION: Alteration ☐ Progress ☐ Regulation ☒
Describe: Meg continues to identify well her way of self-deceiving in controlling emotional closeness both with her daughter and with Jordi. Self-esteem is also observed to be recovered and balanced.

SELF-CARE/HEALTH: Alteration ☐ Progress ☐ Regulation ☒
Describe: Regulation is observed. Meg has lost weight in an orderly manner. Now she is with more energy and an attitude of taking care to exercise. They go for walks with Jordi, 50 minutes three times a week.

Observations: The Self System generates adaptive historical and contextual meanings.

13.2.5.2 Assessment of Dysfunctional Intersubjective Knowledge Domains

Cognition: Change Indicators.

(mark presence: **x**)

Cognitive alterations: Progress ☐ Regulation ☒
Describe: Regulation of rumination, worry and attentional control is maintained. No selective attention or attribution about the benefit of solitude is observed.

Metacognition alterations: Progress ☐ Regulation ☒
Describe: There is a sense of belonging based on her relationship with her partner and a new understanding of her parents' history, which she now knows in greater detail from conversations with her mother. In addition, there is no presence of positive or negative metacognitive beliefs about rumination and avoidance.

Alterations in executive functions: Progress ☐ Regulation ☒
Describe: Optimal regulation in attentional control and cognitive flexibility.

- Functional Narrative Indicator: Integrates knowledge about cognition ☒
- Behavioral Change Indicator: Incorporates changes ☒

Psychological Distress						Psychological Well-Being
High	Moderate	Mild	Neutral	Mild	Moderate	High
-3	-2	-1	0	1	**2**	3
Psychological Dysregulation						Psychological Regulation
High	Moderate	Mild	Neutral	Mild	Moderate	High
-3	-2	-1	0	1	**2**	3

Observations: There is no presence of alterations: cognitive, metacognition, executive functions. Reflects optimally on hypothetical mental states of their partner and others. Similarly, the emerging sense of belonging is essential for their new psychological balance. In short, optimal psychological regulation is maintained and knowledge is incorporated into the emerging functional narrative and behavioral changes in their daily life.

Emotion: Indicators of Change.

(mark presence: **x**)

Alteration of emotional awareness: Progress ☐ Regulation ☒
<u>Describe:</u> Now emotions confer meaning to their experience (greater clarity and understanding) and they use them in decision-making and problem-solving.

Emotional dysregulation: Progress ☐ Regulation ☒

<u>Describe:</u> Emotional regulation strategies indicate flexibility and adaptation: applies cognitive reappraisal and sometimes suppression. There is also no predominance of negative emotions. Meg has been experiencing positive emotions for weeks. Finally, there is presence of adaptive coping both individually and dyadic (with Jordi).

- Functional Narrative Indicator: Integrates knowledge about emotion ☒
- Behavioral Change Indicator: Incorporates Changes ☒

Psychological Distress				Psychological Well-Being		
High	Moderate	Mild	Neutral	Mild	Moderate	High
-3	-2	-1	0	**1**	2	3
Psychological Dysregulation				Psychological Regulation		
High	Moderate	Mild	Neutral	Mild	Moderate	High
-3	-2	-1	0	**1**	2	3

Observations: There is an absence of depressive mood. Continues to incorporate emotional knowledge into functional narrative and incorporates behavioral changes.

Interpersonal: Indicators of Change.

(mark presence: **x**)

Alteration in personal relationships: Progress ☐ Regulation ☒

Describe: There is regulation. With her daughter, there is an existential relationship and she has left behind "being a problem solver". In addition, healthy behavioral changes continue to increase (e.g., she attended a company colleagues' dinner forthe first time).

Alteration in romantic relationships: Progress ☐ Regulation ☒

Describe: Regulation is observed. Healthy behavioral changes continue to increase and diversify, because now she has friends and they go out to dinner.

- Functional Narrative Indicator:
Integrates knowledge about interpersonal relationships ☒

- Behavioral Change Indicator: Incorporates changes ☒

Psychological Distress				Psychological Well-Being		
High	Moderate	Mild	Neutral	Mild	Moderate	High
-3	-2	-1	0	1	**2**	3
Psychological Dysregulation				Psychological Regulation		
High	Moderate	Mild	Neutral	Mild	Moderate	High
-3	-2	-1	0	**1**	2	3

Observations: The incorporation of assertive conversation has been beneficial. In addition, a new dimension of reflection and action translates into Meg increasingly valuing reciprocity and making people in her work environment feel comfortable. It also stands out that with her daughter, there is an existential approach and not focused on achievement and eventual financial aid (if Marcia needed it). Furthermore, she continues to incorporate knowledge into the functional narrative.

Imagination: Indicators of Change.

(mark presence: x)

Interferes with experiential coherence: Progress ☐ Regulation ☒

Describe: Imagination is useful for understanding situations beyond the immediate present.

Interferes with troubleshooting: Progress ☐ Regulation ☒

Describe: Values positively that imagination is very useful for simulating and creatively solving situations.

- Functional Narrative Indicator: Integrates knowledge about imagination ☒

- Behavioral Change Indicator: Incorporates changes ☒

Psychological Distress				Psychological Well-Being		
High	Moderate	Mild	Neutral	Mild	Moderate	High
-3	-2	-1	0	**1**	2	3
Psychological Dysregulation				Psychological Regulation		
High	Moderate	Mild	Neutral	Mild	Moderate	High
-3	-2	-1	0	**1**	2	3

Observations: Imagination continues to be observed as present and regulated. Furthermore, it continues to incorporate knowledge that imagination provides to the functional narrative.

Corporeality: Change indicators.

(mark presence: **x**)

Altered experience: Progress ☐ Regulation ☒

Describe: She highlights that her energy (before she felt lack of energy/fatigue) has been positively boosted with exercise.

Dysfunctional body attitude: Progress ☐ Regulation ☒

Describe: Proud of her gradual and realistic weight loss. She points out that she no longer "attacks the refrigerator" and that she gave up ice cream and sweets with much difficulty, but she achieved it.

- Functional Narrative Indicator: Integrates knowledge about corporeality ☒

- Behavioral Change Indicator: Incorporates changes ☒

Psychological Distress						Psychological Well-Being
High	Moderate	Mild	Neutral	Mild	Moderate	High
-3	-2	-1	0	**1**	2	3
Psychological Dysregulation						Psychological Regulation
High	Moderate	Mild	Neutral	Mild	Moderate	High
-3	-2	-1	0	**1**	2	3

Observations: Meg started a diet a few days ago supported by a nutritionist. In addition, there are advances on the importance of her corporeality. Her change in attitude towards her body self-care is very important. She now exercises and diets, which has been fundamental in her recovery. She continues to incorporate knowledge about the benefits she has felt into the functional narrative and incorporates healthy behavioral changes.

Sexuality: Change indicators.

(mark presence: **x**)

Sexual disconnection with a partner: Progress ☐ Regulation ☒

Describe: The absence of sexual interest is not present. Shows sexual interest and frequency of sexual relations. Similarly, the unsatisfactory sexuality is not present. Indicates that feels pleasure and increased frequency of pleasure.

- Functional Narrative Indicator: Integrates knowledge about sexuality ☒
- Behavioral Change Indicator: Incorporates changes ☒

Psychological Distress						Psychological Well-Being
High	Moderate	Mild	Neutral	Mild	Moderate	High
-3	-2	-1	0	**1**	2	3
Psychological Dysregulation						Psychological Regulation
High	Moderate	Mild	Neutral	Mild	Moderate	High
-3	-2	-1	**0**	1	2	3

Observations: Assertive conversations about sexuality with Jordi have continued. In addition, adjustment of expectations, satisfaction, and sexual interest according to his personal history is observed. Finally, he continues to incorporate knowledge about sexuality into the functional narrative and has incorporated some behavioral changes.

13.2.5.3 Monitoring of the Psychotherapeutic Process

A. Assessment of sessions:

a.1 What changes are observed in the Dysfunctional Narrative?

1. *The dysfunctional narrative is not present*
2. There are no indicators of intersubjective tension

a.2 What characteristics does Functional Narrative have?

Absent: ☐ Emerging: ☐ Stable: ☒

1. *Values and cultivates interpersonal relationships.*
2. *Expresses having energy and desire to do new things in their life and not just dedicate their time to work.*
3. *Takes care of their marital relationship.*
4. *Lives in greater contact with themselves and others. Asks the question "What is the other person thinking?"*

a.3 Represent the domains of second-order intersubjective knowledge in quadrants for psychological evaluation. Indicate the ratings in the boxes (see Table 13.7 and Fig. 13.9).

Table 13.7 Domains of second-order intersubjective knowledge (session 21)

ECF evaluation			ECF intervention	
Discomfort—well-being	Dysregulation—regulation		Discomfort—well-being	Dysregulation—regulation
−3	−2	Cognition [C]	1	1
−3	−2	Emotion [E]	1	1
−1	−1	Interpersonal [I]	2	1
−1	−2	Imagination [Im]	1	1
−1	−2	Corporality [Cor]	1	1
−1	−1	Sexuality [sex]	1	0

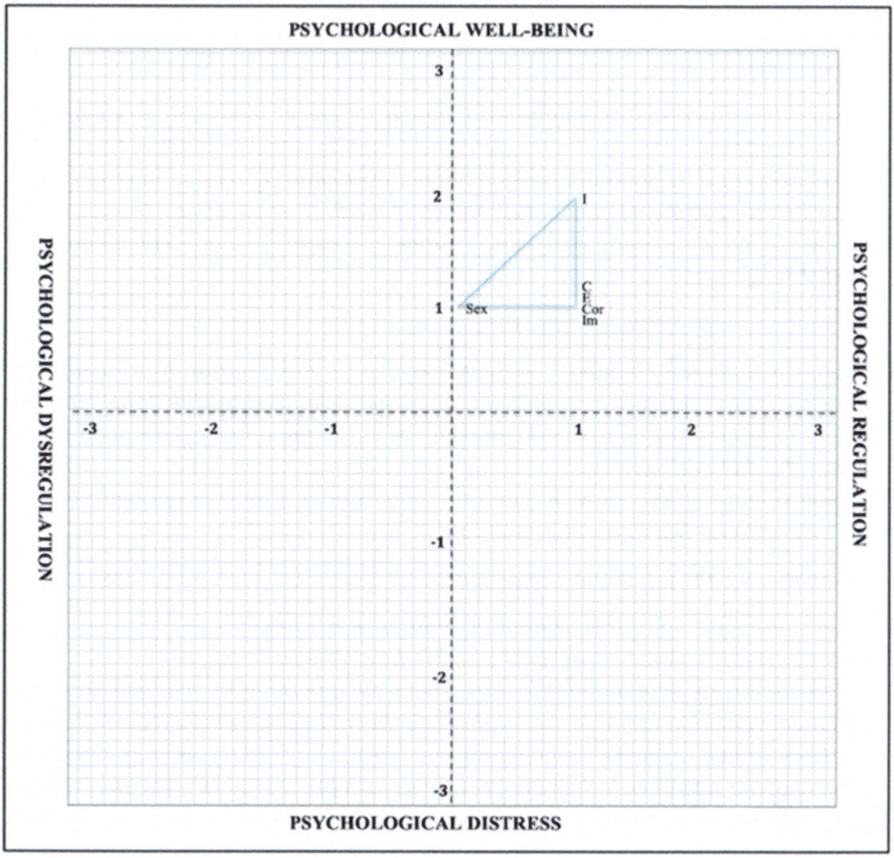

Fig. 13.9 Domains of second-order intersubjective knowledge (session 21)

a.4 Evaluation of therapeutic objectives fulfillment [mark presence: **x**]:

Significant change valued by the patient	x
Significant change valued by the therapist	x
There is agreement on the achievement of objectives between therapist and patient	x

a.5 Change indicators [mark presence: x]:

Behavioral changes	x
Dimensional psychological regulation (quadrant I)	x
Functional narrative	x

General Observations

Meg shows Dimensional Psychological Regulation. The six domains of intersubjective knowledge are in quadrant I "Dimensional Psychological Regulation."

There is a stable presence of an Adaptive Intersubjective Reality Sense articulated and fluid that provides existential perspective and interpersonal regulation.

In relation to the "assessment of therapeutic objectives achievement," there is agreement between patient and therapist, that the agreed therapeutic objectives have been met:

1. *Remission of depressive symptoms. Clinical judgment that coincides with psychometric tests.*
2. *No distress or dysregulation is observed in the domains of intersubjective knowledge involved in the dysfunctional profile of the ECF Evaluation.*
3. *There is balance and satisfaction from the better stable communication with Jordi.*

In relation to the Change Indicators:

1. *Stable behavioral changes: cultivates interpersonal relationships; dedicates time to leisure; takes care of and maintains her relationship with Jordi; stopped being indifferent to others (asks herself "What is the other person feeling?"); follows a diet and exercises.*
2. *Dimensional Psychological Regulation (quadrant I): Presence of regulation.*
3. *The Functional Narrative is now stable.*

Thematically, the following stands out:

1. *Meg continues to perform without difficulties in her job.*
2. *Her marital relationship presents a stable level of well-being.*
3. *The relationship with her mother has gone from intense tension to moderate and open conversation continues regarding the history of her mother's relationship with her father. Likewise, she continues to learn details of the mother's relationship with her unknown father. Meg continues in a process of forgiving her mother for omitting information, lying and telling a distorted story about the father's absence.*

   In relation to the feeling of paternal absence, it takes the form of an existential theme at the present time, that is, it does not present intersubjective tension. In addition, she has started to talk with Marcia about the existence of her maternal grandfather and the omissions in the grandmother's story.

   In conclusion, both the BDI-II and the OQ-45 applied before session 21 show indicators of remission and recovery. The BDI-II shows absence of depressive symptoms and the score of the global scale of the OQ-45 and the three subscales indicate that Meg has stopped belonging to the dysfunctional population (see Psychometric tests: 4th application, graphs 13.5 and 13.6).

13.2.5.4 Psychotherapy Process Assessment Interview [PPAI] (Session 21)

Name: Meg.

Conducted in session: 21

1. We have had ***20*** sessions so far, in terms of usefulness for your well-being, how has the process of psychotherapy been for you?

Very beneficial and useful.

Please, rate:

0	1	2	**3**
No use	Slight use	Moderate use	**High use**

2. Of the Topic(s) we agreed to work on, how much has changed in your opinion? (**If the answer is Yes**) Could you please detail for me?

I don't feel trapped with Jordi anymore. That state is over. Now I feel comfortable and can talk to him. I also feel closer to other people. To be more precise, now I take care of being pleasant with others. And most importantly, I no longer defend myself by distancing myself from people.

Please, rate:

0	1	2	**3**
None	Slight	Moderate	**High**

3. For you, what has been achieved from the agreed therapeutic objectives? In the patient's words: *Not being depressed anymore and valuing interpersonal relationships beyond achievement.*

Please, rate:

0	1	2	**3**
No progress	Slight progress	Moderate progress	**High progress**

4. In general, what changes have you noticed in yourself since you started psychotherapy?

My loneliness was not imposed but chosen by me. I imposed it on myself. Now I cultivate interpersonal relationships and not everything in my life is work. I also cultivate leisure and recreation with Jordi.

(If the answer is YES), Rate how much change you have experienced according to the following scale:

0	1	2	**3**
None	Slight	Moderate	**High**

5. Do you remember having experienced novelty in any session?

Learning about my way of being with people. Now my relationships with others have changed a lot. And now I feel the positive in me and in others. I no longer use sarcasm, for example.

(If the answer is YES), Rate according to the following scale:

0	1	2	**3**
None	Slight	Moderate	**High**

6. What do you believe (your personal theory) has caused the changes you have experienced?

Specify if there are external life situations.

My life is not the same. I am still enthusiastic about my work and I am happy to come home every day. With Jordi, I feel comfortable and nothing of that feeling of "strangeness."

The possibility of working in an NGO has arisen and it is in the city to which Jordi will move. I am considering the possibility of accepting early retirement soon and moving with Jordi.

Please rate if you have had responsibility in the changes according to the following scale:

0	1	2	**3**
None	Slight	Moderate	**High**

7. What psychological explanations (reformulations), that I have conveyed to you in the sessions, have been most helpful to you? Why? (in the patient's words):

- **Reformulation made by the therapist**: *"Moving from worrying to actively taking care of people is beneficial. Now that you talk openly with Jordi about what is happening to you and negotiate, it produces adjustments and positive consequences. For example, telling him that moving to another city is something you see as possible but not yet, since you would have to look for a new job. That it is not an option for you at this moment since you are getting to know each other and you have had many changes. That options can be sought, if he cannot postpone the change of city."*

Psychological reformulation remembered by the patient (in the patient's words): *"Worrying and taking care of understanding people will be relevant to my well-being. As well as negotiating with my partner, it will be beneficial."*

Why? (Patient): *Talking to those close to me about myself is a novelty. I have felt better.*

- **Reformulation made by the therapist**: *"We already know that your job is for you a space of security and of control of interpersonal relationships oriented towards achievement. But we also already know that not everything in life is about achievement and that human contact is relevant for psychological balance and personal well-being both yours and others."*

Psychological reformulation remembered by the patient (in the patient's words): *"My job was a space of security and control, and that relationships were understood as functional to achievement."*

Why? (Patient): "*Observing such a diminished aspect of my life has been very shocking to me."*

- **Reformulation made by the therapist**: *"The story about your father, is only the story told by your mother and accepted by you until not long ago. You also have responsibility in accepting what was told and not only your mother."*

Psychological reformulation remembered by the patient (in the patient's words): *"The story I know about my father is largely a fiction that my mother told me and that I believed."*

Why? (Patient): *My responsibility in not wanting to see what was evident that had great inconsistencies. I realize that I had moments of great doubts in other periods of my life, but I did nothing.*

Please, rate on the following scale how much it has helped you:

0	1	2	**3**
No use	Slight	Moderate	**High**

8. Reflecting on the time you have been in psychotherapy, have there been setbacks in your psychotherapeutic process? Yes: ☐ No: ☒

If the answer is Yes, please specify (in the patient's words): *None.*

Please, rate on the following scale how much of a setback:

0	1	2	3
None	Slight	Moderate	High

9. Of the homework tasks we have agreed upon, is there any that has been impossible, difficult or uncomfortable for you to perform? Yes: ☒ No: ☐

If the answer is Yes, in the patient's words Why?

The task we agreed on to investigate information about my father. It was very difficult to talk to my mother about this matter.

Please, rate on the following scale how difficult/uncomfortable it has been:

0	1	2	**3**
None	Slight	Moderate	**High**

10. What learnings do you consider are due to psychotherapy?

Recognizing my fear, anxiety, sadness, guilt, and anger. Also, understanding others more and better. And feeling bad about my inertia in relation to the story I accepted from my father without questioning anything.

Please rate the learnings according to the following scale:

0	1	2	**3**
None	Mild	Moderate	**High**

11. What expectations do you now have about the psychotherapeutic process? (in the patient's words): *My main interest is to stay better connected with others. I also need to know more about my father's history. I know that my "judgment" about my father, is from my mother. I hope to communicate with my father as soon as possible.*

Please rate the amount of expectations according to the following scale:

0	1	2	**3**
None	Mild	Moderate	**High**

12. We have been working for 17 sessions, do you have any suggestions for me to be able to help you better?

(If the answer is Yes), in the patient's words What suggestion(s)? *I have no suggestions.*

Please rate the number of suggestions according to the following scale:

0	1	2	3
None	Minimum	Some	Many

13. In relation to your awareness of internal time, in the last 2 weeks, is your behavior generally influenced by your current circumstances, by what happened in the past or by the possible future consequences?

- **If the answer is one or more of the temporal dimensions, which one(s)?** *Present and future.*

Could you describe what you indicate in an example? *I am going through a good time and I have future expectations with my partner and father.*

Please rate on the following scale if your internal time causes you discomfort:

0	1	2	3
None	Light	Moderate	High

14. Rate according to the following scale, how have you been in the last 2 weeks?

Psychological distress						Psychological well-being
High	Moderate	Light	Neutral	Light	Moderate	High
-3	−2	−1	0	+1	+2	**+3**

13.2.5.5 Psychometric Tests: Fourth Application

BDI-II and OQ-45 were applied before session 21th (see Results in Table 13.8).

Table 13.8 Results of BDI-II and OQ-45 Results by OQ-45 area (fourth application)

Instrument	Scores	OQ-45 Areas	Scores
BDI–II	5	Symptoms and subjective discomfort	33
		Interpersonal relationships	15
		Social role	11
		OQ-45 global scale	59

Firstly, the BDI-II does not indicate depressive symptomatology. Secondly, in relation to the OQ-45, it is observed that between the first and fourth evaluation, there is a therapeutically significant change in all dimensions evaluated by the OQ-45[2] as shown in the ICC column in Table 13.9. Evolution of overall OQ-45 and BDI-II scores is shown in Figs. 13.10 and 13.11.

[2] In this session, the estimation of therapeutically significant and statistically significant change is made because the patient stopped being symptomatic.

Table 13.9 Evolution of the OQ-45 scores from the first to the fourth application

OQ-45	Scores first application	Scores fourth application	ICC[a]
Area of symptoms and subjective discomfort	72	33	39
Area of interpersonal relationships	27	15	12
Area of social role	20	11	9
OQ-45 global scale	119	59	60

[a] Reliable Change Index (ICC). The difference between the first application and the fourth exceeds the scales established to indicate that the therapeutic change is significant (The established scales are Symptomatology >12; Interpersonal relationships >9; Social Role >8; and global scale >17). In addition, the scores of the fourth application are below the cut-off score. Therefore, the change is also statistically significant

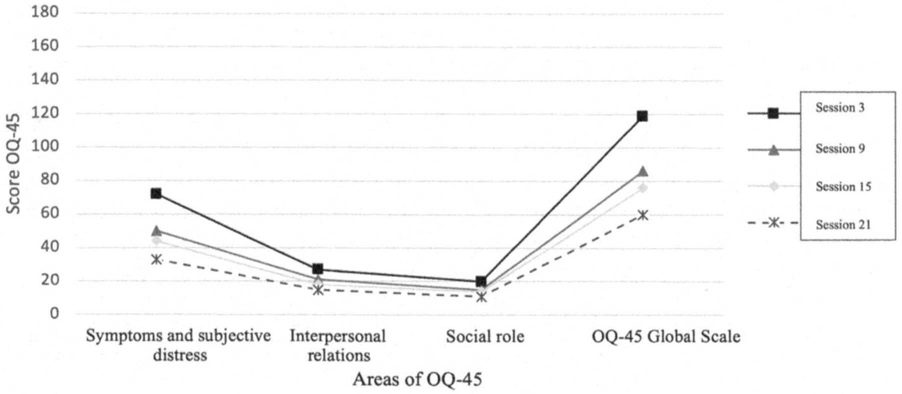

Fig. 13.10 Evolution of the overall OQ-45 score from the first to the fourth application

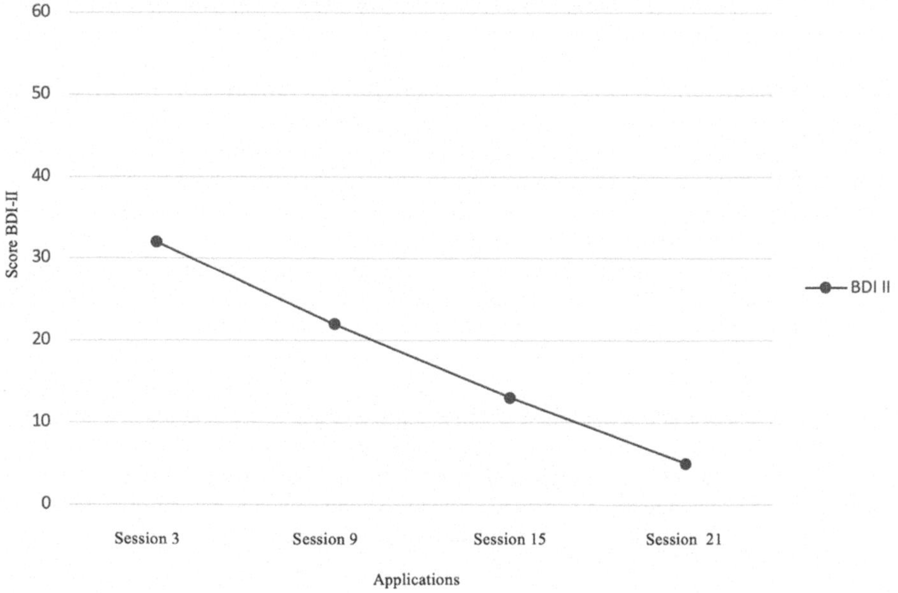

Fig. 13.11 Evolution of the BDI-II score from the first to the fourth application

13.2.6 Case Formulation from an Evolutionary Perspective: Intervention (Session 27)

13.2.6.1 Thematic Conceptualization

Name: Meg.
Conceptualization of sessions No.: 22nd, 23rd, 24th, 25th and 26th (see Box 13.31).
Self System: Clinical Assessment.

(mark presence: x)

SENSE OF AGENCY/EFFICIENCY: Alteration ☐ Progress ☐ Regulation ☒
Describe: Meg has consolidated regulation. She continues feeling in control and confident about what she decides to do and can do. In addition to this, there is consolidation of regulation of efficacy and outcome expectations.

SELF-NARRATIVE/COHERENCE: Alteration ☐ Progress ☐ Regulation ☒
Describe: The self-narrative about her relationship with Jordi remains articulated and provides a renewed continuity to her identity. It presents contextualization, agency, better temporal balance, emotional understanding, self-care, and absence of intersubjective tension. It stands out a genuine interest in her relationship with her partner and in nurturing and cultivating new relationships with common friends.
On the other hand, the self-narrative about the supposed disinterest of her father has disappeared. Now Meg is rewriting her story with many details of how her parents met and developed their love relationship. The main thing is that this knowledge has had a healthy impact to start creating an image of her father.

SENSE OF TIME/BALANCE: Alteration ☐ Progress ☐ Regulation ☒
Describe: Her temporal profile is balanced and fluid. An enriched present is observed and possible futures that she understands as dependent on her decisions.

SELF-ESTEEM/SELF-DECEPTION: Alteration ☐ Progress ☐ Regulation ☒
Describe: Her self-deception is positive and healthy. Meg does not avoid people at her work. She has understood and integrated into her own narrative that she organized herself in that way from her youth and it has not been beneficial for her. Now, she is focused on relating to the people at her work beyond achievement. She also continues to cultivate a richer existential relationship with Marcia.
Finally, she mentions that she has gone out of the office to have coffee with colleagues. She says: "I feel much better with people and I am learning to value them not only for their performance… it is very relevant to me. And I have a better time."

SELF-CARE/HEALTH: Alteration ☐ Progress ☐ Regulation ☒
Describe: Behavioral changes in self-care and health continue. Meg now weighs 77 kilos, that is, overweight. But she is no longer obese type I (BMI: 29) and this is something new for her. She continues with energy and maintains walks with Jordi, 50 minutes three times a week. She bought a German Shepherd (puppy) which has been a wonder according to her description. Finally, she and Jordi practice Yoga that it has allowed both of them to improve their body flexibility.

Observations: The self system is observed with a maintained regulation and psychological flexibility. This allows for the continued integration of information from second-order domains and the creation of new *present and adaptive contextual meanings. All of the above is observed in a stable functional narrative.*

13.2.6.2 Assessment of Dysfunctional Intersubjective Knowledge Domains

Cognition: Change Indicators.

(mark presence: **x**)

Cognitive alterations: Progress ☐ Regulation ☒
Describe: Maintains optimal regulation.

Metacognition alterations: Progress ☐ Regulation ☒
Describe: Maintains optimal regulation.

Alterations in executive functions: Progress ☐ Regulation ☒
Describe: Maintains optimal regulation.

- Functional Narrative Indicator: Integrates knowledge about cognition ☒
- Behavioral Change Indicator: Incorporates changes ☒

Psychological Distress						Psychological Well-Being
High	Moderate	Mild	Neutral	Mild	Moderate	High
-3	-2	-1	0	1	**2**	3
Psychological Dysregulation						Psychological Regulation
High	Moderate	Mild	Neutral	Mild	Moderate	High
-3	-2	-1	0	1	**2**	3

Observations: It presents regulation of the three dimensions. Additionally, it continues to incorporate knowledge into the functional narrative.

Emotion: Indicators of Change.

(mark presence: **x**)

Alteration of emotional awareness: Progress ☐ Regulation ☒
Describe: Emotional awareness is adequate. Now, no problems of emotional clarity or emotional differentiation are observed in the altered emotional profile at the beginning of psychotherapy. Together, a stable realization about the interpersonal function of emotions and a positive valuation of them for problem-solving is observed. Lastly, the absence of dysfunctional mood (depressive) has been consolidated.

Emotional dysregulation: Progress ☐ Regulation ☒

Describe: Emotional regulation strategies indicate flexibility and adequacy, for example: predominantly "cognitive reappraisal" and presence of little "suppression", but both are adequate. In addition, the emotional valence indicates that Meg experiences positive emotions significantly more than negative ones. Finally, there is a flexible presence of coping mechanisms, both individual proactive adaptive and dyadic positive (with Jordi).

- Functional Narrative Indicator: Integrates knowledge about emotion ☒
- Behavioral Change Indicator: Incorporates Changes ☒

Psychological Distress						Psychological Well-Being
High	Moderate	Mild	Neutral	Mild	Moderate	High
-3	-2	-1	0	**1**	2	3
Psychological Dysregulation						Psychological Regulation
High	Moderate	Mild	Neutral	Mild	Moderate	High
-3	-2	-1	0	**1**	2	3

Observations: Uses emotions to give meaning to their experience. Additionally, they continue to incorporate knowledge into the functional narrative.

Interpersonal: Indicators of Change.

(mark presence: **x**)

Alteration in personal relationships: Progress ☐ Regulation ☒

Describe: Maintains and makes healthy adjustments to strengthen the interpersonal relationships they are cultivating with Jordi.

Alteration in romantic relationships: Progress ☐ Regulation ☒

Describe: Maintains and makes healthy adjustments in taking care of their romantic life.

- Functional Narrative Indicator:
Integrates knowledge about interpersonal relationships ☒

- Behavioral Change Indicator: Incorporates changes ☒

Psychological Distress						Psychological Well-Being
High	Moderate	Mild	Neutral	Mild	Moderate	High
-3	-2	-1	0	1	**2**	3
Psychological Dysregulation						Psychological Regulation
High	Moderate	Mild	Neutral	Mild	Moderate	High
-3	-2	-1	0	1	**2**	3

Observations: Their marital relationship has achieved a stable and healthy balance that is expressed in recreation (example: going to the theater), sharing with other couples, and exercising together (going for walks). Their pet "Harry" has greatly helped to motivate their daily exercise (example: they go for walks every day when Jordi gets home from work). And Meg notes that with Marcia a closer relationship is emerging that pleases her a lot. Also in her he continues to have coffee with colleagues and share with some of them. In addition, he continues to incorporate knowledge into the functional narrative and behavioral changes in everyday life.

Imagination: Indicators of Change.

(mark presence: **x**)

Interferes with experiential coherence: Progress ☐ Regulation ☒

Describe: Continues to use emotion in an adaptive way.

Interferes with troubleshooting: Progress ☐ Regulation ☒

Describe: The use of simulation to solve problems has been consolidated, incorporating the probabilities of possible interpersonal scenarios.

- Functional Narrative Indicator: Integrates knowledge about imagination ☒
- Behavioral Change Indicator: Incorporates changes ☒

Psychological Distress				Psychological Well-Being		
High	Moderate	Mild	Neutral	Mild	Moderate	High
-3	-2	-1	0	**1**	2	3
Psychological Dysregulation				Psychological Regulation		
High	Moderate	Mild	Neutral	Mild	Moderate	High
-3	-2	-1	0	**1**	2	3

Observations: Psychological regulation is well rooted. At the same time, he continues to actively incorporate knowledge into the functional narrative and maintains behavioral changes.

Corporeality: Change indicators.

(mark presence: **x**)

Altered experience: Progress ☐ Regulation ☒

Describe: The frequent lack of energy/fatigue is not observed. Maintaining exercise and proper nutrition has contributed to feeling rejuvenated.

Dysfunctional body attitude: Progress ☐ Regulation ☒

Describe: The Insufficient body self-care presents a radical change. Now she takes care of a healthy diet that has allowed her to lose weight. In addition, she takes care of her exercise and being in shape to control her health. Her partner shares with her activities that involve exercise.

- Functional Narrative Indicator: Integrates knowledge about corporeality ☒
- Behavioral Change Indicator: Incorporates changes ☒

Psychological Distress						Psychological Well-Being
High	Moderate	Mild	Neutral	Mild	Moderate	High
-3	-2	-1	0	**1**	2	3
Psychological Dysregulation						Psychological Regulation
High	Moderate	Mild	Neutral	Mild	Moderate	High
-3	-2	-1	0	1	**2**	3

Observations: Has been seeing a diabetologist nutritionist for 2 months. Such a change in attitude is a powerful agent in her new functional narrative.

Sexuality: Change indicators.

(mark presence: **x**)

Sexual disconnection with a partner: Progress ☐ Regulation ☒

Describe: The lack of sexual interest is not present. There is observed satisfactory sexual interest and frequency. Also, the unsatisfactory sexuality is not present. At present she feels pleasure and enjoyment.

- Functional Narrative Indicator: Integrates knowledge about sexuality ☒
- Behavioral Change Indicator: Incorporates changes ☒

Psychological Distress						Psychological Well-Being
High	Moderate	Mild	Neutral	Mild	Moderate	High
-3	-2	-1	0	**1**	2	3
Psychological Dysregulation						**Psychological Regulation**
High	Moderate	Mild	Neutral	Mild	Moderate	High
-3	-2	-1	0	**1**	2	3

Observations: Shows regulation. Continues to inform and incorporate knowledge about sexuality into the functional narrative.

13.2.6.3 Monitoring of the Psychotherapeutic Process

A. Assessment of sessions:

a.1 What changes are observed in the Dysfunctional Narrative?

The Dysfunctional Narrative has not been present since session 20. Discomfort with psychological intimacy with her partner has been overcome and has transformed into a path of learning and personal growth. In addition, Meg has learned about the benefits of proximity and psychological intimacy and considers them necessary for better psychological balance.

a.2 What characteristics does the Functional Narrative have?

Absent: ☐ Emerging: ☐ Stable: ☒

Meg says: "Being and sharing with people is enriching and healthy." Particularly, she values emotional closeness with others and its benefits for being in psychological balance.

a.3 Represent the domains of second-order intersubjective knowledge in quadrants for psychological evaluation. Indicate the assessments in the boxes (see Table 13.10 and Fig. 13.12).

Table 13.10 Domains of second-order intersubjective knowledge (session 27)

ECF evaluation			ECF intervention	
Discomfort—well-being	Dysregulation—regulation		Discomfort—well-being	Dysregulation—regulation
−3	−2	Cognition [C]	2	2
−3	−2	Emotion [E]	1	1
−1	−1	Interpersonal [I]	2	2
−1	−2	Imagination [Im]	1	1
−1	−2	Corporeality [Cor]	1	2
−1	−1	Sexuality [sex]	1	1

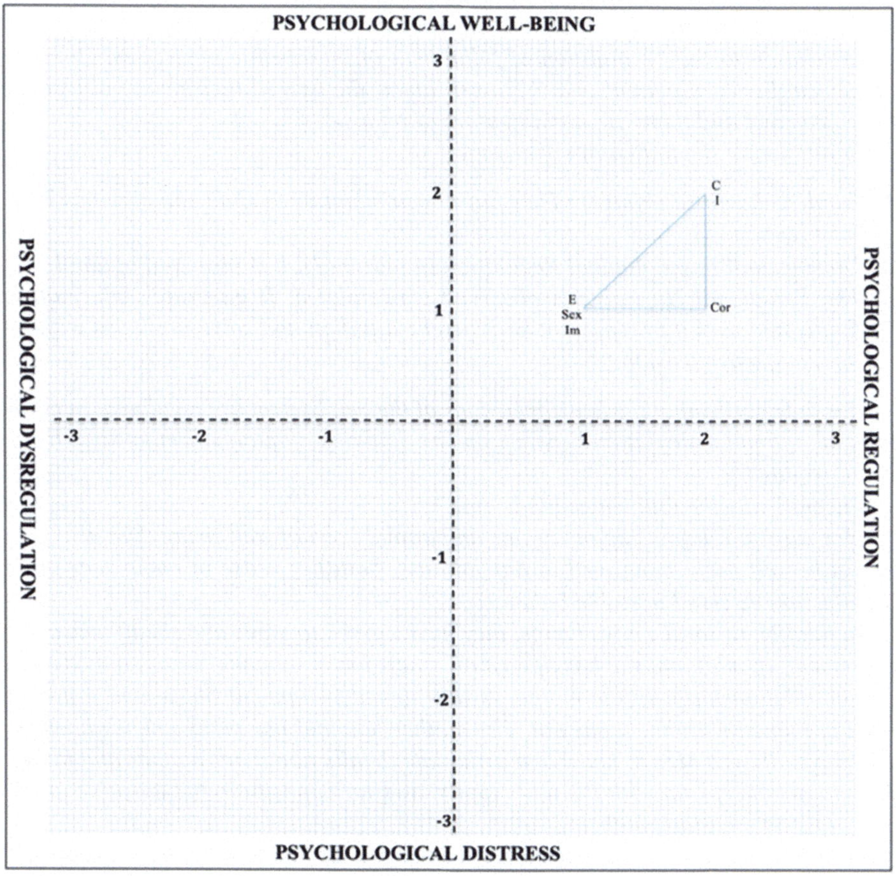

Fig. 13.12 Domains of second-order intersubjective knowledge (session 27)

a.4 Evaluation of therapeutic objectives fulfillment [mark presence: **x**],

Significant change valued by the patient	x
Significant change valued by the therapist	x
There is agreement on the achievement of objectives between therapist and patient	x

a.5 Indicators of change [mark presence: **x**]:

Behavioral changes	x
Dimensional psychological regulation (quadrant I)	x
Functional narrative	x

General Observations

Meg shows maintained Dimensional Psychological Regulation from the previous ECF Intervention. *All six domains of intersubjective knowledge are in quadrant I "Dimensional Psychological Regulation."*

There is a stable presence of an articulated and fluid Adaptive Intersubjective Reality Sense that provides existential perspective and interpersonal regulation.

In relation to the "evaluation of fulfillment of therapeutic objectives," there is agreement between patient and therapist, about the agreed therapeutic objectives have been met and there are no indicators of relapse.

In relation to the Indicators of change:

1. *Stable behavioral changes: They have been maintained since the previous ECF Intervention.*
2. *Dimensional Psychological Regulation (quadrant I): it is observed optimal.*
3. *The Functional Narrative is observed consolidated. It integrates information fluidly and uses it to represent her current situation and solve problems without intersubjective tension.*

It is noteworthy that the five dimensions of the Self System are regulated. In addition, an optimal articulation between the six domains of intersubjective knowledge is appreciated.

Thematically the following stands out:

Her marital relationship maintains an optimal level of well-being. She also perceives herself performing well in her job and, both her sense of competence and dignity, are observed in stable balance.

In relation to Jordi's city change, they have agreed to move and she to take early retirement. In addition, she has agreed on a new job in a humanitarian aid NGO.

The relationship with the mother is in a new development phase and a higher level of human warmth stands out. The mother has told her many unknown events that have allowed Meg to know and articulate details about her mother and father. Marcia also keeps up with the news and shows no opposition, but surprise at the story told by the grandmother.

Meg had her first video conference meeting with her father after session 25. According to her description, the experience has been very emotional and she is aware that it is a process that just begins and that she wants to continue.

On summer vacation she will travel to see her father. From this moment, she refers to her father by his name "Pedro." In the moments when she refers to him, her facial and body expression, is of pleasure.

And essentially, it consists of focusing on interpersonal relationships with the intention of continuing to learn, inform herself, value and weigh different levels of closeness and leisure.

Pharmacologically, Meg has not taken Sertraline for 6 weeks. She completed the 12-month treatment as agreed with her psychiatrist who discharged her. And to date she has not presented difficulties.

There is an absence of depressive symptoms since the previous ECF Intervention. Both the BDI-II and the OQ-45 confirm the clinical judgment (See graph 13.7 and 13.8).

13.2.6.4 Psychotherapy Process Assessment Interview [PPAI] (Session 27)

Name: Meg.
Conducted in session: 27

1. We have had ***26*** sessions, so far, in terms of usefulness for your well-being, how has the process of psychotherapy been for you?

I am happy and very hopeful. I have learned a lot about myself.
Please, score:

0	1	2	**3**
No utility	Slight utility	Moderate utility	**High utility**

2. Regarding the topic we agreed to work on, how much has your opinion changed? (**If the answer is Yes**) Could you please detail for me?

My marital communication is good and we talk a lot. And importantly, we negotiate and reach agreements. I am enjoying and growing as a person.

Now, my topic is to complete the incomplete story that my mother told me, but especially I want to continue getting to know my father.

Please, rate:

0	1	2	**3**
None	Slight	Moderate	**High**

3. For you, what progress have you made in the agreed therapeutic objectives? (In the patient's words): *I'm fine. I'm in a new stage of my personal and family life.*

(**If the answer is Yes**), rate how much progress you have experienced according to the following scale:

0	1	2	**3**
No progress	Slight progress	Moderate progress	**High progress**

4. In general, what changes have you noticed in yourself since you started psychotherapy?

My excess of loneliness has been a chronic problem and for me it was a matter of pride before. Now I continue learning to relate to other people and I also desire it. It is beneficial for me.

Knowing the story of my parents has been very hard but healthy. It was very shocking to talk to him by video conference. I have mixed feelings, but I am calm. That will require time to "digest."

(If the answer is YES), rate how much change according to the following scale:

0	1	2	**3**
None	Mild	Moderate	**High**

5. Do you remember having a novelty experience in any session?

My philosophy of "I solve everything alone" has been forgotten. It's part of my past. Now, when I have problems, I consider others in the possible solutions. For example, with Jordi we talk a lot and agree on what's best for both of us.

(If the answer is YES), score according to the following scale:

0	1	2	**3**
None	Mild	Moderate	**High**

6. What do you believe (your personal theory) has caused the changes you have experienced? Specify if there are external life situations (e.g., job change, city change, etc.)

Valuing how important it is to relate well. I'm still doing well at my job and I value leisure, Yoga, and exercise. Also, I do it with Jordi.

My sense of humor not only have I recovered for some time, but I have also stopped being sarcastic and it has not been easy at all. With Jordi, we have made friends with other couples and we have a social life on weekends.

My belief about "people" has changed and will continue to change. Now I value more and more sharing, enjoying and caring for others.

Please, score if you have had responsibility in the changes according to the following scale:

0	1	2	**3**
None	Mild	Moderate	**High**

7. What psychological explanations (reformulations), that I have transmitted to you in the sessions, have been most helpful to you? Why? (in the patient's words):

***Reformulation made by the therapist**: "The origin of your contempt that you felt with many male people is related to the fact that your mother systematically belittled your father by disqualifying him and telling you that he left from one day to the next, and not giving you information about who he was. From your mother's point of view, she thought it was best since it was not a relationship but rather a casual encounter according to her understanding. We know that they saw each other on several occasions and kept in touch. As you have known, they saw each other for a year and wrote to each other for several months afterwards. It is discrepant the casualness with the relationship time that your mother informed you that it lasted."*

Psychological reformulation remembered by the patient *(in the patient's words): "The origin of the contempt that I sometimes present and its direct relationship with the story and fiction that my mother told me about my father."*

Why? (Patient): *Because the influence of my mother has been essential in my way of understanding and thinking about the relationships of my life so far.*

Reformulation made by the therapist: *"Your mother, as we have seen in the reconstructions, in particular that way of referring to men is often related to your father. That is, the disqualification of interpersonal relationships with boys your age during adolescence and that you remember with quite freshness, she did it because she believed it was a way of defending you from dangers... which were rather her own fears."*

Psychological reformulation remembered by the patient (in the patient's words): *"The issue of disqualifying boys of my age during adolescence has a lot to do with my mother and her way of understanding taking care of me at that time."*

Why? (Patient): *I am much more attached to my mother than I thought and would like, but that's the way it is.*

Please rate on the following scale how much it has helped you:

0	1	2	**3**
No use	Mild	Moderate	**High**

8. If you reflect on the time you have been in psychotherapy, have there been setbacks in your psychotherapeutic process? Yes: ☐ No: ☒

If the answer is Yes, specify (in the patient's words):

Please rate on the following scale how much of a setback:

0	1	2	3
None	Mild	Moderate	High

9. Of the household tasks we have agreed upon, is there any that has been impossible, difficult, or uncomfortable for you to perform? Yes: ☒ No: ☐

If the answer is Yes, in the patient's words, why?

Performing the task we evaluated and considered necessary (session 25[a]) of communicating with my father. I did it via *video conference and it was emotional, somewhat strange at times but not uncomfortable. But I did it and I am very happy about it. Now I know and realize something new, and that is that I physically resemble Pedro, my father.*

Please rate on the following scale how difficult/uncomfortable it has been:

0	1	**2**	3
None	Mild	**Moderate**	High

10. What learnings do you consider are due to psychotherapy?

Recognizing my anger. In particular, the anger about the family secret that has been something new for me. Also, understanding the origins of my loneliness that I thought was chosen. Now I find myself valuing others and I strive to be kind. I am clearly aware that I still have difficulties in "seeing" and "understanding" others.

Please rate the learnings according to the following scale:

0	1	2	**3**
None	Mild	Moderate	**High**

11. What expectations do you now have about the psychotherapeutic process? (in the patient's words):

In the near future I would like to return to explore more the relationship with my father that I hope will develop immediately because he is older. It is a topic that emerged recently but that I feel and think that I should have more interaction and face-to-face conversation with him. Maybe, in a few months I would like to work specifically on the topic and its implications.

Please rate the amount of expectations according to the following scale:

0	1	2	**3**
None	Mild	Moderate	**High**

12. We have been working for 26 sessions, do you have any suggestions for me to be able to help you better? **(If the answer is Yes),** in the patient's words, what suggestion(s)? *No suggestions.*

Please, rate the number of suggestions according to the following scale:

0	1	2	3
None	Minimum	Some	Many

13. In relation to your awareness of internal time, in the last 2 weeks, is your behavior generally influenced by your current circumstances, by what happened in the past or by the possible future consequences? *My present and future are very present.*

- **If the answer is one or more of the temporal dimensions, which one(s)?** *Present and future.*

Could you describe what you indicate in an example? *I have already communicated my acceptance of early retirement. I am excited about the job changes and city that I will make soon. I feel challenged.*

Please, rate on the following scale if your internal time causes you discomfort:

0	1	2	3
None	Mild	Moderate	High

14. Rate according to the following scale, how have you been in the last 2 weeks?

Psychological distress				Psychological well-being		
High	Moderate	Mild	Neutral	Mild	Moderate	High
-3	−2	−1	0	+1	+2	**+3**

13.2.6.5 Psychometric Tests: Fifth Application

BDI-II and OQ-45 were applied before session 27th (see results in Table 13.11 and Figs. 13.13 and 13.14).

Table 13.11 Results of BDI-II and OQ-45 results by OQ-45 area (fifth application)

Instrument	Score	Areas of OQ-45	Score
BDI–II	2	Symptoms and subjective discomfort	16
		Interpersonal relationships	11
		Social role	4
		OQ-45 global scale	31

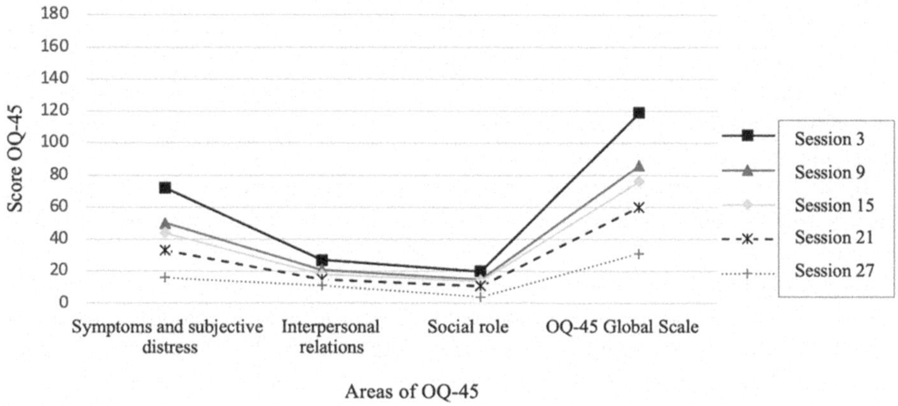

Fig. 13.13 Evolution of OQ-45 score from the first to the fifth application

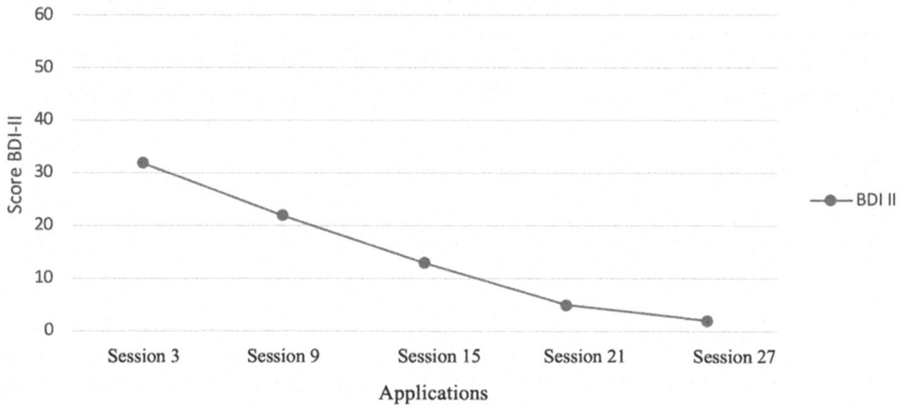

Fig. 13.14 Evolution of BDI-II score from the first to the fifth application

13.3 Follow-Up Sessions

Two follow-up sessions were conducted, the first 1 month later and the second two and a half months later. The first was in person and the second by video conference. In both sessions, the absence of relapses was confirmed. No emerging Dysfunctional Intersubjective Themes were observed.

In a contextual note, the change of city and her new job at the *humanitarian aid NGO* have not presented problems for Meg. Her expectations that her new job would be challenging are being met according to her assessment. In addition, she is seen as comfortable and enthusiastic in "helping" vulnerable population.

On another note, her coping is seen as healthy, both individually and dyadically. With Jordi, they talk about difficulties and how to solve them, so far the small difficulties have been resolved. Also, she continues to enjoy leisure time in company with Jordi, and they continue to enjoy their daily walks with their pet "Harry" who is getting bigger and brings them a lot of joy.

With Marcia, a warmer relationship has been established that is not monothematically focused on achievement. The cultural life in the new city has also been novel and entertaining for both of them.

In their social dimension as a couple, they are gradually cultivating new friendships and have already gone out to dinner on Saturdays with two married couples.

Regarding Pedro, his father, the video conference conversations have continued frequently. Meg describes the encounters as very pleasant and highlights that she is grateful for the opportunities to get to know Pedro and for him to get to know her. She says "*Despite the fact that he is already older, he is self-reliant and very lucid. He handles technology well and I must tell you, he has an extraordinary sense of humor... he makes me laugh. I think I inherited the sarcasm from him... although I haven't told him. Together with Jordi, we are planning a trip during winter vacation to meet Pedro and his family. I am grateful to be getting to know him and to be able to meet him in person... it won't be long now.*"

Lastly, the BDI-II and OQ-45 psychological tests were applied and no indicators of psychological alteration were observed (sixth application, see graph 13.9 and 13.10).

13.3.1 Follow-Up Psychometric Tests: Sixth Application

Table 13.12 and Figs. 13.15 and 13.16 present the results of the psychometric tests carried out in the 29th session.

Table 13.12 BDI-II results by OQ-45 area (sixth application)

Instrument	Score	OQ-45 areas	Score
BDI–II	2	Symptoms and subjective discomfort	13
		Interpersonal relationships	11
		Social role	2
		OQ-45 global scale	26

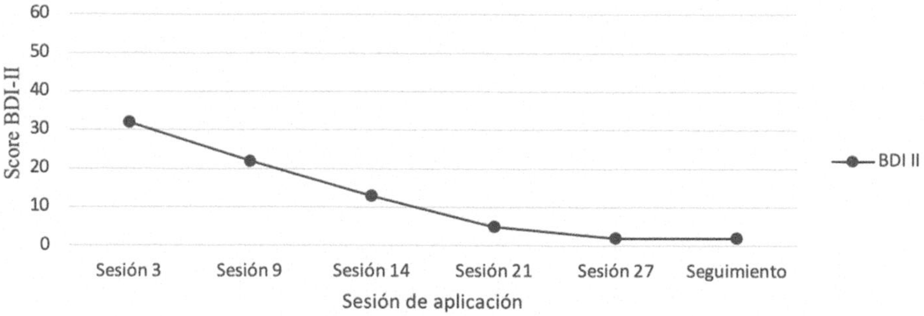

Fig. 13.15 Evolution of depressive symptoms, BDI-II

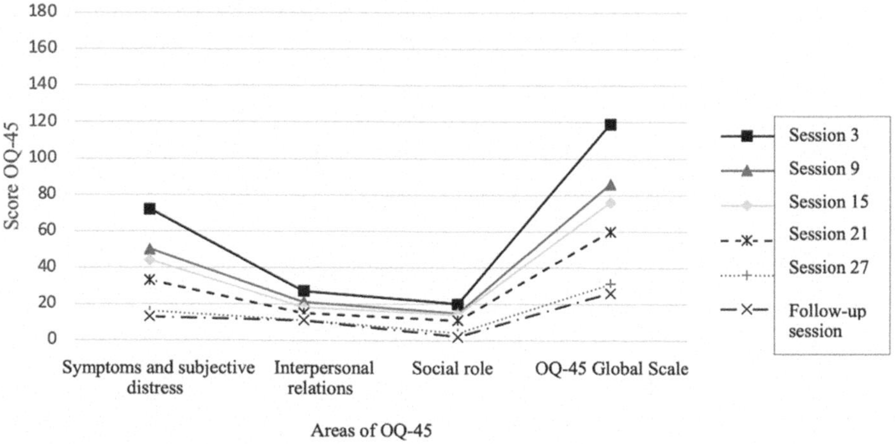

Fig. 13.16 Evaluation of discomfort, OQ-45

References

Beck, A. T., Steer, R. A., & Brown, G. K. (1996). *Manual for the Beck depression inventory-II*. Psychological Corporation.

Dozois, D. J. A., Dobson, K. S., & Ahnberg, J. L. (1998). A psychometric evaluation of the Beck depression inventory–II. *Psychological Assessment, 10*(2), 83–89. https://doi.org/10.1037/1040-3590.10.2.83

von Bergen, A., & de la Parra, G. (2002). OQ-45.2, Cuestionario para evaluación de resultados y evolución en psicoterapia: Adaptación, validación e indicaciones para su aplicación e interpretación. *Terapia Psicológica, 20*(2), 161–176.

Chapter 14
Final Considerations

The *Case Formulation from an Evolutionary Perspective* [ECF] uses a common language based on the intersubjective information processing dimensions that make us a unique species in the animal kingdom: Self System (First Order Intersubjective Knowledge Domains) and seven Second Order Intersubjective Knowledge Domains: Cognition, Emotion, Interpersonal, Imagination, Corporeality, Sexuality, Religiosit y/Spirituality.

The dimensions of the Self System and its wiring with the second order intersubjective domains have a strong relationship with the satisfaction of psychological needs (autonomy, competence, and relationship) and stress coping. The emergence of unhealthy trajectories, such as the presence of a Dysfunctional Intersubjective Theme that is expressed through narratives (see Chap. 13), depends on this self-organizing interaction. We must not lose sight of the fact that motives arise from psychological needs to energize, direct, and sustain the behavior necessary to advance towards greater personal growth and optimal well-being in life.

Narratives are part of our evolution as a species and have implications for psychological well-being and psychological regulation. Narratives give humans many possibilities for creating intersubjective meaning, as they allow us to be in the world in different possible idiographic patterns of conscious self-understanding through narratives about oneself and others with varying degrees of agency (Self System). Therefore, the interpretive possibilities of language/narratives enable the transformation of self-generated information by the person, and received from others, into personal knowledge with degrees of continuity and coherence in a narrative identity in process.

Regarding the advantages that the ECF enables, I list five. First, it facilitates the therapist's participant observation in the dyadic relationship as it provides a map of the patient's dimensional psychological representation that is sensitive, contrastable, perfectible, and communicable in a comprehensible way. Second, it guides the therapist to pay attention to what should not be omitted in their "participant observation" to facilitate change from joint observation, guided reflection, and action

Á. Quiñones Bergeret, *Evolutionary Case Formulation*,
https://doi.org/10.1007/978-3-031-67412-9_14

suggestions for the patient. Third, conceptually it implies understanding psychological problems that arise in life trajectories as processes of intersubjective information/meaning that take shape in a Dysfunctional Intersubjective Theme [TID]. Fourth, communicate a clinical hypothesis with a common language. Fifth, it allows making decisions and designing interventions based on research (paradigmatic/scientific thinking) and adjusted to the patient (narrative/idiographic thinking) with the intention of achieving the gradual emergence of a possible dimensional psychological regulation. Sixth, it allows parsimoniously representing psychological distress and psychological dysregulation in three of the four quadrants (see Chap. 1, Fig. 1.3). This presents the advantage of facilitating the monitoring of the progress made.

On another note, this book intended to answer some questions that were raised in the introduction (see Chap. 1). I list them below and give brief answers that can be reviewed in full in the complete book:

1. **What do we psychotherapists (participant observers) do to facilitate change in a psychotherapeutic process?** Observe and assess altered intersubjective knowledge domains based on two information processing dimensions [Psychological Distress—Psychological Well-being and Psychological Dysregulation—Psychological Regulation] and identify patient strengths. Based on this previously, proceed to design interventions to facilitate the emergence of a new intra and inter-domain regulation of intersubjective knowledge, expressed in a functional narrative free of intersubjective tension.
2. **What do we understand by therapeutic process?** The answer given in this book, which may or may not be liked, is observed in the proposal of the case formulation protocol [ECF]. However, from any grounded psychological perspective, the answer has several possible facets, but it is important to say unequivocally, that the answer should include the active participation of the patient in their process of change explicitly, as occurs through the **PSYCHOTHERAPY PROCESS ASSESSMENT INTERVIEW [PPAI]** in the case of Meg. Let's not forget that human beings live in intersubjectivity.
3. **What should we observe session by session?** Assess the domains of intersubjective knowledge that appear altered (deficit or excess) and that are expressed in a synergistic configuration of information and meaning called Dysfunctional Intersubjective Theme [TID]. It is the observation of the "private world" and that is manifested in the complexity of a nomothetic and idiographic dialectic, in a unique existential trajectory.
4. **How can we describe and assess a complete therapeutic process?** Representing the movement of a constellation of dysfunctional intersubjective knowledge domains that move through four possible quadrants (I Dimensional psychological regulation; II Intrapersonal Dimensional psychological deregulation; III High dimensional psychological deregulation; IV Interpersonal dimensional psychological deregulation).
5. **What do we understand by "changes" in psychotherapy?** A new regulation of the domains of intersubjective knowledge that are deregulated, and that are observed in a Dysfunctional Intersubjective Theme. More specifically, it is to

achieve that the "psychological system" (complex system) resumes a new trajectory of well-being and psychological regulation through the process of *Narrative Scaling*.

To conclude, I explicitly state for the last time the evolutionary stamp of this book ("we are primates and we value images"), and I share an image that I intend to show synthetically the dynamics of the complexity of the psychological system in the processing of information, energy and creation of healthy meanings (see Fig. 14.1).

Finally, I hope that the text will be useful for a practice of psychotherapy with intersubjective and cultural sensitivity. In other words, that people who come to request psychological help feel understood and stimulated to change in a special relational context that we call psychotherapy, and finally, that it contributes to remembering that human beings have a sense of narrative identity that is present until we die and that we should always keep in mind.

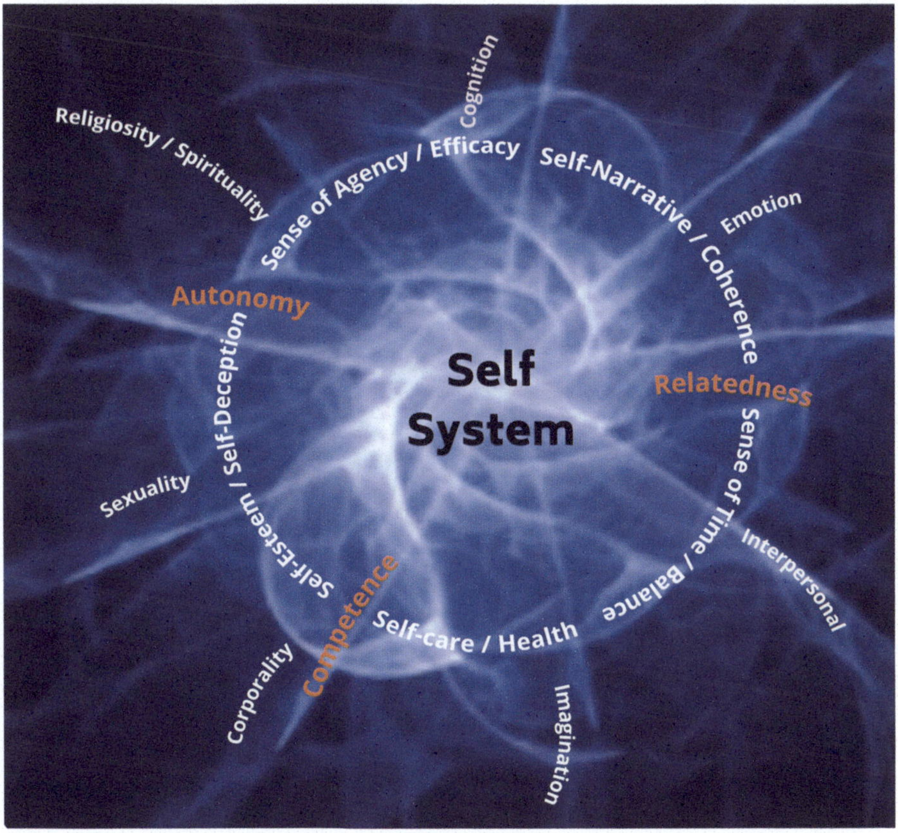

Fig. 14.1 Evolutionary wiring

Appendix: Evolutionary Case Formulation Protocol

Á. Quiñones Bergeret, *Evolutionary Case Formulation*,
https://doi.org/10.1007/978-3-031-67412-9

Section I—EVOLUTIONARY CASE FORMULATION—EVALUATION[1]

Name: .... Date: ....

Conducted in session N°: ____ (integration of information)

Reason for consultation (*in the patient's words*): ....
....
....

THEMATIC CONCEPTUALIZATION

Dysfunctional Intersubjective Theme (co-construction): ....
....

(mark presence: x)

Specify thematic axis(es):

Psychological Intimacy ☐ Death/Finitude of Existence ☐ Surrender ☐ Grandiosity ☐ Inferiority ☐ Righteousness ☐ Power ☐ Failure ☐ Loss ☐ Complacency ☐ Inauthenticity ☐ Freedom ☐ Uncontrollability ☐ Certainty ☐ Mistrust ☐ Perfectionism ☐ Betrayal ☐ Opposition ☐ Loneliness ☐ ☐ Limitation ☐ Sabotaging ☐ Transcending ☐ Contempt ☐ Hypercontrol ☐ Hypercriticism ☐ Discrimination ☐ Jealousy ☐ Competing ☐ Procrastination ☐ Uprootedness ☐ Self-sacrifice ☐ Sexualization ☐ Unworthy ☐ Abandonment ☐ Incompetence ☐ Moral superiority ☐ Fear of aging ☐ Paternal deprivation ☐ Maternal deprivation ☐ Technological addiction ☐ Others: ______________________________

Dysfunctional Narrative:
....
....

Start of Theme(s)?, Course?

Are there relevant life events and/or precipitating stressors?
....
....

Is there frustration of basic psychological needs: competence, autonomy, relationship?
....
....
....

What strengths do you identify in the person?

....

....

SELF SYSTEM: clinical assessment

(mark presence: x)

SENSE OF AGENCY/EFFICACY: Alteration ☐
Describe:..
....
....

SELF-NARRATIVE/COHERENCE: Alteration ☐
Describe:..
....
....

SENSE OF TIME/BALANCE: Alteration ☐
Describe:..
....
....

SELF-ESTEEM/SELF-DECEPTION: Alteration ☐
Describe:..
....
....

SELF-CARE/HEALTH: Alteration ☐
Describe:..
....
....

Observations: ....
....

II. ASSESSMENT OF DYSFUNCTIONAL INTERSUBJECTIVE KNOWLEDGE DOMAINS

[**COGNITION**] Indicate and weigh which processes contribute to discomfort and/or psychological dysregulation: ....
....

(mark presence: x)

Cognitive alterations:

Rumination ☐ Worry ☐ Intolerance to uncertainty ☐ Selective attention ☐

Problematic attributional profile ☐ Absence of realistic expectations ☐

Deficit in problem solving ☐ Others: ____________

Describe: ....

....

Metacognition alterations:

Representation ☐ Differentiation ☐ Decentering ☐ Sharing ☐ Belonging ☐
Integration ☐ Positive metacognitive beliefs ☐

Negative metacognitive beliefs ☐ Others: ____________

Describe: ....

....

Alterations in executive functions:

Cognitive flexibility ☐ Attentional control ☐ Inhibition ☐ Self-monitoring ☐

Planning ☐ Others: _____________

Describe: ....

....

Psychological Distress						Psychological Well-Being
High	Moderate	Mild	Neutral	Mild	Moderate	High
-3	-2	-1	0	1	2	3
Psychological Dysregulation						Psychological Regulation
High	Moderate	Mild	Neutral	Mild	Moderate	High
-3	-2	-1	0	1	2	3

[EMOTION] Indicate and weigh which processes contribute to psychological distress and/or dysregulation.: ....
....

(mark presence: x)

Alteration of emotional awareness:
Emotional profile ☐ Emotional clarity ☐ Emotional differentiation ☐

Understanding emotions ☐

Emotional appraisal in decision making and problem solving ☐

Dysfunctional mood ☐

Others: ______________________________

Describe: ....
....

Emotional Dysregulation:
Regulation strategies ☐ Individual coping ☐ Dyadic coping ☐ Adult attachment ☐
Others: ____________________________________
Describe: ....
....

Psychological Distress						Psychological Well-Being
High	Moderate	Mild	Neutral	Mild	Moderate	High
-3	-2	-1	0	1	2	3
Psychological Dysregulation						Psychological Regulation
High	Moderate	Mild	Neutral	Mild	Moderate	High
-3	-2	-1	0	1	2	3

[INTERPERSONAL] Indicate and weigh what processes contribute to discomfort and/or psychological dysregulation: ....
....

(mark presence: x)

Alteration in personal relationships:

Social skills deficits ☐
Deficit of social support ☐
Lack of friends ☐
Dark Triad personality ☐
Loneliness ☐
Discomfort with people ☐
Constant need for approval ☐
Conflicting labor relations ☐

Others: ___________________

Describe: ....
....

Alteration in romantic relationships:

Decreased confidence ☐
Decreased intimacy ☐
Insecurity ☐
Absence or low admiration ☐
Romantic friendship ☐
Conflict ☐
Diminished passion ☐
Decreased decisiveness/commitment ☐
Fear of abandonment ☐
Decreased cooperation ☐
Intimate partner violence ☐

Others: ___________________

Describe: ....
....

Psychological Distress						Psychological Well-Being
High	Moderate	Mild	Neutral	Mild	Moderate	High
-3	-2	-1	0	1	2	3
Psychological Dysregulation						Psychological Regulation
High	Moderate	Mild	Neutral	Mild	Moderate	High
-3	-2	-1	0	1	2	3

[IMAGINATION] Indicate and weigh what processes contribute to distress and/or psychological dysregulation: ....
....

(mark presence: x)

Imagination interferes with experiential coherence:

Intrusive mental images ☐ Flashbacks ☐ Hotspots ☐
Suicidal flashforwards ☐ Images as an emotional amplifier ☐
Others: ______________________
Describe: ....
....

Imagination interferes with problem solving:

Alteration in mental simulation ☐
Deficit of imagination directed to personal goals ☐
Imagination is a source of self-sabotage ☐
Others: ________________________
Describe: ....
....

Psychological Distress						Psychological Well-Being
High	Moderate	Mild	Neutral	Mild	Moderate	High
-3	-2	-1	0	1	2	3
Psychological Dysregulation						**Psychological Regulation**
High	Moderate	Mild	Neutral	Mild	Moderate	High
-3	-2	-1	0	1	2	3

[**CORPOREALITY**] Indicate and weigh what processes contribute to discomfort and/or psychological dysregulation: ………………………………………………………………………………………
………

(mark presence: x)

Altered experience:

Lack of energy/fatigue ☐ Somatosensory amplification ☐

Interoception disturbances ☐ Alteration of mental representation of the body ☐

Others: ________________________

Describe: ……………………………………………………………………………………………………
………

Dysfunctional body attitude:

Insufficient body self-care ☐ Consequences of sleep on the body ☐

Others: ________________________

Describe: ……………………………………………………………………………………………………
………

Psychological Distress						Psychological Well-Being
High	Moderate	Mild	Neutral	Mild	Moderate	High
-3	-2	-1	0	1	2	3
Psychological Dysregulation						Psychological Regulation
High	Moderate	Mild	Neutral	Mild	Moderate	High
-3	-2	-1	0	1	2	3

[SEXUALITY] Indicate and weigh what processes contribute to discomfort and/or psychological deregulation: ....

....

(mark presence: x)

Sexual disconnection with a partner:

Absence of sexual interest ☐ Sexual performance anxiety ☐
Poor sexual communication ☐ Sexual dysfunction ☐
Sexual stress ☐ Unsatisfactory sexuality ☐
Others: ________________________________

Describe: ....

....

Disconnection with others:

Pornography abuse ☐ Sexual addiction ☐
Excessive masturbation ☐
Others: ________________________________

Describe: ....

....

Psychological Distress						Psychological Well-Being
High	Moderate	Mild	Neutral	Mild	Moderate	High
-3	-2	-1	0	1	2	3
Psychological Dysregulation						Psychological Regulation
High	Moderate	Mild	Neutral	Mild	Moderate	High
-3	-2	-1	0	1	2	3

[**RELIGIOSITY/SPIRITUALITY**] Indicate and weigh what processes contribute to discomfort and/or psychological dysregulation: ....
....

(mark presence: x)

Existential tension:

Negative religious and spiritual coping ☐

Religious and/or spiritual beliefs interfere with re-signifying events ☐

Others: ____________________________
Describe: ....
....

Dysfunctional religious attachment:

Anxious/ambivalent attachment ☐

Avoidant attachment ☐

Others: ____________________________
Describe: ....
....

Psychological Distress						Psychological Well-Being
High	Moderate	Mild	Neutral	Mild	Moderate	High
-3	-2	-1	0	1	2	3
Psychological Dysregulation						Psychological Regulation
High	Moderate	Mild	Neutral	Mild	Moderate	High
-3	-2	-1	0	1	2	3

III. REPRESENTATION OF DYSFUNCTIONAL INTERSUBJECTIVE KNOWLEDGE DOMAINS

a.1 Indicate the ratings in the boxes for: Psychological Distress-Psychological Well-being (D-W) and Psychological Deregulation-Psychological Regulation (D-R). Also, represent the second order intersubjective knowledge domains in the quadrants for psychological evaluation.

ECF - Evaluation		
SECOND- ORDER INTERSUBJECTIVE KNOWLEDGE DOMAINS	Distress - Wellbeing	Deregulation-Regulation
Cognition [C]		
Emotion [E]		
Interpersonal [I]		
Imagination [Im]		
Corporeality [Cor]		
Sexuality [Sex]		
Religiosity/Spirituality [R/E]		

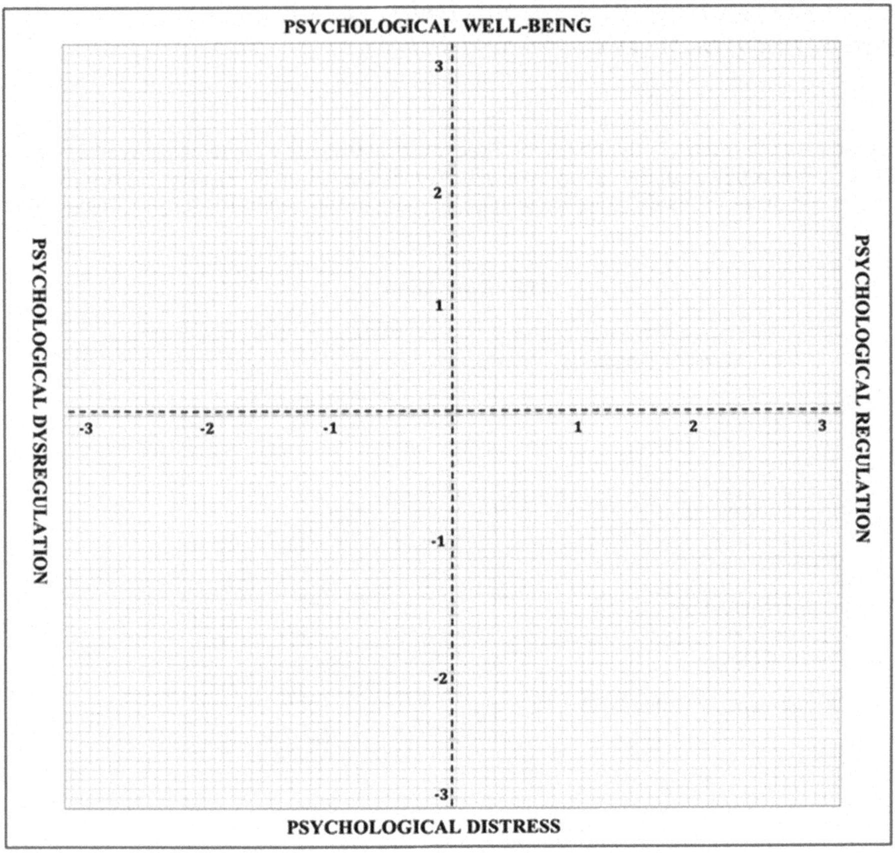

a.2 Indicate the agreed Therapeutic Objectives:

....

....

....

....

....

a.3 Main psychological reformulations communicated to the patient:

....

....

....

....

....

a.4 Psychological Clinical Hypothesis:

The dysfunctional intersubjective theme ".. ...." shapes the dimensional psychological deregulation that is located in the quadrant ....., and is produced by the synergy of the following second-order intersubjective knowledge domains that behave dysfunctionally in the present:..
....
....

General observations:

....
....
....
....
....
....
....
....
....

Section 2—EVOLUTIONARY CASE FORMULATION—INTERVENTION[2]

Date: ....

Name: ....

Conceptualization of the sessions: ....

I. THEMATIC CONCEPTUALIZATION

SELF SYSTEM: clinical assessment

(mark presence: x)

SENSE OF AGENCY/EFFICIENCY: Alteration ☐ Progress ☐ Regulation ☐
Describe:..
....
....

SELF-NARRATIVE/COHERENCE: Alteration ☐ Progress ☐ Regulation ☐
Describe: ....
....
....

SENSE OF TIME/BALANCE: Alteration ☐ Progress ☐ Regulation ☐
Describe: ....
....
....

SELF-ESTEEM/SELF-DECEPTION: Alteration ☐ Progress ☐ Regulation ☐
Describe: ....
....
....

SELF-CARE/HEALTH: Alteration ☐ Progress ☐ Regulation ☐
Describe: ....
....
....

Observations: ....

....

II. ASSESSMENT OF DYSFUNCTIONAL INTERSUBJECTIVE KNOWLEDGE DOMAINS

Change indicators

(mark presence: x)

Cognitive alterations: Progress ☐ Regulation ☐
Describe: ....
....

Metacognition alterations: Progress ☐ Regulation ☐
Describe: ....
....

Alterations in executive functions: Progress ☐ Regulation ☐
Describe: ....
....

- Functional Narrative Indicator: Integrates knowledge about cognition ☐
- Behavioral Change Indicator: Incorporates changes ☐

Psychological Distress						Psychological Well-Being
High	Moderate	Mild	Neutral	Mild	Moderate	High
-3	-2	-1	0	1	2	3
Psychological Dysregulation						Psychological Regulation
High	Moderate	Mild	Neutral	Mild	Moderate	High
-3	-2	-1	0	1	2	3

Observations: ....
....

EMOTION: Change indicators

(mark presence: x)

Alteration of emotional awareness: Progress ☐ Regulation ☐

Describe: ....

....

Emotional dysregulation: Progress ☐ Regulation ☐

Describe: ....

....

- Functional Narrative Indicator: Integrates knowledge about emotion ☐

- Behavioral Change Indicator: Incorporates Changes ☐

Psychological Distress				Psychological Well-Being		
High	Moderate	Mild	Neutral	Mild	Moderate	High
-3	-2	-1	0	1	2	3
Psychological Dysregulation				**Psychological Regulation**		
High	Moderate	Mild	Neutral	Mild	Moderate	High
-3	-2	-1	0	1	2	3

Observations: ....

....

INTERPERSONAL: Change indicators

(mark presence: x)

Alteration in personal relationships: Progress ☐ Regulation ☐

Describe: ....

....

Alteration in romantic relationships: Progress ☐ Regulation ☐

Describe: ....

....

- Functional Narrative Indicator:
Integrates knowledge about interpersonal relationships ☐

- Behavioral Change Indicator: Incorporates changes ☐

Psychological Distress						Psychological Well-Being
High	Moderate	Mild	Neutral	Mild	Moderate	High
-3	-2	-1	0	1	2	3
Psychological Dysregulation						Psychological Regulation
High	Moderate	Mild	Neutral	Mild	Moderate	High
-3	-2	-1	0	1	2	3

Observations: ....

....

IMAGINATION: Change indicators

(mark presence: x)

Interferes with experiential coherence: Progress ☐ Regulation ☐

Describe: ....

....

Interferes with troubleshooting: Progress ☐ Regulation ☐

Describe: ....

....

- Functional Narrative Indicator: Integrates knowledge about imagination ☐

- Behavioral Change Indicator: Incorporates changes ☐

Psychological Distress						Psychological Well-Being
High	Moderate	Mild	Neutral	Mild	Moderate	High
-3	-2	-1	0	1	2	3
Psychological Dysregulation						Psychological Regulation
High	Moderate	Mild	Neutral	Mild	Moderate	High
-3	-2	-1	0	1	2	3

Observations: ....

....

CORPOREALITY: Change indicators

(mark presence: x)

Altered experience: Progress ☐ Regulation ☐

Describe: ....
....

Dysfunctional body attitude: Progress ☐ Regulation ☐

Describe: ....
....

- Functional Narrative Indicator: Integrates knowledge about corporeality ☐

- Behavioral Change Indicator: Incorporates changes ☐

Psychological Distress						Psychological Well-Being
High	Moderate	Mild	Neutral	Mild	Moderate	High
-3	-2	-1	0	1	2	3
Psychological Dysregulation						Psychological Regulation
High	Moderate	Mild	Neutral	Mild	Moderate	High
-3	-2	-1	0	1	2	3

Observations: ....
....

SEXUALITY: Change indicators

(mark presence: x)

Sexual disconnection with a partner: Progress ☐ Regulation ☐

Describe: ....

....

Sexual disconnection with others: Progress ☐ Regulation ☐

Describe: ....

....

- Functional Narrative Indicator: Integrates knowledge about sexuality ☐

- Behavioral Change Indicator: Incorporates changes ☐

Psychological Distress						Psychological Well-Being
High	Moderate	Mild	Neutral	Mild	Moderate	High
-3	-2	-1	0	1	2	3
Psychological Dysregulation						Psychological Regulation
High	Moderate	Mild	Neutral	Mild	Moderate	High
-3	-2	-1	0	1	2	3

Observations: ....

....

RELIGIOSITY/SPIRITUALITY: Change indicators

(mark presence: x)

Existential tension: Progress ☐ Regulation ☐

Describe: ....
....

Dysfunctional religious attachment: Progress ☐ Regulation ☐

Describe:..
....

- Functional Narrative Indicator: Integrates knowledge about religiosity/spirituality ☐

- Behavioral Change Indicator: Incorporates changes ☐

Psychological Distress						Psychological Well-Being
High	Moderate	Mild	Neutral	Mild	Moderate	High
-3	-2	-1	0	1	2	3
Psychological Dysregulation						Psychological Regulation
High	Moderate	Mild	Neutral	Mild	Moderate	High
-3	-2	-1	0	1	2	3

Observations: ....
....

III. MONITORING OF THE PSYCHOTHERAPEUTIC PROCESS

A. Assessment of sessions:

a.1 What changes are observed in the Dysfunctional Narrative?

....

....

....

....

a.2 What characteristics does the Functional Narrative have?

Absent ☐ Emerging ☐ Stable ☐

....

....

....

....

....

....

a.3 Represent the domains of second-order intersubjective knowledge in quadrants for psychological evaluation. Indicate the assessments in the boxes:

ECF - Evaluation			ECF - Intervention	
Distress-Well-being	Dysregulation - Regulation	Second- order intersubjective knowledge domains	Distress – Well-being	Dysregulation -Regulation
		Cognition [C]		
		Emotion [E]		
		Interpersonal [I]		
		Imagination [Im]		
		Corporeality [Cor]		
		Sexuality [Sex]		
		Religiosity/Spirituality [R/E]		

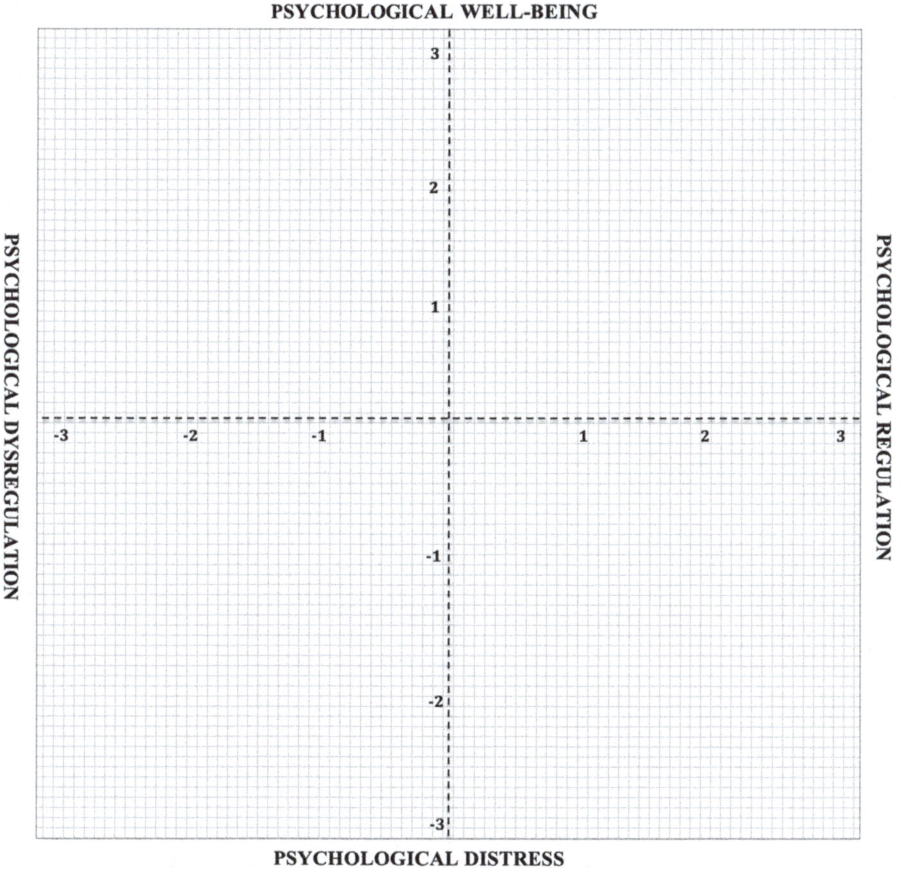

a.4. Assessment of therapeutic objectives fulfillment [mark presence: x]

Significant change valued by the patient	
Significant change valued by the therapist	
There is agreement on the achievement of objectives between therapist and patient	

a.5 Indicators of change [mark presence: x]

Behavioral changes	
Dimensional psychological regulation (quadrant I)	
Functional narrative	

General observations:

....
....
....
....
....
....
....
....
....
....
....
....
....

Section 3—PSYCHOTHERAPY PROCESS ASSESSMENT INTERVIEW [PPAI][3]

Name: ____________________________ Conducted in session: ___

Read to the patient:

The purpose of the interview is to jointly evaluate your therapeutic process to date. In order to obtain additional information that is useful to us to accurately assist you. In the next session, I will inform you of the results and we can discuss them together.

1. We have had __ sessions. So far, in terms of usefulness for your well-being, how has the psychotherapy process been for you?

....

....

....

....

Please, rate:

0	1	2	3
None	Mild	Moderate	High

2. Of the Topic(s) we agreed to work on, how much has changed in your opinion? (If the answer is Yes) Could you describe, please?

....

....

....

....

Please, rate:

0	1	2	3
None	Mild	Moderate	High

3. For you, what progress have you made on the agreed therapeutic objectives? (in the patient's words): ....

....

....

....

(If the answer is Yes) Score how much progress you have experienced according to the following scale:

0	1	2	3
None	Mild	Moderate	High

[3] © Álvaro Quiñones Bergeret, 2021
Intellectual Property Registration No. 2021-A-9588

4. In general, what changes have you noticed in yourself since you started psychotherapy?

....

....

....

....

(If the answer is Yes) Score how much change you have experienced according to the following scale:

0	1	2	3
None	Mild	Moderate	High

5. Do you remember having had an experience of novelty in any session?

....

....

....

....

(If the answer is Yes) Score according to the following scale:

0	1	2	3
None	Mild	Moderate	High

6. What do you believe (according to your personal theory) has caused the changes you have experienced? Specify if there are external life situations (example: job change, change of city, etc.)

....

....

....

....

Please, score if you have had responsibility in the changes according to the following scale:

0	1	2	3
None	Mild	Moderate	High

7. Which psychological explanations (reformulations), that I have conveyed in the sessions, have been most helpful to you?

Psychological reformulation made by the therapist (the therapist must write it):

....

....

....

....

Psychological reformulation remembered by the patient (in the patient's words): ....
....
....
....

Why? (in the patient's words): ....
....
....
....

Please, rate on the following scale how much it has helped you:

0	1	2	3
None	Mild	Moderate	High

8. If you reflect on the time you have been in psychotherapy, have there been psychological setbacks? Yes: ☐ No: ☐

(If the answer is Yes), specify (in the patient's words): ....
....
....
....

Please, rate on the following scale how much of a setback:

0	1	2	3
None	Mild	Moderate	High

9. Of the homework tasks we have agreed on, is there any that has been impossible, difficult or uncomfortable for you to perform? Yes: ☐ No: ☐

(If the answer is Yes) in the patient's words, why?...
....
....
....

Please rate on the following scale how difficult/uncomfortable it has been:

0	1	2	3
None	Mild	Moderate	High

10. What learnings do you consider are due to psychotherapy? ....
....
....
....

Please rate the learnings according to the following scale:

0	1	2	3
None	Mild	Moderate	High

11. What expectations do you now have about the psychotherapeutic process? (in the patient's words): ....
....
....
....

Please rate the amount of expectations according to the following scale:

0	1	2	3
None	Mild	Moderate	High

12. We have been working for ___ sessions, do you have any suggestions for me, so that I can help you better? (If the answer is Yes), in the patient's words, what suggestion(s)?
....
....
....
....

Please rate the number of suggestions according to the following scale:

0	1	2	3
None	Minimal	Some	Many

13. In relation to your awareness of internal time, in the last two weeks, is your behavior generally influenced by your current circumstances, by what happened in the past, or by the possible future consequences?

If the answer is one or more of the temporal dimensions, which one(s)?
....
....
....
....

Could you describe what you indicate in an example? ....
....
....
....

Please, rate on the following scale if your internal time causes you discomfort:

0	1	2	3
None	Mild	Moderate	High

14. Rate according to the following scale, how have you been psychologically in the last two weeks? Please, score:

PSICHOLOGICAL DISTRESS PSICHOLOGICAL WELLBEING

-3	-2	-1	0	+1	+2	+3
High	Moderate	Mild	Neutral	Mild	Moderate	High

Index

Á. Quiñones Bergeret, *Evolutionary Case Formulation*,
https://doi.org/10.1007/978-3-031-67412-9